HONG KONG AS AN ACTOR IN INTERNATIONAL ECONOMIC LAW

This open access book unveils Hong Kong's pivotal role in the realm of international economic law.

Unique to this book is its focus on the interplay between Hong Kong's historical roots and institutional contexts, integrated into its exploration of unilateral, bilateral, and multilateral economic approaches. What sets this book apart is its in-depth treatment of Hong Kong's distinct position as China's Special Administrative Region. It showcases the balance the territory maintains: the autonomy it enjoys, its own robust legal and economic systems, all while being intertwined with broader global interests. Hong Kong's position as China's economic gateway, coupled with its adaptability amidst technological evolutions and international tensions, positions it uniquely in the global economic arena. With the Asia-Pacific economy's rapid evolution and the Greater Bay Area's development, Hong Kong's role is illuminated as increasingly pivotal.

This book exposes challenges confronting Hong Kong, from political changes to the ramifications of the National Security Law, while emphasising its continued relevance and growing influence. As Hong Kong threads its path in a globalised world, its prowess in international economic law remains a cornerstone of its identity. Will the territory sustain its prominence amidst evolving challenges and global shifts? The answers lie within, and further research awaits as we track its unfolding narrative.

Specifically tailored for academics, diplomats, and researchers in international law, relations, economics, and finance, this book offers a vital perspective. Anyone with a vested interest in international economic law and policy will find this comprehensive exploration invaluable.

Studies in International Trade and Investment Law: Volume 32

Studies in International Trade and Investment Law

This series offers a forum for publication of original and scholarly analyses of emerging and significant issues in international trade and investment law – broadly understood to include the whole of the law of the WTO, the public international law of foreign investment, the law of the EU common commercial policy and other regional trade regimes, and any legal or regulatory topic that interacts with global trade and foreign investment. The aim of the series is to produce works which will be readily accessible to trade and investment law scholars and practitioners alike.

Recent titles in this series:

Regional Economic Integration and Dispute Settlement in East Asia: The Evolving Legal Framework
Anna G Tevini

The EU, World Trade Law and the Right to Food: Rethinking Free Trade Agreements with Developing Countries
Giovanni Gruni

Patent Games in the Global South: Pharmaceutical Patent Law Making in Brazil, India and Nigeria
Amaka Vanni

The Nationality of Corporate Investors under International Investment Law
Anil Yilmaz Vastardis

The Regulation of Product Standards in World Trade Law
Ming Du

Investors' International Law
Edited by Jean Ho and Mavluda Sattorova

Rethinking, Repackaging, and Rescuing World Trade Law in the Post-Pandemic Era
Edited by Amrita Bahri, Weihan Zhou and Daria Boklan

Flexible Regional Economic Integration in Africa: Lessons and Implications for the Multilateral Trading System
Timothy Masiko

International Investment Law: An Analysis of the Major Decisions
Edited by Hélène Ruiz Fabri and Edoardo Stoppioni

State Capitalism and International Investment Law
Edited by Panagiotis Delimatsis, Georgios Dimitropoulos and Anastasios Gourgourinis

The European Union and International Investment Law: The Two Dimensions of an Uneasy Relationship
Francesco Montanaro

Financial Market Infrastructure and Economic Integration: A WTO, FTAs, and Competition Law Analysis
George A Papaconstantinou

International Trade Law and Global Data Governance: Aligning Perspectives and Practices
Neha Mishra

Hong Kong as an Actor in International Economic Law

Multilateralism, Bilateralism and Unilateralism

Julien Chaisse

•HART•
OXFORD • LONDON • NEW YORK • NEW DELHI • SYDNEY

HART PUBLISHING
Bloomsbury Publishing Plc
Kemp House, Chawley Park, Cumnor Hill, Oxford, OX2 9PH, UK
1385 Broadway, New York, NY 10018, USA
29 Earlsfort Terrace, Dublin 2, Ireland

HART PUBLISHING, the Hart/Stag logo, BLOOMSBURY and the Diana logo are trademarks of Bloomsbury Publishing Plc

First published in Great Britain 2024

A catalogue record for this book is available from the British Library.

Library of Congress Cataloging-in-Publication data

Names: Chaisse, Julien, author.

Title: Hong Kong as an actor in international economic law : multilateralism, bilateralism, and unilateralism / Julien Chaisse.

Description: Oxford, UK ; New York, NY : Hart Publishing, 2024. | Series: Studies in international trade and investment law; volume 32 | Includes bibliographical references and index. | Summary: "This open access book explains why Hong Kong adopts a triangular approach (combining unilateralism, bilateralism, and multilateralism) in its external trade and investment relations, describing how it applies the methods necessary to manage the triple-track strategy, and identifying the legal, political, and economic implications of this approach. The book explores the evolving role of Hong Kong in contemporary regional and global affairs and makes recommendations on how Hong Kong can improve its effectiveness in securing its regional policy goals"—Provided by publisher.

Identifiers: LCCN 2024004852 (print) | LCCN 2024004853 (ebook) | ISBN 9781509968169 (hardback) | ISBN 9781509968206 (paperback) | ISBN 9781509968176 (Epub) | ISBN 9781509968183 (ebook)

Subjects: LCSH: Foreign trade regulation—China—Hong Kong. | Investments, Foreign—Law and legislation—China—Hong Kong. | Taxation—Law and legislation—China—Hong Kong. | Commercial law—China—Hong Kong. | Dispute resolution (Law)—China—Hong Kong.

Classification: LCC KNQ9379.3 .C43 2024 (print) | LCC KNQ9379.3 (ebook) | DDC 343.512507—dc23/eng/20240205

LC record available at https://lccn.loc.gov/2024004852

LC ebook record available at https://lccn.loc.gov/2024004853

ISBN:		
	HB:	978-1-50996-816-9
	ePDF:	978-1-50996-818-3
	ePub:	978-1-50996-817-6

Typeset by Compuscript Ltd, Shannon
Printed and bound in Great Britain

Acknowledgements

I am pleased to present my latest scholarly contribution, entitled *Hong Kong as an Actor in International Economic Law: Multilateralism, Bilateralism and Unilateralism*. This publication endeavours to provide a comprehensive examination of Hong Kong's role and participation in the area of international economic law, covering the fields of international trade law, international investment law and international tax law.

Given its distinct status as a significant international financial centre and a Special Administrative Region of China, Hong Kong occupies a unique position in the global economy. Despite this position, Hong Kong has proactively participated in several international economic initiatives, such as negotiating and concluding free trade agreements, engaging in multilateral trade negotiations and representing China in international economic organisations.

This book investigates Hong Kong's involvement in international economic law from three different standpoints: multilateralism, bilateralism and unilateralism. By critically analysing Hong Kong's involvement in various international economic forums, I examine its accomplishments and challenges in promoting its economic interests and protecting its economic rights.

Furthermore, this book does not rely solely on primary and secondary legal sources. It is the outcome of an extensive research project, for which I was the principal investigator, which involved numerous interviews and interactions with field experts from 2019 to 2022. This project, 'Anatomy of Hong Kong's International Trade Law', was given financial support by Hong Kong's Research Grants Council (RGC Ref No. 11606820). Furthermore, my knowledge of Hong Kong law has expanded substantially due to my interactions with friends and colleagues since relocating from Europe to Hong Kong in 2009. Hong Kong has played a pivotal role in my life during the past 15 years and they have given me an outstanding learning experience.

I wish to thank Wing Shi Tsang, Kehinde Olaoye, Xuchiang Ji, Mary Ng, and David Tang, alongside many other colleagues, for their support and expertise. Their contributions, combined with a shared interest in international economic law and Hong Kong, have been valuable to the development of this book. It has been a privilege to work with such experienced and skilled professionals.

In particular, I deeply appreciate Hart's support and I would like to give special recognition to Sinead Moloney (Editorial Director), Roberta Bassi (Senior Commissioning Editor) and Verity Stuart (Assistant Editor) for their exceptional contributions throughout the publication process. Their unwavering dedication to quality and excellence is evident on every page of this book, which I hope will be a valuable addition to the prestigious 'Studies in International Trade and

Investment Law' series, edited by Gabrielle Marceau, Krista Nadakavukaren Schefer, Federico Ortino and Gregory Shaffer. It is an honour to be affiliated with such a distinguished series and academic publishing house.

Additionally, I would like to express my sincere gratitude to Dr David Wilmshurst, who has edited the book's contents and whose invaluable assistance significantly aided me in refining this monograph. Dr Wilmshurst worked as an Administrative Officer in the pre-1997 Hong Kong Government and his insightful comments, astute suggestions and valuable feedback helped to shape this book into its final form.

This book presents an in-depth analysis of Hong Kong's engagement in international economic law. It is my sincere hope that it will be of interest not only to scholars and students in the field of international economic law, but also to policymakers, practitioners and anyone curious about the unique role of Hong Kong in the global economy.

Hong Kong
April 25, 2024

Contents

PART III
MULTILATERAL ENGAGEMENT: HONG KONG'S ROLE IN GLOBAL ECONOMIC INSTITUTIONS

PART IV
RESOLVING ECONOMIC CONFLICTS: DISPUTE SETTLEMENT IN HONG KONG'S INTERNATIONAL RELATIONS

Abbreviations

ADR	Alternative Dispute Resolution
APEC	Asia-Pacific Economic Cooperation
ASEAN	Association of Southeast Asian Nations
BEPS	Base Erosion and Profit Shifting
BIT	Bilateral Investment Treaty
BRI	Belt and Road
CETA	Comprehensive Economic and Trade Agreement
CJEU	Court of Justice of the European Union
CPC	Cooperative Patent Classification
CSR	Corporation Social Responsibility
DoJ	Department of Justice
DSU	Dispute Settlement Understanding
DTA	Double Taxation Agreement
EU	European Union
FDI	Foreign Direct Investment
FTA	Free Trade Agreement
FTZ	Free Trade Zone
GATT	General Agreement on Tariffs and Trade
GATS	General Agreement on Trade in Services
GDP	Gross Domestic Product
ICC	International Chamber of Commerce
ICJ	International Court of Justice
ICSID	International Centre for Settlement of Investment Disputes
IDSD	Investor State Dispute Settlement
IEL	International Economic Law (IEL)

IIA	International Investment Agreements
ISDS	Investor-State Dispute Settlement
MAP	Mutual Agreement Procedure
MFN	Most Favoured Nation
MIGA	Multilateral Investment Guarantee Agency
ML	Multilateral Investment
MNE	Multinational Enterprises
NAFTA	North American Free Trade Agreement
NGO	Non-governmental Organisation
OBOR	One Belt One Road
OECD	Organisation for Economic Co-operation and Development
PRC	People's Republic of China
RCEP	Regional Comprehensive Economic Partnership
SOE	State-owned Enterprise
SAR	Special Administrative Region
TFEU	Treaty on the Functioning of the European Union
TRIMS	Agreement on Trade-Related Investment Measures
TRIPs	Agreement on Trade-Related Aspects of Intellectual Property Rights
UN	United Nations
UNCITRAL	United Nations Commission on International Trade Law
UNCTAD	United Nations Conference on Trade and Development
US	United States of America
USMCA	United States-Mexico-Canada Agreement
WHO	World Health Organisation
WIPO	World Intellectual Property Organisation
WTO	World Trade Organisation

Table of Cases

WTO Cases

ICSID Cases

HK Cases

Other

Table of Legislation

International treaties

HK legislation

1

Hong Kong as an Actor in International Economic Law: An Introduction

I. HONG KONG'S UNIQUE ROLE IN INTERNATIONAL ECONOMIC LAW: MULTILATERALISM, BILATERALISM AND UNILATERALISM

HONG KONG'S EXCEPTIONAL status as a Special Administrative Region (SAR) of China affords it a unique position in the realm of international economic policy.[1] It maintains a separate legal and economic system from mainland China, which encompasses its own customs territory, trade policy, autonomous monetary policy and currency.[2] This distinctiveness renders the territory an enticing location for businesses seeking to operate within the region. Though modest in size, Hong Kong wields considerable influence on the global economy, owing to its location on the south-eastern coast of China. With its thriving and affluent economy, Hong Kong has a significance not only for China but also for the Asia Pacific region and the world at large, rendering itself an understudied yet crucial player in international economic law (IEL).[3]

Hong Kong's remarkable economic prosperity can be attributed to an complex network of historical influences, geographical benefits, a proficient workforce and astute government policies. The economy of Hong Kong is widely recognised as prosperous and dynamic, not just in China but also in the Asia Pacific region and the wider world. This view is supported by several indicators such as GDP growth, investment inflows and the territory's high rankings in global economic rankings. Hong Kong is a vital player in IEL, despite being under-studied. The strategic location of Hong Kong at the crossroads of the

[1] Basic Law of the Hong Kong Special Administrative Region, Chapter I: General Principles (Adopted at the Third Session of the Seventh National People's Congress on April 4, 1990); The Joint Declaration on the Question of Hong Kong (signed 19 December 1989) 1399 UNTS.

[2] Zhang Youyu, 'The Reasons for and Basic Principles in Formulating the Hong Kong Special Administrative Region Basic Law and its Essential Contents and Mode of Expression (1988) 2 *Journal of Chinese Law* 5.

[3] William H Overholt, 'A Decade Later: Hong Kong's Economy Since 1997' (2007) *Hong Kong Journal*. Available at: https://carnegieendowment.org/hkjournal/PDF/2007_fall/4.pdf.

Asia Pacific region has been one of the reasons for its economic success. It acts as a gateway to mainland China and a hub for regional trade and investment. The territory has a highly developed financial sector, generally recognised as one of the most efficient and competitive in the world. The Hong Kong Stock Exchange is one of the largest in Asia and is home to several multinational corporations. Hong Kong's legal system is efficient, transparent and independent; these advantages create a stable environment for business and investment. Hong Kong's commitment to free trade and open markets makes it an attractive destination for foreign companies looking to do business in the region which has contributed to its economic success. Hong Kong's government has actively pursued policies to promote innovation and entrepreneurship, which has led to the growth of a vibrant start-up ecosystem.

However, Hong Kong faces several challenges, such as its high cost of living and limited land resources, which have led to a shortage of affordable housing and a high degree of income inequality. Hong Kong also faces competition from other economies in the region, such as Singapore, which have similar advantages in terms of their location, financial sector and commitment to free trade. Recent political developments, such as the imposition of the National Security Law in 2020 and the arrests of politicians from the opposition parties and activists, have also cast a shadow over Hong Kong's civil liberties and economic future. Concerns have been raised about the territory's autonomy and the potential impact on its business environment. The future of civil liberties in Hong Kong is also in question. In a nutshell, while Hong Kong's economy has for many decades been regarded as prosperous and dynamic, recent political developments have raised concerns about the territory's autonomy and its business environment, which could have implications for its future economic growth.

Hong Kong's position as a major port at the heart of the Asia Pacific region has been critical to its growth as a key trading hub.[4] Its strategic location has allowed it to become a gateway to China and the rest of Asia, connecting it to both the mainland and the global economy.[5] Although Hong Kong did not merge with China's economy after the 1997 handover, the two economies have become closely intertwined. Hong Kong's role as a gateway for foreign investment and trade has been crucial in facilitating China's economic expansion. Conversely, China's growth has presented new opportunities for Hong Kong, especially in the financial sector. This has established Hong Kong as a vital hub for financial services, attracting numerous leading banks and financial organisations.

[4] Hong Kong Government, 'The Port' (2022) Hong Kong: The Facts. Available at: www.gov.hk/en/about/abouthk/factsheets/docs/The-Port.pdf, accessed 2 February 2024.

[5] Jiangyu Wang, 'China's Impact on Hong Kong's Position as an International Financial Centre: The Legal and Policy Dimensions' in DC Donald, J Wang and JP Vanderwolk, *A Financial Centre for Two Empires: Hong Kong's Corporate, Securities and Tax Laws in its Transition from Britain to China* (Cambridge, Cambridge University Press, 2014).

However, recent political developments have not only clouded Hong Kong's future but could also undermine China's reputation as an attractive destination for foreign investment. While the strong interdependence between the two economies provides opportunities for growth, it also presents challenges, especially in the need to maintain a competitive edge in a rapidly changing economic landscape. It is essential for both China and Hong Kong to work together to address these challenges if they are to maintain their success.

Hong Kong's economy has greatly benefited from its highly educated and skilled workforce, which includes professionals in finance, technology and professional services.[6] The territory puts a strong emphasis on education and has impressive literacy rates. These advantages help to attract top talent from all over the world and contribute to its economic growth. Countries such as the United States, Japan and the United Kingdom have been investing in Hong Kong for decades, attracted by its strategic location, well-established legal system and favourable business environment. However, recent political and social unrest has led to a loss of confidence among some investors, prompting them to seek alternative investment destinations.[7] In addition to foreign investors, Hong Kong also attracts a diverse range of professionals from around the world, drawn to its dynamic business environment, high quality of life and opportunities for career advancement. However, these recent political developments and the economic impact of the pandemic have also led many skilled professionals to consider leaving Hong Kong. If this trend continues over the long term, it could have significant implications for the territory's economy. Hong Kong needs to address these challenges to maintain its competitiveness and ensure its continued economic growth and success.

Government policies have always been instrumental in driving Hong Kong's remarkable economic growth. One of the primary drivers of this growth has been its low tax rates, which have encouraged numerous businesses to set up operations in the territory. This has fostered a strong and diverse business environment, which has contributed to Hong Kong's status as a global financial hub. The government has also implemented policies aimed at limiting its intervention in the economy, creating a free-market environment that has allowed businesses to flourish in a competitive and open market. Furthermore, Hong Kong's network of Double Taxation Agreements (DTAs) with various countries has facilitated international trade and investment by eliminating or reducing the double taxation of income, providing greater certainty to businesses operating

[6] Jane Knight, 'Education Hubs: International, Regional and Local Dimensions of Scale and Scope (2013) 49(3) *Comparative Education* 374.

[7] Cheryl Arcibal, 'Once a shining light, foreign investors abandon Hong Kong office space as slowing economy weighs on sentiment' (*South China Morning Post*, 13 May 2022). Available at: www.scmp.com/business/article/3177531/once-shining-light-foreign-investors-abandon-hong-kong-office-space, accessed 2 February 2024;Pak Yiu, 'Global companies moving top posts out of Hong Kong' (*The Nikkei Asia*, 17 August 2022). Available at: https://asia.nikkei.com/Spotlight/Coronavirus/Global-companies-moving-top-posts-out-of-Hong-Kong-survey, accessed 2 February 2024.

in Hong Kong and helping to prevent tax evasion and avoidance.[8] With the establishment of DTAs, businesses have been able to enjoy a more favourable tax environment, which has fuelled economic growth. The government has invested in infrastructure and transportation to facilitate economic expansion, exemplified by the construction of the Hong Kong-Zhuhai-Macau Bridge, which has diminished travel time between Hong Kong and the Western Pearl River Delta region.[9] However, these advantages have been undermined in recent years in other areas. The United States has revoked the preferential treatment previously granted to Hong Kong, including exemptions from certain tariffs and export controls, after the implementation in 2020 of the National Security Law, which has significantly curtailed freedom of expression in Hong Kong.[10] The termination of this special status has had a particularly negative impact on the financial sector. Many US companies have re-evaluated their operations in Hong Kong and some have chosen to move to other destinations. The loss of special status has also damaged Hong Kong's reputation as an attractive location for foreign investment.

Although the US decision to revoke its special status indeed poses a significant challenge, Hong Kong has consistently exhibited resilience in times of adversity and continues to serve as an essential centre for trade and commerce. This resilience can be attributed to various factors, including the territory's robust legal and regulatory framework, strategic geographical location and well-developed infrastructure. Firstly, Hong Kong's legal and regulatory system, underpinned by the rule of law and an independent judiciary, provides a stable environment for businesses to operate and thrive. This strong foundation ensures that the territory remains an attractive destination for foreign investors, despite the termination of its special status by the United States. Secondly, Hong Kong's strategic geographical position at the heart of the Asia-Pacific region offers unparalleled access to some of the world's largest and fastest-growing markets. This connectivity, along with the territory's status as a gateway to Mainland China, enables Hong Kong to maintain its position as a crucial hub for trade and investment. Finally, the development of the Greater Bay Area (GBA) initiative

[8] Michael Littlewood 'Tax Treaty Disputes in Hong Kong' in Eduardo Baistrocchi (ed), *A Global Analysis of Tax Treaty Disputes* (Cambridge, Cambridge University Press, 2007).

[9] Brian Scanlon, 'The Geopolitics of Infrastructure and the Unmaking of an Island: The Hong Kong-Zhuhai- Macau Bridge' (2023) *Geopolitics* 1.

[10] In the context of the United States revoking Hong Kong's preferential treatment, including exemptions from specific tariffs and export controls, the Chinese imposition of the National Security Law plays a significant role. This situation can be further understood by examining the US statutory framework on Hong Kong's status. As outlined in the US–Hong Kong Policy Act, the President has the authority to suspend the application of an American law that grants Hong Kong distinct treatment compared to China. This suspension can be initiated if the President determines that Hong Kong lacks sufficient autonomy to justify such different treatment. Congressional Research Service, 'Revoking Hong Kong's Preferential Trade Status: Legal Framework and Implications' (Updated 2 April 2021). Available at: https://crsreports.congress.gov/product/pdf/lsb/lsb10488, accessed 2 February 2024.

adds another dimension to Hong Kong's resilience and potential for growth. The GBA consists of nine cities in Guangdong Province, together with Hong Kong and Macau. These cities, with a combined population of over 70 million people, constitute a dynamic economic powerhouse. This ambitious development plan aims to foster innovation, economic integration and sustainable development across the region, thereby enhancing Hong Kong's role as a key player in the global economy.

This book examines the distinctive role of Hong Kong as a SAR of China, within the sphere of IEL.[11] This comprehensive investigation probes deep into Hong Kong's legal framework, domestic policies and its interactions with other countries and regions by scrutinising its involvement in unilateral, bilateral and multilateral endeavours. The forthcoming context and background information set the stage for this profound analysis, illuminating the historical, geographical and political factors that have shaped Hong Kong's economy and help to account for its far-reaching influence on the global economic stage.

This book presents a comprehensive analysis of Hong Kong's engagement in IEL by scrutinising the legal framework of its economic policies, their domestic repercussions and its relationships with other countries and regions. The book situates Hong Kong's connection with trade, investment and taxation.

Analysing Hong Kong's trade sector, the book examines the unilateral trade regime, its bilateral and multilateral free trade agreements (FTAs) and its participation in the World Trade Organisation (WTO). It also assesses Hong Kong's role as a global supply chain hub, owing to its proximity to mainland China.[12] Hong Kong's unilateral trade regime, which promotes free trade and open markets, has been instrumental in driving its economic growth. In addition, Hong Kong has entered into bilateral and multilateral FTAs with various countries and regions, such as the ASEAN Free Trade Area, which has helped to promote trade and investment. However, Hong Kong's long-term economic trends have been affected by protectionist measures implemented by some countries, which have constrained the territory's ability to export its goods and services. Market forces have played a significant role in Hong Kong's economy, with the territory serving as a global hub for finance, trade and commerce.

[11] The official name of Hong Kong is the Hong Kong Special Administrative Region of the People's Republic of China (HKSAR) since 1997, when it was returned to China by the British. However, in accordance with legal arrangements, Hong Kong continued to be a WTO Member on and after 1 July 1997, using the name 'Hong Kong, China'. For the purposes of this book, we simply use the name 'Hong Kong' which refers to the HKSAR or Hong Kong, China, depending on the political context. The name Hong Kong, given to the territory by its British colonisers, is an approximation of the Cantonese pronunciation of 'Heung Kong' ('Fragrant Harbour'), its name in Chinese. The putonghua pronunciation of this name, once rarely heard in Hong Kong but now increasingly common, is 'Xianggang'. The city which grew up on the north shore of Hong Kong Island in the early decades of the colonial period was officially known as Victoria, but this name gradually fell out of use and is rarely, if ever, heard nowadays.

[12] Yun Wing Sung, 'Hong Kong as Trading Partner' (2011) in *The China-Hong Kong Connection: The Key to China's Open Door Policy* (Cambridge, Cambridge University Press, 2011).

Hong Kong is a major trading partner with many countries, particularly with mainland China, which accounts for a significant portion of its trade flows. In recent years, Hong Kong has also diversified its exports to include high-value-added services, such as finance and logistics. Overseas investment and trade have also been essential components of Hong Kong's economic success. A significant inflow of foreign direct investment (FDI) has contributed to the territory's growth. Hong Kong has attracted FDI from a wide range of countries, including the United States, Japan and mainland China. Despite these strengths, Hong Kong's trade sector has faced challenges, particularly in recent years with the global economic slowdown and the impact of the Covid-19 pandemic. These challenges have highlighted the need for Hong Kong to diversify its economy and adapt to changing global trade dynamics. Overall, Hong Kong's trade sector plays a crucial role in its economy, with a focus on promoting free trade and open markets. However, the territory faces challenges in the form of protectionism, internal problems and external economic pressures. The government must continue to pursue policies that promote economic diversification to ensure Hong Kong's long-term economic growth and success.

Analysing Hong Kong's investment arena, the book explores Hong Kong's approach to foreign investment, including the absence of general investment legislation governing foreign investment admission. It also examines foreign investment screening mechanisms and the role of the Hong Kong Court of Final Appeal in addressing sovereign immunity issues.[13] The book considers Hong Kong's investment regime, which includes various bilateral and multilateral agreements such as Bilateral Investment Treaties (BITs), Preferential Trading Agreements (PTAs), the International Centre for Settlement of Investment Disputes (ICSID), the United Nations Commission on International Trade Law (UNCITRAL) and the Multilateral Investment Guarantee Agency (MIGA. Hong Kong's liberal approach to foreign investment has attracted significant FDI inflows from overseas, particularly in the financial and services sectors and there is no general domestic investment legislation governing foreign investment admission. However, recent global trends towards protectionism and internal political disputes have presented challenges to Hong Kong's foreign investment structure and have created uncertainties for the territory's economy. Despite these challenges, Hong Kong continues to remain a crucial hub for international trade and commerce, with its strategic location and efficient logistics infrastructure facilitating its trading activities. Hong Kong is a major trading partner with China, exporting significant amounts of electronics, clothing and textiles, as well as to other major markets such as the US, Japan and the EU. Market forces have played a significant role in Hong Kong's economic success, with the government playing a limited role in the economy. The territory's free-market approach has enabled businesses to thrive, while its legal system

[13] Zeng Huaqun, 'Initiative and Implications of Hong Kong's Bilateral Investment Treaties' (2010) 11 *The Journal of World Investment & Trade* 696.

and regulatory framework provide a high level of protection for investors. The government has also implemented policies aimed at supporting businesses and attracting investment, such as tax incentives and investment promotion schemes. Despite its open and liberal approach to foreign investment, however, Hong Kong's economy is vulnerable to the impact of global economic trends, protectionism and internal problems, which could negatively impact its long-term economic growth.

Moving away from the areas of trade and investment, the book examines in depth Hong Kong's taxation regulatory environment, discussing its principal tax institutions, membership in regional tax organisations and DTAAs with other countries. The low tax rates and limited tax base of Hong Kong's tax system have been essential in driving the territory's economic success, making it an attractive destination for businesses and foreign investment. This has created a competitive and open business environment that has helped to establish Hong Kong as a global financial hub.[14] The book also examines the evolving global consensus on multinational corporation taxation and its implications for Hong Kong's economic policies. The ongoing discussions around the taxation of multinational corporations could have a significant impact on Hong Kong's tax regime and its ability to attract foreign investment, which is crucial to its economy. To address issues facing the tax regime in Hong Kong, the government has implemented policies aimed at supporting businesses and promoting economic growth, including tax incentives and investment promotion schemes. Nonetheless, these policies may need to be updated to ensure Hong Kong remains globally competitive. In conclusion, Hong Kong's tax structure has been a crucial factor in its economic success. The government's commitment to maintaining a low tax regime and limited tax base has attracted businesses and investment to the territory, reinforcing its status as a global financial hub. However, the changing global consensus on multinational corporation taxation and the ongoing challenges facing the territory's economy call for a constant evaluation of its tax policies to ensure its continued sustainability and competitiveness in the global economy.

The book provides an in-depth analysis of Hong Kong's participation in IEL, focusing on its unilateral, bilateral and multilateral approaches to trade, investment and taxation to contribute to broader debates on IEL and its role in shaping the global economic order.

A. Hong Kong's Economic Resilience

The reawakening of Asia has not only been characterised by its rapid economic growth, but also by a social shift highlighting the revival of global relations

[14] Littlewood 'Tax Treaty Disputes in Hong Kong' (n 8).

between Asia and other parts of the world. In the case of Hong Kong, its economy has been shaped by several factors, including its colonial legacy, its unique status as an SAR of China and its position as a leading financial hub in the Asia-Pacific region. Hong Kong is currently viewed as a vital component of China's overall progress and is playing a pivotal role in the Belt and Road Initiative (BRI), which seeks to enhance economic connectivity and encourage collaboration between China and other nations.[15] Moreover, Hong Kong has become a significant participant in the global financial system. Its stock exchange is one of the largest in the world by market capitalisation. Its location and logistics infrastructure have enabled it to function as a gateway to China and a crucial centre for international trade and commerce. Hong Kong is broadening its economic relations with other countries and regions, including the ASEAN and EU groupings and China's Greater Bay Area, which is expected to become a significant economic force in coming years. Hong Kong's present status is determined by its distinct association with China and its role in the global financial system. Its future growth prospects depend on its ability to navigate successfully through the ongoing challenges and maintain its competitiveness in the global economy.

With over seven million inhabitants, Hong Kong is one of the world's most densely populated cities. It boasts a highly skilled and educated workforce.[16] The services sector dominates the territory's economy, accounting for more than 90 per cent of its GDP, with financial services, trade and logistics as the main growth drivers.[17] However, the current challenges facing Hong Kong's economic stability should not be underestimated. The Covid-19 pandemic has further compounded these challenges, with the tourism and retail sectors being particularly hard hit. Additionally, the territory is facing stiff competition from other global financial hubs, including Singapore and Shanghai.

In conclusion, while Hong Kong's highly skilled and educated workforce and services sector have been crucial factors in its economic success, it faces significant challenges that require attention. The government's efforts to promote economic growth and development, coupled with its expanding network of economic partnerships, will be crucial in ensuring the sustainability and continued success of Hong Kong's economy amidst the ongoing challenges posed by political unrest, Covid-19, intense competition and global trends in taxation and protectionism.

[15] Ching Kwan Lee, *Hong Kong: Global China's Restive Frontier* (Cambridge, Cambridge University Press, 2022).

[16] Philip Bowring 'Hong Kong as an International Commercial Centre' in W Cohen and L Zhao (eds), *Hong Kong under Chinese Rule: The Economic and Political Implications of Reversion* (Cambridge, Cambridge University Press, 1997).

[17] AHK Hong Kong, 'Back to the Future: Re-industrialisation in Hong Kong, (*German Industry and Commerce*, 29 May 2019). Available at: https://hongkong.ahk.de/news/news-details/back-to-the-future-re-industrialisation-in-hong-kong, accessed 2 February 2024.

B. Hong Kong's Multifaceted Role in International Economic Law

Since the 1980s, Hong Kong has been one of the world's most open economies. Its highly liberalised trade and investment regime has made it a hub for international trade and investment.[18] The territory has been a member of the WTO since its inception in 1995 and has signed a range of bilateral and multilateral FTAs with other countries and regions, including mainland China, the Association of Southeast Asian Nations (ASEAN) and EFTA.[19]

Hong Kong's economic policies have been shaped not only by its engagement with the global economic order but also by its unique position as an SAR.[20] Hong Kong operates under a unique political system characterised as 'One Country, Two Systems'. This principle was established when Britain handed back Hong Kong to China in 1997.[21] Under this system, Hong Kong has retained a high degree of autonomy in its economic and legal affairs, while its political system remains separate from that of mainland China. This means that Hong Kong has its own government, legal system and economy and maintains a separate identity from mainland China. The "One Country" aspect of the system means that Hong Kong is a part of China and follows the overall policies of the Chinese government. However, under the 'two systems' aspect, Hong Kong is able to maintain its own political, legal and economic systems. This allows Hong Kong to enjoy a high degree of autonomy and to function as a separate entity from mainland China. However, there have been growing concerns about the erosion of Hong Kong's autonomy, particularly after the imposition of a controversial National Security Law following widespread protests in 2019 against an extradition bill.[22] Despite these challenges, the 'One Country, Two Systems' principle remains a crucial aspect of Hong Kong's identity and autonomy. It allows the territory to maintain its unique economic and legal systems while still being a part of China. The system has contributed to Hong Kong's success as a global financial hub and a gateway to mainland China and will continue to play a significant role in the territory's future.

[18] Julien Chaisse and Georgios Dimitropoulos, 'Domestic Investment Laws and International Economic Law in the Liberal International Order' (2023) 22 *World Trade Review* 1; see also Nie G Mac and Enbao Wang, 'Hong Kong: The World's Freest Economy and its Liberal Policy' in Stuart Nagel (ed) *Handbook of Global Economic Policy* (New York, Routledge, 2000).

[19] Mainland and Hong Kong Closer Economic Partnership Arrangement (signed 29 June 2003, entry into force 29 June 2003) (CEPA); Free Trade Agreement between Hong Kong, China and the Association of Southeast Asian Nations (signed 28 March 2018, entry into force 11 June 2019).

[20] Li Pang Kwong, *Hong Kong from Britain to China: Political Cleavages, Electoral Dynamics and Institutional Changes* (London, Routledge, 2001).

[21] Shi Jiuyong, 'Autonomy of the Hong Kong Special Administrative Region' (2004) 10 *Leiden Journal of International Law* 191.

[22] Brain CH Fong, 'Practicing Autonomy within a Communist State: Hong Kong's Autonomy from Handover to Anti-Extradition Bill Movement, 1997–2019' (2020) 53 *Communist and Post Communist Studies* 68.

However, Hong Kong's position as a financial centre has come under scrutiny in recent years, with concerns about its role in facilitating money laundering and other financial crimes.[23] In 2019, the Financial Action Task Force (FATF) reviewed Hong Kong's anti-money laundering and counter-terrorist financing regime, commending its legal framework, but criticising its patchy enforcement record and the effectiveness of its risk management systems.[24] Hong Kong has one of the lowest tax rates in the world and its simple and transparent tax system has made it a popular destination for multinational corporations.[25] The territory has also entered into various DTAAs with other countries, providing for the elimination of double taxation and the prevention of fiscal evasion.[26] However, there has been a growing global consensus on the need for multinational corporations to pay their fair share of taxes, with concerns about the use of tax havens and other aggressive tax planning strategies.[27]

Given Hong Kong's economic significance and its role in shaping the global economic order, there is a need for a comprehensive analysis of the territory's participation in IEL. This book aims to provide such an analysis, examining the legal framework of Hong Kong's economic policies, their impact on its domestic economy and its relations with other countries and regions.

The core contention of this book is that Hong Kong, as an SAR of China, plays a complex and pivotal role in international economic law. This role is established through its dynamic involvement in unilateral, bilateral and multilateral initiatives. The territory's unparalleled historical, political and legal backdrops have paved the way for its emergence as a formidable player in global economic governance, enabling it to actively shape international norms and policies.

Predictions these days about Hong Kong's future, whether optimistic or pessimistic, nearly always reflect the deepening geopolitical tensions between China and the West. The book seeks to pick its way through the morass of self-serving rhetoric on both sides and tries to focus firmly on contemporary realities.

[23] Eva Gibson, 'A Financial History of Hong Kong' in *A Regulatory Design for Financial Stability in Hong Kong* (Cambridge, Cambridge University Press, 2022). The system has been successful in maintaining Hong Kong's unique identity and economic success, but it has also faced challenges in recent years. There have been concerns about the erosion of Hong Kong's autonomy, as well as the suppression of civil liberties and the rule of law. The controversial extradition bill in 2019 sparked widespread protests and unrest in Hong Kong, while many residents felt that their freedoms were under threat.

[24] FATF, 'Hong Kong, China's Measures to Combat Money Laundering and Terrorist Financing' (2019). Available at: www.fatf-gafi.org/en/publications/Mutualevaluations/Mer-hong-kong-china-2019.html, accessed 2 February 2024.

[25] Andrew Halkyard, 'Treating Taxpayers Right: Taxpayers' Rights with Special Reference to Hong Kong' (2001) 9 *Asia Pacific Law Review* 133.

[26] Inland Revenue Department (Hong Kong SAR) 'Comprehensive Doble Taxation Agreements Concluded'. Available at: www.ird.gov.hk/eng/tax/dta_inc.htm, accessed 2 February 2024.

[27] Hansrudi Lenz, 'Aggressive Tax Avoidance by Managers of Multinational Companies as a Violation of Their Moral Duty to Obey the Law: A Kantian Rationale' (2020) 165 *Journal of Business Ethics* 681.

Several critical aspects and supporting evidence from the context substantiate this primary thesis:

1. Hong Kong's extraordinary status as an SAR, functioning under the 'One Country, Two Systems' principle, sets it apart from both mainland China and other jurisdictions. Not only does it encapsulate the territory's colonial legacy and its incorporation into the Chinese state, but it also underpins the development and advancement of its unique ideas and norms in international economic law.[28]
2. Illustrating Hong Kong's unilateral engagement, the territory has consistently championed free trade and open markets, pledging to nurture an open economic landscape.[29] Hong Kong has preserved its own discrete customs territory, legal system and currency – the Hong Kong dollar, which is freely convertible and has been linked to the US dollar since 1983.[30]
3. On a bilateral level, Hong Kong has forged robust economic connections with countries across the globe, encompassing the negotiation of numerous FTAs and BITs.[31] For example, Hong Kong has signed FTAs with ASEAN and Australia, thereby bolstering its trade and investment ties within the Asia-Pacific region.[32]
4. In a multilateral context, Hong Kong actively engages in a variety of international economic organisations and forums, including the WTO, the Asia-Pacific Economic Cooperation (APEC), and the World Economic Forum (WEF). Through these avenues, Hong Kong can influence global economic policies and advocate for its interests on the international stage.[33]

The book maintains that Hong Kong plays a crucial and diverse role in international economic law through its involvement in unilateral, bilateral and multilateral endeavours. This position is buttressed by the territory's distinctive

[28] Stefan H.C. Lo et al, 'Interface between Hong Kong and International and Chinese Law' in *Hong Kong Legal System*, 2nd edn (Cambridge, Cambridge University Press, 2019).

[29] Lawrence Mills, *Protecting Free Trade: The Hong Kong Paradox 1947–1997* (Hong Kong, Hong Kong University Press, 2012).

[30] John Greenwood, 'The Monetary Framework Underlying the Hong Kong Dollar Stabilization Scheme' (2009) 99 *The China Quarterly* 631.

[31] WTO, Regional Trade Agreements Database: Hong Kong, China. Available at: https://rtais.wto.org/UI/PublicSearchByMemberResult.aspx?membercode=344, accessed 2 February 2024; UNCTAD Investment Policy Hub, 'International Investment Agreements Navigator: Hong Kong, China SAR'. Available at: https://investmentpolicy.unctad.org/international-investment-agreements/countries/93/hong-kong-sar-china, accessed 2 February 2024.

[32] Paul Krugman, 'The Move Towards Free Trade Zones' (1991) 76 *Economic Review* 5; see also Mr. Eduardo Pedrosa, 'Free Trade Agreements in East Asia: A Way toward Trade Liberalization' (*PECC Forum*, 21 January 2011). Available at: https://www.pecc.org/blog/entry/free-trade-agreements-in-east-asia-a-way-toward-trade-liberalization, accessed 2 February 2024; see also ASEAN-Hong Kong FTA (see note: 17); Free Trade Agreement Between Australia and Hong Kong, China (entry into force 17 January 2020).

[33] Commerce and Economic Development Bureau 'Participation in International Organisations'. Available at: www.cedb.gov.hk/en/trade-and-investment/participation-in-international-organisations.html, accessed 2 February 2024.

historical, political and legal contexts, as well as its proactive engagement in shaping international norms and policies. The book's organisation, theoretical framework and methodology all contribute to a thorough and discerning examination of Hong Kong's standing within the realm of international economic governance. The author has deconstructed the research around Hong Kong to devise new perspectives and orientations surrounding the international economic law literature.

II. IDEAS, NORMS AND SOCIAL PROCESSES IN HONG KONG'S INTERNATIONAL ECONOMIC LAW

In today's globalised world, IEL and policy play a critical role in shaping the economic fortunes of nations and the prosperity of their citizens.[34] Hong Kong, an SAR of China, has a distinct legal and institutional framework that sets it apart from mainland China and other jurisdictions. This framework not only symbolises the territory's colonial heritage and its assimilation into the Chinese state but also lays the foundation for developing and promoting its own ideas and norms within the realm of international economic law.

The book uses both analytical and comparative approaches to provide a profound exploration of the subject matter and facilitate a solid comprehension of the intricate legal and policy environment in Hong Kong's international economic relations. The analytical approach scrutinises the historical, legal and institutional contexts, as well as the fundamental principles, objectives and challenges shaping Hong Kong's international economic law. The comparative approach offers a more extensive context for understanding Hong Kong's international economic law and policy by contrasting the territory's approach with those of other jurisdictions and international norms.

A. Conceptual Framework

To analyse more deeply Hong Kong's stance within the sphere of IEL, this book utilises constructivism as its primary conceptual framework. Constructivism is a social theory that accentuates the significance of ideas, norms and social interactions in shaping the behaviour of international relations actors, encompassing states and non-state entities.[35] By concentrating on the interaction between

[34] Moshe Hirsch, 'Linkages Between International Economic Law and Foreign Policy' in Tomer Broude et al (eds), *The Politics of International Economic Law* (Cambridge, Cambridge University Press, 2011).

[35] Dora Kostakopoulou, 'Constructivisms and Institutional Constructivism' in *Institutional Constructivism in Social Sciences and Law: Frames of Mind, Patterns of Change* (Cambridge, Cambridge University Press, 2018).

ideational aspects and social processes, constructivism offers a valuable perspective for examining the intricate forces that mould Hong Kong's international economic law and policy.

Hong Kong's exceptional historical, political and legal context renders it a fertile environment for investigating the creation and dissemination of ideas and norms in international economic law. Constructivism facilitates a more refined understanding of the role of Hong Kong's various public and private actors in shaping its international economic law. By recognising the significance of social interactions among policymakers, businesses, civil society and international institutions, constructivism reveals the ways in which these actors contribute to the formation, interpretation and enforcement of Hong Kong's international economic law. Furthermore, this approach highlights the role of agency and reflexivity in constructing ideas and norms, emphasising that Hong Kong's IEL is not a static outcome of structural forces but rather an ongoing, dynamic process of social negotiation and contestation.[36]

Constructivism accentuates the importance of norm diffusion and socialisation in Hong Kong's international economic law. As a key participant in the global economy and an active member of various international organisations, Hong Kong is exposed to an array of international norms and practices that influence its domestic legal and policy framework. Constructivism helps to elucidate the mechanisms through which these norms and practices are transmitted, adapted and resisted and how they interact with local ideas and norms to generate a unique, hybrid form of international economic law in Hong Kong. By concentrating on the ideational and social dimensions of Hong Kong's IEL, constructivism offers valuable insights into the wider implications of the territory's legal and policy decisions. By examining how Hong Kong's ideas, norms and values shape its engagement with international economic governance, this book can provide insights into the effectiveness, legitimacy and resilience of Hong Kong's international economic law amidst evolving global norms and power dynamics.

By situating ideas, norms and social interactions at the core of its analysis, constructivism enables a rich and nuanced comprehension of the diverse forces that shape Hong Kong's legal and policy landscape in the domain of international economic governance of the twenty-first century. Employing constructivism as its main conceptual framework, this book aspires to furnish readers with a thorough and insightful examination of Hong Kong's international economic law and policy, while also contributing to the wider theoretical and empirical literature on the role of ideas, norms and social processes in international relations.

[36] Y C Jao, 'Building Prosperity: A Five-Part Economic Strategy for Hong Kong's Future. By Sri International' (2009) 122 *The China Quarterly* 329.

B. Methodology

In the introductory segment of this thorough investigation into Hong Kong's IEL and policy, it is imperative to delineate and substantiate the methodology employed throughout the book. The primary methodology encompasses a fusion of analytical and comparative approaches, allowing for a profound exploration of the subject matter and facilitating a solid comprehension of the intricate legal and policy landscape in Hong Kong's international economic relations.

The analytical approach is vital for unravelling the complexities of Hong Kong's IEL and policy. This method involves scrutinising the historical, legal and institutional contexts, as well as the fundamental principles, objectives and challenges shaping Hong Kong's international economic law. Through the analytical lens, readers will acquire valuable insight into the driving forces and motivation underpinning Hong Kong's legal and policy decisions, thus enabling them to appreciate the unique nature of the territory's international economic governance.

Employing the analytical approach, the book critically assesses Hong Kong's unilateral trade, foreign investment and tax regimes, illuminating their origins, development and repercussions. Furthermore, the analytical methodology facilitates an understanding of the interplay between Hong Kong's domestic legal system and the wider international economic law landscape, enabling readers to grasp how the territory navigates intricate global challenges and opportunities.

Conversely, the comparative approach offers a more extensive context for understanding Hong Kong's IEL and policy by contrasting the territory's approach with those of other jurisdictions and international norms. Engaging in comparative analysis, the book allows readers to discern the similarities and disparities between Hong Kong's approach and the international standards governing economic relations. This methodology not only accentuates the unique aspects of Hong Kong's IEL but also demonstrates how the territory adheres to, or deviates from, global trends and practices.

The comparative methodology proves particularly pertinent in examining Hong Kong's bilateral and multilateral economic relations, such as its FTAs, BITs and participation in the WTO. By contrasting Hong Kong's approach to these agreements and institutions with those of other jurisdictions, the book imparts a comprehensive understanding of the territory's legal and policy stance within the global economic landscape. This comparison also helps to pinpoint potential areas for enhancement or reform and evaluates the implications of Hong Kong's choices for its international economic relations.

By juxtaposing Hong Kong's approach to dispute settlement mechanisms and its involvement in international legal proceedings with other jurisdictions, the book elucidates the territory's strategy in managing international economic disputes and its adherence to global standards in resolving such conflicts.

The book builds upon the work of scholars, including the author, who have conducted research in the past. The proliferation of trade, investment and tax agreements in recent years has generated extensive literature on why states prefer one level of negotiation over others. Additionally, an emerging body of literature has examined whether the growth of bilateral and regional agreements should be seen as a positive or negative development.[37] The primary challenge confronting trade, investment and tax negotiators in the coming years, however, is how to amalgamate these levels or venues of negotiation, including state-led and 'hybrid' regulatory regimes involving both state and non-state actors.[38]

The amalgamation of analytical and comparative approaches constitutes the principal methodology for this book, presenting a comprehensive and robust examination of Hong Kong's international economic law and policy. The analytical approach examines in depth the underpinning principles, objectives and challenges shaping the territory's international economic governance, while the comparative approach positions Hong Kong's approach within the broader purview of global trends and practices.

Together, these methodologies will equip readers with a thorough understanding of Hong Kong's IEL and policy landscape, as well as the intricate interplay between the territory's domestic legal system and the wider international economic law framework. By employing these complementary approaches, the book offers a nuanced and well-rounded analysis of Hong Kong's unique position within the realm of international economic governance, allowing readers to appreciate the territory's significance as an actor in IEL.

III. OVERVIEW

The book aims to provide readers with a thorough and insightful examination of Hong Kong's international economic law and policy, while also contributing to the wider theoretical and empirical literature on the role of ideas, norms and social processes in international relations. By situating these at the core of its analysis, the book enables a rich and nuanced comprehension of the diverse forces that shape Hong Kong's legal and policy landscape in the domain of

[37] G. Richard Shell, 'Trade Legalism and International Relations Theory: An Analysis of the World Trade Organization' (1995) 44 *Duke Law Journal* 829; See generally Neda Zawahri and Sara McLaughlin Mitchell, 'Fragmented Governance of International Rivers: Negotiating Bilateral versus Multilateral Treaties' (2011) 55 *International Studies Quarterly* 835, 842; Dirk De Bièvre and Marcel Hanegraaff, 'Non-state Actors in Multilateral Trade Governance' in Bob Reinalda (ed), *Ashgate Research Companion to Non-state Actors* (London, Routledge, 2011).

[38] Bas Arts, 'Non-state Actors in Global Environmental Governance. New Arrangements beyond the State' in M. Koenig-Archibugi and M. Zürn (eds), *New Modes of Governance in the Global System* (London, Palgrave Macmillan, 2005); see also Markus Thiel and Jeffery Maslanik, 'Transnational Actors' (2017 Print version) *Oxford Research Encyclopedia of International Studies.*

international economic governance. It offers valuable insights into the wider implications of the territory's legal and policy decisions on its position in the global economy and its capacity to tackle the challenges and opportunities of the twenty-first century.

This comprehensive book provides an in-depth analysis of Hong Kong's international economic law, addressing the various aspects that contribute to its unique characteristics. The book is divided into four main parts, each focusing on a different dimension of Hong Kong's international economic relations and highlighting how these aspects are shaped by the territory's historical and institutional factors and together, support the main thesis of the book.

A. Unilateral Foundations: Domestic Trade, Investment and Taxation in Hong Kong

Part I considers Hong Kong's domestic trade regime, unilateral foreign investment regime and unilateral tax regime. It examines the historical context and the legal framework that underpin Hong Kong's approach to international economic governance. By analysing the intricacies of these regimes, the book highlights the unique nature of Hong Kong's unilateral economic policies and the ways in which they support the main thesis – that Hong Kong's international economic law is shaped by its distinct historical and institutional factors. The concept of unilateral economic law refers to a jurisdiction's ability to implement its own economic policies, without necessarily following international trade and investment laws.[39] Hong Kong is a prime example of a region that has established its own unilateral economic policies. These policies cover trade, investment and tax and have been developed based on Hong Kong's unique historical and institutional factors. Hong Kong's approach to international economic governance has been shaped by its colonial history and its current political and economic status as an SAR of China. Hong Kong has benefited by its position adjacent to Shenzhen and Zhuhai, two of China's Special Economic Zones (SEZs), which are areas within the region where businesses are given preferential treatment and regulatory flexibility in order to encourage investment and trade. They are governed by their own set of laws and regulations, which are

[39] Julien Chaisse and Georgios Dimitropoulos, 'Special Economic Zones in International Economic Law: Towards Unilateral Economic Law' (2021) 24 *Journal of International Economic Law* 229. This article explains that unilateral economic law refers to a jurisdiction's use of its domestic legal system to promote trade and investment in a way that diverges from traditional international economic law. This approach emerged as a response to the limitations of traditional international economic law in addressing developing countries' needs. Unilateral economic law has evolved to include policies such as free trade zones, investment incentives and tax breaks, which are tailored to individual countries' economic development goals. While unilateral economic law may diverge from traditional international economic law, it remains subject to international legal norms and principles.).

distinct from those that apply in Hong Kong. Another difference is its approach to foreign investment. Unlike many other countries, Hong Kong does not have a comprehensive foreign investment law or regulatory regime. Instead, it relies on a piecemeal approach, whereby it establishes individual investment agreements with other countries on a bilateral basis. This allows Hong Kong to maintain a high degree of control over its investment policies while still attracting foreign investment. Finally, Hong Kong's unilateral economic policies also extend to its unique tax system, which is based on a territorial principle, meaning that it only taxes income that is earned within the region. This makes it an attractive location for multinational corporations looking to minimise their tax liabilities. Overall, Hong Kong's approach to unilateral economic law is based on its unique historical and institutional factors. By implementing its own economic policies, Hong Kong has been able to maintain a high degree of control over its economic development while still attracting foreign investment and trade.

B. Bilateral Endeavours: Strengthening Hong Kong's Economic Relations

Exploring the bilateral aspects of Hong Kong's international economic relations, Part II focuses on the trends, prospects and challenges associated with bilateral trade, investment treaties and tax treaties. It investigates the evolution of Hong Kong's FTAs, BITs and tax treaties, revealing the impact of these agreements on its international economic law. This underscores the significance of Hong Kong's bilateral relationships in shaping its economic policies and contributes to the main thesis by demonstrating how these relationships are influenced by its unique history and institutional structure. Bilateral economic law refers to the legal rules that regulate economic relations between two countries, covering areas such as trade, investment and taxation. The primary goal of such agreements is to encourage economic cooperation and growth by reducing barriers to trade and investment. FTAs are a key form of bilateral economic law, aimed at liberalising trade by eliminating tariffs and other trade barriers between the signatory countries. For example, the 2010 FTA between Hong Kong and New Zealand abolished tariffs on most traded goods, making it easier and cheaper for both economies to do business with each other.

BITs are another crucial component of bilateral economic law. These agreements offer legal protection to investors from one jurisdiction investing in another by providing provisions on investment protection, dispute resolution and the promotion of investment. For example, the 2003 BIT between Hong Kong and Germany guarantees that investors from both economies will be treated fairly and equitably in each other's jurisdictions. Tax treaties also form a significant part of bilateral economic law. These agreements govern the taxation of income earned by residents of one jurisdiction in the other jurisdiction, with the aim of preventing double taxation, eliminating tax evasion and encouraging cross-border investment. For instance, the 1995 tax treaty between Hong Kong and the United States ensures that residents of both economies are not subjected to double taxation on their income. In conclusion, bilateral economic law plays a pivotal role in regulating economic activity between two countries. FTAs, BITs and tax treaties are essential legal frameworks that foster international economic cooperation, promote economic growth and offer legal protection to investors. As such, they significantly influence the economic policies of countries, facilitating trade and investment and shaping their economic relations with other nations.

C. Multilateral Engagement: Hong Kong's Role in Global Economic Institutions

Part III analyses Hong Kong's participation in multilateral economic institutions, such as the WTO, the ICSID and the Organisation for Economic Co-operation and Development (OECD). It investigates Hong Kong's role in these organisations and its approach to multilateralism in the realms of trade, investment and taxation. This part demonstrates that Hong Kong's multilateral relations are also influenced by its distinctive historical and institutional context and reinforces the main thesis. Multilateral international economic law refers to a complex system of rules, regulations and agreements that govern economic transactions between multiple countries. This system encompasses various aspects of the global economy, including trade, investment and taxation and aims to promote cooperation and coordination among nations for mutual benefit. One of the most compelling arguments in favour of multilateralism in international economic law is that it provides a stable and predictable global economic environment. By establishing common rules and procedures, multilateral institutions like the WTO can provide a framework for resolving disputes and preventing conflicts that could otherwise escalate into costly and damaging trade wars. Furthermore, multilateralism in international economic law can help level the playing field between developed and developing countries.

By providing a forum for negotiations and agreements that take into account the differing needs and capabilities of different nations, multilateral institutions can promote a more equitable and sustainable global economic system. A prime example of the benefits of multilateralism in IEL has been the WTO's success in promoting global trade and reducing barriers to entry for developing countries. The organisation's establishment in 1995 has led to increased economic growth and development in many countries, making it a significant force for positive change in the global economy. In addition, multilateral institutions like the OECD and ICSID play an essential role in promoting international investment and providing mechanisms for resolving investment disputes in a fair and transparent manner. These institutions contribute to creating a stable and secure environment for cross-border investments and are essential in facilitating international trade and economic growth. In conclusion, multilateral IEL is crucial in promoting global economic cooperation, stability and development. Through institutions like the WTO, OECD and ICSID, nations can work together to establish common rules and procedures that benefit all parties involved. Multilateralism can ensure a level playing field, promote a more sustainable economic system and provide mechanisms for resolving disputes in a fair and transparent manner. By embracing multilateralism, nations can work together to create a more prosperous and equitable global economy.

D. Resolving Economic Conflicts: Dispute Settlement in Hong Kong's International Relations

The final section of the book considers Hong Kong's active involvement in several international economic dispute resolution mechanisms, such as the WTO Dispute Settlement Mechanism (DSM), investor-state dispute settlement and international tax disputes. Through a comprehensive overview of Hong Kong's participation in these mechanisms, this section highlights the challenges and opportunities that arise due to its unique position. The thesis of the book is further supported by demonstrating how Hong Kong's historical and institutional factors have shaped its approach to dispute resolution. Hong Kong's involvement in these international economic dispute resolution mechanisms is essential as it enables the territory to safeguard its interests and rights in the global economic environment. For instance, the WTO DSM is a crucial platform for Hong Kong to settle trade disputes with other WTO members, ensuring that its trade interests are protected. Additionally, investor-state dispute settlement mechanisms provide a means for Hong Kong investors to seek remedies in case of disputes with foreign governments. Given its status as a major financial centre, Hong Kong's involvement in international tax dispute resolution mechanisms is critical. Tax disputes can significantly impact the territory's economy, making it essential to have robust mechanisms in place to resolve them. Hong Kong has entered into several DTAAs with other countries and territories, enabling it to resolve tax disputes through negotiation and consultation. Overall, Hong Kong's participation in these international economic dispute resolution mechanisms is vital to safeguard its economic interests and rights in the global arena. As a financial hub and gateway to China, the territory must have strong mechanisms in place to resolve disputes and maintain its competitive edge. Therefore, it is imperative to understand the challenges and opportunities that arise from Hong Kong's unique position in these mechanisms.

The book provides a comprehensive understanding of Hong Kong's unique position in the global economy and the intricacies of its legal framework. By examining the territory's unilateral, bilateral and multilateral policies, as well as its approach to international economic dispute resolution, it aims to offer valuable insights to academics, policymakers and practitioners alike. As the chapters progress, readers will not only gain a deeper appreciation of Hong Kong's IEL but also a broader understanding of the underlying factors that have shaped it over time, ultimately contributing to the richness and complexity of this fascinating field of study.

Part I

Unilateral Foundations: Domestic Trade, Investment and Taxation in Hong Kong

Within the sphere of international economics, unilateralism refers to the ability of jurisdictions to make decisions and carry out actions autonomously, without the need for cooperation with other nations or international organisations.[1] This approach is founded on the principle of self-determination and often mirrors a nation's strategic priorities or political philosophy. By contrast, multilateralism denotes collaboration and coordination among various countries and global bodies with the aim of establishing a more interconnected and fair international economic system.[2]

Unilateralism can take several forms, ranging from protectionist trade policies to the creation of independent economic institutions.[3] Although asserting control over their own economy can be advantageous for countries, unilateral actions may occasionally disrupt the global economic balance or provoke retaliatory measures from other nations.[4] Import tariffs, export subsidies and non-tariff barriers are prime examples of unilateralism. These measures are frequently implemented to shield domestic industries, uphold national security, or guard sensitive sectors from foreign competition.

Expert insights indicate that, in specific situations, unilateralism can yield positive results, such as fostering self-reliance, boosting domestic growth and preserving cultural or national identity.[5] The merits and demerits of unilateralism need to be meticulously evaluated, taking into account the particular needs, resources and goals of each jurisdiction.

Multilateralism encourages the development of a stable, predictable and rules-based global economic framework. Through harmonised efforts, such

[1] Douglas Kriner, 'Unilateralism Unleashed? Polarization and the Politics of Executive Action,' in Robert Lieberman, Suzzanne Mettler and Kenneth Roberts (eds), *Democratic Resilience: Can the United States Withstand Rising Polarization?* (Cambridge, Cambridge University Press, 2021) 118.

[2] Abdur Chowdhury, Xuepeng Liu, Miao Wang and MCS Wong, 'The Role of Multilateralism of the WTO in International Trade Stability' (2021) 20 *World Trade Review* 668.

[3] Edward D Mansfield, Helen V Milner and Peter B Rosendorff, 'Why Democracies Cooperate More: Electoral Control and International Trade Agreements' (2002) 56 *International Organization* 477.

[4] Joost Pauwelyn, 'New Trade Politics for the 21st Century' (2008) 11 *Journal of International Economic Law* 559.

[5] David A Gantz, '*Liberalizing International Trade after Doha: Multilateral, Plurilateral, Regional and Unilateral Initiatives*' (New York, Cambridge University Press, 2013).

as trade agreements, investment treaties and regulatory alignment, countries can nurture mutually advantageous relationships, augment economic interdependence and enable the effective distribution of resources.[6] By participating in multilateral cooperation, nations can tackle intricate global challenges, such as climate change, income inequality and financial instability, which demand a joint and collaborative approach.

In conclusion, unilateralism and multilateralism embody two different strategies for international economic relations, each with its own unique ramifications and results. Achieving the right balance between these approaches is crucial for governments to negotiate the intricacies of the global economy and secure sustainable growth and development.

Part I of this book utilises a constructivist framework to analyse the unique legal and economic system of Hong Kong as a Special Administrative Region (SAR) of China. This approach enables a comprehensive understanding of Hong Kong's unilateral foundations in trade, investment and taxation. The first chapter examines Hong Kong's unilateral trade regime, exploring its open and liberal system characterised by low tariffs and minimal non-tariff barriers. While Hong Kong formulates its trade policy independently, the territory's adherence to World Trade Organisation (WTO) rules and agreements ensures a consistent and open approach. The second chapter investigates Hong Kong's unilateral investment regime, emphasising the territory's capacity to determine its investment policies independently. Hong Kong's open and liberal investment environment promotes stability and predictability, attracting international investors and contributing to its competitive edge in the global market. However, as a WTO member, Hong Kong is also bound by the organisation's rules and agreements, which prohibits discrimination against foreign investors and confers protection upon their rights. Finally, the third chapter discusses Hong Kong's unilateral taxation system, where the territory independently establishes its tax policies without coordination with other nations or international organisations. This fiscal autonomy, combined with Hong Kong's low tax rates and territorial tax system, makes the territory an appealing destination for multinational corporations and overseas investors. In conclusion, Part I presents an in-depth examination of Hong Kong's unilateral foundations in domestic trade, investment and taxation, using the constructivist framework to clarify the interplay of ideas, norms and shared understanding that shape these policies. This analysis provides valuable insights into Hong Kong's unique legal and economic environment and its implications for the territory's position in the international economic landscape.

[6] John Owen, 'Economic Interdependence and Regional Peace' in Thazha Varkey Paul (ed), *International Relations Theory and Regional Transformation* (Cambridge, Cambridge University Press, 2012) 107.

2

Trade on the Frontier: Hong Kong's Unilateral Trade Regime and its Evolution

THIS CHAPTER DELVES into the fascinating history and development of Hong Kong's trade regime and aims to offer readers a comprehensive understanding of how Hong Kong, a small territory-state, emerged as a vital player on the global stage and the factors that have contributed to its remarkable economic growth. In this chapter, we will embark on a journey to explore the evolution of Hong Kong's trade policies, the driving forces behind its global integration and the territory's involvement in international trade affairs.

The discussion is set against the backdrop of Hong Kong's extraordinary transformation from a small fishing village into a thriving metropolis renowned for its free-market economy and an international trade hub. This chapter highlights the significance of Hong Kong's unilateral trade regime in paving the way for its ascent as a global trade powerhouse.

The inclusion of constructivism as a theoretical framework enriches the analysis by allowing for an examination of how Hong Kong's identity as a global trade hub has been socially constructed and sustained through its trade policies and practices. A constructivist approach provides a means to explore how Hong Kong's unique historical experiences and cultural values have influenced the formation of its trade regime and continue to shape its interactions with the international community. By employing constructivism, a more nuanced understanding of Hong Kong's trade regime and its ability to adapt to a changing international economic governance can be gained. This approach not only offers a comprehensive analysis of Hong Kong's trade policies but also emphasises the significance of considering the broader social and cultural context in which these policies have been formulated and implemented.

The main objectives of this chapter can be summarised as follows: Firstly, to trace the emergence of Hong Kong on the global stage by examining its historical foundations and the key milestones that have shaped its trade regime. This includes an analysis of the territory's early years under British rule, the establishment of its free port status and the subsequent development of its export-oriented economy. Secondly, to explore Hong Kong's economic growth by focusing on its involvement in international trade affairs. This section will discuss Hong Kong's accession to the General Agreement on Tariffs and Trade (GATT) and its participation in the World Trade Organisation (WTO). The discussion will also encompass the territory's bilateral and multilateral trade agreements, as well as its engagement in regional economic forums and partnerships. Lastly, the chapter will trace the evolution of Hong Kong's unilateral trade regime, evaluating the territory's trade policy adjustments in response to shifting global economic trends and challenges. The impact of significant events on Hong Kong's trade policies and its ability to maintain its status as a global trade and financial hub will be examined closely.

I. CHARTING NEW HORIZONS: HONG KONG'S EMERGENCE ON THE GLOBAL STAGE

Over the years, Hong Kong has established itself as a prominent player on the global stage, forging a unique position as an international financial and trade hub.[1] Its rich history, strategic location and thriving economy have enabled Hong Kong to successfully tackle the challenges and seize the opportunities presented by an ever-changing world.

Through an exploration of its unique historical background and the pivotal role of the Basic Law, a deeper comprehension of the contextual factors that have shaped Hong Kong's global presence can be attained. Furthermore, this section aims to examine the strategies and mechanisms employed by Hong Kong to engage with external affairs, showcasing the approaches that have enabled the territory to uphold and enhance its influence on the world stage. To provide a comprehensive understanding, the section begins with a concise overview of Hong Kong's history, to supply the essential context for comprehending its growth and development. Subsequently, the section discusses the significance of the Basic Law as the constitutional foundation of Hong Kong's governance and its role in shaping the territory's external relations. It also scrutinises Hong Kong's participation in external affairs, highlighting the diverse channels and platforms through which it engages in international dialogue and collaboration. By offering a thorough analysis of these key aspects, the section aims to provide a well-rounded understanding of Hong Kong's emergence and its ongoing role in global affairs.

[1] Hong Kong Monetary Authority, 'Hong Kong as an international finance centre'. Available at: www.hkma.gov.hk/eng/key-functions/international-financial-centre/hong-kong-as-an-international-financial-centre/, accessed 9 February 2024.

A. Setting the Scene: An Historical Overview

Hong Kong Island, Kowloon and the New Territories have long been a part of China.[2] Hong Kong has witnessed substantial economic transformations over the past century, going from a fishing and agricultural hamlet to one of the major sources of foreign direct investment (FDI) and one of the world's top financial centres.

In 1840, during the First Opium War, British troops entered Hong Kong Island for the first time.[3] The Treaty of Nanjing, by which China legally ceded the Island to Britain, allowed Britain to occupy Hong Kong Island in 1842.[4] After Britain forced the Qing government to sign the Convention of Peking, Kowloon was forcibly captured by British forces during the Second Opium War in 1860 and annexed.[5] With the 1898 Convention for the Extension of Hong Kong Territory, a sizable portion of Chinese territory south of the Shenzhen River and north of Boundary Street, consisting of 235 islands, was given under a 100-year lease, effectively establishing full imperial rule over Hong Kong.[6]

Hong Kong was administered as a crown colony while it was ruled by the British, where British legal institutions, including a British civil service and courts were established.[7] Commercial factors and the building of a military-controlled trading centre in the Far East were the primary drivers behind the British annexation.[8] The Joint Declaration on the Question of Hong Kong was signed by the governments of China and the United Kingdom on 19 December 1984. Britain undertook to restore Hong Kong to China and the PRC declared that it would resume the exercise of sovereignty over Hong Kong on 1 July 1997.[9] In order to prepare for the transfer, many transitional arrangements between 1984 and 1997 were created.

In accordance with Article 31 of the PRC Constitution, the PRC officially commenced exercising control over Hong Kong as a Special Administrative Region on July 1, 1997.[10] The Basic Law, the main constitutional document

[2] Liu Shuyong, 'Hong Kong: A Survey of Its Political and Economic Development over the Past 150 Years' (1997) 151 *The China Quarterly* 583.

[3] James Yu TC, 'The Struggle with Foreign Powers, 1840–1914' (1927) 26 *Current History* 383.

[4] Treaty of Peace, Friendship, Commerce and Indemnity between Great Britain and China (Signed at Nanking, 29 August 1842, Ratifications exchanged at Hong Kong, 26 June 1843).

[5] Convention of Peace and Friendship between Great Britain and China (Signed at Peking, 24 October 1860).

[6] Wen-Sze King, 'The Lease Convention between China and the Foreign Powers' (1916) 1 *Chinese Social and Political Science Review* 24, 25.

[7] Stefan H C Lo, Kevin Kwok-yin Cheng and Wing Hong Chui, *The Hong Kong Legal System*, 2nd edn (Cambridge, Cambridge University Press, 2019) 21.

[8] Tzu-nang Chiu, *The Port of Hong Kong: A Survey of its Development* (Hong Kong, Hong Kong University Press, 1973) 13.

[9] Roda Mushkat, 'The Dynamics of International Legal Regime Formation: The Sino-British Joint Declaration on the Question of Hong Kong Revisited' (2011) 22 *European Journal of International Law* 1119.

[10] Yash Ghai, *Hong Kong's New Constitutional Order: The Resumption of Chinese Sovereignty and the Basic Law* (Hong Kong, Hong Kong University Press, 1997).

governing Hong Kong, acknowledges that Hong Kong shall be governed in accordance with the maxim 'One Country, Two Systems' and that the socialist system and policies would not be implemented in Hong Kong for a period of 50 years.[11]

With the exception of foreign and defence concerns, Hong Kong remains highly autonomous and has the authority to manage external affairs, including trade affairs.[12] It is the only SAR in China where the common law system is practised. It is distinctive because it preserves a common law system within a socialist and civil law framework, adhering to liberal economic ideas.[13] This gives Hong Kong a unique status in the international law domain. Priority has been placed on the rule of law, promotion as a centre for international dispute resolution, judicial independence, economic integration with the Chinese Mainland and stability as a global financial hub in Hong Kong policy.[14] The third-ranked host economy for FDI inflows in 2022 was Hong Kong.[15]

There are various instances where Hong Kong has actively participated in the activities associated with the WTO. It has contributed to the dispute resolution regime[16] or implemented WTO policies by utilising international dispute settlement provisions contained in bilateral investment treaties (BITs).[17] Hong Kong has abided by the principles of the WTO, as witnessed by the shift

[11] Ji Pengfei, 'Explanations on The Basic Law of the Hong Kong Special Administrative Region of the People's Republic of China (Draft) and its Related Documents (Addressing the Third Session of the Seventh National People's Congress on 28 March 1990). See also Matthieu Burnay and Florian Couveinhes-Matsumoto, 'One Country, Two International Status? The Evolution of Hong Kong's International Positioning from Western Imperialism to Chinese Authoritarianism' (2022) 64 *German Yearbook of International Law* 243; Johannes Chan, 'State Succession to Human Rights Treaties: Hong Kong and the International Covenant on Civil and Political Rights' (1996) 45 *The International and Comparative Law Quarterly* 928; Roda Mushkat, 'Scrapping Hong Kong Legislature: An International Law Perspective' (1997) 27 *Hong Kong Law Journal* 12.

[12] Xianggang Ji Ben Fa (The Basic Law of the Hong Kong Special Administrative Region of the People's Republic of China) (date of signature 19 December 1984; entry into force 1 July 1997) (hereinafter referred as Basic Law), Chapter 1: General Principles, art 12.

[13] Roda Mushkat, 'The Future of Hong Kong's International Legal Personality: Does International Law Matter – A Post-Handover Snapshot' (1998) 22 *Southern Illinois University Law Journal* 291; See T *se Chu-Fai v Governor of the Metropolitan Reception Centre* (1997) 150 ALR 566. Also see: Stephen D. Krasner, 'The Hole in the Whole: Sovereignty, Shared Sovereignty and International Law' (2004) 25 *Michigan Journal of International Law* 1095.

[14] HKSAR Government, 'Speech by CE-elect at Bauhinia Culture International Forum (English only) (with photos/video)' (*The Government of the Hong Kong Special Administrative Region Press Releases*, 16 June 2022). Available at: www.info.gov.hk/gia/general/202206/16/P2022061600310.htm, accessed 9 February 2024.

[15] UNCTAD, 'World Investment Report 2022: International Tax Reforms and Sustainable Investment' (2022) 9.

[16] WTO, 'Member Information: Hong Kong, China and the WTO'. Available at: www.wto.org/english/thewto_e/countries_e/hong_kong_china_e.htm (accessed 9 February 2024).

[17] Christophe Hillion and Ramses A Wessel, 'The European Union and International Dispute Settlement: Mapping Principles and Conditions' in Marise Cremona, Anne Thies, Ramses A Wessel (eds), *The European Union and International Dispute Settlement*, 1st edn (Portland, Hart Publishing 2017) 15. The contracting parties of 20 BITs are: United Arab Emirates, Chile, Canada, Kuwait, Finland, Thailand, UK, Korea, Japan, Austria, BLEU (Belgium-Luxembourg Economic Union), Germany, France, Italy, New Zealand, Switzerland, Sweden, Denmark, Australia, The Netherlands.

from diplomatic procedures to adjudicative methods such as the mutual agreement procedure (MAP) while dealing with the double taxation agreement.[18]

In the past few years, events in Hong Kong have exacerbated the complexities of the 'One Country, Two Systems' regime.[19] These circumstances highlight that Hong Kong's outward autonomy is constrained not just politically and economically, but legally as well.[20] The legal limitations underscore the pre-eminence of the People's Republic of China as the ruling authority, while relegating Hong Kong to a position of a non-state entity with considerably limited political clout. Although Hong Kong enjoys a remarkable degree of external influence and self-governance for a non-sovereign entity, its global capabilities remain circumscribed. Historically, since 1949, Hong Kong's interaction with China, although marred with sporadic political disputes, has often been characterised by a reciprocal economic advantage. However, the dynamics of this relationship have undergone a radical transformation since the revolution of 1949.

B. Foundational Framework: The Basic Law

The Basic Law of the Hong Kong Special Administrative Region (Hong Kong) was promulgated on 4 April 1990 under the Decree of the President of the

[18] OECD, *Making Dispute Resolution More Effective-MAP Peer Review Report, Hong Kong, China (stage 1): Inclusive Framework on BEPS: Action 14, OECD/G20 Base Erosion and Profit Shifting Project* (Paris, OECD Publishing, 2019).

[19] Albert HY Chen, 'The Basic Law and The Development of The Political System in Hong Kong' (2007) 15 *Asia Pacific Law Review* 19. See also the former Hong Kong's Secretary of Justice stated that '[t]he National Security Law does not derogate from any of the provisions of the Basic Law that seek to strengthen Hong Kong's roles as an international financial centre and a global investment hub. Hong Kong will continue to maintain its status as a free port and protect in accordance with law the right of private ownership of property as well as the ownership of enterprises and the investments from outside Hong Kong. As provided under the Basic Law, Hong Kong will continue to be a separate customs territory and participate in the World Trade Organisation in the name of 'Hong Kong, China'. Furthermore, with the authorisation of the CPG, Hong Kong continues to, under the framework of the Basic Law, conclude free trade agreements and international investment agreements with overseas jurisdictions and participate in appropriate capacities in the work of international organizations. International commerce and investment activities can only thrive under a stable and rule of law-based social environment. It is a pivotal measure that can restore Hong Kong to a harmonious, diverse and inclusive international metropolis where business, as well as international trade and investment activities can be conducted as usual and the legitimate rights and interests of Hong Kong residents and foreigners are safeguarded and can be exercised freely without concerns. Following the enactment of the National Security Law, Hong Kong continues to enjoy its high degree of autonomy in matters such as finance, trade and economic policies.' Teresa Cheng, 'National Security Law – A New Horizon for the Successful Implementation of 'One Country, Two Systems'' (2020) 4 *China Law Magazine* Available at: www.doj.gov.hk/en/community_engagement/speeches/20200824_sj1.html, accessed 9 February 2024.

[20] Xiaobing Xu and George D. Wilson, 'The Hong Kong Special Administrative Region as a Model of Regional External Autonomy' (2000) 32 *Case Western Reserve Journal of International Law* 1, 12. See also Matthieu Burnay and Florian Couveinhes-Matsumoto, 'One Country, Two International Status? The Evolution of Hong Kong's International Positioning from Western Imperialism to Chinese Authoritarianism' (2022) 64 *German Yearbook of International Law* 243.

People's Republic of China (PRC), No. 26 and came into effect on 1 July 1997.[21] The Basic Law has the legal status of a statute enacted by the highest constitutional power of China.[22] But in practice, the Basic Law remains a transnational legal instrument with domestic, regional and international dimensions.

Chapter VII of the Basic Law, entitled External Affairs, provides legal authority for Hong Kong's international trade law policymaking.[23] Article 115 provides that '*The Hong Kong Special Administrative Region shall pursue the policy of free trade and safeguard the free movement of goods, intangible assets and capital.*'[24] These two articles underscore the importance of Hong Kong SAR as a global and regional financial capital. Of particular importance is Article 114 which provides that '*The Hong Kong Special Administrative Region shall maintain the status of a free port and shall not impose any tariff unless otherwise prescribed by law*'.[25]

The legal basis for the Hong Kong government to conclude economic agreements stems from the Hong Kong Basic Law. Under Article 109, the Hong Kong government has to create a suitable economic and legal environment to preserve Hong Kong's reputation as an international financial centre.[26] Furthermore, Articles 116 and 151 allow the Hong Kong government to use the name 'Hong Kong, China' when engaging in international organisations and international trade agreements, expanding and sustaining economic and trade relations and developing and enforcing agreements in these areas with third countries and international organisations.[27]

Hong Kong has been enlarging its economic agreement networks,[28] with a growing focus on establishing and consolidating the territory's economic and commerce relationships with countries belonging to the Association of Southeast Asian Nations ('ASEAN') and nations which have joined the Belt and Road Initiative ('BRI'). These are evidenced when the former Chief Executive Carrie Lam explicitly mentioned that her government was eager to promote stronger business, trade and investment ties with ASEAN countries during the 2021 Policy Address[29] and the plan to create the Steering Group on Integration

[21] Xianggang Ji Ben Fa (Basic Law) (n 18).

[22] Danny Gittings, *Introduction to the Hong Kong Basic Law*, 2nd edn (Hong Kong, Hong Kong University Press, 2013) 37.

[23] Xianggang Ji Ben Fa (Basic Law) (n 18) Chapter VII: External Affairs.

[24] ibid Chapter V: Economy, art 115.

[25] ibid art 114.

[26] ibid art 109.

[27] ibid art 116.

[28] Teresa Cheng, 'From Special Economic Zones to Greater Special Economic Region – Hong Kong Special Administrative Region as a Model for Legal Infrastructure Design' (2019) 26 *Transnational Corporations Journal* 63, 74.

[29] Office of the Chief Executive, 'The Chief Executive's 2021 Policy Address – Building a Bright Future Together' (2021). Available at: www.policyaddress.gov.hk/2021/eng/pdf/PA2021.pdf, accessed 9 February 2024.

into National Development,[30] which would encourage mutual business and trade cooperation between Hong Kong and the nations along the BRI and develop appropriate policies to achieve such an objective.[31] Past Policy Addresses delivered by the Chief Executive have also indicated and acknowledged the continual active role that the government had played in broadening its international markets,[32] exploring new opportunities for Hong Kong businesses and highlighting Hong Kong's comparative advantages to incentivise Chinese and international investors and businesses to enter Hong Kong.[33] Additionally, the government's intention to apply for accession to the Regional Comprehensive Economic Partnership ('RCEP') was emphasised in the 2018 Policy Address and all subsequent addresses,[34] while its commitment to expand Hong Kong market access to foreign investors and companies through the signature of Free Trade Agreements (FTAs), Investment Promotion Protection Agreements (IPPAs) and other economic agreements has been explicitly mentioned.[35]

For economic agreements, the general practice in Hong Kong is to first lobby and explore the possibility of an agreement with a third country. Once negotiations are announced to be commenced on a particular date, various documents may be released soon afterwards, including a Joint Statement by Hong Kong's Secretary for Commerce and Economic Development, a press release announcing the launching of negotiations and a consultation paper to solicit public opinions.[36] After the agreement's conclusion, various steps may need to be taken for the agreement to enter into force in Hong Kong.

C. Global Connections: Hong Kong's External Affairs

Article 151 of the Basic Law serves as a critical reference for comprehending Hong Kong's nuanced role within the international economic environment.

[30] Office of the Chief Executive, 'The Chief Executive's 2022 Policy Address – 2022.10.19' (2022) para 36. Available at: www.policyaddress.gov.hk/2022/public/pdf/policy/policy-full_en.pdf, accessed 9 February 2024.

[31] ibid.

[32] Office of the Chief Executive, 'The Chief Executive's 2019 Policy Address – Treasure Hong Kong. Our Home' (2019). Available at: www.policyaddress.gov.hk/2019/eng/pdf/PA2019.pdf, accessed 9 February 2024.

[33] Office of the Chief Executive, 'The Chief Executive's 2018 Policy Address – Striving Ahead Rekindling Hope' (2018) para 82. Available at: www.policyaddress.gov.hk/2018/eng/pdf/PA2018.pdf, accessed 9 February 2024.

[34] See, eg, Office of the Chief Executive, 'The Chief Executive's 2021 Policy Address – Building a Bright Future Together' para 47 and Office of the Chief Executive, 'The Chief Executive's 2022 Policy Address – 2022.10.19' (n 11) para 44.

[35] Office of the Chief Executive, 'The Chief Executive's 2017 Policy Address – We Connect for Hope and Happiness' (2017) para 47. Available at: www.policyaddress.gov.hk/2017/eng/pdf/PA2017.pdf, accessed 9 February 2024.

[36] See Trade and Industry Department, 'Hong Kong's Free Trade Agreements (FTAs)' (*Trade and Industry Department, The Government of the Hong Kong Special Administrative Region*, 24 February 2023). Available at: www.tid.gov.hk/english/ita/fta/index.html, accessed 5 March 2024.

This chapter establishes that 'The Hong Kong Special Administrative Region possesses the authority to independently cultivate and maintain relationships and to establish and execute agreements under the appellation "Hong Kong, China" with international entities, states and relevant global organisations in relevant domains. These encompass areas such as economy, trade, finance, currency, maritime affairs, communications, tourism, cultural exchanges, and sports.'[37] This provision elucidates Hong Kong's unique position as a Special Administrative Region within the People's Republic of China, allowing it to independently engage with other countries and international entities in various fields. This level of autonomy, particularly in sectors such as trade, finance and communications, suggests an unprecedented and distinctive status for a non-sovereign entity. However, it is also noteworthy that the extent and execution of this autonomy might be influenced by the larger geopolitical dynamics and relationships of the People's Republic of China.

In light of this, it is noteworthy to mention that Hong Kong is a signatory to 263 multilateral agreements currently in force.[38] A large majority of these treaties were applicable to Hong Kong prior to 1 July 1997 and continue to apply from that date.[39] Fewer treaties have been applied to the Hong Kong SAR after 1 July 1997.[40]

Moving from the domain of multilateral agreements, it is important to consider the application of Article 153. According to this article, any international agreement to which China is a party (or becomes a party) requires the consultation of the Hong Kong SAR Government before its extension to Hong Kong.[41] Since 1997, international economic law has been an area of pronounced activity. This is evident in the Outline Development Plan for the Guangdong-Hong Kong-Macao Greater Bay Area, issued on 18 February 2019.[42] The Plan intends to fortify and advance Hong Kong's standing as an international hub for finance, trade and transportation, including its prominence as a global aviation nexus. It further aims to enhance Hong Kong's position as a leading offshore hub for Renminbi (RMB) transactions and its role as a global centre for asset and risk management. Additionally, it aspires to position Hong Kong as the preferred choice for legal and dispute resolution services in the Asia-Pacific region, shaping it into an international metropolis.[43]

[37] See art 151.

[38] According to the DoJ, HK is a party to 263 multilateral agreements (latest figures on 1 December 2022). See Department of Justice, 'Multilateral Agreements' (*Department of Justice, The Government of the Hong Kong Special Administrative Region*, 1 December 2022). Available at: www.doj.gov.hk/en/external/treaties.html, accessed 9 February 2024.

[39] ibid.

[40] ibid.

[41] Xianggang Jiben Fa (Basic Law) (n 18), art 153.

[42] Greater Bay Area, 'Outline Development Plan for the Guangdong-Hong Kong-Macao Greater Bay Area' (*Greater Bay Area*, 18 February 2019). Available at: www.bayarea.gov.hk/filemanager/en/share/pdf/Outline_Development_Plan.pdf, accessed 9 February 2024.

[43] ibid 12.

Further reinforcing Hong Kong's unique status in international affairs, we must take into account Article XII of the Marrakesh Agreement. This states that 'any State or separate customs territory possessing full autonomy in the conduct of its external commercial relations may accede to the WTO'. Concurrently, Article 152 of the Basic Law asserts that 'the Central People's Government shall take the necessary steps to ensure that the Hong Kong SAR shall continue to retain its status in an appropriate capacity in those international organizations of which the PRC is a member and in which Hong Kong participates in one capacity or another'.[44]

Articles 2 and 12 of the Basic Law significantly underline Hong Kong's elevated level of autonomy in administration, permitting the systems in place before the 1997 handover to persist until 2047.[45] Consequently, China has, in general, maintained a 'hands-off' approach in its governance of Hong Kong, except for defence and foreign affairs.[46] In this sense, Hong Kong has formulated its trade policy for free trade,[47] where little to no custom duties are imposed on imported goods, whilst also being able to enjoy preferential treatment in the areas of tariffs and customs.

In this respect, while pursuing a separate international and trade policy from that of China under Article XII of the Marrakesh Agreement Hong Kong has also maintained a membership with the WTO that is independent of China, under the name of 'Hong Kong, China'.[48] Consequently, under its individualised WTO membership, Hong Kong has participated in various disputes, both as a third party[49] and as a complainant.[50] Furthermore, Hong Kong has its separate trade policy reviews from China, where the reviews are tailored to address the situation and unique issues present in Hong Kong. Hong Kong has also participated in China's trade policy review meetings[51] and vice versa.[52] In this sense, in the resolution and discussion of issues relating to international trade law, Hong Kong has free reign over this matter; and China will not launch a dispute at the WTO-level on behalf of Hong Kong, nor represent it in the WTO disputes.

[44] Chapter VII: External Affairs, art 152.

[45] ibid art 5.

[46] HKSAR Government, 'One Country, Two Systems' (*The Government of the Hong Kong Special Administrative Region Press Releases*, July 2002). Available at: www.info.gov.hk/info/sar5/e12.htm, accessed 9 February 2024.

[47] Trade and Industry Department, 'Hong Kong's Trade Policy' (*Trade and Industry Department, The Government of the Hong Kong Special Administrative Region*, 11 November 2022). Available at: www.tid.gov.hk/english/trade_relations/trade_policy/trpolicy.html, accessed 9 February 2024.

[48] ibid.

[49] Hong Kong has been a third party in 22 cases, including DS 564 United States – Certain Measures on Steel and Aluminium Product.

[50] Hong Kong has been a complainant in two cases, namely, DS 29 Turkey – Restrictions on Imports of Textile and Clothing Products and DS 597 – United States – Origin Marking Requirement.

[51] Trade Policy Review Body – 11 and 13 July 2018 – Trade Policy Review – China – Minutes of the Meeting (21 November 2018) WT/TPR/M/375. Available at: http://docsonline.wto.org.

[52] Trade Policy Review Body – 26 and 28 November 2018 – Trade Policy Review – Hong Kong, China – Minutes of the Meeting (6 March 2019) WT/TPR/M/380. Available at: http://docsonline.wto.org.

II. THE ENGINE OF GROWTH: HONG KONG'S INVOLVEMENT IN INTERNATIONAL TRADE AFFAIRS

Within the ever-changing global economic environment, Hong Kong has consistently assumed a critical position in influencing international trade dynamics. The main aim of this section is to explore the diverse aspects of Hong Kong's engagement in international trade affairs. By scrutinising the essential organisations, regulations and legislation that preside over its trade ecosystem, readers will acquire an improved comprehension of the intricate workings of Hong Kong's trade system. Furthermore, the section will examine the roles of governmental and non-governmental organisations in shaping trade policy, providing valuable insights into the primary decision makers and influencers moulding Hong Kong's trade landscape. Additionally, the section will underscore recent developments, demonstrating how Hong Kong continues to negotiate the challenges and opportunities brought by a rapidly shifting global economy. The framework of this section is devised to deliver an exhaustive investigation into Hong Kong's involvement in international trade affairs. Commencing with an overview of the principal organisations and rules governing the world economy, the section discusses the organisation of foreign trade institutions and legislation, shedding light on the essential elements of Hong Kong's trade infrastructure. Subsequently, the role of governmental and non-governmental organisations in devising trade policy is assessed, offering a glimpse into the mechanisms and actors contributing to Hong Kong's tactical trade decisions. In conclusion, the section discusses recent developments, depicting the ongoing evolution and adaptability of Hong Kong's trade landscape.

A. Architects of Prosperity: Key Organisations and Rules Shaping the World Economy

According to Article 31 of the PRC Constitution, Hong Kong is a sovereign Special Administrative Region operating under the tenet of 'One Country, Two Systems'.[53] The Basic Law promises that Hong Kong will not adopt socialist practices and that the previous capitalist system and way of life will endure for 50 years without alteration.[54] Predominantly, Hong Kong's policy-makers centre around the HKSAR Government – the Chief Executive, the Departments of Justice, Administration and Finance, the heads of the 13 policy bureaux within the government and the Executive Council.

As an executive-led government, the HKSAR Government is in charge of the creation and enforcement of policies, as well as the preparation and proposal

[53] Roda Mushkat, *One Country, Two International Legal Personalities: The Case of Hong Kong* (Hong Kong, Hong Kong University Press, 1997).

[54] Chapter 1: General Principles, art 5.

of draft legislation.[55] Under Article 64 of the Basic Law, the government is accountable to the Legislative Council.[56] Among other requirements, it is obliged to make regular addresses on its policies and respond to queries made by Legislative Council members.[57] Finally, the government is required to consider public opinions fully when making any policy decisions to ensure their alignment with public objectives.[58] In this sense, the Legislative Council remains an important source for the demonstration of public views, where public hearings are conducted to gather public opinions on legislative bills and public policies.[59] Apart from public hearings, the government has also often introduced a public consultation period when it is planning to negotiate an agreement[60] or introduce a bill to the Legislative Council[61] in a bid to solicit public opinion.

As the leader of Hong Kong, the Chief Executive is answerable to the Central People's Government.[62] The Central People's Government appoints the Chief Executive following local elections for a five-year term that is extendable for an additional five years. The Chief Executive executes the Basic Law, names judges, approves legislation and spending plans, enacts laws, decides on governmental policies and issues executive orders.[63] He is also in charge of delivering an annual Policy Address to the Legislative Council,[64] which is broadcasted to the public in real-time.[65] The Policy Address is important, since it outlines the policy initiatives that are to be initiated and implemented by the current government and the solutions that are proposed to tackle existing issues in Hong Kong. Policy addresses on the policy initiatives of different bureaus are also delivered to the corresponding Legislative Council panels. For example, the Policy Initiatives

[55] Government Information Centre, 'Policy Address' (*The 2005–06 Policy Address, The Government of the Hong Kong Special Administrative Region*, 12 October 2005). Available at: www.policyaddress.gov.hk/05-06/eng/p5.htm, accessed 9 February 2024.

[56] Xianggang Jiben Fa (Basic Law) (n 18), Chapter IV: Political Structure, art 64.

[57] HKSAR Government, 'LCQ2: The Relationship among the Executive Authorities, the Legislature and the Judiciary' (*The Government of the Hong Kong Special Administrative Region Press Releases*, 27 January 2010). Available at: www.info.gov.hk/gia/general/201001/27/P201001270155.htm, accessed 9 February 2024.

[58] ibid.

[59] Legislative Council, Public Engagement. in Legislative Council (ed), *A Companion to the History, Rules and Practices of the Legislative Council of the Hong Kong Special Administrative Region* (The Legislative Council Commission 2016), para 16.8. Available at: www.legco.gov.hk/general/english/procedur/companion/chapter_16/chapter_16.html, accessed 9 February 2024.

[60] Trade and Industry Department, 'Consultation Papers' (*Trade and Industry Department, The Government of the Hong Kong Special Administrative* Region, 24 November 2022). Available at: www.tid.gov.hk/english/aboutus/noticeboard/consultpaper.html, accessed 9 February 2024.

[61] 'Legislative Council, Legislative Process' in Legislative Council (ed), *A Companion to the History, Rules and Practices of the Legislative Council of the Hong Kong Special Administrative Region* (The Legislative Council Commission 2016) para 11.39. Available at: www.legco.gov.hk/general/english/procedur/companion/chapter_11/chapter_11.html, accessed 9 February 2024.

[62] Chapter IV: Political Structure, art 43.

[63] ibid art 48.

[64] ibid art 64.

[65] News.gov.hk, 'CE to Deliver Policy Address' (*News.gov.hk*, 17 October 2022). Available at: www.news.gov.hk/eng/2022/10/20221017/20221017_190644_997.html, accessed 9 February 2024.

of Commerce and Economic Development Bureau have been delivered to the Legislative Council Panel on Commerce, Industry, Innovation and Technology.[66] Hong Kong's Chief Executive serves as the head of government.[67] He oversees several bureaux, divisions and commissions in addition to the departments of administration, finance and justice.

Hong Kong has a two-tiered system of representational government and judiciary, together with three branches of government headed by a Chief Executive and an Executive Council.[68] The Executive Council is a board of 37 advisers, who are either high-ranking government officials, Legislative Council members or public figures.[69] Under Article 56 of the Basic Law, the Council has to be consulted before the Chief Executive makes decisions relating to policies, introduces draft legislation into the Legislative Council, produces subordinate legislation or disbands the Legislative Council.[70] During this consultation, the Chief Executive and the Executive Council would typically meet weekly,[71] with the latter providing advice to the former. However, should the Chief Executive

[66] See, eg, Commerce and Economic Development Bureau, 'Legislative Council Panel on Commerce, Industry, Innovation and Technology, 2022 Policy Address – Policy Initiatives of Commerce and Economic Development Bureau' (*Legislative Council of the Hong Kong Special Administrative Region of the People's Republic of China*, October 2022) LC Paper No CB(1)718/2022(03). Available at: www.legco.gov.hk/yr2022/english/panels/ci/papers/ci20221107cb1-718-3-e.pdf, accessed 9 February 2024.

[67] Arts 43 and 60.

[68] GovHK, 'Government Structure' (*GovHK, The Government of the Hong Kong Special Administrative Region*, September 2022). Available at: www.gov.hk/en/about/govdirectory/govstructure.htm, accessed 9 February 2024; GovHK, 'Organisation Chart of the Government of the Hong Kong Special Administrative Region' (*GovHK, The Government of the Hong Kong Special Administrative Region*, 1 July 2022). Available at: www.gov.hk/en/about/govdirectory/govchart/index.htm, accessed 9 February 2024.

[69] Basic Law, art 55. This states: Members of the Executive Council of the Hong Kong Special Administrative Region shall be appointed by the Chief Executive from among the principal officials of the executive authorities, members of the Legislative Council and public figures. Their appointment or removal shall be decided by the Chief Executive. The term of office of members of the Executive Council shall not extend beyond the expiry of the term of office of the Chief Executive who appoints them.

Members of the Executive Council of the Hong Kong Special Administrative Region shall be Chinese citizens who are permanent residents of the Region with no right of abode in any foreign country.

The Chief Executive may, as he or she deems necessary, invite other persons concerned to sit in on meetings of the Council.

[70] ibid, art 56. This states: The Executive Council of the Hong Kong Special Administrative Region shall be presided over by the Chief Executive.

Except for the appointment, removal and disciplining of officials and the adoption of measures in emergencies, the Chief Executive shall consult the Executive Council before making important policy decisions, introducing bills to the Legislative Council, making subordinate legislation, or dissolving the Legislative Council.

If the Chief Executive does not accept a majority opinion of the Executive Council, he or she shall put the specific reasons on record.

[71] Executive Council, 'Executive Council' (*Executive Council, The Government of the Hong Kong Special Administrative Region*, 8 April 2022). Available at: www.ceo.gov.hk/exco/eng/index.html, accessed 9 February 2024.

decide not to accept any opinions held by the majority of the Executive Council, he must provide a written explanation of the reasons for not doing so. The 90-member Legislative Council, which is in charge of making laws, approving public spending, overseeing the administration's performance and supporting the appointment and removal of judges, sits in the centre.[72]

At the regional level, 18 councils with a total of 479 seats advise the HKSAR Government on issues pertaining to the welfare of the populace, the provision and use of public facilities and services and the undertaking of environmental improvement projects as well as the promotion of recreational, cultural and communal activities within the districts.[73] Departments and the Government Secretariat make up the Administration, which is the government's executive branch. Legislative proposals are initiated and policies are developed by the Government Secretariat Bureaux. As well as delivering direct services to the community, departments also enforce laws and regulations. Judges have the authority to make decisions.[74]

In the context of the formulation of international policy, leaving aside the Chief Executive and the Executive Council, the Department of Justice and the Commerce and Economic Development Bureau are the most relevant departments within Hong Kong government. The Department of Justice is in charge of judicial affairs and consists of six divisions, including the International Law Division. This division is comprised of the Treaties & Law Unit and the Mutual Legal Assistance Unit.[75] The Treaties & Law Unit, besides advising the government on international law issues, also negotiates agreements relating to the handover of fugitive criminals, reciprocal legal help in criminal proceedings and the removal of convicted people on behalf of the HKSAR Government,[76] and gives legal support in bilateral and multilateral negotiations, such as investment promotion and protection.[77]

The Commerce and Economic Development Bureau is responsible for Hong Kong's commercial affairs and for policy formulation relating to Hong Kong's commerce, economy and industry,[78] such as in the areas of trade and investment facilitation and intellectual protection.[79] The relevant policies

[72] ibid art 73.

[73] ibid art 97.

[74] ibid art 90.

[75] A discussion of the Mutual Legal Assistance Unit is outside the scope of this section.

[76] Department of Justice, 'International Law Division' (*Department of Justice, The Government of Hong Kong Special Administrative Region*, 14 November 2022). Available at: www.doj.gov.hk/en/about/orgchart_ild.html, accessed 9 February 2024.

[77] ibid.

[78] Commerce and Economic Development Bureau, 'Our Portfolio' (*Commerce and Economic Development Bureau, The Government of the Hong Kong Special Administrative Region*, 1 July 2022). Available at: www.cedb.gov.hk/en/about-us/our-portfolio.html, accessed 9 February 2024.

[79] ibid.

are introduced and enforced by the Permanent Secretary for Commerce and Economic Development.[80]

The Commerce and Economic Development Bureau oversees the work of several departments. These include the Trade and Industry Department (TID), Invest Hong Kong (InvestHK) and the Economic and Trade Offices (ETOs). In the context of international policy, the TID is responsible for maintaining and promoting Hong Kong's trade and economic relationships with its trading partners, while also maintaining the territory's trade environment and policies and ensuring they comply with Hong Kong's international obligations.[81] In doing so, the TID has organised and assisted in Hong Kong's attendance at the WTO and other international organisations,[82] and provided services relating to certificates of origin and the licensing and registration of certain products, such as rice and textiles.[83] It has also prepared briefing papers for members of the panels under the Legislative Council, which form the basis for discussions during panel meetings.[84]

InvestHK is a governmental department which aims to introduce investment projects from abroad that would be strategically advantageous to Hong Kong's economic development and encourage foreign investors to stay in the territory continuously for development purposes.[85] The objectives are achieved through activities such as the hosting of seminars aimed at promoting Hong Kong as an investment destination to bridge the gap between China and third countries.[86]

[80] Commerce and Economic Development Bureau, 'Permanent Secretary for Commerce and Economic Development' (*Commerce and Economic Development Bureau, The Government of the Hong Kong Special Administrative Region*, 1 July 2022). Available at: www.cedb.gov.hk/en/about-us/permanent-secretary-for-commerce-and-economic-development.html, accessed 9 February 2024.

[81] Trade and Industry Department, 'Our Mission and Values' (*Trade and Industry Department, The Government of the Hong Kong Special Administrative Region*, 11 November 2022). Available at: www.tid.gov.hk/english/aboutus/deptprofile/mission.html, accessed 9 February 2023.

[82] Trade and Industry Department, 'International Trade Organisations' (*Trade and Industry Department, The Government of the Hong Kong Special Administrative Region*, 11 November 2022). Available at: www.tid.gov.hk/english/ito/index.html, accessed 9 February 2024.

[83] Trade and Industry Department 'An Introduction to the Trade and Industry Department' (*Trade and Industry Department, The Government of the Hong Kong Special Administrative Region*, April 2022). Available at: www.tid.gov.hk/english/aboutus/deptprofile/files/intro_TID.pdf, accessed 9 February 2024.

[84] See, eg, Trade and Industry Department, 'World Trade Organization: Key Outcomes of the Twelfth Ministerial Conference' (*Legislative Council of the Hong Kong Special Administrative Region of the People's Republic of China*, October 2022) LC Paper No CB(1)673/2022(05). Available at: www.legco.gov.hk/yr2022/english/panels/ci/papers/ci20221018cb1-673-5-e.pdf, accessed 9 February 2024.

[85] InvestHK, 'About InvestHK' (*InvestHK, The Government of the Hong Kong Special Administrative Region*, 6 October 2022). Available at: www.investhk.gov.hk/en/about-investhk.html, accessed 9 February 2024.

[86] InvestHK, 'InvestHK Hosts Seminar to Update Foreign Companies about Foreign Investment Policy and Business Environment in Mainland' (*InvestHK, The Government of the Hong Kong Special Administrative Region*, 14 October 2022). Available at: www.investhk.gov.hk/en/news/investhk-hosts-seminar-update-foreign-companies-about-foreign-investment-policy-and-business.html, accessed 9 February 2024.

Conversely, the ETOs are 14 offices that are currently established in third countries to represent Hong Kong, increase global awareness of Hong Kong's advantages, further Hong Kong's economic interests in third countries and assist foreign companies planning to do business in the territory.[87] For example, among other objectives, the London ETO aims to facilitate both bilateral trade and investment between Hong Kong and the United Kingdom, Russia and the Scandinavian countries.[88] Thus, it has hosted talks regarding business opportunities in Hong Kong.[89]

There are many ways in which principal Hong Kong organisations have addressed or discussed issues relating to international trade law. For example, the interrelationship between the HKSAR Government and the Legislative Council has meant that the former must address and engage in discussions with members of the Legislative Council and where issues relating to international economic law have been raised by the members for the government to address. This will be discussed in further detail in section 5. Correspondingly, the Department of Justice's Treaties & Law Unit has provided advice to the government on issues relating to public international law, including international trade law,[90] as well as how cooperative treaties, such as that of customs, are to be drafted and interpreted.

Recently, Hong Kong launched a dispute at the WTO-level to protest against changes by the US in origin marking requirements[91] – this will be further explained in section 6. Procedurally however, after the US Customs and Excise Department's notice that goods manufactured in Hong Kong were required to bear the label of origin 'Made in China', instead of 'Made in Hong Kong' from 25 September 2020 onwards, the HKSAR Government issued a statement objecting to the measures on 11 August 2020.[92] It then formally challenged the new origin marking requirements on 16 September 2020 with the US Government. During a meeting with both parties on the same day,

[87] Commerce and Economic Development Bureau, 'Economic and Trade Offices' (*Commerce and Economic Development Bureau, The Government of the Hong Kong Special Administrative Region*, 1 July 2022). Available at: www.cedb.gov.hk/en/trade-and-investment/economic-and-trade-offices.html, accessed 9 February 2024.

[88] Hong Kong Economic and Trade Office (London), 'Our Responsibilities' (*Hong Kong Economic and Trade Office (London), The Government of the Hong Kong Special Administrative Region*, 14 December 2022). Available at: www.hketolondon.gov.hk/responsibilities.php, accessed 9 February 2024.

[89] Hong Kong Economic and Trade Office (London), 'London ETO Events' (*Hong Kong Economic and Trade Office (London), The Government of the Hong Kong Special Administrative Region*, 14 December 2022). Available at: www.hketolondon.gov.hk/london-event.php, accessed 9 February 2024.

[90] ibid.

[91] *United States: Origin Marking Requirement – Communication from Hong Kong, China* (2 February 2023) WT/DS597/10.

[92] HKSAR Government, 'HKSARG strongly Objects to US' New Rule on Origin Marking of Hong Kong Products' (*The Government of the Hong Kong Special Administrative Region Press Releases*, 11 August 2020). Available at: www.info.gov.hk/gia/general/202008/11/P2020081100732.htm, accessed 9 February 2024.

the Secretary for Commerce and Economic Development requested the US Consul General to Hong Kong and Macau to deliver a letter, containing the HKSAR Government's official position on the matter and its request for the US to withdraw the measures, to the US Trade Representative.[93] Follow ups were also conducted by both Hong Kong ETOs in Washington, DC and Geneva,[94] with the Permanent Representative of Hong Kong to the WTO reiterating the HKSAR Government's objection to the new labelling requirements, whilst noting the American failure to withdraw them,[95] as well as the adverse impacts that these measures would have on both businesses and consumers alike.[96] Consultations commenced on 24 November 2020, but both Hong Kong and the US failed to resolve the dispute during the consultation process. Therefore, the Permanent Representative of Hong Kong to the WTO, on two consecutive Dispute Settlement Body (DSB) meetings, requested the DSB to allow for the establishment of a panel to analyse the labelling requirements, which, in the view of the HKSAR Government, were a violation of the US' obligations under the WTO covered agreements,[97] whilst emphasising the need for doing so. The request was granted on 22 February 2021[98] and a panel was established on the same day.[99]

B. The Trade Ecosystem: Organisation of Foreign Trade Institutions and Legislature

Hong Kong is a distinct customs territory which, in accordance with the Basic Law, participates independently in the relevant international organisations and international trade agreements, such as the WTO Agreements, under the name 'Hong Kong, China'. The Basic Law mandates that Hong Kong maintains its

[93] HKSAR Government, 'HKSAR Government Formally Takes Issue with US Government over its new requirement on origin marking' (*The Government of the Hong Kong Special Administrative Region Press Releases*, 16 September 2020). Available at: www.info.gov.hk/gia/general/202009/16/P2020091600513.htm?fontSize=1, accessed 9 February 2024.

[94] HKSAR Government, 'HKSAR Government Officially Launches Dispute Settlement Procedures in accordance with WTO Mechanism on US' New Requirement on Origin Marking' (*The Government of the Hong Kong Special Administrative Region Press Releases*, 30 October 2020). Available at: www.info.gov.hk/gia/general/202010/30/P2020103000455.htm?fontSize=1, accessed 9 February 2024.

[95] General Council – Held in the Centre William Rappard and in virtual format on 13 October 2020 – Minutes of Meeting (25 November 2020) WT/GC/M/187 para 12.11. Available at: http://docsonline.wto.org.

[96] ibid para 12.12.

[97] Dispute Settlement Body – Held in the Centre William Rappard on 25 January 2021 – Minutes of Meeting (12 March 2021) WT/DSB/M/448 para 5.2. Available at: http://docsonline.wto.org; Dispute Settlement Body – Held in the Centre William Rappard on 22 February 2021 – Minutes of Meeting (24 March 2021) WT/DSB/M/449 para 5.2. Available at: http://docsonline.wto.org.

[98] Dispute Settlement Body – Held in the Centre William Rappard on 22 February 2021 (n 103) para 5.5.

[99] ibid.

free port status, promotes a free trade agenda, safeguards the free movement of money, products and intangible assets and be permitted to issue its own certificates of origin for commodities.[100]

Issues pertaining to international economic law are discussed and policy documents are created by the Legislative Council Panel on Commerce and Industry. As mentioned earlier, out of the 14 ETOs, with the exception of the Geneva ETO, which represents Hong Kong, China at the World Trade Organisation and the Trade Committee of the Organisation for Economic Cooperation and Development, 11 of the 14 ETOs address bilateral matters (including economic and cultural concerns) between Hong Kong and the nations that come within their purview.[101] The ETOs coordinate different promotional efforts with other Hong Kong agencies abroad to highlight Hong Kong's advantages and draw attention to recent developments in the territory.

Prior to the transfer of sovereignty in 1997, Hong Kong Government Offices handled the economic interests of the territory in its primary trade markets, while the corresponding British embassy or high commission handled consular matters. This is how the Hong Kong Economic and Trade Offices (HKETOs) came to be. The Hong Kong Government's Councils and Administration Branch took control of the Hong Kong Government Offices in 1982. These offices had sites in London, Brussels, Washington and Geneva. In order to make it apparent that they did not exercise diplomatic or consular functions prior to the handover, the British and Chinese governments agreed that these offices should be renamed 'Hong Kong Economic and Trade Offices'.[102,103]

The political structure of the Hong Kong SAR is 'executive-led', based on the pertinent provisions of the Hong Kong Basic Law, according to Wang Shuwen, a member of the committee which formulated the law.[104] The Hong Kong Basic Law helps to protect this political system, which grants the Chief Executive enormous authority and significant position.[105]

According to the Second Report of the Task Force on Constitutional Development in 2004, the executive power and the legislature are frequently able to 'regulate' (ie, work as a mutual check) but are not able to 'co-ordinate' (ie, completely complement) each other. Under the current configuration, the Chief Executive does not have any established support in the Legislative Council. As a result, the executive-led system and administrative efficiency have suffered.

[100] Xianggang Jiben Fa (Basic Law) (n 18), Chapter VI: Economic System

[101] Establishment of Five New Economic and Trade Offices (ETOs) and the ETO Policy Division in the Commerce, Industry and Tourism Branch of the Commerce and Economic Development Bureau (LC Paper No CB(1)1238/17-18(08)).

[102] 'Official Report of Proceedings' (Hong Kong Legislative Council, 16 June 1982), Available at: www.legco.gov.hk/yr81-82/english/lc sitg/hansard/h820616.pdf, accessed 9 February 2024.

[103] ibid.

[104] Wang Shuwen, *Introduction to the Basic Law of the Hong Kong Special Administration Region* (Central Party School of the CPC Press, 1997) 207. (NB: During the colonial era, Hong Kong's political system was initially referred to as 'executive led.).

[105] Hong Kong Economic and Trade Office Act 1996. Available at: www.legislation.gov.uk/ukpga/1996/63/schedule, accessed 9 February 2024.

The key to the Legislative Council's authority is its ability to veto any legislative or appropriation proposal made by the executive branch.[106] Due to its significant influence, the Legislative Council can negotiate with and exert pressure on the administration about a range of policy issues, compelling it to change its policies in the public and social interest in response to its requirements.

C. Influencers and Decision-makers: The Role of Governmental and Non-Governmental Organisations in Trade Policy Formulation

The Legislative Council has a member who represents the Hong Kong Chamber of Commerce. Hong Kong legislation ought to require participation from the general public in the legislative process in line with PRC law. The people of Hong Kong have a right to provide drafters with feedback on suggested phrasing and to have that opinion carefully considered when legislation is being drafted.[107]

Proposed draft bills and their accompanying rationales are generally disclosed following the sessions during which they are deliberated. This occurs within a standard window of not less than 30 days, designated for written responses. However, this procedure can be avoided if there is concurrence from the Council of Chairpersons, which comprises the chairperson, deputy chairpersons and the secretary-general of the Standing Committee of the National People's Congress (NPCSC), to abstain from publication. In recent years, all legislation within the People's Republic of China (PRC) has undergone at least one public consultation phase and, in certain instances, two. These periods of public comment facilitate national dialogue and offer a platform for citizen engagement in the legislative process. The drafts of the proposed legislations, inclusive of any revisions or amendments, are made accessible online, promoting transparency and fostering public discourse.[108]

However, the effectiveness of this public participation in amending proposed laws can sometimes be questioned, as illustrated by the PRC's Cyber-security and Foreign NGO Laws. These enactments show that, despite public involvement, substantial improvements to draft laws may be minimal. This critique echoes the backlash following the abandonment of the Hong Kong National Security Bill

[106] Ghai, *Hong Kong's New Constitutional Order* (n 16) 292; Albert Hung Yee Chen, 'The Executive Authorities and the Legislature in the Political Structure of the Hong Kong SAR' (2014) 6 *Academic Journal of Once Country, Two Systems* 80. Available at: www.mpu.edu.mo/cntfiles/upload/docs/research/common/1country_2systems/academic_eng/issue4/09.pdf.

[107] Jamie P Horsley, 'Chinese Law Requires Public Consultation in Lawmaking: What Does it Mean for the Hong Kong National Security legislation?' (*Brookings*, 8 June 2020). Available at: www.brookings.edu/blog/order-from-chaos/2020/06/08/chinese-law-requires-public-consultation-in-lawmaking-what-does-it-mean-for-the-hong-kong-national-security-legislation/, accessed 9 February 2024.

[108] ibid.

2003. Widely perceived as a blueprint for current versions under drafting, the Bill was predominantly criticised for insufficient public participation. Yet, for the majority of Hong Kong residents, this comment-seeking procedure conducted by the NPCSC may well represent their only avenue for direct involvement in the legislative process.[109]

As the previous discussion has underscored the potential limitations of public participation in legislative modifications, such as seen in the cases of the PRC's Cyber-security and Foreign NGO Laws, it leads us to another vital facet of citizen engagement in governance: the power of judicial review. This not only ensures a system of checks and balances but also provides a different, yet significant, avenue for public influence over governance in Hong Kong.

Indeed, the right of Hong Kong citizens to challenge executive decisions by resorting to the judicial process forms an essential part of their participation in governance. This method of public oversight over the executive is maintained and safeguarded by the region's legal framework, as articulated in the Basic Law. As such, the continuity of the Common Law, as stipulated by the Basic Law, ensures that administrative review remains a component of common law. Article 35 of the Basic Law is widely considered as the legal foundation for administrative review.[110]

In exploring this essential capacity for judicial review in Hong Kong, one must also consider how the legal precedent of this special administrative region compares with that of other jurisdictions. In particular, the role and influence of the judiciary within the legislative process, as a balancing mechanism, becomes a significant point of comparison. Specifically, the Hong Kong courts' interpretations are held in similar respect as their counterparts in the U.S., allowing them to review the compatibility of laws passed by the legislature with the Basic Law. This contrasts with the UK's longstanding principle of parliamentary sovereignty, where courts may not possess the same scope of authority. As the Hong Kong courts have highlighted, unlike in the UK where legislative supremacy is the norm, Hong Kong has the capability for laws to be re-examined. This fact further underscores the critical role of feedback gathered during consultation periods in shaping policies and legislative outcomes.

D. Navigating the Future: Recent Developments in Hong Kong's Trade Landscape

This section discusses recent developments in Hong Kong's trade landscape, examining the notable changes and challenges that have transpired since 2019.

[109] Horsley, 'Chinese Law Requires Public Consultation in Lawmaking' accessed 9 February 2024 (n 113).

[110] Xianggang Jiben (Basic Law) (n 18) Chapter III: Fundamental Rights and Duties of the Residents, art 35, '… Hong Kong residents shall have the right to institute legal proceedings in the courts against the acts of the executive authorities and their personnel'.

A pivotal issue that has significantly impacted Hong Kong's international trade relations is the withdrawal of its special trading status by the United States. This decision was prompted by concerns over China's perceived encroachment on Hong Kong's autonomy and liberties. As a result, Hong Kong's trade environment has undergone significant transformations, necessitating a re-evaluation of its position within the global market.

In 2022, Hong Kong was the third top host economy for FDI inflows.[111] However, much has changed since 2019. Particularly, the foremost international trade law issue post-2019 stemmed from the withdrawal of Hong Kong's special trading status with the US, as a result of what the latter considered as China's erosion of the high level of autonomy and liberties accorded to Hong Kong.[112]

From late March 2019 to early January 2020, the territory saw widespread protests. These were initially launched against the introduction of the Hong Kong Extradition Bill to close certain legal loopholes[113] but, during the third quarter of 2019, they developed into a campaign to protest against what the protesters perceived as a gradual erosion of democracy and freedoms in Hong Kong.[114] The proposed Extradition Bill, if enacted by the Legislative Council, would have allowed those named in Chinese extradition requests to be extradited back to China; at the time there was no extradition treaty with Hong Kong.[115] This was a concern for many, as it was perceived that those so extradited could face discretionary detention and unfair legal proceedings under the Chinese legal system.[116] Because of what was happening in Hong Kong, a series of legislative bills was introduced in the US Congress which eventually became part of US law.[117] These included the Hong Kong Human Rights and Democracy Act, which necessitated a certification by the US Secretary of State that Hong Kong was still autonomised from China, thus special and preferential treatment granted by the US should still be warranted.[118]

[111] UNCTAD, 'World Investment Report 2022' (n 21) 9.

[112] Bureau of East Asian and Pacific Affairs, '2020 Hong Kong Policy Act Report' (*US Department of State*, 28 May 2020). Available at: www.state.gov/2020-hong-kong-policy-act-report/, accessed 9 February 2024.

[113] Eric Kleefeld, 'Hundreds of Thousands Attend Protest in Hong Kong over Extradition Bill' (*Vox*, 9 June 2019). Available at: www.vox.com/world/2019/6/9/18658650/hong-kong-protest-march-china-extradition-bill-2019, accessed 9 February 2024.

[114] Helier Cheung, 'Hong Kong Extradition: How Radical Youth Forced the Government's Hand' (*BBC*, 17 June 2019). Available at: www.bbc.com/news/world-asia-china-48655474 accessed 9 February 2024.

[115] BBC, 'Hong Kong-China Extradition Plans Explained' (*BBC*, 13 December 2019). Available at: www.bbc.com/news/world-asia-china-47810723, accessed 9 February 2024.

[116] ibid.

[117] See, eg, US Congress, 'S.1838 – Hong Kong Human Rights and Democracy Act of 2019' (*Congress.gov*). Available at: www.congress.gov/bill/116th-congress/senate-bill/1838/actions, accessed 9 February 2024 and US Congress, 'S.2710 – A Bill to Prohibit the Commercial Export of Covered Munitions Items to the Hong Kong Police Force' (*Congress.gov*). Available at: www.congress.gov/bill/116th-congress/senate-bill/2710, accessed 9 February 2024.

[118] 22 USC §5725: Secretary of State report regarding the autonomy of Hong Kong.

On 28 May 2020, the adoption of a decision which authorised the introduction of a national security law in Hong Kong[119] prompted the US Secretary of State, Mike Pompeo, to declare that as a consequence of its implementation, which eroded Hong Kong's autonomy from China, preferential treatment should no longer be accorded to the territory.[120] Subsequently, on 14 July 2020, President Donald Trump signed the Executive Order on Hong Kong Normalisation, which removed the special treatment that had been granted to Hong Kong.[121] One of these was the suspension of the application of s 201(a) of the 1992 Act towards s 304 of the Tariff Act 1930,[122] which had allowed goods manufactured in Hong Kong entering the US market to continue to bear the label of origin 'Made in Hong Kong' after the handover to China in 1997.[123] In this regard, from 25 September 2020 onwards, there was a regime change in labelling requirements, where Hong Kong-manufactured goods would now have to be marked instead as 'Made in China'.[124] Consequently, having taken the view that the changes in labelling requirements were a breach of the US' WTO obligations, as mentioned in section 2, the HKSAR Government requested consultations with the US on this matter[125] and then the establishment of a WTO panel on 14 January 2021 when a mutually satisfactory solution had failed to be reached.[126]

Chapter 2 has offered a comprehensive exploration of Hong Kong's trade regime, focusing on its historical development and the factors that have contributed to its continued success. The main findings of the chapter can be categorised into four key areas: Hong Kong's engagement with international affairs, its participation in international trade affairs, the role of various organisations and institutions in shaping trade policy and recent developments in Hong Kong's trade landscape. The chapter has emphasised Hong Kong's active engagement with international affairs, particularly in the realm of trade, as a vital component of its global presence. The analysis highlighted how Hong Kong's unique historical, legal and political background has contributed to its distinctive approach to international trade, enabling it to maintain a competitive edge in

[119] Nectar Gan, 'China Approves Controversial National Security Law for Hong Kong' (CNN, 28 May 2020). Available at: www.edition.cnn.com/2020/05/28/asia/china-npc-hk-security-law-intl-hnk/index.html, accessed 9 February 2024.

[120] Bureau of East Asian and Pacific Affairs, (n 118), n 169.

[121] Exec Order No. 13936, 85 Fed Reg 43413 (17 July 2020) sec 3(c). Available at: www.federalregister.gov/documents/2020/07/17/2020-15646/the-presidents-executive-order-on-hong-kong-normalization.

[122] ibid sec 2(f).

[123] Country of Origin Marking of Products of Hong Kong, 62 Fed Reg 30927 (5 June 1997).

[124] Country of Origin Marking of Products of Hong Kong, 85 Fed Reg 48551 (11 August 2020).

[125] *United States: Origin Marking Requirement – Request for Consultation by Hong Kong China* (3 November 2020) WT/DS597/1, G/L/1365, G/RO/D/8, G/TBT/D/53. Available at: http://docsonline.wto.org.

[126] *United States: Origin Marking Requirement – Request for the Establishment of a Panel by Hong Kong, China* (15 January 2021) WT/DS597/5. Available at: http://docsonline.wto.org.

the global market. In conclusion, Chapter 2 has offered an in-depth analysis of Hong Kong's unilateral trade regime and its evolution, demonstrating the territory's unique position in the global trading system. The key lessons from this chapter contribute to the book's broader conceptual framework and main theme, emphasising Hong Kong's ongoing transformation as an international financial and trade centre.

3

Forging Pathways: Hong Kong's Unilateral Foreign Investment Landscape

THIS CHAPTER DISCUSSES the complexities and intricacies of Hong Kong's unique approach to foreign investment. As a SAR of China with a separate legal system and substantial autonomy in its economic affairs, Hong Kong has historically pursued a liberal and open investment environment.

To enrich the analysis of Hong Kong's foreign investment regulatory environment, this chapter employs a constructivist theoretical framework. Constructivism, as a social theory, emphasises the role of ideas, norms and beliefs in shaping actors' behaviours and decisions in the international arena. The approach allows us to examine the ways in which Hong Kong's identity as an attractive investment destination has been socially constructed and sustained through these policies and initiatives.

This chapter has three main objectives. Firstly, it seeks to discuss the absence of general legislation for foreign investment admission in Hong Kong and how this has influenced the territory's approach to attracting and regulating foreign investments. Secondly, it aims to examine the various strategies and initiatives undertaken by Hong Kong to champion global investment, including investment promotion, bilateral investment treaties, and other policy measures. Thirdly, it explores the delicate balance Hong Kong must strike between fostering growth and addressing the issue of foreign investment screening, particularly with regard to national security concerns. In addition to these core objectives, the chapter also discusses the concept of sovereign immunity in Hong Kong, outlining the legal considerations at play during the suit recognition and execution stages of investment disputes. This analysis provides valuable insights into the implications of immunity both for foreign investors and for the Hong Kong government.

Chapter 3 is structured into several sections, each addressing a specific aspect of Hong Kong's foreign investment regulatory environment. In Section I, the absence of comprehensive legislation for foreign investment admission is thoroughly discussed, highlighting the unique regulatory framework that governs foreign investment in Hong Kong. Section II examines the strategies and initiatives implemented by Hong Kong to foster and promote global investment, showcasing the territory's proactive approach to attracting foreign capital. In Section III, the focus shifts to the challenges associated with striking a balance between economic growth and the need for foreign investment screening. This section explores the complexities and considerations involved in effectively managing and regulating foreign investment to ensure sustainable development. Lastly, Section IV discusses the concept of sovereign immunity in Hong Kong. Subsections IV(A) and (B) specifically address the stages of suit recognition and execution. These provide an in-depth analysis of the legal mechanisms and procedures governing the recognition and enforcement of foreign judgments in Hong Kong, shedding light on the jurisdiction's approach to sovereign immunity. Through this structure, Chapter 3 aims to provide a comprehensive understanding of the intricacies and challenges associated with foreign investment in Hong Kong.

I. NAVIGATING INVESTMENT: THE ABSENCE OF GENERAL LEGISLATION FOR FOREIGN INVESTMENT ADMISSION

In the complex world of global finance, the regulatory environment plays a crucial role in determining the attractiveness of a jurisdiction for foreign investment. Interestingly, Hong Kong stands out for its unique approach to foreign investment admission, characterised by the absence of any general legislation governing this domain. This distinctive feature of Hong Kong's investment landscape has enabled the territory to offer unparalleled flexibility and adaptability to foreign investors, fostering an environment conducive to the influx of foreign capital. In this section, we will explore the reasons behind this legislative void and the implications it has for investors and consider how Hong Kong has successfully navigated investment matters in the absence of a comprehensive regulatory framework for foreign investment admission.

States usually enact diverse laws impacting foreign investment. While several forms of domestic legislation affect investment, Domestic Investment Law (DIL), in particular, is a subset of domestic legislation that seeks to promote and regulate foreign investment.[1] DILs are unilateral pieces of legislation enacted at the domestic level that seek to safeguard both domestic and international investors.[2] Further, the trend towards 'de-globalisation',[3] particularly in the aftermath of the 2008 global financial crisis[4] and the Covid-19

[1] In its database, UNCTAD counts 186 investment laws; see UNCTAD, 'Investment Laws Navigator'. Available at: https://investmentpolicy.unctad.org/investment-laws, accessed 2 February 2024.

[2] See Julien Chaisse and Georgios Dimitropoulos, 'Special Economic Zones in International Economic Law: Towards Unilateral Economic Law' (2021) 24 *Journal of International Economic Law* 229.

[3] Walden Bello, *Deglobalization: Ideas for a New World Economy* (London, Zed Books, 2002).

[4] See IRC Trade Task Force, 'Understanding the Weakness in Global Trade: What is the New Normal?' (Occasional Paper Series No 178, September 2016). Available at: www.ecb.europa.eu/pub/pdf/scpops/ecbop178.en.pdf, accessed 2 February 2024.

pandemic,[5] has called into question the assumptions that underpin modern IEL. As a result, DILs have started playing an increasingly important role in boosting and facilitating foreign investment by providing FDI incentives.[6]

DILs can take a variety of forms (specific or general) in order to regulate foreign investment. There are two main types of specialised domestic investment law, namely outright prohibition and screening.[7] Some countries may restrict foreign investment or ownership in certain industries or sectors, either with or without a formal review process.[8] Investment screening regulations (which have grown increasingly common) aim to prevent or limit foreign investors' entry or subject them to particular conditions.[9] Apart from specialised DILs, there are several other laws that impact foreign investment directly and indirectly, such as laws governing data,[10] SEZs, property laws and arbitration laws.[11] However, such regulations are part of a jurisdiction's overall legal structure and are not always intended to promote and facilitate foreign investment as narrowly as DILs.

DILs have prominently been used to support investor-state disputes in international arbitration. On the one hand, investment tribunals have considered DIL obligations as unilaterally adopted international obligations of the host state.[12] On the other hand, DILs might be classified as domestic law.[13] Consequently, DILs can be classified in either way, in both cases with significant

[5] Douglas Irwin, 'The Pandemic adds Momentum to the Deglobalisation Trend' (*Voxeu*, 5 May 2020) Available at: https://voxeu.org/article/pandemic-adds-momentum-deglobalisation-trend, accessed 2 February 2024.

[6] Krista Tuomi, 'Review of Investment Incentives Best Practice in Attracting Investment' (*International Growth Centre*, 2012). Available at: www.theigc.org/publication/review-of-investment-incentives-best-practice-in-attracting-investment/, accessed 2 February 2024.

[7] See with a tripartite differentiation Markus Burgstaller, 'Sovereign Wealth Funds and International Investment Law' in Chester Brown and Kate Miles (eds), *Evolution in Investment Treaty Law and Arbitration* (Cambridge, Cambridge University Press, 2011).

[8] See Federal Law No 57 of 2008 'Procedures for Foreign Investments in the Business Entities of Strategic Importance for Russian National Defence and State Security'.

[9] See Georgios Dimitropoulos, 'National Security: The Role of Investment Screening Mechanisms' in Julien Chaisse, Leïla Choukroune and Sufian Jusoh (eds), *Handbook of International Investment Law and Policy* (Singapore, Springer 2019).

[10] States often justify the need to regulate cross-border data flows by the need to protect personal sensitive information and reduce data breaches. Nevertheless, protectionist intents or effects are never far off. See, for example, Andrew D Mitchell and Theodore Samlidis, 'Cloud Services and Government Digital Sovereignty in Australia and Beyond' (2022) 30 *International Journal of Law and Information Technology* 1. As a result, CBDF domestic laws increasingly affect the eco-system of domestic investment law.

[11] See Nathan Arentsen and Matthew S Weber, 'UNCITRAL Model Law: Still a Model or Second Best?' (*Kluwer Arbitration Blog*, 1 July 2014). Available at: http://arbitrationblog.kluwerarbitration.com/2014/07/01/uncitral-model-law-still-a-model-or-second-best/, accessed 2 February 2024.

[12] *Lighthouse Corporation Pty Ltd v East Timor*, ICSID Case No ARB/15/2, Award (22 December 2017) [151]; *CEMEX Caracas Investments BV v Venezuela*, ICSID Case No ARB/08/15, Decision on Jurisdiction (30 December 2010) [77]–[79]; *Mobil Corporation v Venezuela*, ICSID Case No ARB/07/27, Decision on Jurisdiction (10 June 2010) [83]–[85]; *SPP v Egypt*, ICSID Case No ARB/84/3, Decision on Preliminary Objections to Jurisdiction (27 November 1985) [258]–[265].

[13] C Eckart, *Promises of States under International Law* (Oxford, Hart Publishing, 2012) 223.

implications for their use in investor-state claims. Notably, based on varying circumstances, DILs may end up reflecting international law norms on either characterisation.

Hong Kong has a unique foreign investment law regime because of its autonomy as an SAR. Hong Kong through its Basic Law has maintained openness to trade and foreign investment on the basis of a free-market economy and a liberal investment regime. For this reason, Hong Kong has contributed to jurisprudence on state succession and international investment treaties (IIAs). Other significant contributions include treaty practice on public health exceptions. Foreign investment has played an important role in sustaining Hong Kong's economic growth and in fostering Hong Kong's development as an international trade, financial, and business centre. Hong Kong participated as an observer in the Multilateral Agreement on Investment (MAI) negotiations.

According to the United Nations Conference on Trade and Development's (UNCTAD) World Investment Report 2020, Hong Kong is the world's second-largest recipient of FDI, with a significant percentage destined for mainland China.[14] However, Hong Kong does not have a foreign investment law. The government advocates a free-market economy and a policy of little government intervention. There is no defined procedure for international investors seeking investment approval. Due to Hong Kong's free market philosophy, there is no specific investment statute guiding foreign investment admission.[15] Furthermore, there is no legal or practical distinction between investments made by foreign-controlled corporations and those made by local interests. Foreign companies and individuals can incorporate in Hong Kong, register foreign operations as branches, and open representative offices without facing discrimination or unnecessary regulation.[16] Many countries have chosen to build investment-specific legislative frameworks. Hong Kong, by contrast, advocates a *laissez faire* market economy and has chosen not to have a law specific to foreign investment. Its general law does not differentiate between domestic and foreign investors.[17]

In order to promote and safeguard foreign investments, laws governing foreign investment have also been passed in economies in transition. Some nations, like Kazakhstan, Uzbekistan and Kyrgyzstan, have recently updated their foreign investment laws to provide crucial protection and assurances for

[14] 'Trade Policy Review Body – Hong Kong, China' (1999) 11 *World Trade and Arbitration Materials* 92.

[15] Terry Miller, Anthony B Kim and James M Roberts, '2018 Report of Index of Economic Freedom' (*The Heritage Foundation*) 215. At the same time, Hong Kong has only signed a limited number of FTAs and BITs; see UNCTAD, 'Investment Policy Hub: Hong Kong, China SAR'. Available at: https://investmentpolicy.unctad.org/international-investment-agreements/countries/93/hong-kong sar-China, accessed 2 February 2024.

[16] US Department of State, '2021 Investment Climate Statements' (2021). Available at: www.state.gov/reports/2021-investment-climate-statements/, accessed 2 February 2024.

[17] Mark Williams, 'Foreign Investment in China: Will the Anti-monopoly Law Be a Barrier or a Facilitator?' (2009) 45 *Texas International Law Journal* 127.

investors.[18] The new 'Law on Foreign Investments' of the Kyrgyz Republic guarantees non-discrimination, a just and equal legal system, protection against expropriation of foreign investments, the freedom to dispose of their investments and the income they generate and compensation for losses incurred in the event of armed conflict or other similar situations.[19] Therefore, efforts in these nations to enhance foreign investment legislation are focused on developing an entire legal framework that is compliant with international standards and includes components governing local investments as well.

II. CHAMPIONING GLOBAL INVESTMENT: STRATEGIES AND INITIATIVES

As a premier international financial centre, Hong Kong has consistently prioritised the promotion of global investment as a key aspect of its economic strategy. In this section, we will explore the various methods and approaches employed by Hong Kong to attract and facilitate foreign investment. By examining the incentives, policies, and institutional support mechanisms that have contributed to Hong Kong's success in this domain, the section aims to provide readers with a comprehensive understanding of the territory's proactive and strategic approach to fostering a thriving investment environment.

Investment promotion policies actively work to draw potential investors' attention to available investment opportunities, supply capital, employment, skills, technology, and exports, and boost a territory's or nation's productivity, innovation, and salaries.[20] Investment promotion agencies (IPAs) are typically a component of a nation's larger national foreign investment promotion strategy, which over time becomes a key component of a nation's growth and development strategy.[21]

Investment generation, image enhancement, investment facilitation and investment retention are traditional roles that have been systematically linked to IPAs.[22] They frequently have a multi-year investment attraction plan which

[18] UT Isayev, 'Session VII: Foreign Investment during the Transition: How to Attract It, and How to Make the Best Use of It' (27–28 May 1998) Presentation to the International Monetary Fund-Kyrgyz Republic Conference on Challenges to Economies in Transition: Stabilization, Growth, and Governance (Bishkek) 3–4. Available at: www.imf.org/external/np/eu2/kyrgyz/pdf/isayev.pdf, accessed 2 February 2024.

[19] ibid.

[20] Millennium Cities Initiative, 'Tools, Techniques and Resources for Investment Promotion'. Availableat:http://mci.ei.columbia.edu/initiatives/private-sector-development/overview-of-investment-promotion/#:~:text=Investment%20promotion%20actively%20seeks%20to,as%20well%20as%20foreign%20companies, accessed 2 February 2024.

[21] Carlos Portales Undurraga and Cristian Rodriguez Chiffelle, 'Investment Promotion Agencies: Investment Attraction, Policy Role, and Response to Crises' in J Chaisse, L Choukrone and S Josh (eds), *Handbook of International Investment Law and Policy* (Singapore, Springer, 2021).

[22] Louis T Wells and Alvin G Wint Jr, 'Marketing a Country: Promotion as a Tool for Attracting Foreign Investment' (2000) Foreign Investment Advisory Service Occasional Paper No 13, World Bank Group. Available at: https://documents.worldbank.org/en/publication/documents-reports/

prioritises promoting investment into particular industries and place a greater emphasis on the Sustainable Development Goals (SDGs).[23] Although all IPAs' primary goal is to encourage inbound FDI, they increasingly include other functions linked to enhance the investment climate.[24] Thus, the IPA's mission is to improve the probability of an investor selecting the Agency's region.

InvestHK is the HKSAR Government department responsible for FDI, assisting international enterprises to establish and expand in Hong Kong.[25] InvestHK has industry experts in a variety of priority sectors. The Investment Officers are divided into nine specialist sector teams that cover Hong Kong's four pillar industries as well as six new growth sectors: Business & Professional Services, Consumer Products, Creative Industries, Financial Services, Fintech, Information & Communications Technology, Innovation & Technology, Tourism & Hospitality and Transport & Industrial.[26] It established an aftercare team to monitor clients' requirements following the establishment or expansion of their businesses. Aftercare services prove very beneficial, as investors who are already active in the local market should be seen as the most convenient source of further investments and as middlemen between IPAs and new investors.[27] The latter is taking place as a result of their business relationships, references, and expertise, which can encourage new potential foreign investors to invest in the host jurisdiction.[28] Thereby, by providing aftercare services, the IPAs also perform a function of business networking.

In addition, the Department maintains an international network of workers and representatives situated in 31 significant commercial locations across the world that cover its target markets. Overall, the Department's professionals in Hong Kong and abroad collaborate to support customers' business establishment and expansion in Hong Kong. InvestHK works on a long-term basis with clients and is accessible to assist them at any level of their business development in Hong Kong.[29] InvestHK works closely with its parent bureau to formulate

documentdetail/884891468763824660/marketing-a-country-promotion-as-a-tool-for-attracting-foreign-investment-revised-edition, accessed 2 February 2024.

[23] See Gudrun Zagel, 'Achieving Sustainable Development Objectives in International Investment Law' in Chaisse, Choukrone and Josh (eds), *Handbook of International Investment Law and Policy* (Singapore, Springer, 2021).

[24] UNESCAP, 'Outward Foreign Direct Investment and Home Country Sustainable Development' (20 April 2020) Studies in Trade, Investment and Innovation no 93, 54. Available at: www.unescap.org/publications/studies-trade-investment-and-innovation-no-93-outward-foreign-direct-investment-and, accessed 2 February 2024.

[25] See www.investhk.gov.hk/; www.legco.gov.hk/yr04-05/english/sec/library/0405in03e.pdf.

[26] RTHK, 'NSL not a top concern for investors: InvestHK chief' (*RTHK*, 25 March 2022). Available at: https://news.rthk.hk/rthk/en/component/k2/1640706-20220325.htm, accessed 2 February 2024.

[27] Algirdas Miškinis and Mariya Byrka, 'The Role of Investment Promotion Agencies in Attracting Foreign Direct Investment' (2014) 93 *Ekonomika* 41.

[28] ibid.

[29] InvestHK, 'Hong Kong: Where Work Opportunities Connect'. Available at: www.investhk.gov.hk/sites/default/files/2022.11-corporate-brochure-en.pdf, accessed 2 February 2024.

these operational rules but has significant autonomy. It is effectively filling a policy void by producing a restricted set of on-the-ground industry policy initiatives and instruments in an environment where the government maintains a low policy profile.[30]

III. BALANCING GROWTH: THE ISSUE OF FOREIGN INVESTMENT SCREENING

International investment opportunities can occasionally come with risks, especially to the host countries' vital security interests. Governments are beginning to take these risks more seriously, and an increasing number of nations are putting in place procedures that permit the advance scrutiny of specific investment proposals.[31] Investment screening is the process of the government evaluating foreign investment deals and refusing or mandating the divestiture of interests considered unsuitable.[32] State authorities may assess FDI based on a range of factors. Investments were historically screened primarily on the basis of their potential to produce a 'net economic advantage' for the host economy.[33] By contrast, current investment screening has been primarily based on national security concerns, ie whether a certain transaction is likely to jeopardise national security.[34]

In response to growing political concerns, several nations have implemented new policies and processes or strengthened those already in existence that are explicitly devoted to national security-related investment screening. In at least 13 nations, new regulatory frameworks were adopted between January 2011 and September 2019.[35] In 15 jurisdictions during this same time period, there were at least 45 substantial adjustments to the screening systems that were already in place.[36] Legislative changes pertaining to these various investment screening methods primarily concentrate on expanding the screening scope, extending the statutory timeframes for the length of screening operations, or increasing the disclosure duties of foreign investors during screening procedures.

[30] ibid.

[31] OECD, 'Investment screening in times of COVID-19 and beyond' (7 July 2020) Available at: www.oecd.org/coronavirus/policy-responses/investment-screening-in-times-of-covid-19-and-beyond-aa60af47/, accessed 2 February 2024.

[32] Sarah Bauerle Danzman and Sophie Meunier, 'The Big Screen: Mapping the Diffusion of Foreign Investment Screening Mechanisms' (28 August 2021) Princeton School of Public and International Affairs. Available at: www.internationalpoliticaleconomysociety.org/sites/default/files/paper uploads/2021-10-20-00_43_32-sbauerle@indiana.edu.pdf, accessed 2 February 2024.

[33] ibid.

[34] ibid.

[35] UNCTAD, 'National Security-Related Screening Mechanisms for Foreign Investment' (December 2019) Investment Policy Mentor. Available at: https://unctad.org/system/files/official-document/diaepcbinf2019d7_en.pdf, accessed 2 February 2024.

[36] ibid.

These days, investment screening increasingly includes the acquisition of domestic technology and know-how by foreigners, including those in the fields of artificial intelligence, robotics, semiconductors, cloud computing, and 5G. Recently, security-related screening methods have also been used or are being considered to limit foreign investors' access to sensitive information about local residents.[37]

Foreign investment is usually regarded as a driver of job creation and economic growth, and recipient countries around the world have generally welcomed it.[38] Nonetheless, there have been cases where such investments have been deemed to be a risk to national security or other equally important goals of the recipient countries (such as public order and security, and in practice, economic reasons).[39] Many governments, including the United States, Australia, Canada, and Japan, have FDI screening systems in place and have lately enhanced them. Furthermore, the European Union (EU) as a whole lacks a comparable common mechanism, and less than half of EU member states currently have foreign investment laws in place, allowing them to examine investments on the basis of national security or public order. As a result, the implementation in early 2019 of an EU-wide coordination and information exchange framework for screening inward FDI in domains of strategic relevance to the EU represents a watershed moment.[40]

A jurisdiction's investment law framework may consist of specialist legislation dedicated to international investors or of more broad legislative instruments that may have an impact on foreign investment flows. In general, there are three types of investment laws: (1) general investment rules that do not differentiate between domestic and foreign investors; (2) specialised investment laws with identical treatment; and (3) foreign laws with varied treatment. Hong Kong falls into the first category because it lacks general foreign investment legislation guiding foreign investment admittance. Hong Kong maintains an open policy towards foreign investment and does not have an investment screening mechanism for the protection of national interests. However, Hong Kong's National Security Law, which took effect on 30 June 2020, may continue to have a significant deterrent effect on foreign investments.[41]

Regardless, notifications/approvals from regulators/authorities are required for investing in the following sectors: banking, insurance, stocks and futures,

[37] ibid.

[38] Manuel R Agosin and Roberto Machado, 'Foreign Investment in Developing Countries: Does it Crowd in Domestic investment?' (2005) 33 *Oxford Development Studies* 149.

[39] Foreign Investment Watch, 'Multi-jurisdiction Guide for Screening of Foreign Investments' (August 2019). Available at: https://foreigninvestmentwatch.com/guidance/, accessed 2 February 2024.

[40] Regulation (EU) 2019/452 of the European Parliament and of the Council of 19 March 2019 establishing a framework for the screening of foreign direct investments into the Union, (2019) OJ L 79I/1.

[41] The Law of the People's Republic of China on Safeguarding National Security in the Hong Kong Special Administrative Region 2020.

provident funds, and telecommunications. These notifications primarily concern shareholding and are made at the discretion of the respective governing bodies. In comparison to other large capital-exporting and importing economies, Hong Kong has had comparatively few sector-specific foreign investment restrictions. Its IIAs indicate the core industries that are deemed vital.[42]

Following the entry into force of the EU's FDI Screening Regulation on 11 October 2020, inward FDIs have increasingly been scrutinised by host-country governments on the grounds of national security concerns.[43] Since the Regulation was first implemented, FDI in the EU has undergone changes. According to the European Commission's report, all (except two) EU Member States now have screening procedures in place or are in the process of implementing them. However, traders may be pleased to learn that the bulk of FDI creates no problems and is authorised rapidly at both the Member State and Commission levels, according to the report.[44]

The distinctiveness of FDI policies and their associated screening systems vary greatly across countries but converge on a noteworthy trait – a prevalent undertone of ambiguity and vagueness.[45] This characteristic, particularly prominent in matters of national security, has emerged as an intrinsic aspect of most nations' FDI policy frameworks. There is reason to believe that this ambiguity is deliberate and is designed to leave space for power negotiations and diplomatic manoeuvering.[46]

IV. SOVEREIGN IMMUNITY IN HONG KONG

Sovereign immunity is a critical aspect of international law, which provides protection to states and their assets from legal proceedings in foreign courts. As an SAR within the People's Republic of China, Hong Kong operates under the 'One Country, Two Systems' framework, maintaining its own legal system and courts separate from those of Mainland China. This unique arrangement raises important questions and challenges regarding the application of sovereign immunity within Hong Kong's jurisdiction. In this section, we will explore the

[42] See Hong Kong-Canada SAR BIT (date of signature 10 February 2016; entry into force 6 September 2016), art 16; Hong Kong-Chile SAR BIT (date of signature 18 November 2016; entry into force 14 July 2019), art 18.

[43] Christina Boswell, 'Migration Control in Europe After 9/11: Explaining the Absence of Securitization' (2007) 45 *Journal of Common Market Studies* 589.

[44] 'Report Published on Efficacy of EU's Framework for Foreign Direct Investment Screening' (HKTDC Research, 14 September 2022). Available at: https://research.hktdc.com/en/article/MTE2ODI1NTA5MQ, accessed 2 February 2024.

[45] Zenobia T Chan and Sophie Meunier, 'Behind the Screen: Understanding National Support for a Foreign Investment Screening Mechanism in the European Union' (2021) 17 *The Review of International Organizations* 1.

[46] Keyan Lai, 'National Security and FDI Policy Ambiguity: A Commentary' (2021) *Journal of International Business Policy* 496.

concept of sovereign immunity as it pertains to Hong Kong, specifically focusing on the Hong Kong Court of Final Appeal's approach towards this legal principle and its implications for foreign investment and international relations.

Sovereign immunity remains important both in international law and international relations[47] and 'has to be viewed together with the principle that each State possesses sovereignty over its own territory, the jurisdiction of the State over events and persons within that territory'.[48] In practice, sovereign immunity is a limited right of States. According to Article 5 of the UN Convention on the Jurisdictional Immunities of States and Their Property (hereinafter 'UNCSI'), 'a State enjoys immunity, in respect of itself and its property, from the jurisdiction of the courts of another State subject to the provisions of the present Convention'.[49] However, there is a difference between immunity from a suit and immunity from execution. The International Court of Justice (ICJ) holds that jurisdictional immunity does not indicate immunity from enforcement.[50]

Recognition of an investment award is separate from recognition of execution. In *FG Hemisphere Associates LLC v DR Congo*, the Hong Kong Court of Final Appeal held that the recognition of an investment award is a separate stage from the recognition of its execution.[51] Through its pleadings for immunity, the Democratic Republic of the Congo tried to resist the recognition of an arbitration award in Hong Kong. The court by majority held that well-established common law principles recognised that a waiver of immunity for the enforcement of arbitral awards must be evinced in respect of both jurisdictional immunity and immunity of property from execution, which are distinct immunities enjoyed by a State.[52]

A. Suit Recognition Stage: Immunity Considerations

(i) If Immunity is Involved

Referring to the FG Hemisphere decision, the Hong Kong Court of Appeal (Hong Kong Court of Final Appeal, hereinafter 'HKCFA') has held that when enforcing an award under the Convention on the Recognition and Enforcement of Foreign Arbitral Awards (NYC), the relevant court exercises an adjudicative function in which the party seeking enforcement bears the burden of addressing

[47] According to the reasoning of the International Court of Justice (ICJ) in *Jurisdictional Immunities of the State (Germany v Italy: Greece Intervening)*, Judgment, 2012 ICJ Rep 99, para 57 (Feb 3) [hereinafter *Jurisdictional Immunities of the State*].

[48] ibid.

[49] GA Res 59/38, annex, United Nations Convention on Jurisdictional Immunities of States and Their Property art 5 (2 December 2004).

[50] *Jurisdictional Immunities of the State* (n 47) para 113.

[51] *Congo v FG Hemisphere Associates LLC*, [2011] 14 HKCFAR 95, para 383.

[52] ibid paras 379, 382–83.

possible defences and the party resisting enforcement retains the right to resist enforcement based on aforesaid defences.[53] Based on this reasoning, when recognising an NYC award, the Forum State can invoke its adjudicative power to decline recognition if certain conditions are met.

(ii) Waiver

According to UNCSI Article 7(1)(b), immunity from a suit can be contractually waived in advance.[54] However, in this case, the Court of Final Appeal in the *FG Hemisphere* case held that the contract, which is the arbitration agreement to waive the state immunity, is insufficient.[55] In this regard, it held that the threshold of waiver of immunity is high and requires explicit words or conduct of an impleaded state indicating such a waiver.[56] The debtor state needs to exempt the Forum State from offering immunity to another state.[57] In this regard, the majority of the HKCFA in the FG Hemisphere case held that international agreements cannot occasion a waiver of immunity by a non-party state according to the *pacta tertiis* rule.[58]

B. Execution Stage: Evaluating Immunity Implications

As has been discussed above, immunity from execution is a distinct stage from immunity from a suit. The German Federal Constitutional Court in the *Philippine Embassy Bank Account* case has stated that immunity from execution is not curtailed in international law, unlike immunity from jurisdiction, since forced execution entails more severe consequences for the foreign state.[59] As a general rule, the exception of a waiver is available in cases of immunity from execution. However, in *FG Hemisphere*, the court stated that the arbitral agreement itself cannot be regarded as a waiver of immunity from execution.[60] Overall, the HKCFA case is significant because it is a dispute that highlights the

[53] *FG Hemisphere Associates LLC v Congo*, [2010] 2 HKLRD 66, para 174.

[54] International Law Commission Report on the Work of its Forty-Third Session, UN Doc A/46/10, at 27 (1991).

[55] *FG Hemisphere Associates LLC*, 14 HKCFAR 95, para 390 (2011).

[56] ibid para 392.

[57] See also the observation of the Supreme Court of the Netherlands in *NN v The State of The Netherlands* (14 October 2016, ECLI:NL:HR:2016:2371, 15/01944) that it is the forum State's responsibility to afford immunity to the debtor State.

[58] Adrian Lai, 'State Immunity in the Context of Enforcement of Investment Arbitration Awards' in Julien Chaisse, Leila Choukroune and Sufian Jusoh (eds), *Handbook of International Investment Law and Policy* (Singapore, Springer, 2021). See also the judgment of the Hong Kong Court of First Instance on this issue by Reyes J, *FG Hemisphere Associates. LLC v Congo* [2009] 1 HKLRD 410, para 116.

[59] August Reinisch, 'European Court Practice Concerning State Immunity from Enforcement Measures' (2006) 17(4) *European Journal of International Law* 803, 807.

[60] *FG Hemisphere Associates LLC* [2011] 14 HKCFAR 95, paras 378–79.

complexities of Hong Kong's unique sovereignty as a participant in international dispute settlement. By recognising the position of the PRC that an international convention signed by the PRC did not recognise restrictive state immunity and that the PRC only recognised the doctrine of absolute state immunity, Hong Kong's constitutional courts gave full interpretation to Hong Kong's precarious international standing.

Hong Kong recognises international arbitration for investment disputes between itself and investors and has embraced the model legislation for domestic and international commercial arbitration developed by the United Nations Commission on International Trade Law (UNCITRAL).[61] It has a Memorandum of Understanding with mainland China for reciprocal enforcement of arbitral awards based on the New York Convention.[62] In resolving investor-state disputes, Hong Kong has adopted dynamic approaches. Firstly, Hong Kong has signed a limited number of BITs but has in recent years started setting new model BIT standards that are very different from the BIT model adopted by China. Secondly, as an applicable territory under China's membership of the International Centre for Settlement of Investment Disputes (ICSID) Convention and NYC, Hong Kong has provided avenues for its residents to use other multilateral conventions to promote the enforcement of arbitral awards. Lastly, by analysing and limiting the immunity exercised in Hong Kong, the role of Hong Kong as a place to enforce awards can be protected.

The main findings of this chapter can be summarised through four key areas: the absence of general investment legislation, the promotion of international investment, the foreign investment screening mechanism and the approach of the Hong Kong Court of Final Appeal towards sovereign immunity. The chapter highlighted the absence of any general investment legislation governing the admission of foreign investment in Hong Kong. This unique situation is attributable to the territory's commitment to free-market principles and its open-door policy towards foreign investments. The absence of overarching legislation has implications for the flexibility and adaptability of Hong Kong's investment landscape, allowing it to swiftly respond to global economic changes and market trends. In conclusion, Chapter 3 offers key insights into Hong Kong's unilateral foreign investment landscape, underscoring the territory's unique legal and regulatory environment.

[61] US Department of State, '2022 Investment Climate Statements: Hong Kong' (2022). Available at: www.state.gov/reports/2022-investment-climate-statements/hong-kong/, accessed 2 February 2024.
[62] ibid.

4

Tax Haven or Tax Haven't? Exploring Hong Kong's Unilateral Tax Regime

In today's rapidly evolving global tax landscape, the unique characteristics and complexities of a jurisdiction's tax regime play a crucial role in determining its attractiveness as an investment destination.[1] Hong Kong, with its strategic location and reputation as an international financial centre, has long been a magnet for foreign investors and its autonomous tax regime has undoubtedly contributed to its continued success. In this chapter, we shall undertake a comprehensive examination of Hong Kong's unilateral tax system, discussing its institutional framework, incentives, compliance measures and impact on cross-border transactions and investments.

Hong Kong has an autonomous taxation framework which is low and simple and also enacts its tax regulations and laws. The tax rates suggest that Hong Kong's corporate and personal income tax rates are 'among the lowest in the world'[2] since the personal tax rates (tax levied on an individual's income, ie salary and wages) range from 2–17 per cent, while corporate tax (levied on a company's income or capital) in Hong Kong is 8.25 per cent or 16.5 per cent, depending on the volume of the assessable profits of the corporation.[3] Furthermore, Hong Kong does not levy any estate duty, tax on capital gains or VAT in its territory.[4] The financial separation, commonly known as the 'fiscal firewall', between the HKSAR Government and the Central People's Government (CPG) is legally defined by Articles 106 and 108 of the Basic Law.[5] Article 106 states that Hong

[1] OECD, 'Addressing the Tax Challenges of the Digital Economy' (OECD 2014) 32. Available at: www.oecd-ilibrary.org/fundamental-principles-of-taxation5jxv8zhcggxv.pdf, accessed 30 September 2023.

[2] 'Is Tax Reform Required in Hong Kong?' Available at: www.taxreform.gov.hk/eng/pdf/Chapter_01.pdf, accessed 30 September 2023.

[3] GovHK, 'Tax Return Filing, Enquiry & Payment' (*GovHK*). Available at: www.gov.hk/en/residents/taxes/taxfiling/?subcat=taxrates, accessed 30 September 2023.

[4] HSBC Expat 'Tax in Hong Kong'. Available at: www.expat.hsbc.com/expat-explorer/expat-guides/hong-kong/tax-in-hong-kong/, accessed 30 September 2023.

[5] Richard Cullen and Antonietta Wong, 'Globalization and the Hong Kong Revenue Regime', in Arthur J Cockfield (ed), *Globalization and Its Tax Discontents: Tax Policy and International Investments* (Toronto, University of Toronto Press, 2010) 171.

Kong is to maintain autonomous finances. The revenues procured by the Hong Kong SAR are designated exclusively for its own usage and no revenues need be remitted to the Central People's Government. It is also stipulated that the Central People's Government is not authorised to impose taxes within the confines of the Hong Kong SAR.

Hong Kong's tax policy provides for imposing a tax only on business profits under profits tax, property rental income under property tax and employment income under salaries tax.[6] Any income that does not come under any of these heads will not be taxable. The issue of multiple taxation has been addressed by Hong Kong to a large extent by restricting tax layers and tax rates on savings and investments.[7] The taxation regime recognises the territorial source principle of taxation, meaning that profit taxes will be levied on profits originating in or flowing from Hong Kong. Therefore, offshore profits are not subject to profits tax. Moreover, the neutral tax framework that Hong Kong has adopted enables it not only to levy tax uniformly but also preserve economic activity.[8] All these facets combined ensure the success of Hong Kong as a lucrative destination for international transactions and a wealth/asset management centre.

Chapter 4 provides a thorough analysis of Hong Kong's tax system, exploring key components and mechanisms that contribute to its efficacy and stability. It examines the institutions responsible for tax policies and administration, highlighting their role in attracting domestic and international investors. It discusses the tax incentives and exemptions tailored to promote growth and innovation across sectors. It also explores Hong Kong's compliance measures to combat tax evasion and avoidance, emphasising its commitment to international standards. The chapter also investigates the impact of Hong Kong's tax regime on cross-border transactions and investments, emphasising its role in facilitating global financial activities. The chapter concludes by examining Hong Kong's participation in tax organisations and its proactive approach to shaping regional tax policies. This comprehensive overview aims to provide valuable insights for experts, practitioners, policymakers and investors interested in understanding Hong Kong's tax system and its implications for the global economy. The analysis sheds light on the unique features, challenges and opportunities presented by Hong Kong's tax regime.

I. PILLARS OF HONG KONG'S TAX SYSTEM: KEY INSTITUTIONS AND MECHANISMS

Taxation is one of Hong Kong's most essential international economic policies. To fit the ever-changing worldwide taxation landscape, Hong Kong must

[6] 'Prevailing Tax Policy' (*Financial Services and the Treasury Bureau*). Available at: www.fstb.gov.hk/en/treasury/general/prevailing-tax-policy.htm, accessed 30 September 2023.

[7] 'The Tax System of Hong Kong' (*IRET Policy Bulletin*, 28 December 2010). Available at: http://iret.org/pub/BLTN-95.PDF, accessed 30 September 2023.

[8] ibid.

be competitive and aggressive in its tax policy.[9] Hong Kong has long attracted foreign investment due to its straightforward tax system and low tax rate. Countries like Singapore adopt tax incentives to attract multinational companies.[10] As states compete for tax revenue, a more sophisticated and appealing tax structure is essential,[11] with a more liberal reduction in withholding taxes perhaps being an option.[12] China's Hainan Free Trade Port, a project announced in 2018,[13] will compete with Hong Kong in terms of trade, investment, capital flows and movement of people and data by 2035.[14] To allow Hong Kong to remain a hub of international influence, the tax-free shopping policy for the outlying islands[15] and the departure tax rebate policy should be modified.[16] A proactive tax framework will facilitate both inward and outward investment under the Belt and Road initiative.[17]

This section provides a comprehensive overview of the primary institutions responsible for formulating, implementing and administering tax policies in the territory, while also examining the essential mechanisms that contribute to the overall efficacy and stability of the system. By elucidating the roles and responsibilities of these key institutions, it offers valuable insights into the inner workings of Hong Kong's tax system and the factors that make it uniquely attractive to both domestic and international investors. Additionally, it highlights the principles and strategies that have shaped the territory's tax landscape, enabling it to strike a delicate balance between revenue generation and fostering a business-friendly environment.

The body responsible for tax collection in Hong Kong is the Inland Revenue Department (IRD). The composition of the IRD is similar to other national

[9] Antony KF Ting and Daniel HK Ho, 'Tax Consolidation: Does It Have to Be Complex for Hong Kong' (2012) 42 *Hong Kong Law Journal* 158.

[10] Justin Dabner, 'Are Taxation Incentives Designed to Attract Regional Corporate Headquarters Likely to Be Effective' (1996) 2 *International Trade and Business Law Annual* 21.

[11] Andrew Halkyard, 'Treating Taxpayers Right: Taxpayers' Rights with Special Reference to Hong Kong' (2001) 9 *Asia Pacific Law Review* 133; Julien Chaisse and Xueliang Ji, '"Soft Law" in International Law-Making: How Soft International Taxation Law is Reshaping International Economic Governance' (2018) 13 *Asian Journal of WTO Law and Health Policy* 463.

[12] Kunka Petkova, Andrezej Stasio and Martin Zagler, 'On the Relevance of Double Tax Treaties' (2020) 27 *International Tax and Public Finance* 590.

[13] English translation of President Xi Jinping's report at the 19th National Congress of the Communist Party, *Secure a Decisive Victory in Building a Moderately Prosperous Society in All Respects and Strive for the Great Success of Socialism with Chinese Characteristics for a New Era*. Available at: www.hnftp.gov.cn/xwzx/ywsd/202002/t20200224_3260171.html, accessed 16 November 2020.

[14] Sidney Leng and William Zheng, 'China unveils plan to make Hainan a free trade hub like Hong Kong, Singapore as risks of US decoupling loom' (*South China Morning Post*, 2 June 2020). Availableat:www.scmp.com/economy/china-economy/article/3087206/china-unveils-plan-make-hainan-free-trade-hub-hong-kong, accessed 30 September 2023.

[15] Ministry of Finance, *Support Hainan to Comprehensively Deepen the Reform and Opening up of the Implementation Plan for Fiscal and Taxation Policies*. Available at: www.hnftp.gov.cn/zcfg/zcwj/ss/202002/t20200226_3261459.html, accessed 27 August 2020.

[16] Daniel Ho, 'Boosting Hong Kong's Competitiveness in the BEPS Era' (2017) 43 *International Tax Journal* 17, 19.

[17] ibid 26.

revenue bodies. Staffed by almost 2930 officers across the department,[18] the IRD is headed by a Commissioner, supported by two Deputy Commissioners in the Commissioner's Unit. Apart from the Headquarters Unit, there are four more Units, all headed by an Assistant Commissioner.[19]

The IRD is responsible for enforcing several ordinances, including the Stamp Duty Ordinance, the Inland Revenue Ordinance and the Estate Duty Ordinance.[20] In accordance with the provisions of the Inland Revenue Ordinance (IRO), the IRD levies three separate direct taxes on income: properties tax, salaries tax and profits tax.[21] In recent years profit tax has accounted for the greatest proportion of the HKSAR Government's income.[22] The IRO establishes certain requirements which must be met while filing returns and maintaining due diligence. The Commissioner is authorised to take punitive action if these requirements are not met. Actions can range from the imposition of a penalty to prosecution.[23]

Since 2001, the model followed by IRD is a 'assess first, audit later' approach. The benefit of this approach is that it is a computerised system which helps in processing tax assessments automatically.[24] This system requires issuing tax assessments or statements of loss first and then submitting the return. These are subject to audits or investigation at a later stage.[25]

Taxpayers may file an objection with the IRD if they wish to dispute the assessment. An appeal to the Board of Review (IRO) (the Board) can be filed if the dispute pertains to the Commissioner or the assessment of additional tax. The time limit for this is within one month of the transmission of the written determination or notice of assessment. The Board may confirm, increase, reduce or annul the disputed assessment or refer the matter back to the Commissioner with its review. If either party is still not satisfied at this stage, they have the option to appeal to the Court of First Instance of the High Court against such decision on a question of law.[26]

[18] 'Organization Chart' (*Inland Revenue Department*). Available at: www.ird.gov.hk/eng/abo/org.htm, accessed 30 September 2023.

[19] 'Organization Chart' (*Inland Revenue Department*). Available at: www.ird.gov.hk/eng/abo/org_02.htm#ciroffice accessed 30 September 2023.

[20] 'Ordinances Administered' (*Inland Revenue Department*). Available at: www.ird.gov.hk/eng/abo/ord.htm, accessed 30 September 2023.

[21] Inland Revenue Ordinance (Cap. 112). Available at: www.elegislation.gov.hk/hk/cap112, accessed 30 September 2023.

[22] 'Five Major Revenue Sources of the Government' (*Financial Services and the Treasury Bureau*) Available at: www.fstb.gov.hk/en/treasury/general/five-major-revenue-sources-of-the-government.htm, accessed 30 September 2023.

[23] 'Penalty Policy' (*Inland Revenue Department*). Available at: www.ird.gov.hk/eng/pol/ppo.htm, accessed 30 September 2023.

[24] 'Commissioner's Overview' (*Inland Revenue Department*). Available at: www.ird.gov.hk/dar/2007-08/table/eng/ch1.pdf, accessed 30 September 2023.

[25] ibid.

[26] 'Objections and Appeals' (*GovHK*). Available at: www.gov.hk/en/residents/taxes/taxfiling/object/objections.htm, accessed 30 September 2023.

The IRO helps in reducing tax compliance costs by codifying its rules in a single document.[27] The IRD regularly issues Departmental Interpretation and Practice Notes for public knowledge, thereby maintaining a transparent taxation system.[28] Hong Kong has an efficient tax collection practice and prides itself on having one of the lowest tax collection costs in the world.[29]

II. TAX INCENTIVES AND EXEMPTIONS: ENCOURAGING GROWTH AND INNOVATION

Hong Kong's tax regime has long been recognised for its simplicity and competitiveness, making the territory an attractive destination for businesses and investors alike. One of the key components of the territory's tax policy is its use of targeted tax incentives and exemptions designed to encourage growth, stimulate innovation and promote economic development. In this section, we will explore the various tax incentives and exemptions offered by Hong Kong, examining their impact on different industries, research and development (R&D) activities and small and medium-sized enterprises (SMEs).

Hong Kong's government recognises the importance of certain sectors in driving economic growth and has introduced tailored tax incentives to support their development. For example, the territory's thriving maritime industry benefits from a concessionary profits tax rate for ship leasing management activities, while the aircraft leasing sector enjoys a similarly reduced tax rate for qualifying profits. These targeted incentives serve to strengthen Hong Kong's position as a regional hub for these industries, attracting investment and fostering growth.

In addition to industry-specific incentives, Hong Kong's tax policy also seeks to promote innovation and R&D by offering tax breaks for eligible activities. The territory's Enhanced Tax Deduction Scheme for R&D expenditure, introduced in 2018, provides a 300 per cent tax deduction for the first HKD2 million of qualifying R&D expenditure and a 200 per cent deduction for the remainder. This incentive encourages businesses to invest in research and innovation, boosting Hong Kong's status as a leading centre for technological advancement.

Moreover, Hong Kong recognises the vital role played by SMEs in its economy and has implemented a range of tax incentives and exemptions to support their growth. For instance, the territory's two-tiered profits tax system, which came into effect in 2018, offers a lower tax rate of 8.25 per cent on the first HKD 2 million of assessable profits, while the standard 16.5 per cent rate is

[27] 'The Tax System of Hong Kong' (*IRET Policy Bulletin*, 28 December 2010). Available at: http://iret.org/pub/BLTN 95.PDF, accessed 30 September 2023.

[28] 'Departmental Interpretation and Practice Notes' (*Inland Revenue Department*). Available at: www.ird.gov.hk/eng/ppr/dip.htm, accessed 30 September 2023.

[29] Anthony Au-Yeung, 'Understanding the Hong Kong Tax System' (1982) 8 *International Tax Journal* 337.

applied to the remainder. This preferential tax treatment provides a significant boost to SMEs, enabling them to reinvest their earnings into further growth and development.

Hong Kong's tax regime also includes various exemptions designed to encourage investment and economic growth.[30] For example, the territory does not impose a capital gains tax, which can be particularly advantageous for investors and businesses involved in mergers and acquisitions. Similarly, Hong Kong does not levy a dividend tax or a value-added tax (VAT), reducing the overall tax burden on businesses and promoting a favourable investment climate.[31]

However, it is important to note that these tax incentives and exemptions are not without their challenges. While they undoubtedly contribute to Hong Kong's attractiveness as a business destination, they may also lead to concerns about tax revenue and potential abuse. To address these issues, the territory's IRD employs a stringent set of eligibility criteria and reporting requirements to ensure that businesses claiming tax incentives and exemptions are genuinely engaged in qualifying activities. Furthermore, the IRD actively participates in international tax initiatives, such as the Base Erosion and Profit Shifting (BEPS) project, to combat tax evasion and avoidance.

In conclusion, Hong Kong's tax incentives and exemptions play a crucial role in encouraging growth and innovation within the territory. By offering targeted tax breaks for specific industries and R&D activities, as well as preferential treatment for SMEs, Hong Kong fosters a dynamic and competitive business environment that attracts investment and drives economic development. However, it is essential for the territory to continue balancing these incentives with robust compliance measures and international cooperation to ensure the integrity and fairness of its tax system.

III. ADDRESSING TAX EVASION AND AVOIDANCE: HONG KONG'S COMPLIANCE MEASURES

Tax evasion and avoidance pose significant challenges to the global economy, eroding the tax base and undermining public trust in the fairness of tax systems.[32] In response, Hong Kong has taken proactive measures to strengthen its compliance

[30] Also unexceptionally, art 108 specifically authorises and requires the SAR to 'enact laws … concerning types of taxes, tax rates, tax reductions, allowances and exemptions and other matters of taxation'. (In other respects, as will be seen, art 108 is exceptional.)

[31] Article 108 of the Basic Law provides: 'The Hong Kong Special Administrative Region shall practise an independent taxation system. The Hong Kong Special Administrative Region shall, taking the low tax policy previously pursued in Hong Kong as reference, enact laws on its own concerning types of taxes, tax rates, tax reductions, allowances and exemptions and other matters of taxation.'

[32] Mathew N Murray, 'Would Tax Evasion and Tax Avoidance Undermine a National Retail Sales Tax?' in J Slemrod (ed), *Tax Policy in the Real World* (Cambridge, Cambridge University Press, 2010).

framework and align its tax policies with international best practices. In this section, we explore the various measures implemented by the territory to address tax evasion and avoidance, highlighting its commitment to transparency, information exchange and cooperation with international initiatives.

One of the key components of Hong Kong's approach to tackling tax evasion and avoidance is its participation in the BEPS project, led by the Organisation for Economic Co-operation and Development (OECD) and the G20. BEPS refers to tax planning strategies that exploit gaps and mismatches in tax rules to artificially shift profits to low or no-tax jurisdictions. By joining the BEPS project, Hong Kong has committed to implementing a series of measures aimed at combating harmful tax practices, preventing treaty abuse and enhancing dispute resolution mechanisms.

In line with its BEPS commitments, Hong Kong has amended its existing laws and introduced new regulations. An important recent development is the introduction of the Transfer Pricing Regime, which requires multinational enterprises (MNEs) to comply with the arm's-length principle when determining the pricing of transactions between related parties. This measure is designed to prevent MNEs from manipulating the pricing of intra-group transactions to shift profits to low-tax jurisdictions and avoid paying their fair share of tax.

Hong Kong has also adopted the Country-by-Country (CbC) Reporting framework, which requires large MNEs to report financial and tax-related information on a country-by-country basis. This initiative enhances the transparency of MNEs' global operations and enables tax authorities to better assess the risk of tax avoidance. To facilitate information exchange between tax jurisdictions, Hong Kong has signed the Multilateral Competent Authority Agreement on the Exchange of CbC Reports, signalling its commitment to international cooperation in the fight against tax evasion and avoidance.

Additionally, Hong Kong has taken significant steps to enhance the transparency of its tax system and improve the exchange of tax-related information with other jurisdictions. The territory has entered into numerous bilateral agreements for the exchange of information (EOI) on tax matters and has adopted the Common Reporting Standard (CRS) for the automatic exchange of financial account information. Under the CRS framework, Hong Kong's financial institutions are required to identify and report information on financial accounts held by tax residents of reportable jurisdictions to the IRD. This information is then exchanged with the tax authorities of the relevant jurisdictions on an annual basis, enabling more effective detection and deterrence of tax evasion.

To further strengthen its compliance measures, Hong Kong has implemented rigorous anti-money laundering (AML) and counter-terrorist financing (CTF) regulations.[33] These regulations require financial institutions and designated

[33] FATF, 'Hong Kong, China's measures to combat money laundering and terrorist financing' (2019). Available at: www.fatf-gafi.org/en/publications/Mutualevaluations/Mer-hong-kong-china-2019.html.

non-financial businesses to establish robust systems and controls to detect and prevent illicit activities, including tax evasion. Furthermore, the territory's regulatory authorities, such as the IRD and the Hong Kong Monetary Authority, actively collaborate with their international counterparts to share information and combat cross-border financial crimes.

In addition to these legislative and regulatory measures, Hong Kong has adopted a risk-based approach to tax compliance, enabling the IRD to focus its resources on high-risk taxpayers and areas of concern. The territory's 'assess first, audit later' approach to tax administration allows for the efficient processing of tax returns, while also ensuring that audits and investigations are conducted where necessary. This approach, combined with the IRD's ongoing efforts to educate taxpayers and raise awareness of compliance requirements, contributes to the effectiveness of Hong Kong's tax compliance framework.

In sum, Hong Kong has implemented a robust set of measures to address tax evasion and avoidance, demonstrating its commitment to maintaining a fair and transparent tax system. By participating in international initiatives such as the BEPS project, adopting the CRS framework and entering numerous EOI agreements, the territory has strengthened its cooperation with other tax jurisdictions and enhanced the effectiveness of its compliance measures. Furthermore, the introduction of transfer pricing regulations, CbC reporting requirements and comprehensive AML and CTF rules has bolstered Hong Kong's efforts to combat harmful tax practices and promote fiscal responsibility.

Hong Kong's proactive approach to addressing tax evasion and avoidance has not only contributed to the stability and integrity of its tax system but has also helped maintain its reputation as a trusted and compliant international financial centre. The territory's ongoing efforts to refine and adapt its tax policies in response to the evolving international tax law framework reflect its determination to uphold the principles of transparency, fairness and compliance with international standards.

As the global economy continues to evolve, Hong Kong must remain vigilant and responsive to emerging challenges and opportunities in the realm of taxation. By continually reviewing and enhancing its compliance measures, fostering international cooperation and promoting a culture of tax compliance among its residents and businesses, the territory can ensure that its tax system remains robust and effective in the face of a rapidly changing global environment.

IV. THE IMPACT OF HONG KONG'S TAX REGIME ON CROSS-BORDER TRANSACTIONS AND INVESTMENTS

Hong Kong's unique tax regime has long been recognised for its simplicity, low rates and territorial source principle, all of which contribute to the territory's attractiveness as an international business hub. In this section, we explore the impact of Hong Kong's tax system on cross-border transactions and investments, focusing on how the territory's approach to taxation fosters an environment conducive to international trade and investment.

As a leading global financial centre, Hong Kong has been successful in attracting foreign investments, thanks in part to its favourable tax regime. The territory's low and straightforward tax rates, coupled with the absence of taxes on capital gains, dividends and interest income, have made Hong Kong a preferred destination for international investors. Additionally, the territorial source principle, which taxes only income derived from within Hong Kong, has further encouraged foreign investors to channel their funds through the territory. The territory's extensive network of double taxation avoidance agreements (DTAAs) has also played a significant role in facilitating cross-border investments.[34] By reducing the tax burden on income arising from international transactions, DTAAs promote trade and investment between Hong Kong and its treaty partners. Furthermore, these agreements help prevent tax evasion and provide a level of certainty for investors regarding the tax treatment of their cross-border activities.

Hong Kong's tax system is particularly supportive of cross-border transactions, both in terms of trade and financial services. The territory's commitment to international tax transparency and compliance has also contributed to the growth of cross-border transactions. By adopting global standards, such as the BEPS project and the CRS, Hong Kong has demonstrated its commitment to combating tax evasion and avoidance, thereby enhancing its reputation as a reliable and trustworthy financial centre.

Hong Kong's tax regime has also played a key role in promoting innovation and entrepreneurship in the territory. The government has implemented various tax incentives and exemptions aimed at encouraging R&D activities, such as enhanced tax deductions for R&D expenditure and profits tax exemptions for certain qualifying debt instruments. These tax incentives, along with the territory's overall favourable tax environment, have not only attracted innovative enterprises to establish their presence in Hong Kong but also spurred local companies to invest in R&D and other value-adding activities. Consequently, this has fostered a vibrant ecosystem of innovation and entrepreneurship, further cementing Hong Kong's position as a leading global business centre.

While Hong Kong's tax regime has been successful in facilitating cross-border transactions and investments, the territory must also adapt to the changing global tax landscape. For example, the ongoing global efforts to reform international corporate taxation, such as the proposed global minimum tax under the BEPS project, could potentially impact Hong Kong's attractiveness as a tax-efficient jurisdiction. To address these challenges, Hong Kong must continue

[34] Michael Littlewood, 'Tax Treaty Disputes in Hong Kong' in Eduardo Baistrocchi (ed), *A Global Analysis of Tax Treaty Disputes* (Cambridge, Cambridge University Press, 2007); see also Hansrudi Lenz, 'Aggressive Tax Avoidance by Managers of Multinational Companies as a Violation of Their Moral Duty to Obey the Law: A Kantian Rationale' (2020) 165 *Journal of Business Ethics* 681.

to refine its tax policies and strengthen its international tax cooperation. By actively engaging in global tax policy discussions and adopting international tax standards, the territory can ensure its tax regime remains competitive and attractive to international investors, while also upholding the principles of transparency, fairness and compliance with global norms.

Hong Kong's tax regime has played a pivotal role in promoting cross-border transactions and investments, thanks to its low and simple tax rates, territorial source principle and extensive network of DTAAs. By continuing to actively participate in international tax forums, adopting global tax standards and refining its tax policies, Hong Kong can maintain its competitive edge as a leading global financial centre. As the territory navigates the evolving international tax regime, it must strike a balance between fostering an attractive tax environment for international investors and ensuring compliance with international norms and standards. This approach will enable Hong Kong to remain a preferred destination for cross-border transactions and investments while reinforcing its reputation as a transparent and responsible financial hub.

In the face of growing international scrutiny and regulatory changes, Hong Kong has the opportunity to further enhance its tax regime by adopting targeted measures that support specific sectors, such as green finance and digital innovation. For instance, the government could consider implementing tax incentives for environmentally friendly projects or for companies engaged in developing advanced technologies. By doing so, Hong Kong can attract more investment and talent in these high-growth areas, while also aligning its tax policies with global sustainability goals and technological advances.

Another important aspect for Hong Kong to consider is the strengthening of its dispute resolution mechanisms in tax matters. As cross-border transactions and investments become more complex, there is an increasing likelihood of tax disputes arising between taxpayers and tax authorities. Enhancing its tax dispute resolution framework, such as through the adoption of arbitration procedures under its DTAAs, can provide greater certainty for taxpayers and contribute to Hong Kong's overall attractiveness as an investment destination.

To sum up, Hong Kong's tax regime has had a significant impact on facilitating cross-border transactions and investments, contributing to the territory's status as a prominent global financial centre. As the global tax environment continues to evolve, Hong Kong must adapt its tax policies and practices to maintain its competitive edge while adhering to international standards. By doing so, the territory can continue to foster innovation, attract foreign investment and support its long-term economic growth and development.

This section has considered Hong Kong's participation in various tax organisations and its proactive role in shaping tax policies and practices across the region. As an influential financial centre, Hong Kong's involvement in these organisations not only contributes to the harmonisation and alignment of regional tax policies but also enables the territory to stay abreast of evolving international tax norms and standards. This section has provided valuable insights into how Hong Kong leverages its regional ties to further refine and adapt its tax system in response to the changing global tax landscape. In doing so, it has underscored the territory's ongoing efforts to maintain its competitive edge as a thriving business hub while upholding the principles of transparency, fairness and compliance with international standards.

V. STRENGTHENING REGIONAL TIES: HONG KONG'S ROLE IN TAX ORGANISATIONS

As part of its commitment to promoting strategic dialogue on taxation policy, promoting knowledge sharing, improving cooperation and coordination in tax administration and policy in the region and achieving the Sustainable Development Goals, the Asian Development Bank (ADB) established the Asia-Pacific Tax Hub in 2021 as an 'open and inclusive' forum.[35] Since Hong Kong is a member of the ADB, the Asia-Pacific Tax Hub can benefit it, especially with the fall in regional tax revenues. In 1992, the Asia Oceania Tax Consultants' Association (AOTCA) was formed, composed of tax consultants, lawyers and other professionals.[36] AOTCA's members include the Hong Kong Institute of Certified Public Accountants and the Taxation Institute of Hong Kong, who meet annually to discuss tax-related issues. The AOTCA International Tax Conference, which took place in Hong Kong in 2016, discussed tax transparency, BEPS and fair taxation issues.[37] APTF, co-founded by the International Trade and Investment Centre in 2005, has witnessed active participation from Hong Kong.[38] In addition to private and public stakeholders, APTF brings together experts in the field to discuss the implications of changes in the international tax regime and tax-related issues in the region.

Through its initiatives, Hong Kong, which has evolved into Asia's preferred International Finance Centre, actively participates in several regional and international forums seeking to promote financial stability.[39] As a result, Asia is now better positioned in the international standard-setting process. It could further improve its position by participating in and promoting policy debates and by offering recommendations on issues affecting the region. This is supported by

[35] '*Asia Pacific Tax* Hub an open and inclusive forum' (*Asia Times*, 13 April 2022). Available at: https://asiatimes.com/2022/04/asia-pacific-tax-hub-an-open-and-inclusive-forum/, accessed 30 September 2023.

[36] See www.aotca.org/about/, accessed 30 September 2023.

[37] AOTCA, 'AOTCA Hong Kong 2016 – International Tax Conference Program'. Available at: www.nichizeiren.or.jp/eng/pdf/AOTCA2016-InternationalTaxConferenceProgram.pdf, accessed 30 September 2023.

[38] International Trade and Investment Center, 'Reach' (*International Trade and Investment Center*). Available at: www.iticnet.org/reach, accessed 30 September 2023.

[39] 'Why Complementarity Matters for Stability – Hong Kong SAR and Singapore as Asian Financial Centers' (*IMF*, 2014). Available at: www.imf.org/external/pubs/ft/wp/2014/wp14119.pdf, accessed 30 September 2023.

the European Union's experience,[40] which has shown that recommendations and representations by state legislators can help influence regional policy, promote inter-state cooperation, help build principles and ensure they are being complied with, all to the benefit of the whole region.

The chapter's analysis highlighted the territory's commitment to maintaining a business-friendly environment while adhering to global tax standards and fostering regional cooperation. Hong Kong's tax system is underpinned by a robust institutional framework, which ensures the efficacy and stability of its tax policies and practices. Key institutions such as the IRD play a vital role in administering and implementing tax regulations in a transparent and efficient manner. The territory's tax incentives and exemptions are strategically designed to encourage growth and innovation across various sectors. These measures contribute to Hong Kong's attractiveness as an investment destination and help create a competitive business environment.

Hong Kong demonstrates a strong commitment to addressing tax evasion and avoidance through the implementation of robust compliance measures. The territory's adherence to international tax standards and focus on transparency reflects its dedication to preserving the integrity of its tax system. The impact of Hong Kong's tax regime on cross-border transactions and investments is significant, as the territory's tax policies and practices contribute to its status as a leading global financial centre. The overall implications of the analysis suggest that Hong Kong's unilateral tax regime successfully balances the need for a competitive, business-friendly environment with its obligations to uphold international tax standards and foster regional cooperation. The territory's approach to taxation demonstrates a clear understanding of the challenges and opportunities presented by an increasingly interconnected global economy.

PART I CONCLUSION

The main findings of Part I provide a comprehensive overview of Hong Kong's domestic policies and practices in trade, investment and taxation. The analysis identifies the core strengths and challenges of the territory's economic framework, highlighting its commitment to fostering a competitive and business-friendly environment while adhering to international standards. Hong Kong's trade policies are characterised by their openness, which facilitates a vibrant and diverse trading environment. The territory's commitment to free trade and minimal market intervention has contributed significantly to its status as a leading global trade hub. Hong Kong's investment regime is driven by a

[40] European Parliament, 'The EU's Role in International Economic for a' (*European Parliament*, 2015). Available at: www.europarl.europa.eu/RegData/etudes/BRIE/2015/563475/IPOL_BRI(2015)563475_EN.pdf, accessed 30 September 2023.

strong institutional framework, clear regulations and a pro-business attitude. This environment has attracted significant foreign direct investment which has enabled the territory to maintain its position as a prominent financial centre. The territory's tax system strikes a balance between low tax rates, a simple structure, transparency and international compliance. This approach plays a vital role in attracting businesses and investors to Hong Kong while upholding global tax standards.

However, it is important to acknowledge some critical comments and challenges that deserve attention. Some critics argue that Hong Kong's heavy reliance on trade leaves it vulnerable to global economic fluctuations and disruptions, emphasising the need to diversify the economy and reduce the dependence on external trade for long-term sustainability. Income inequality remains a significant issue, despite Hong Kong's robust economic growth. Critics contend that the territory's economic policies have disproportionately benefited the wealthy, leading to a widening wealth gap and social tensions. Addressing income inequality and promoting inclusive growth should be priorities to ensure a more equitable society.

The overall implications of the analysis suggest that Hong Kong's unilateral foundations have successfully created a thriving domestic economic environment by prioritising free trade, investment attractiveness and a competitive tax regime. These factors have collectively contributed to the territory's economic success and its ability to navigate an increasingly interconnected global economy. Moving forward to Part II, which centres on fortifying Hong Kong's economic relations through bilateral endeavours, an exploration of the territory's involvement in international trade agreements, investment treaties and tax cooperation initiatives will ensue. This comprehensive examination aims to offer a more encompassing perspective of Hong Kong's economic landscape, shedding light on the intricate interplay between its unilateral foundations and bilateral undertakings in shaping the trajectory of its economy.

Part II

Bilateral Endeavours: Strengthening Hong Kong's Economic Relations

PART II OF the book focuses on the territory's bilateral initiatives within the realms of trade, investment and taxation. Utilising the conceptual framework of constructivism, Part II examines how Hong Kong's economic relations with its bilateral partners have evolved and the ways in which prevalent norms and ideas in international economic law both influence and are shaped by these interactions. By investigating the interplay between Hong Kong's economic policies, legal instruments and the broader global context, this section aims to provide a comprehensive understanding of the territory's strategic approach to cultivating economic alliances. Constructivism, as a theoretical approach, argues that state behaviour is primarily driven by the norms, ideas and social processes that constitute the international system. In the context of international economic law, this implies that the emergence, interpretation and evolution of legal norms depend on the collective understanding and shared values of the actors involved in the system. As a result, Hong Kong's bilateral engagements can be viewed as manifestations of the prevailing norms and ideas that underpin its economic relations, as well as its role as a norm-shaper within the international economic law landscape. In accordance with this constructivist perspective, Part II systematically investigates Hong Kong's bilateral endeavours in trade, investment and taxation, illustrating how the territory has strategically utilised its unique position within the international economic law framework to establish strong, mutually beneficial partnerships.

Through a detailed examination of the substantive provisions of Hong Kong's FTAs, Bilateral Investment Treaties (BITs) and Double Taxation Avoidance Agreements (DTAAs), this section offers valuable insights into the underlying norms and ideas driving the development and implementation of these legal instruments. Analysing the impact of these agreements on Hong Kong's economic policies and the territory's overall economic relations with its partners, this section highlights the critical role of constructivist dynamics in shaping the course of Hong Kong's bilateral endeavours. This analysis also contributes to a more nuanced understanding of how Hong Kong has navigated the complexities of the international economic law landscape in pursuit of its strategic interests and adaptation to the evolving global context. In sum, Part II provides a thorough and insightful examination of Hong Kong's bilateral endeavours in the domains of trade, investment and taxation, while emphasising the vital role of constructivist dynamics in shaping the territory's approach to strengthening its economic relations. By situating these developments within the broader context of the book's central themes, this section illuminates the interconnections between Hong Kong's unilateral foundations, bilateral engagements and multilateral aspirations within the realm of international economic law.

Chapter 5 commences with an exploration of Hong Kong's FTAs, offering an overview of the territory's trade policy, its FTA network and recent developments in trade policy. The discussion then moves to Hong Kong's unique trading relationship with the United States and analyses the implications of the Regional Comprehensive Economic Partnership (RCEP) for Hong Kong's future trade policy. Chapter 6 discusses Hong Kong's Bilateral Investment Treaties (BITs), emphasising the crucial role of international investment treaties in Hong Kong's economic policy, as well as providing an overview of the territory's existing BITs. Finally, Chapter 7 investigates Hong Kong's bilateral tax relations, examining the territory's taxation regime from both historical and contemporary perspectives and considering the substantive rules of Hong Kong's tax agreements. By weaving a cohesive and engaging narrative, Part II unravels the intricate web of bilateral relationships underpinning Hong Kong's economic policy and showcases the territory's strategic approach to forging powerful economic alliances in the international arena.

5

Crossing Borders: Hong Kong's Free Trade Agreements and their Impact

THE ROLE OF Hong Kong as an economic actor in the international arena is influenced by a complex interplay of factors, including its historical and political context, its position within the 'One Country, Two Systems' framework and its evolving relationship with both regional and global trading partners. This chapter examines Hong Kong's engagement with FTAs and their impact on its economic landscape through the lens of constructivism, a theoretical framework that emphasises the importance of ideas, norms and social processes in shaping the behaviour of actors in international relations.

Until recently, trade liberalisation has been a defining characteristic of the world since 1945.[1] The decades that followed the end of the Second World War saw the enactment of various agreements, including the Bretton Woods agreement and the General Agreement on Tariffs and Trade (GATT) and the hosting of a series of multilateral trade negotiations in the GATT.[2] However, since then, the long World Trade Organisation (WTO) multilateral negotiations on trade liberalisation have led to frustration with the process, which may have driven the demand for FTAs,[3] particularly in Asia. Despite implementing a free trade regime, Hong Kong is no exception. Since its first FTA with China in 2003, it has signed seven others, while negotiations for a ninth one will commence in the first quarter of 2023. It has also applied for early accession to the RCEP. If its accession application is approved, it will become part of the largest free trade area in the world.

This chapter begins by providing an overview of Hong Kong's trade policy, highlighting its historical roots and current issues, while establishing the context for its engagement with FTAs. It then explores the trends in the Asia-Pacific

[1] Andrew Walker, 'Is Free Trade Good or Bad?' (*BBC*, 18 January 2017). Available at: www.bbc.com/news/business-38209407, accessed 2 February 2024.

[2] Office of the Historian, 'Bretton Woods GATT, 1941–1947' (*Office of the Historian, Foreign Service Institute, United States Department of State*). Available at: www.history.state.gov/milestones/1937-1945/bretton-woods, accessed 2 February 2024.

[3] Alan O Sykes, 'The Law, Economics and Politics of Preferential Trading Arrangements: An Introduction' (2010) 46 *Stanford Journal of International Law* 171, 173.

region and their implications for Hong Kong's trade policy, as well as offering a general commentary on Hong Kong's approach to FTAs. The core of the chapter presents a comprehensive analysis of Hong Kong's FTA network, discussing the details of each agreement and the specific provisions that have shaped the relationships with its trading partners. Additionally, the chapter discusses the United States–Hong Kong Special Trading Status, its origins and benefits and the recent revocation of this status. In the latter part of the chapter, the focus shifts to contemporary developments in trade policy, including ongoing negotiations and potential future FTAs. A special emphasis is placed on the RCEP and its potential implications for Hong Kong's trade policy. The chapter concludes by synthesising the key findings and offering insights into the broader implications of Hong Kong's FTA engagements within the constructivist framework, linking these developments to the overarching themes of the book.

I. UNFOLDING HONG KONG'S TRADE POLICY LANDSCAPE

Free trade is practised in Hong Kong, which is widely recognised as having one of the most liberal economies in the world. Tariffs are kept to a bare minimum and there is a comparatively limited amount of government participation in commercial transactions. In addition to being a vital centre for international commerce and investment, Hong Kong is also an important gateway to Mainland China for a large number of foreign businesses. Hong Kong is also a signatory to several free trade agreements with various partners elsewhere in the world, in addition to being a member of the WTO.

A jurisdiction's trade policy may include the imposition of tariffs and other forms of trade restrictions, the negotiation of FTAs with other nations and involvement in international trade organisations.[4] FTAs are agreements between two or more nations to lower or abolish trade obstacles, such as tariffs and quotas, to enhance commerce between the countries that are parties to the agreement. FTAs may include both bilateral and multilateral trade pacts. In addition to provisions regarding intellectual property rights, labour standards and environmental protection, FTAs may also include provisions on other trade-related concerns. It is common practice for national trade strategies to involve the negotiation and implementation of FTAs as a means of expanding access to foreign products and services for local consumers and the opening of new markets for domestic goods and services.

The first bilateral FTA during modern times was concluded in the nineteenth century, when Britain and France signed an agreement on trade liberalisation on

[4] FTAs are agreements where two or more nations come to an understanding of the imposition of obligations on a variety of issues, including trade in goods and services and investment protection. International Trade Administration, 'Free Trade Agreement Overview' (*International Trade Administration*). Available at: www.trade.gov/free-trade-agreement-overview, accessed 2 February 2024.

23 January 1860. The Cobden–Chevalier Treaty, as it is known from the names of its two negotiators, removed trade barriers, reduced tariffs and granted to both parties most-favoured-nation status.[5] Crucially, it sparked what Krasner and other scholars have seen as a golden age of trade liberalisation[6] and led to the promulgation of similar agreements, especially in Europe, where 56 FTAs were signed within a span of 15 years.[7] Some economists have doubted whether this landmark agreement did as much to promote trade as has sometimes been claimed. However, recent quantitative assessments based on gravity models that also included domestic trade have indicated that the Cobden–Chevalier Treaty had increased both trade flows and the welfare of nations.[8]

Hong Kong has entered into FTAs in order to expand access for its customers to goods and services offered by foreign companies, as well as to open up new markets for the company's products and services. FTAs make it simpler and less expensive for firms in Hong Kong to export their wares to other countries, as well as for consumers in Hong Kong to purchase goods from other countries. This is accomplished by lowering or removing trade obstacles, such as tariffs and quotas. Additionally, Hong Kong may expand its position as a gateway to Mainland China and other markets for many foreign businesses by negotiating FTAs with other nations and regions. This is because Hong Kong is a key centre for worldwide commerce and investment. Having these agreements in place not only enables it to compete with other nations that have accords of a similar kind but also gives it an extra edge over other countries.

A. A Primer on Free Trade Agreements

FTAs can be difficult to evaluate from a political as well as an economic point of view, for a number of different reasons. When seen through the lens of politics, FTAs often include negotiations and compromises between various industries and geographical areas within a nation. For instance, lowering tariffs on a certain commodity may be beneficial to one sector of the economy but detrimental to another. In addition, FTAs often include provisions on other policy areas, such as intellectual property rights, labour standards and environmental protection, which may garner differing degrees of support from various interest

[5] Gene M Grossman, 'The Purpose of Trade Agreements' (2016) NBER Working Paper No 22070. Available at: www.nber.org/system/files/working_papers/w22070/w22070.pdf, accessed 2 February 2024.

[6] Stephen D Krasner, 'State Power and the Structure of International Trade' (1976) 28 *World Politics* 317, 325.

[7] Markus Lampe, 'Explaining Nineteenth-Century Bilateralism: Economic and Political Determinants of the Cobden-Chevalier Network' (*World Trade Organization*, 11 January 2011). Available at: www.wto.org/english/res_e/publications_e/wtr11_forum_e/wtr11_11jan11_e.htm, accessed 2 February 2024.

[8] Jacopo Timini, 'Revisiting the 'Cobden-Chevalier Network' Trade and Welfare Effects' (2022) *Explorations in Economic History* 1, 6, 11.

groups, depending on the specifics of the terms. As a result, it may be difficult to accurately forecast whether an FTA is politically feasible and this viability might shift over time.

The effects of a FTA might also be challenging to evaluate from an economic point of view. The exact trade obstacles that are being removed, the composition of the economies that are participating and the condition of the economy as a whole all influence the economic implications of a FTA. In addition, it may be difficult to quantify the economic effects of a FTA and those effects may also vary substantially depending on the particular set of assumptions and methods that were used in the research. Furthermore, the intricacies of FTAs, which may take the form of lengthy, cumbersome papers that include a great number of technical specifics and legal rules, can also be a source of concern. Considering these factors, it is impossible to forecast the success of these agreements. Their efficacy can only be judged over the course of time and by careful observation of the results of the deal. FTAs are designed to eliminate and reduce barriers, including tariffs and quotas, while enabling trade and investment facilitation and the consolidation of ties between trading and economic partners.[9] While these agreements facilitate trade flows, the actual trade gains and effect on welfare will depend on the interaction between the trade creation and trade diversion effects.[10]

From a legal perspective, free trade agreements (FTAs) are important for several reasons. Firstly, FTAs serve as a foundation for establishing legal norms that govern commercial interactions between participating nations. These agreements encompass a range of trade-related issues, including intellectual property rights, labour standards, environmental protection and laws on tariffs and trade barriers. By providing this comprehensive legal framework, FTAs help to ensure predictability and stability in trade relations, thereby encouraging firms to engage in freer investment and trade activities. Secondly, FTAs provide a structured mechanism for resolving disputes that may arise among participating nations. Instead of resorting to trade penalties or actions that could adversely affect broader relationships, FTAs incorporate dispute resolution procedures that enable nations to address disagreements in a calm and orderly manner.

[9] Department of Foreign Affairs and Trade, 'About FTAs' (*Australian Government, Department of Foreign Affairs and Trade*). Available at: www.dfat.gov.au/trade/about-ftas/about-free-trade-agreements, accessed 2 February 2024.

[10] Jacob Viner, 'The Economics of Customs Unions' in Paul Oslington (ed), *The Customs Union Issue* (Oxford University Press 2014) 55; Kimberly A Clausing, 'Trade Creation and Trade Diversion in the Canada – United States Free Trade Agreement' (2001) 34 *The Canadian Journal of Economics* 677, 679. Trade creation happens when the reduction of trade barriers between FTA partners leads to increased trade flows, as a result of these countries trading on comparative advantage terms, whereby imports of higher costs from an FTA member are replaced with imports of lower costs from another FTA member. This leads to a better allocation of resources and an improvement in welfare. Contrarily, trade diversion happens when preferential tariff concessions cause trade to be redirected from a non-FTA country whose exports are low cost to an FTA member state whose exports are more expensive.

This helps maintain a harmonious trade environment and promotes peaceful resolution of conflicts. Thirdly, FTAs facilitate collaboration among nations on trade-related matters of mutual concern and enable coordination of policies governing their respective trade sectors. This cooperation may extend to addressing technical trade barriers, implementing sanitary and phytosanitary measures and fostering capacity development. By working together, nations can tackle common challenges and enhance the efficiency and effectiveness of their trade practices. Lastly, FTAs can serve as a template for other nations to follow in their own negotiations and conclusion of trade agreements. They provide valuable guidance on the provisions that can be included in such agreements, particularly for developing nations that may lack the financial resources and expertise required to independently negotiate and finalise trade accords. FTAs act as a reference point and offer a framework for crafting effective trade agreements. Overall, free trade agreements are recognised as essential legal instruments that contribute to establishing a predictable and stable commercial environment. They provide a comprehensive legal framework for trade relations, offer mechanisms for dispute resolution, facilitate cooperation on trade-related issues and can serve as a model for other nations. The coordination and harmonisation achieved through FTAs promote the growth of international trade and foster economic development.

The WTO keeps a close eye on FTAs, in many cases to satisfy itself that they conform to its own norms. FTAs have the potential to contain terms that are not in line with WTO regulations. One example of this would be the application of discriminatory treatment to products and services originating from countries that are not members of the WTO. This may result in a diversion of commerce and may be detrimental to the interests of nations who are not members of the agreement but are nonetheless parties to it. For instance, if an FTA lowers tariffs on commodities traded between two nations, this may provide an incentive for other countries to buy these items via the FTA's member countries rather than importing them directly themselves. This may provide the member nations an unfair advantage, which can hurt the commercial interests of the countries who are not members of the organisation.

The lack of openness around FTAs is another concern. WTO members are obligated to notify the organisation of any trade agreements that they negotiate and to submit information on the terms of these agreements. However, this does not always happen, making it difficult for other members of the WTO to fully understand the repercussions of these agreements. As a result, an element of unpredictability is introduced in the international trade system. FTAs also have the potential to contribute to problems caused by fragmentation in the global trading system. The development of FTAs may result in a patchwork of distinct trade laws and regulations, which can make it more difficult for firms to manage the many rules and regulations and can result in higher expenses associated with compliance. This may be especially difficult for small and medium-sized enterprises (SMEs), since these companies often lack the resources necessary to manage the many laws and regulations. Additionally, FTAs have the potential to cause inconsistencies with other international laws and agreements. For instance, an FTA that contains intellectual property rights provisions may not be compatible with other international accords or policies on intellectual property rights, such as those enacted by the World Intellectual Property Organisation (WIPO). This may lead to misunderstandings and make it more difficult to reach a worldwide consensus on these matters.

Recognised as an effective and useful tool to promote trade and investment liberalisation,[11] the nature of FTAs complements the GATT, whose remit explicitly mentions the entry of 'reciprocal and mutually advantageous arrangements directed to the substantial reduction of tariffs and other barriers to trade and to the elimination of discriminatory treatment in international commerce' to achieve the WTO's objectives. However, FTAs also contradict the WTO. On the face of it, they erode the most-favoured-nation principle under GATT, Article I, and the General Agreement on Trade in Services (GATS), Article II, because members of an FTA receive more favourable treatment in trade than non-members.[12] Furthermore, although the WTO has often emphasised multilateralism and considers regionalism to be an exception, the proliferation of FTAs has meant that regionalism may soon become the norm[13] and a substitute for multilateralism.[14] This thus poses a threat to the existing multilateral trade system.[15]

Under GATT, Article XXIV, and GATS, Article V the conclusion of an FTA is not prohibited, as long as the conditions stipulated are met. In particular, the effect of the imposition of tariffs by members of the free trade area on countries which are not part of the FTA must be less restrictive than any tariffs imposed before the inception of the relevant free trade area.[16]

B. Asia's Trade Trends: Implications for Hong Kong

As a key actor in international economic law, Hong Kong's trade policy and its engagement in FTAs must be understood within the broader context of the

[11] Ministry of Foreign Affairs of Japan, 'Global Trend Towards Regional Trade Agreements (RTA)' (*Ministry of Foreign Affairs of Japan*) 8. Available at: www.mofa.go.jp/region/asia-paci/korea/fta/report0310-3.pdf, accessed 2 February 2024.

[12] Congressional Research Service, 'Free Trade Agreements and the WTO Exceptions' (*Congressional Research Service*, 2 July 2008) 1. Available at: www.everycrsreport.com/files/20080702_RS21554_79458f5c4fb11a879a916b4b60cd2ba87b525df9.pdf, accessed 2 February 2024.

[13] Richard Baldwin and Theresa Carpenter, 'Regionalism: Moving from Fragmentation towards Coherence' in Thomas Cottier and Panagiotis Delimatsis (eds), *The Prospects of International Trade Regulation: From Fragmentation to Coherence* (Cambridge, Cambridge University Press, 2011) 148.

[14] ibid 148, 150–51.

[15] Julien Chaisse and Mitsuo Matsushita, 'Maintaining the WTO's Supremacy in the International Trade Order: A Proposal to Refine and Revise the Role of the Trade Policy Review Mechanism' (2013) 16 *Journal of International Economic Law* 9, 29.

[16] General Agreement on Tariffs and Trade (15 April 1994) LT/UR/A-1A/1/GATT/1, art XXIV(5)(b).

rapidly evolving trade landscape in the Asia-Pacific region. This section discusses the key trends and developments that have characterised trade in Asia, specifically examining their implications for Hong Kong's trade policy and its role as a vital hub in the region's economic integration.

The section begins by outlining the major trade trends that have emerged in the Asia-Pacific region over recent years, including the rise of regional FTAs, the increasing importance of global value chains and the shift towards digital trade. It explores the driving forces behind these trends, such as economic growth, technological advancements and the pursuit of economic diversification. The analysis highlights how these trends have shaped the trade dynamics in the region, as well as the strategies and priorities of its key trading partners. Next, the section considers the specific implications of these trends for Hong Kong's trade policy. It investigates how Hong Kong has adapted its trade strategy to navigate the changing regional landscape, including the pursuit of new FTAs, the expansion of its existing FTA network and the adoption of digital trade initiatives. The analysis also considers the challenges and opportunities that these trends pose for Hong Kong, such as the need to maintain its competitive edge as a trading hub, address emerging trade barriers and capitalise on the growth of digital trade. In examining the implications of Asia's trade trends for Hong Kong, the section seeks to demonstrate the intricate connections between the region's trade dynamics and Hong Kong's trade policy. It underscores the importance of understanding these trends in order to effectively analyse and predict the future trajectory of Hong Kong's trade engagements and its role in international economic law.

Historically, the number of FTAs in the Asia Pacific (APEC) region has been relatively low. A mere 29 FTAs were in force in 1998.[17] Yet, the past decades have seen a growing number of Asian countries participating in FTAs. For example, by June 2023, 195 FTAs with at least one APEC jurisdiction remained in force.[18] Thus, many countries, such as Japan and South Korea, have made significant efforts to sign FTAs.[19]

In contrast to the rest of the world, Asia has traditionally favoured the usage of bilateral FTAs, instead of plurilateral FTAs. Statistics from the Asian Development Bank indicate that although the first agreement since its tracking

[17] APEC Policy Support Unit, 'Trends and Developments in Provisions and Outcomes of RTA/FTAs Implemented in 2018 by APEC Economies' (*APEC*, March 2020) 1, 40. Available at: www.apec.org/docs/default-source/publications/2020/3/trends-and-developments-in provisions-and-outcomes-of rta-ftas-implemented-in-2018-by-apec-economies/220psutrends-and-developments-in-provisions-and-outcomes-of-rtaftas-implemented-in-2018-by-apec-econ.pdf?sfvrsn=19cd760d_1, accessed 2 February 2021.

[18] ESCAP, 'Preferential Trade Agreements in Asia and the Pacific 2022/2023: Trends and Developments' (*ESCAP*, 18 June 2023). Available at: www.repository.unescap.org/rest/bitstreams/756c42fd-3d72-4aa5-b9bc-229f806239c9/retrieve, accessed 25 June 2024.

[19] Ministry of Foreign Affairs of Japan, 'Global Trend Towards Regional Trade Agreements (RTA)' (*Ministry of Foreign Affairs of Japan*) 8. Available at: www.mofa.go.jp/region/asia-paci/korea/fta/report0310-3.pdf, accessed 2 February 2024.

began in 1975 was of a plurilateral nature, by 2022, bilateral FTAs outnumbered plurilateral FTAs by almost 2.65 to 1.[20] This may be because negotiations for plurilateral agreements tend to be longer and more complex than those for bilateral treaties.[21] For example, the negotiations around the now-defunct Trans-Pacific Partnership took seven years to conclude.[22]

Historically, FTAs in Asia have predominantly focused on trade in goods, particularly on the elimination of customs duties and tariffs.[23] However, a recent analysis of the existing FTAs indicated that the majority contained key chapters, such as trade in goods and services, sanitary and phytosanitary measures and general provisions. Statistics from between 2008 to 2016 have also demonstrated that more than half of the FTAs in place contained provisions or a chapter on investment protection,[24] and there were an increasing number of FTAs in Asia where WTO-plus commitments were included in the text.[25] For example, the EU–Korea FTA has chapters on sustainable development and labour;[26] these can also be seen in the United States–Singapore FTA.[27]

There is also a growing trend in Asia regarding the conclusion of digital economy agreements and the inclusion of a chapter on electronic commerce. For example, the first bilateral digital economy agreement was signed between Japan and the United States on 7 October 2019,[28] while the first multilateral digital economy agreement, the 'Digital Economy Partnership Agreement', was signed on 12 June 2020.[29] Presently, there are five digital economy agreements,

[20] ADB, 'Table 3 FTAs by Scope (cumulative)' (*ADB*, 26 August 2022). Available at: www.aric.adb.org/fta-trends-by-scope, accessed 2 February 2024.

[21] Masahiro Kawai and Ganeshan Wignaraja, 'Asian FTAS: Trends and Challenges' (2009) ADBI Working Paper Series No 144. Available at: www.adb.org/sites/default/files/publication/155999/adbi-wp144.pdf, accessed 2 February 2024.

[22] Export.gov, 'The Trans-Pacific Partnership' (*Export.gov*, 1 December 2015) 2016. Available at: www.export.gov/peru/eg_pe_092418.asp, accessed 2 February 2024.

[23] Matteo Dian, 'The Strategic Value of the Trans-Pacific Partnership and the Consequences of Abandoning it for the US Role in Asia' (2017) 54 *International Politics* 583, 589.

[24] ADB, 'Table 7 FTAs in effect with investment chapter or clause (2008–2015)' (*ADB*, December 2016). Available at: www.aric.adb.org/fta-trends-with-investment, accessed 2 February 2024.

[25] Pasha L Hsieh, 'The RCEP, New Asian Regionalism and the Global South' (2017) IILJ Working Paper 2017/4. Available at: www.iilj.org/wp-content/uploads/2017/12/Hsieh-IILJ_2017_4_MegaReg.pdf, accessed 2 February 2024.

[26] Directorate-General for External Policies, Policy Department, 'Workshop: Trade and Economic Relations with Asia' (*European Parliament*, 7 March 2016). Available at: www.europarl.europa.eu/RegData/etudes/STUD/2016/535024/EXPO_STU(2016)535024_EN.pdf, accessed 2 February 2024.

[27] Enterprise Singapore, 'United States (USSFTA) Legal Text' (Enterprise Singapore, September 2022). Available at: www.enterprisesg.gov.sg/-/media/esg/files/non-financial-assistance/for-companies/free-trade-agreements/ussfta/legal-text/ussfta_legal_text.pdf, accessed 2 February 2024.

[28] Matthew Pereira, 'U.S.–Japan Digital Trade Agreement and U.S.–Japan Trade Agreement Finalized' (*Trade and Manufacturing Monitor*, 11 October 2019). Available at: www.ustrademonitor.com/2019/10/u-s-japan-digital-trade-agreement-and-u-s-japan-trade-agreement-finalized/, accessed 2 February 2024.

[29] New Zealand Foreign Affairs & Trade, 'The Digital Economy Partnership Agreement is a New Initiative with Chile and Singapore.' (*New Zealand Foreign Affairs & Trade*). Available at: www.mfat.govt.nz/en/trade/free-trade-agreements/free-trade-agreements-in-force/digital-economy-partnership-agreement-depa/overview/, accessed 2 February 2024.

to all of which at least one APEC member is a party.[30] Similarly, since the conclusion of the Singapore–Australia FTA, the first FTA that contained a chapter on e-commerce,[31] references to e-commerce can now be seen in the legal text of some of the largest free trade areas, such as RCEP and the Comprehensive and Progressive Agreement for Trans-Pacific Partnership.[32]

In conclusion, Asia's trade trends have significant implications for Hong Kong, as its approach to free trade agreements and economic integration closely mirrors those of other countries in the Asia-Pacific region. Trade liberalisation, economic cooperation and the pursuit of strategic partnerships remain central to the region's economic growth and development. Hong Kong's network of agreements with partners such as China, New Zealand and ASEAN reflects its commitment to expanding its global market access and enhancing the competitiveness of its businesses. Additionally, Hong Kong's focus on economic complementarity and adherence to WTO principles underscores its dedication to fostering non-discriminatory trade practices and maintaining a rules-based international trading system. As Hong Kong continues to navigate the evolving trade landscape in the Asia-Pacific region, it must remain agile and responsive to emerging trends and challenges. By doing so, it can ensure its continued integration into regional and global markets, ultimately contributing to its sustained economic growth, development and prosperity.

C. Hong Kong's FTA Journey: A General Overview

Various dimensions of Hong Kong's approach to FTAs resemble those of other countries in the Asia-Pacific region. Trade liberalisation and the reduction of trade barriers are central to Hong Kong's economy, as they are to the economics of other countries in the region. This is evidenced by the agreements Hong Kong has pursued, which aim to eliminate tariffs and other trade impediments to facilitate the movement of goods and services between the parties involved.

Hong Kong, like other Asia-Pacific economies, has constructed a network of agreements with numerous nations and regions. These encompass agreements with countries such as China and New Zealand, as well as with the Association of Southeast Asian Nations (ASEAN).

Like other Asia-Pacific economies, Hong Kong is interested in economic integration and has incorporated provisions in its agreements that encourage

[30] ESCAP, 'Trade Agreements in Asia and the Pacific: Bigger, Deeper, Digital and more Supportive of Sustainable Development? 2022/2023' (*ESCAP*, 10 November 2022) 1, 7. Available at: www.repository.unescap.org/rest/bitstreams/36eb72af-40b8-4a25-86bd-a1602f30e582/retrieve, accessed 2 February 2024.

[31] Duncan McCann, 'e-Commerce Free Trade Agreements, Digital Chapters and the Impact on Labour' (*International Trade Union Confederation*, 2019) 1, 7. Available at: www.ituc-csi.org/IMG/pdf/digital_chapters_and_the_impact_on_labour_en.pdf, accessed 2 February 2024.

[32] Deborah Elms, 'Managing Digital Trade in Asia' (*East Asia Forum*, 20 April 2021). Available at: www.eastasiaforum.org/2021/04/20/managing-digital-trade-in-asia/, accessed 2 February 2024.

economic cooperation in the form of investment, service provision and other types of economic collaboration. Alongside other economies in the Asia-Pacific region, Hong Kong has sought to conclude agreements with strategic partners to enhance its access to international markets and improve the competitiveness of its businesses globally.

Recognising the importance of trade for its economic growth and development, Hong Kong has actively pursued trade agreements to boost both economic growth and commerce. Hong Kong, like other Asia-Pacific economies, has aimed to establish agreements with countries and regions that exhibit economic complementarity. This is exemplified by its agreements with China, which is its largest trading partner and the primary source of both imports and exports.

Hong Kong has also sought to conclude agreements with countries and regions that demonstrate economic complementarity. Alongside other Asia-Pacific economies, Hong Kong has focused on finalising trade agreements with nations and regions that endorse non-discriminatory trade and adhere to the principles set forth by the WTO.

Hong Kong has currently signed eight FTAs. Additionally, plans for the commencement of negotiations for a new FTA with Peru have been made[33] and the Hong Kong government is also seeking to negotiate an FTA with Thailand.[34] The eight FTAs include two with China and New Zealand and one with Switzerland, Liechtenstein, Norway and Iceland, the Member States of the European Free Trade Association (EFTA). The remaining five were concluded with Chile, Macao, the Association of Southeast Asian Nations (ASEAN), Georgia and Australia.[35] These latter FTAs will be detailed in the following section.

Presently, however, Hong Kong does not have FTAs with most of its important trading partners or those countries with the largest trading volume – these include the United States, Taiwan, the United Kingdom and India. However, Hong Kong has submitted an application for early accession to the RCEP (this will be covered in further detail in section III). Consequently, upon Hong Kong joining the free trade area, the lack of an FTA with Japan and South Korea, which were Hong Kong's fifth and sixth largest trading partners by total trade in 2021 and are also RCEP members, will be remedied.

[33] Trade and Industry Department, 'Hong Kong's Free Trade Agreements (FTAs)' (*Trade and Industry Department, The Government of the Hong Kong Special Administrative Region*, 5 January 2023). Available at: tid.gov.hk/english/ita/fta/index.html, accessed 2 February 2024.

[34] Council Business Division 1, Legislative Council Secretariat, 'Legislative Council Panel on Commerce and Industry – Minutes of Meeting held on Friday, 19 February 2021, at 10:45 am in Conference Room 3 of the Legislative Council Complex' (*Legislative Council of the Hong Kong Special Administrative Region of the People's Republic of China*, 15 April 2021) LC Paper No CB (1)798/20-21 1, 8. Available at: www.legco.gov.hk/yr20-21/english/panels/ci/minutes/ci20210219.pdf, accessed 2 February 2024.

[35] Trade and Industry Department, 'Hong Kong's Free Trade Agreements (FTAs)' (*Trade and Industry Department, The Government of the Hong Kong Special Administrative Region*, 24 February 2023). Available at: tid.gov.hk/english/ita/fta/index.html, accessed 5 March 2024.

A number of observations can be made from the list of Hong Kong's FTAs. Firstly, although Hong Kong is a WTO member that does not apply tariffs, this does not mean that FTAs are not needed. Concluding FTAs will be a useful tool for Hong Kong to strengthen its existing ties and create new ones, expand its trade and business networks and consolidate its position internationally[36] without being marginalised by the rest of the world. These agreements also expose Hong Kong businesses to unexplored commercial opportunities, giving them a chance to tap into the markets of other countries[37] in more favourable circumstances.[38] Reciprocally, the conclusion of FTAs facilitates trade and foreign direct investment flows from the businesses of Hong Kong's FTA counterparts into Hong Kong.[39] FTAs also allow Hong Kong to address various WTO-plus issues, including intellectual property rights (IPR), investment facilitation and transparency in trade-in services. These are important to protect the interests of Hong Kong businesses ensuring that they can enjoy preferential treatment in these areas. Crucially, partaking in FTAs will allow Hong Kong to resolve the free-riding problem. A lot of countries have been able to benefit from Hong Kong's lack of customs duties and tariffs. Yet, the opposite cannot be said to be true: reciprocal treatment largely does not exist and Hong Kong's exports are subjected to third country tariffs. Therefore, FTAs will enable Hong Kong to have a more level playing field, where its exports could also benefit from zero to minimal tariffs and customs duties and gain better access to third countries' markets.

Additionally, out of Hong Kong's FTAs, including the countries which are members of ASEAN, five are with the territory's key trading partners. Thus, the existence of FTAs with Georgia, New Zealand, Chile and Peru is at first sight surprising, given that they are far from being Hong Kong's top trading partners. However, an analysis of these countries and their economic relationship with Hong Kong indicates the reason why FTAs with these four countries is desirable. Both Chile and Peru are ranked highly in trade volume in Hong Kong's trade with South America – in 2021, Chile and Peru were Hong Kong's third- and fifth-largest trade in goods partners in Latin America respectively.[40]

[36] Trade and Industry Department, 'Legislative Council Brief – Free Trade Agreement between Hong Kong and Georgia' (*Trade and Industry Department, The Government of the Hong Kong Special Administrative Region*, 28 June 2018) CR WT 324/27/3 1, 1–6. Available at: www.tid.gov.hk/english/ita/fta/hkgefta/files/GEHKFTA_Legco_Brief.pdf, accessed 2 February 2024.

[37] See, eg, HKSAR Government, 'Hong Kong to Commence Free Trade Agreement Negotiation with Peru (with photos)' (*The Government of the Hong Kong Special Administrative Region Press Releases*, 16 November 2022). Available at: www.info.gov.hk/gia/general/202211/16/P2022111600587.htm, accessed 2 February 2024.

[38] BrandHK, 'Trade Agreements' (*BrandHK*, 31 August 2021). Available at: www.brandhk.gov.hk/en/doing-business/trade-agreements, accessed 2 February 2024.

[39] Trade and Industry Department, 'Legislative Council Brief – Free Trade Agreement between Hong Kong and Georgia' 4.

[40] Trade and Industry Department, 'Free Trade Agreement between Hong Kong, China and Chile' (*Trade and Industry Department, The Government of the Hong Kong Special Administrative Region*,

Similarly, New Zealand, whilst only the 40th largest trading partner of Hong Kong, is the largest economy in Oceania after Australia and thus remains a crucial trading partner in the region. Contrastingly, Georgia is deemed as an emerging market with some strategic significance, given that it is one of the Belt and Road countries.[41]

Furthermore, although Hong Kong's trade policy is completely different from that of China, the list of Hong Kong's existing FTAs almost exactly mirrors that of China.[42] The only difference is that Hong Kong has an FTA with all of the EFTA states. Even then, China has two out of four FTAs with the EFTA states – Iceland and Switzerland; its FTA with Switzerland also applies to Liechtenstein.[43] It is also pursuing FTA negotiations with Norway.[44]

While it would be desirable for Hong Kong to conclude FTAs with certain key trading partners with large volumes of trade, in reality, there may be certain restrictions. This is particularly the case with the United States, which had the third-largest total trade volume with Hong Kong in 2021. Such a move would, however, be unlikely due to political reasons, as the territory has been regarded as a pawn in the US–China rivalry.[45] Nevertheless, there are other countries, less closely aligned with US policy, with which Hong Kong ought to and could conclude an FTA. Singapore,[46] for example, was Hong Kong's fourth-largest trading partner in 2021[47] and is an FTA partner of China.[48]

11 November 2022). Available at: www.tid.gov.hk/english/ita/fta/hkclfta/index.html, accessed 2 February 2024; HKSAR Government, 'Public Consultation on Free Trade Agreement with Peru Starts' (*The Government of the Hong Kong Special Administrative Region Press Releases*, 24 November 2022). Available at: www.info.gov.hk/gia/general/202211/24/P2022112200515.htm, accessed 2 February 2024.

[41] Trade and Industry Department, 'Hong Kong to Negotiate Free Trade Agreements with Georgia and Maldives' (Trade and Industry Department, The Government of the Hong Kong Special Administrative Region, 11 November 2022). Available at: www.tid.gov.hk/english/aboutus/noticeboard/maldivesgeorgiafta.html, accessed 2 February 2024.

[42] China has currently signed 17 FTAs: ASEAN, Singapore, Pakistan, New Zealand, Chile, Peru, Costa Rica, Iceland, Switzerland, Maldives, Mauritius, Georgia, Korea, Australia, Cambodia, Hong Kong and Macao.

[43] Free Trade Agreement between the Swiss Confederation and the People's Republic of China, art 2.1(1).

[44] Ministry of Commerce, People's Republic of China, 'China-Norway FTA' (*China FTA Network*). Available at: http://fta.mofcom.gov.cn/topic/ennorway.shtml, accessed 2 February 2024.

[45] Yen Nee Lee, 'Hong Kong is a 'Pawn' in US–China Rivalry, Says Former Diplomat' (CNBC, 28 May 2020). Available at: www.cnbc.com/2020/05/28/hong-kong-is-a-pawn-in-us-china-rivalry-ex-singapore-diplomat-says.html, accessed 2 February 2024.

[46] William Choong, 'Singapore and the United States: Speaking Hard Truths as a Zhengyou' (*Fulcrum*, 7 April 2022) Available at: www.fulcrum.sg/singapore-and-the-united-states-speaking-hard-truths-as-a-zhengyou/, accessed 2 February 2024.

[47] Trade and Industry Department, 'Hong Kong's Principal Trading Partners in 2021' (*Trade and Industry Department, The Government of the Hong Kong Special Administrative Region*, 11 November 2022). Available at: www.tid.gov.hk/english/trade_relations/mainland/trade.html, accessed 2 February 2024.

[48] International Trade Administration, 'China – Trade Agreements' (*International Trade Administration*, 4 January 2022). Available at: www.trade.gov/country-commercial-guides/china-trade-agreements, accessed 2 February 2024.

Finally, there are very few FTAs between Hong Kong and the countries of Central Asia. This can be explained by the fact that they are not Hong Kong's biggest trading partners. Additionally, most are members of the BRI.[49] As Hong Kong is also a member of the initiative, which aims to liberalise trade,[50] the Central Asian countries will already have been covered. Of course, Hong Kong signed its first Central Asian FTA with Georgia in 2018, so future FTAs with countries in the region cannot be ruled out.

II. MAPPING HONG KONG'S FTA NETWORK

The rise of Hong Kong as a significant actor in international commerce can be attributed to its calculated efforts in establishing a varied and expansive array of FTAs. These accords serve as a fundamental aspect of Hong Kong's trade strategy, bolstering its competitive edge and promoting its further assimilation into regional and global trade structures. This section discusses the complexities surrounding Hong Kong's FTA framework, scrutinising the legal, economic and political facets of its bilateral and multilateral trade affiliations.

In this analysis, we undertake an exhaustive examination of the eight FTAs that form the backbone of Hong Kong's trade infrastructure, assessing the extent, primary stipulations and characteristics of each pact. The discussion commences with an inquiry into the pivotal FTA between Hong Kong and Mainland China, which established the groundwork for Hong Kong's successive trade accords. Subsequently, we will analyse Hong Kong's FTAs with other trade partners, including New Zealand, the European Free Trade Association (EFTA), Chile, Macao, Georgia and Australia, underlining the resemblances and differences between these accords and their strategic ramifications for Hong Kong's trade policies.

A. The Closer Economic Partnership with Mainland China (2003)

The Closer Economic Partnership Arrangement (CEPA) is a comprehensive and pioneering free trade agreement between Hong Kong and Mainland China, first established in 2003.[51] As the first bilateral trade agreement signed by the Chinese government, CEPA aims to bolster economic ties and facilitate cross-border

[49] David Sacks, 'Countries in China's Belt and Road Initiative: Who's In and Who's Out' (*Council on Foreign Relations*, 24 March 2021). Available at: www.cfr.org/blog/countries-chinas-belt-and-road-initiative-whos-and-whos-out, accessed 2 February 2024.

[50] Belt and Road Initiative, 'Trade' (*Belt and Road Initiative*). Available at: http://onebeltoneroad.com/en/intro/trade, accessed 2 February 2024.

[51] Ministry of Commerce, People's Republic of China, 'Mainland and Hong Kong Closer Economic and Partnership Arrangement' (*China FTA Network*). Available at: http://fta.mofcom.gov.cn/topic/enhongkong.shtml, accessed 2 February 2024.

trade and investment between the two regions, further strengthening the 'One Country, Two Systems' principle.[52]

The CEPA encompasses four broad domains: product trade, services trade, investment and economic and technical cooperation. For product trade, each consignment of goods exported to the Mainland is accompanied by a Certificate of Origin. If the CEPA rules of origin are adhered to, all items of Hong Kong origin can benefit from zero-tariff preference upon importation into the Mainland. Regarding services trade, Hong Kong service suppliers are granted preferential status when entering the Mainland market across various service categories. Additionally, numerous agreements and arrangements have been made between regulatory agencies in the Mainland and Hong Kong concerning the reciprocal recognition of professional qualifications. In the area of investment, Hong Kong investors receive preferential treatment in non-service industries within the Chinese mainland. The Investment Agreement not only facilitates investment but also actively promotes and safeguards it. Lastly, in terms of economic and technical cooperation, both parties have agreed to intensify collaboration across 22 sectors to address emerging trends, support development, foster cooperation and streamline and advance trade and investment between the two parties.

Since its inception, CEPA has undergone several amendments and supplementary agreements to address evolving economic needs and expand its scope. As a result, the agreement has significantly enhanced trade and investment flows between Hong Kong and Mainland China, leading to mutual benefits and closer economic integration.

In summary, CEPA represents a crucial milestone in the economic relationship between Hong Kong and Mainland China. By leveraging the strengths and advantages of both regions, the agreement has facilitated economic growth and development, while setting a precedent for further regional and global trade cooperation.

B. Pioneering Trade with New Zealand (2010)

The first FTA that Hong Kong signed with a foreign economy was the Closer Economic Partnership Agreement (CEP Agreement) between Hong Kong and New Zealand. It is an extensive and high-quality FTA that covers a broad range of issues of importance to both Hong Kong and New Zealand. After its CEPA with the Mainland, Hong Kong's FTA with New Zealand entered into force on 1 January 2011.

As the first FTA between Hong Kong and a third country, the Hong Kong–New Zealand CEP Agreement encompasses a wide range of areas, including

[52] Trade and Industry Department, 'Overview of Mainland and Hong Kong Closer Economic Partnership Arrangement' (*Trade and Industry Department, The Government of the Hong Kong Special Administrative Region*, 11 November 2022). Available at: www.tid.gov.hk/english/cepa/cepa_overview.html, accessed 2 February 2024.

trade in goods and services, government procurement and IPR.[53] The agreement opens the doors for Hong Kong businesses to enter New Zealand's market. As a result of tariff eliminations and the securement of various preferential treatment, including in the area of trade in services, economic benefits accrued to both parties, including an increase in mutual trade flows.[54]

C. Strengthening Ties with EFTA Member States (2011)

The high volume of trade between Hong Kong and the European Union makes it crucial for respective customs administrations to work together in order to facilitate legal trade flows and maintain supply chain security. An Agreement on Cooperation and Mutual Administrative Assistance in Customs Matters was signed by Hong Kong and the European Community (as it was then called) on 13 May 1999.[55]

An FTA encompassing issues including trade facilitation and IPR enforcement was also signed by Hong Kong in 2011 with the four EFTA Member States.[56] The EFTA Member States and Hong Kong discussions began in January 2010 and ended in March 2011. A comprehensive assortment of subjects is covered under the FTA, including trade in commodities (industrial and processed agricultural products, fish and other marine products), trade in services, investment, protection of IPR, government procurement, competition and trade and the environment.[57] The agreements creating the free trade area between the two sides also include bilateral agreements on agricultural goods between the various EFTA Member States and Hong Kong.[58] A separate labour arrangement was reached in conjunction with the FTA.[59]

[53] Trade and Industry Department, 'Hong Kong, China – New Zealand Closer Economic Partnership Agreement' (*Trade and Industry Department, The Government of the Hong Kong Special Administrative Region*, 14 November 2022). Available at: www.tid.gov.hk/english/ita/fta/hknzcep/index.html, accessed 2 February 2024.

[54] Trade and Industry Department, 'Legislative Council Brief – Hong Kong – New Zealand Closer Economic Partnership Agreement' (*Trade and Industry Department, The Government of the Hong Kong Special Administrative Region*, 29 March 2010) CR WT 324/9/1 1, 6–7. Available at: www.tid.gov.hk/english/ita/fta/hknzcep/files/LegCoBriefs_HKC_NZCE.pdf, accessed 2 February 2024.

[55] Agreement between the European Community and Hong Kong, China on Cooperation and Mutual Administrative Assistance in Customs Matters (1999) OJ L 151/21.

[56] European Commission, 'EU – Hong Kong Customs Cooperation' (*European Commission*). Available at: www.ec.europa.eu/taxation_customs/customs-4/international-affairs/third-countries/hong-kong_en, accessed 2 February 2024.

[57] Trade and Industry Department, 'Free Trade Agreement between Hong Kong, China and the Member States of the European Free Trade Association' (*Trade and Industry Department, The Government of the Hong Kong Special Administrative Region*, 11 November 2022). Available at: www.tid.gov.hk/english/ita/fta/hkefta/index.html, accessed 2 February 2024.

[58] EFTA, 'EFTA States and Hong Kong, China sign Free Trade Agreement' (*EFTA*, 21 June 2011). Available at: www.efta.int/Free-Trade/news/EFTA-States-and-Hong-Kong-China-sign-Free-Trade-Agreement-808, accessed 2 February 2024.

[59] ibid.

D. Connecting with Chile (2012)

Negotiations for an FTA with Chile commenced on 19 December 2011. The discussions emphasised trade and investment liberalisation and facilitation, but they also touched upon a wide variety of other subjects.[60] Chile and Hong Kong are both pro-free trade and share the objective of advancing international trade liberalisation and enhancing the multilateral trading system as WTO members.[61] The Hong Kong Government wanted to establish a comprehensive and high-quality FTA which complies with WTO rules and principles.

In July 2009, Hong Kong and Chile completed a Joint Feasibility Study (JFS) on the possibility of initiating FTA negotiations. According to the assessment, expanding trade and economic ties between Chile and Hong Kong would be beneficial for the two economies. In July 2011, there were exploratory discussions about the potential of establishing formal FTA negotiations and their frameworks, based on the results and recommendations of the JFS.[62] The following key areas and related issues were covered by the negotiations: removal or reduction of tariffs; liberalisation of non-tariff barriers, such as technical trade barriers, sanitary and phytosanitary measures, anti-dumping, safeguards and countervailing measures; a set of adaptable rules of origin that would facilitate bilateral trade; a set of customs facilitation procedures; liberalisation of trade in services; and liberalisation as well as promotion and protection.

The 2012 FTA between Chile and Hong Kong, which became legally binding on 9 October 2014, now incorporates an Investment Agreement. The Investment Agreement's ratification should increase investor trust and increase investment flows between Chile and Hong Kong.[63] Overall, the FTA expanded market access, boosted commerce and created a better business climate for its members, since there was great potential for expanding trade and investment with Chile. An FTA between Hong Kong and Chile provided businesspeople in Hong Kong with more and better market opportunities in Chile and also a gateway to the developing market in South America,[64] with advantages for Hong Kong in terms of trade, revenue and employment.

[60] Trade and Industry Department, 'Negotiation of a Free Trade Agreement between Hong Kong and Chile Consultation Document' (*Trade and Industry Department, The Government of the Hong Kong Special Administrative Region*, 11 November 2022). Available at: www.tid.gov.hk/english/aboutus/noticeboard/chile_agreement.html, accessed 2 February 2024.

[61] ibid.

[62] Trade and Industry Department, 'Negotiation of a Free Trade Agreement between Hong Kong and Chile Consultation Document' (*Trade and Industry Department, The Government of the Hong Kong Special Administrative Region*, 11 November 2022). Available at: www.tid.gov.hk/english/aboutus/noticeboard/chile_agreement.html, accessed 2 February 2024.

[63] Trade and Industry Department, 'Hong Kong and Chile Sign Investment Agreement' (*Trade and Industry Department, The Government of the Hong Kong Special Administrative Region*, 16 November 2016). Available at: www.tid.gov.hk/english/aboutus/presspeech/press/2016/20161119.html, accessed 2 February 2024.

[64] Trade and Industry Department, 'Free Trade Agreement between Hong Kong, China and Chile' (n 50).

E. Reinforcing Relations with Macao (2017)

The establishment of the Closer Economic Partnership Arrangement (CEPA) between Hong Kong and Mainland China has proven to be a successful model for fostering economic collaboration and integration within the region. In light of its success, Hong Kong sought to reinforce its regional connections by signing a similar agreement with Macao, its neighbouring Special Administrative Region (SAR). In 2017, the two SARs entered into a Free Trade Agreement, further strengthening their bilateral economic ties and promoting cooperation across various sectors.

Formal discussions for a Hong Kong–Macao CEPA were initiated in November 2015 between Hong Kong and Macao. After three rounds of negotiations and subsequent discussions, the principal language and schedule of responsibilities were agreed on 29 June 2017 and the HK–Macao CEPA became effective on 27 October 2017. The trade in goods and services liberalisation measures stated therein came into effect on 1 January 2018.[65]

The HK–Macao CEPA provides more legal certainty for market access and treatment because of its extensive scope and responsibilities, which go beyond those established by Hong Kong and Macao under the WTO. Long-standing bilateral trade relationships exist between Hong Kong and Macao. The trade regimes in both economies have been significantly relaxed. The HK–Macao CEPA will help the economic growth and collaboration of both nations by giving Hong Kong's service providers better market access and predictability when conducting business in Macao.[66] However, for a highly specialised economy, free trade can not only lead to macroeconomic advantages, but also increase sensitivity to external shocks.

F. Strengthening Relations with ASEAN (2017)

The Association of Southeast Asian Nations (ASEAN) has emerged as a prominent and dynamic economic region, boasting rapid growth and significant potential for further development. Recognising the importance of fostering strong ties with this thriving region, Hong Kong has embarked on a mission to strengthen its economic relations with ASEAN member states. In 2017, a milestone was achieved when Hong Kong and ASEAN signed an FTA and a related Investment Agreement, marking a new era of enhanced cooperation and integration between the two parties.

[65] Trade and Industry Department, 'Hong Kong Special Administrative Region and Macao Special Administrative Region Closer Economic Partnership Arrangement (HK–Macao CEPA)' (*Trade and Industry Department, The Government of the Hong Kong Special Administrative Region*, 11 November 2022). Available at: www.tid.gov.hk/english/ita/fta/hkmacao/index.html, accessed 2 February 2024.

[66] ibid.

ASEAN was the second-largest trading partner of Hong Kong in terms of goods in 2021 and the third largest in terms of services in 2020.[67] 2021 saw HK$1,246.8 billion in total product trade between Hong Kong and ASEAN, whereas 2020 saw HK$94.6 billion in total services trade.[68]

Hong Kong and ASEAN commenced discussing the FTA and an investment agreement in July 2014. Hong Kong and ASEAN concluded negotiations after ten rounds in September 2017 and signed the accords on 12 November 2017. The accords expanded Hong Kong's network of free trade and investment agreements to cover all significant Southeast Asian economies.

The agreements include a wide range of issues, including investment, economic and technical cooperation, commerce in goods and services, a dispute resolution framework and other domains. New business opportunities and enhanced trade and investment flows between Hong Kong and ASEAN have been generated as a result of the agreements' enhanced market access, clearer legal definitions and fair and equal treatment in trade and investment.

G. Exploring Opportunities with Georgia (2018)

One of the most significant trading partners for Hong Kong is Georgia. A total of HK$311 million of products was exchanged between Hong Kong and Georgia in 2021.[69] In terms of commodities trade, Georgia ranked 117th among Hong Kong's trading partners worldwide in 2021.[70] Hong Kong was Georgia's 30th-largest trading partner in goods trade in 2020.

The Hong Kong–Georgia FTA encompasses a broad variety of subjects in its 18 chapters, including investment, trade in products and services, dispute resolution procedures and other pertinent sectors. Due to domestic sensitivity, Georgia removed all import taxes on goods of Hong Kong origin, with the exception of 3.4 per cent of tariff lines, predominantly agricultural goods, such as fruits, nuts and their preparations, beverages and spirits.

Both the Sino–Georgia and Hong Kong–Georgia FTAs feature chapters on trade in services, under which both parties promise to gradually open their markets to one another in conformity with WTO obligations. These chapters

[67] Trade and Industry Department, 'Free Trade Agreement between Hong Kong, China and the Association of Southeast Asian Nations' (*Trade and Industry Department, The Government of the Hong Kong Special Administrative Region*, 4 January 2023). Available at: www.tid.gov.hk/english/ita/fta/hkasean/index.html, accessed 2 February 2024.

[68] ibid.

[69] Trade and Industry Department, 'Free Trade Agreement between Hong Kong, China and Georgia' (*Trade and Industry Department, The Government of the Hong Kong Special Administrative Region*, 11 November 2022). Available at: www.tid.gov.hk/english/ita/fta/hkgefta/index.html, accessed 2 February 2024.

[70] ibid.

are in addition to product trade. There are several areas where there is consensus, such as trade, competition, IPR, investment and e-commerce.[71]

These FTAs have increased access to the Georgian market for both Hong Kong and Mainland businesses and simplified the regulations. They also promise to act as a gateway to the BRI-adopted Caucasian region of Eurasia. Additionally, they will increase trade and investment between Georgia, other Eurasian nations, Mainland China and Hong Kong.

H. Engaging with Australia (2019)

Hong Kong's trade with Australia is significant. In terms of total services traded, the country was Hong Kong's eighth-largest trading partner in 2020 with an approximate worth of HK$28.9 billion.[72] In terms of total products traded, Australia was Hong Kong's 20th-largest trading partner in 2021 with HK$52.6 billion. As of the end of 2020, Australia ranked 20th among the sources of inbound direct investment into Hong Kong, with a stock of HK$29.5 billion and 10th among destinations for outbound direct investment, with a stock of HK$142.4 billion.

The FTA and Investment Agreement negotiations between Australia and Hong Kong commenced in May 2017 and concluded on 15 November 2018. The two agreements were signed on 26 March 2019.[73] Australia and Hong Kong then began the legal verification procedure to ensure that the texts were clear and precise. The FTA became legally enforceable on 17 January 2020.[74]

The agreements encompass a diverse range of fields, including high-quality agreements on investment, government contracts, IPR, competition and other pertinent areas. They also have a broad reach and cover trade in goods, services and other areas. They will increase business opportunities and enhance trade and investment flows between Hong Kong and Australia, while also providing Hong Kong traders and investors with legal certainty and more advantageous access to the Australian market.

[71] Louis Chan, 'Georgia: A Free Trade Partner' (*HKTDC Research*, 19 July 2018). Available at: www.research.hktdc.com/en/article/NDMxNDMyNDMw#:~:text=Under%20the%20Sino%2DGeorgia%20FTA,total%20imports%20from%20Mainland%20China, accessed 2 February 2024.

[72] Trade and Industry Department, 'Free Trade Agreement between Hong Kong, China and Australia (*Trade and Industry Department, The Government of the Hong Kong Special Administrative Region*, 11 November 2022). Available at: www.tid.gov.hk/english/ita/fta/hkaufta/index.html#:~:text=Hong%20Kong%20and%20Australia%20commenced,signed%20on%2026%20March%202019, accessed 2 February 2024.

[73] Ashurst, 'Australia-Hong Kong Free Trade Agreement & Investment Agreement (2019)' (*Ashurst*, 4 July 2019). Available at: www.ashurst.com/en/news-and-insights/legal-updates/australia-hong-kong-free-trade-agreement-and-investment-agreement-(2019)/, accessed 2 February 2024.

[74] Trade and Industry Department, 'Free Trade Agreement between Hong Kong, China and Australia'.

III. THE US–HONG KONG SPECIAL TRADING STATUS: AN HISTORICAL OVERVIEW

Historically, Hong Kong had experienced strong economic and financial ties with the United States ('the US'); for 28 years, it had also enjoyed a so-called 'Special Trading Status' with the latter. However, the 2014 Hong Kong protests dealt a blow to the bilateral relationship when a bill to amend the act that granted Hong Kong its Special Trading Status was introduced in Congress. The watershed moment came when the 2019 Hong Kong Extradition Bill protests erupted in the first quarter of 2019 and continued into early 2020. This turbulent period and its aftermath saw the deterioration of the economic relationship between Hong Kong and the US and delivered the final blow to Hong Kong's Special Trading Status. In 2020 this status was revoked, much to the dismay of Hong Kong's politicians[75] and businesses.[76] This section examines the origin of Hong Kong's Special Trading Status with the US and its benefits to both parties, before discussing the events surrounding its revocation in June 2020.

A. Origin and Benefits

Hong Kong's Special Trading Status originated in the US–Hong Kong Policy Act 1992 ('1992 Act'), which became a part of US law on 5 October 1992.[77] The crux of the 1992 Act was that, after its return to China on 1 July 1997, Hong Kong would still be afforded separate treatment from China in trade and economic matters.[78] This Special Trading Status was granted in recognition of Hong Kong's much-touted high level of autonomy from China and China's promise that, for at least 50 years after the handover in 1997, the existing socio-economic and legal status quo would remain unchanged.[79]

To give an overview of the 1992 Act's key economic provisions, under section 103(1), Hong Kong was to be viewed as separate from China in import quotas, certificates of origin and other trade matters; such matters within the territory were also to be sovereign from China. Specifically, the act required the US to trade with Hong Kong non-discriminatorily, to recognise certificates of origin

[75] HKSAR Government, 'LCQ 17: Impacts of the Revocation of Hong Kong's Special Trade Status' (*The Government of the Hong Kong Special Administrative Region Press Releases*, 17 June 2020). Available at: www.info.gov.hk/gia/general/202006/17/P2020061700355.htm/, accessed 2 February 2024.

[76] The American Chamber of Commerce in Hong Kong, 'Response of Amcham HK to President Trump's Revocation of Hong Kong's Special Trading Status' (*AmCham*, 17 July 2020). Available at: www.amcham.org.hk/news/response-amcham-hk-president-trumps-revocation-hong-kongs-special-trading-status/, accessed 2 February 2024.

[77] US Congress, 'S.1731 – United States-Hong Kong Policy Act of 1992' (*Congress.gov*). Available at: www.congress.gov/bill/102nd-congress/senate-bill/1731/actions/, accessed 2 February 2024.

[78] Commerce between United States and Hong Kong, 22 USC §5713, cl. 1.

[79] United States–Hong Kong Policy Act of 1992, 22 USC §5701(1)(C).

for goods from Hong Kong and to permit the continual free exchange between US and Hong Kong dollars. Finally, Hong Kong's access to sensitive technologies would still be supported, as long as these technologies were neither used nor exported for improper means. Crucially, under section 201(a), the manner of application of US legislation in Hong Kong would remain unchanged after the handover in 1997.[80] However, under section 202, this application could be revoked by a US President's Executive Order[81] – this was the basis for the eventual rescission of Hong Kong's Special Trading Status with the US.

Through the 1992 Act, Hong Kong enjoyed a separate US tariff regime from China, with its status as an individual customs territory recognised by the US.[82] This privilege allowed the territory's economy to flourish. The ability to import sensitive technologies distinguished Hong Kong from China as a business location, even if US knowledge-intensive goods only made up a small percentage of the territory's total imports.[83] Consequently, many Chinese companies which could not access these particular goods directly from China operated in the territory to take advantage of this access to sensitive technologies.[84] Additionally, since the US distinguished Hong Kong from its tariff regime with China, this meant that any US tariffs against China did not apply to Hong Kong.[85] This was particularly significant as, during the US–China trade war, Hong Kong was unaffected by the imposition by the US of punitive tariffs of up to 25 per cent on Chinese exports worth over $250 billion.[86] Correspondingly, the low US tariff levels that it enjoyed for its exports and the inapplicability of tariffs on Chinese exports transformed Hong Kong into a key re-export transit point. In 2019, out of exports worth HK$306 billion from Hong Kong to the US, 98 per cent of aggregate exports were re-exports from China and other third countries.[87]

For the US, the preferential treatments under the 1992 Act meant that any American commercial interests in the territory after the 1997 handover were protected and Hong Kong's status as an Indo-Pacific hotspot, both financially

[80] Continued application of United States law, 22 USC §5721(a).

[81] ibid; Presidential Order, 22 USC § 5722.

[82] Participation in multilateral organisations, rights under international agreements and trade status, 22 USC §5712(3).

[83] Mark Williams, 'How Much Does Hong Kong's Special Status Matter?' (*Capital Economics*, 11 November 2019). Available at: www.admin.capitaleconomics.com/publications/china-economics/china-economics-update/how-much-does-hong-kongs-special-status-matter, accessed 2 February 2024.

[84] Kenji Kawase and Zach Coleman, 'Hong Kong's Special Trade Status with the US: Five Things to Know' (*Nikkei Asia*, 29 May 2020). Available at: www.asia.nikkei.com/Spotlight/Hong-Kong-protests/Hong-Kong-s-special-trade-status-with-the-US-Five-things-to-know, accessed 2 February 2024.

[85] *Fortune*, 'Can Hong Kong Leverage Its Special Trade Status against China?' (*The News Lens International Edition*, 19 August 2019). Available at: www.international.thenewslens.com/feature/likantielab/123671, accessed 2 February 2024.

[86] Kenneth Rapoza, 'Imaging Hong Kong without Its U.S. Special Status Deal' (*Forbes*, 29 May 2020). Available at: www.forbes.com/sites/kenrapoza/2020/05/29/imaging-hong-kong-without-its-us-special-status-deal/?sh=4560f1851c9d, accessed 2 February 2024.

[87] ibid.

and strategically, was preserved. This thus provided stability and continuity for the many foreign nationals and businesses that were still located in the territory after 1997. For American business newcomers, the Special Trading Status was an attractive opportunity to establish their presence in Hong Kong. In 2021, Hong Kong played host to seventy of the world's 100 largest banks[88] and 1,260 US businesses, more than half of which were regional operations. Crucially, Hong Kong imposed a 0 per cent tariff on US exports, which the jurisdiction benefited from – goods worth $30.8 billion were exported from the US to Hong Kong and in 2019, the latter became the former's second-largest trading partner relative to trade surplus.

B. Revocation of Hong Kong's Special Trading Status

Although Hong Kong was able to enjoy the benefits of the 1992 Act for almost three decades, the protests of 2019 and early 2020 severely tested its ties with the US and ultimately resulted in the revocation by the US of its Special Trading Status.

Protests first began in late March 2019, when the government attempted to introduce its controversial Hong Kong Extradition Bill. As time grew, the protest morphed into a wider movement on freedoms, rights and democracy.[89] Thus, despite the bill's suspension on 9 July, protests did not diminish. In response to what was happening in Hong Kong, the Hong Kong Human Rights and Democracy Act ('HKHRDA') was re-introduced in the Senate on 13 June 2019 and became a part of US law on 27 November 2019.[90] Amongst other requirements, the HKHRDA required the Secretary of State to certify annually Hong Kong's autonomy from China as grounds for granting special treatment under the 1992 Act[91] and the Secretary of Commerce to evaluate annually whether the Hong Kong Government had complied with both US and United Nations sanctions and US export control laws and to release a report on the matter.

On 28 May 2020, China's National People's Congress adopted a decision on the promulgation of national security legislation in Hong Kong aimed at

[88] US Department of State, '2022 Investment Climate Statements: Hong Kong' (2022). Available at: www.state.gov/reports/2022-investment-climate-statements/hong-kong/, accessed 2 February 2024.

[89] Daniel Victor and Mike Ives, 'Why Are People Protesting in Hong Kong?' (*The New York Times*, 15 October 2019). Available at: www.nytimes.com/2019/10/15/world/asia/what-are-hong-kong-protests-about.html, accessed 2 February 2024.

[90] US Congress, 'S.1838 – Hong Kong Human Rights and Democracy Act of 2019' (*Congress.gov*). Available at: www.congress.gov/bill/116th-congress/senate-bill/1838/actions, accessed 2 February 2024. On the same day that the HKHRDA was signed into law, a bill prohibiting the export of crowd-control munitions to the Hong Kong Police Force was also signed.

[91] Secretary of State report regarding the autonomy of Hong Kong, 22 USC §§5725; Reporting requirement, §§5731.

prohibiting acts that were considered to endanger China's national security.[92] On the same day, the US Secretary of State reported that the provision of differential treatment to Hong Kong was no longer warranted, as the unilateral imposition of the National Security Law in Hong Kong had undermined the territory's autonomy.[93] Consequently, President Donald Trump, on 29 May 2020, announced that he had directed his administration to commence the process of removing Hong Kong's Special Trading Status and its preferential treatment,[94] which led to the US Secretary of Commerce suspend the special treatment given to Hong Kong by his department.[95] The culminating result, however, was the Executive Order on Hong Kong Normalisation, which was issued and signed on 14 July 2020 and which eliminated the differential treatments that had been conferred to Hong Kong as a result of US policy exemptions, including in the areas of exports.[96]

Table 5.1 Chronological Overview of Hong Kong's Legislative Changes and Associated International Reactions (2014–2022)

13 November 2014	The Hong Kong Human Rights and Democracy Act ('HKHRDA') bill is first introduced in the Senate, as a response to the 2014 Hong Kong protests.
29 March 2019	The Fugitive Offenders and Mutual Legal Assistance in Criminal Matters Legislation (Amendment) Bill 2019 ('HK Extradition Bill') is first published.
31 March 2019	The first protest in relation to the HK Extradition Bill occurs.
April 2019 – approximately early 2020	Various protests in Hong Kong are held. The number of protests peaked around November 2019 and suffered a gradual decline as a result of the Covid-19 pandemic – the first case in Hong Kong was confirmed on 23 January 2020.
13 June 2019	The HKHRDA bill is once again introduced in the US Senate. Amongst other obligations, the HKHRDA requires certain US departments to assess whether the change in Hong Kong's circumstances warranted a change of its Special Trading Status.

(continued)

[92] Lily Kuo, 'Chinese Parliament Approves Controversial Hong Kong Security Law' (*The Guardian*, 28 May 2020). Available at: www.theguardian.com/world/2020/may/28/china-vote-npc-national-security-laws-hong-kong-us-protest, accessed 2 February 2024.

[93] Bureau of East Asian and Pacific Affairs, '2020 Hong Kong Policy Act Report' (*US Department of State*, 28 May 2020). Available at: www.state.gov/2020-hong-kong-policy-act-report/, accessed 2 February 2024.

[94] BBC, 'Trump Targets China over Hong Kong Security Law' (*BBC News*, 30 May 2020). Available at: www.bbc.co.uk/news/world-us-canada-52856876, accessed 14 May 2024.

[95] US Department of Commerce, 'Statement from U.S. Secretary of Commerce Wilbur Ross on Revocation of Hong Kong Special Status' (US Department of Commerce, 29 June 2020) 2017–2021. Available at: www.commerce.gov/news/press-releases/2020/06/statement-us-secretary-commerce-wilbur-ross-revocation-hong-kong.html, accessed 2 February 2024.

[96] Exec Order No 13936, 85 Fed Reg 43413 (17 July 2020) sec 3(c).

Table 5.1 *(Continued)*

15 June 2019	The then Chief Executive, Carrie Lam announces that the second reading of the HK Extradition Bill would be delayed for an unspecified time.
9 July 2019	Carrie Lam declares the HK Extradition Bill to be 'dead'.
23 October 2019	The HK Extradition Bill is formally withdrawn.
24 October 2019	A bill that would prohibit the export of crowd-control munitions to the Hong Kong Police Force is introduced in the Senate.
19 November 2019	The Senate votes unanimously to pass the HKHRDA.
	The Senate votes unanimously to pass the bill prohibiting crowd-control munitions to the Hong Kong Police Force.
20 November 2019	The House votes unanimously to pass the HKHRDA.
	The House votes unanimously to pass the bill prohibiting crowd-control munitions to the Hong Kong Police Force.
27 November 2019	President Trump signs the HKHRDA bill, which becomes a legally binding act.
	President Trump signs the bill that prohibits the export of crowd-control munitions to the Hong Kong Police Force. This becomes a legally binding act.
28 May 2020	China's National People's Congress passes the 'Decision of the National People's Congress on Establishing and Improving the Legal System and Enforcement Mechanisms for the Hong Kong Special Administrative Region to Safeguard National Security', which approves the introduction of the National Security Law in Hong Kong.
	The US Secretary of State releases a report, which concludes that the change in Hong Kong's status meant that the granting of special treatment should cease.
29 May 2020	President Trump announces a plan to revoke Hong Kong's Special Trading Status with the US and to impose sanctions against certain governmental officials in Hong Kong.
29 June 2020	The US Department of Commerce rescinds the special status it had granted to Hong Kong.
30 June 2020	China's National People's Congress Standing Committee passes the National Security Law of Hong Kong, bypassing the standard process for enacting legislation in the territory.
	The Hong Kong National Security Law becomes effective.
1 July 2020	The Hong Kong Autonomy Act bill, which seeks to impose sanctions on government officials who had played a role in undermining the autonomy of Hong Kong, is introduced in the US House of Representatives.

(continued)

Table 5.1 *(Continued)*

	The House of Representatives passes the Hong Kong Autonomy Act bill.
2 July 2020	The Senate passes the Hong Kong Autonomy Act bill unanimously.
14 July 2020	President Trump signs the Hong Kong Autonomy Act bill into law.
	President Trump signs the Executive Order on Hong Kong Normalisation, which seeks to 'end special conditions and preferential treatment' granted to Hong Kong. This essentially revokes Hong Kong's Special Trading Status with the US.
15 July 2020	China's Foreign Ministry announces a series of countersanctions, in retaliation to what it described as 'gross interference in China's internal affairs' by the US.[97]
11 August 2020	Citing the Executive Order on Hong Kong Normalisation, the US Customs and Border Protection issues a notice, notifying the public regarding a change in labelling requirements for exports manufactured in Hong Kong. Such products can no longer be marked with 'Hong Kong' as their place of origin but must be marked with 'China' instead.
19 August 2020	Three bilateral treaties between the US and Hong Kong are unilaterally suspended or terminated by the US.
30 October 2020	Hong Kong requests consultations with the US regarding the change in labelling requirements for goods imported from Hong Kong to the US at the World Trade Organisation; see DS 597.
9 November 2020	The US indicates that it is willing to enter into consultations with Hong Kong regarding DS 597. However, such consultations would be without prejudice to the jurisdiction's position that the change in labelling requirements for goods imported to the US from Hong Kong related to national security matters and thus 'not susceptible to review or capable of resolution by WTO dispute settlement'.[98]
24 November 2020	Consultations regarding DS 597 are held, but they fail to resolve the dispute.

(continued)

[97] Ministry of Foreign Affairs of the People's Republic of China, 'The Ministry of Foreign Affairs: The Chinese Side Firmly Opposes the US Side's Signing of the "Hong Kong Autonomy Act"' (*Ministry of Foreign Affairs of the People's Republic of China*, 15 July 2020). Available at: www.fmprc.gov.cn/mfa_eng/gjhdq_665435/3376_665447/3432_664920/3435_664926/202007/t20200716_590947.html, accessed 2 February 2024.

[98] *United States: Origin Marking Requirement – Communication from the United States* (13 November 2020) WT/DS597/2.

Table 5.1 *(Continued)*

14 January 2021	Hong Kong submits a request for the establishment of a panel for DS 597.
22 February 2021	A panel for DS 597 is established.
31 March 2021	The 2021 Hong Kong Policy Act Report is released, which concludes that special treatment should not be accorded to Hong Kong.
29 April 2021	A panel for DS 597 is composed.
31 March 2022	The 2022 Hong Kong Policy Act Report is released, which concludes that special treatment should not be accorded to Hong Kong.

Source: Compiled by the author from various public sources.

Notably, the Executive Order suspends the application of section 201(a) of the 1992 Act towards section 304 of the Tariff Act 1930.[99] Section 304 concerns import-marking requirements and provides that the origin of imports to the US have to be indicated in English in a visible, permanent and clear manner.[100] However, after Hong Kong's handover to China, products manufactured in Hong Kong were to continue to be marked as originating from 'Hong Kong' rather than from 'China'.[101] Based on the suspension of the applicability of section 201(a) of the 1992 Act to section 304 of the Tariff Act 1930, the US Customs and Borders Protection issued a notice on 11 August 2020, that goods manufactured in Hong Kong entering into the US market on or after 25 September 2020 would be required to have their origin marked as 'China'.[102] Subsequently, Hong Kong launched a challenge at the WTO level and requested that a WTO panel be established on 14 January 2021.[103]

In the aftermath of the demise of Hong Kong's Special Trading Status with the US, far-reaching consequences have been projected. Nonetheless, during the 2020 Report, it was concluded that it was unlikely the recertification and regranting of Hong Kong's Special Trading Status with the US would occur in the future, in light of the situation.[104] Subsequent Hong Kong Policy Act Reports have also concluded that Hong Kong did not warrant special treatment granted under the 1992 Act.[105] Consequently, whether Hong Kong will regain

[99] ibid s 2(f).

[100] Marking of imported articles and containers, 19 USC § 1304(a).

[101] Country of Origin Marking of Products of Hong Kong, 62 Fed Reg 30927 (5 June 1997).

[102] Country of Origin Marking of Products of Hong Kong, 85 Fed Reg 48551 (11 August 2020).

[103] *United States: Origin Marking Requirement – Request for the establishment of a panel by Hong Kong, China* (15 January 2021) WT/DS597/5.

[104] Bureau of East Asian and Pacific Affairs, '2020 Hong Kong Policy Act Report' (*US Department of State*, 28 May 2020). Available at: www.state.gov/2020-hong-kong-policy-act-report/, accessed 2 February 2024.

[105] Bureau of East Asian and Pacific Affairs, '2021 Hong Kong Policy Act Report' (*US Department of State*, 31 March 2021). Available at: www.state.gov/2021-hong-kong-policy-act-report/, accessed

its lost Special Trading Status with the US sometime in the future remains to be seen. However, the likelihood of doing so, at least in the short term, looks remote.

IV. CONTEMPORARY TRADE POLICY DEVELOPMENTS

On 2 February 2023, it was announced that John Lee, Hong Kong's Chief Executive, would embark on a trip to the Middle East from 4–11 February 2023, with two days spent in Riyadh, Saudi Arabia, two days in Abu Dhabi, the United Arab Emirates (UAE) and three in Dubai, UAE.[106] The delegation that accompanied him included high-ranking government officials including the Secretary for Financial Services and the Treasury, the Secretary for Commerce and Economic Development and the Acting Commissioner for Belt and Road,[107] as well as representatives from various industries, including finance and banking, technology, logistics and transport.[108]

The trip's objectives, which have been described as multifaceted, included the development of business opportunities in both Saudi Arabia and the UAE and the construction and consolidation of Hong Kong's relationship with both countries. The trip also served as an opportunity to invite companies, both big and small, to come to and invest in Hong Kong.[109] However, Lee was also quick to emphasise that rather than focusing on a single entity, the trip's target audience included all companies and people that the Hong Kong delegation had encountered and that the formation of collaborative relationships with different sectors was also one of the purposes of the trip. Consequently, throughout the trip, the spirit of one of the key catchphrases of the current administration, 'to tell good stories of Hong Kong'[110] was adhered to and embodied. It was central to Lee's message that Hong Kong had multiple distinctive advantages – including China's backing – and was also highly connected to the rest of the world. He

2 February 2024; US Department of State, '2022 Hong Kong Policy Act Report' (*US Department of State*, 31 March 2022). Available at: www.state.gov/2022-hong-kong-policy-act-report/, accessed 2 February 2024.

[106] HKSAR Government, 'CE to Visit Saudi Arabia and UAE' (*The Government of the Hong Kong Special Administrative Region Press Releases*, 2 February 2024). Available at: www.info.gov.hk/gia/general/202302/02/P2023020200473.htm, accessed 2 February 2024.

[107] ibid.

[108] Iris Ouyang, 'Chief Executive John Lee's Middle East Delegation Comprises 30 Heavyweights from Finance, Tech and Logistics Sectors' (*South China Morning Post*, 6 February 2023). Available at: www.scmp.com/business/banking-finance/article/3209281/chief-executive-john-lees-middle-east-delegation-comprises-30-heavyweights-finance-tech-and, accessed 2 February 2024.

[109] HKSAR Government, 'Transcript of Remarks by CE at Media Sessions in Dubai (with Photos/Video)' *The Government of the Hong Kong Special Administrative Region Press Releases*, 10 February 2023). Available at: ww.info.gov.hk/gia/general/202302/10/P2023021000502.htm, accessed 7 March 2024.

[110] See Office of the Chief Executive, 'The Chief Executive's 2022 Policy Address – 2022.10.19' paras 143–48.

hoped that every company in the Middle East region would take advantage of Hong Kong's opportunities.[111]

During its stay in Riyadh, the Hong Kong delegation attended various exhibitions, including the 'The Line Experience' exhibition, which featured designs of the NEOM, a planned smart territory project funded by Saudi Arabia's Public Investment Fund.[112] Multiple meetings were also held between John Lee and various personnel from the Saudi Arabian government, the Cooperation Council for the Arab States of the Gulf ('CCASG') and businesses alike. These included the Saudi Arabian Minister of Investment, the Secretary-General of the CCASG and the President and Chief Executive Officer of Saudi Aramco.[113] Topics such as the implementation in Saudi Arabia of BRI infrastructure projects and cooperation between Saudi Arabia and Hong Kong in the areas of economy, finance and technology were discussed.[114]

As with his itinerary in Saudi Arabia, apart from attendance at the Abu Dhabi–Hong Kong Business Forum and networking luncheon hosted by the Abu Dhabi Chamber of Commerce & Industry, John Lee spent much time during the Abu Dhabi part of his Middle East trip in meetings with various officials including the territory's Investment Authority Managing Director and on visits to various premises, including the UAE's sovereign wealth fund and companies located in Abu Dhabi.[115] Discussions were held regarding cooperation and collaboration between Hong Kong and the UAE, particularly economically and commercially. Hong Kong's comparative advantages under China's support and the 'One Country, Two Systems', as well as its unique position as a connector between the GBA and the BRI with the rest of the world, were conveyed to the relevant parties,[116] while the commercial opportunities that existed in Hong Kong were also promoted.

Similar activities were also conducted in Dubai, during which the Hong Kong delegation visited the Museum of the Future,[117] the Dubai Holding and the Burj

[111] 'CE Continues UAE Visit' (*news.gov.hk*, 9 February 2023). Available at: www.news.gov.hk/eng/2023/02/20230209/20230209_084056_941.html, accessed 2 February 2024.

[112] HKSAR Government, 'CE Begins Visit Programme in Saudi Arabia (with Photos/ Video)' (*The Government of the Hong Kong Special Administrative Region Press Releases*, 6 February 2023). Available at: www.info.gov.hk/gia/general/202302/06/P2023020600104.htm, accessed 2 February 2024.

[113] 'CE Boosts Ties in Saudi Arabia' (*news.gov.hk*, 7 February 2023). Available at: www.news.gov.hk/eng/2023/02/20230207/20230207_100533_806.html?type=category&name=finance&tl=t, accessed 2 February 2024.

[114] ibid.

[115] News.gov.hk, 'CE Begins Abu Dhabi Visit' (*news.gov.hk*, 8 February 2023). Available at: www.news.gov.hk/eng/2023/02/20230208/20230208_094211_229.html, accessed 2 February 2024.

[116] HKSAR Government, 'CE Continues Visit in Abu Dhabi and Starts Dubai Visit (with Photos/ Video)' *The Government of the Hong Kong Special Administrative Region Press Releases*, 9 February 2023. Available at: www.info.gov.hk/gia/general/202302/09/P2023020800799.htm, accessed 2 February 2024.

[117] News.gov.hk, 'CE Meets UAE Officials' (*news.gov.hk*, 10 February 2023). Available at: www.news.gov.hk/eng/2023/02/20230210/20230210_095500_526.html, accessed 2 February 2024.

Al Arab Jumeirah.[118] Such visits allowed the delegation to better understand how businesses evolved in Dubai. Crucially, it also allowed the Hong Kong delegation to present the current policies and actions of the Hong Kong government so as to court business and investment.[119] The Dubai leg of John Lee's Middle East trip also featured meetings with the Minister of State for Foreign Trade, the Vice-President and Prime Minister and Ruler of Dubai and the Chairman of Dubai Holding, during which the BRI and the role that Hong Kong could play to help the UAE in the development and materialisation of its projects with China were also discussed.

Overall, 13 Memorandums of Understanding ('MOUs') and Letters of Intent ('LOI') were signed between Hong Kong companies or organisations and their Saudi Arabian and UAE counterparts.[120] These included MOUs between the Hong Kong Trade Development Council ('HKTDC') and the Abu Dhabi Chamber of Commerce & Industry and the Federation of Hong Kong Industries and the Abu Dhabi Chamber of Commerce & Industry. Significantly, MOUs were signed between HKTDC and the Dubai Chamber of Commerce & Industry ('Dubai Chamber') and between HKTD and Invest in Sharjah. In the former, it was agreed that mutual support in various areas, including trade enquiries, would be provided and that cooperation would be enhanced on business opportunities in industries where both parties have shared interests.[121] Additionally, the Dubai Chamber announced that it would open an office in Hong Kong. This would facilitate bilateral trade flows between Hong Kong and Dubai, while allowing Dubai to establish a firmer footprint in the Asia-Pacific region. Similarly, the MOU with Invest in Sharjah aims to enhance cooperation, particularly in information sharing regarding investment and trade matters.[122]

Multiple negotiations are also ongoing. On 5 February 2023, John Lee announced that negotiations for an IPPA between Saudi Arabia and Hong Kong and an MOU on the facilitation of FDI cooperation would commence,[123] while

[118] News.gov.hk, 'Middle East Visit Fruitful: CE' (*news.gov.hk*, 10 February 2023). Available at: www.news.gov.hk/eng/2023/02/20230210/20230210_135407_131.html, accessed 2 February 2024.

[119] ibid.

[120] HKTDC Media Room, 'Hong Kong's Middle East Mission Lays Groundwork for New Business Opportunities' (*HKTDC*, 10 February 2023). Available at: www.mediaroom.hktdc.com/en/press-release/detail/20485/Hong%20Kong%E2%80%99s%20Middle%20East%20mission%20lays%20groundwork%20for%20new%20business%20opportunities, accessed 2 February 2024.

[121] Dubai Chamber, 'Dubai Chambers Inaugurates New Office in Hong Kong to Drive Mutual Economic and Business Growth' (*Dubai Chamber*, 9 February 2023). Available at: www.dubaichamber.com/en/media-center/news/dubai-chambers-inaugurates-new-office-in-hong-kong-to-drive-mutual-economic-and-business-growth/, accessed 2 February 2024.

[122] World Business Outlook, 'Hong Kong and Sharjah Announces a Strategic Investment Alliance' (*World Business Outlook*, 10 February 2023). Available at: www.worldbusinessoutlook.com/hong-kong-and-sharjah-announces-a-strategic-investment-alliance/, accessed 8 March 2024.

[123] HKSAR Government, 'Speech by CE at Kingdom of Saudi Arabia-Hong Kong Investment Forum and Chinese New Year Gala Dinner (English only) (With Photo/Video)' (*The Government of the Hong Kong Special Administrative Region Press Releases*, 6 February 2023). Available at: www.info.gov.hk/gia/general/202302/06/P2023020600055.htm, accessed 2 February 2024.

there would also be a formalisation of cooperation agreements between Hong Kong's business chambers and the HKTDC and their Saudi Arabia equivalent.[124] He noted that the new IPPA would facilitate investment flows between Hong Kong and Saudi Arabia, while also boosting investors'.[125] Additionally, both the agreement and the MOU would help accelerate Hong Kong's commercial and investment engagement.[126] The Hong Kong government is also exploring the possibility of commencing negotiations with the UAE for an FTA, having already signed an IPPA with the country in March 2020. However, formal discussions on this matter have yet to be entered.[127] Finally, on 9 February 2023, it was announced that the Hong Kong and UAE governments were discussing the possibility of concluding an MOU regarding green and sustainable finance.[128]

As a result of some of the most stringent Covid-19 social distancing rules and other restrictions,[129] for the past three years or so, Hong Kong has largely been isolated from the rest of the world. It has also suffered from a massive exodus of foreign companies and a significant brain drain, as many individuals have fled from the territory because of its measures during the pandemic and the passage of the National Security Law in response to the 2019/2020 protests.[130] Consequently, the trip is symbolically significant, as it signals to the world that Hong Kong is finally opening up again. As restrictions are lifted, this could incentivise those who had left the territory to return.

Trade and FDI are regarded as key drivers of economic recovery and development.[131] Thus, one of the most obvious implications of John Lee's Middle East trip would be a potentially positive impact on trade and investment flows to Hong Kong – this would aid its economic recovery, which had been severely impacted by the 2019/2020 political crisis,[132] the Covid-19 pandemic and the

[124] ibid.

[125] News.gov.hk, 'CE Begins Visit in Saudi Arabia' (*news.gov.hk*, 6 February 2023). Available at: www.news.gov.hk/eng/2023/02/20230206/20230206_102337_811.html, accessed 2 February 2024.

[126] ibid.

[127] Natalie Wong, 'Free-Trade Agreement 'Logical Next Step' for Hong Kong and United Arab Emirates, Territory Leader John Lee Says' (*South China Morning Post*, 9 February 2023). Available at: www.scmp.com/news/hong-kong/article/3209568/hong-kong-and-united-arab-emirates-set-commence-talks-bilateral-free-trade-agreement-territory-leader, accessed 2 February 2024.

[128] HKSAR Government, 'Speech by CE at United Arab Emirates-Hong Kong Business Forum and Chinese New Year Gala Dinner (English Only) (With Photos/Videos)' (*The Government of the Hong Kong Special Administrative Region Press Releases*, 9 February 2023). Available at: www.info.gov.hk/gia/general/202302/09/P2023020900034.htm, accessed 10 March 2024.

[129] BBC, 'Hong Kong's Tough Covid Laws Threatened by Virus Surge' (*BBC*, 10 February 2022). Available at: www.bbc.com/news/world-asia-china-60329578, accessed 2 February 2024.

[130] Logan Wright, 'Fractured Foundations: Assessing Risks to Hong Kong's Business Environment' (*Atlantic Council Geoeconomics Center*, 7 March 2023) 1, 7. Available at: www.atlanticcouncil.org/wp-content/uploads/2023/03/Fractured-foundations-Assessing-risks-to-Hong-Kongs-business-environment.pdf, accessed 2 February 2024.

[131] Siva S Makki and Agapi Somwaru, 'Impact on Foreign Direct Investment and Trade on Economic Growth: Evidence from Developing Countries' (2004) 86 *American Journal of Agricultural Economics* 795.

[132] Finbarr Bermingham, 'Hong Kong's Status as Trade Hub Based on Political Stability, EU Figures in Protest-Racked Territory Warn' (*South China Morning Post*, 27 November 2019). Available at:

resulting restrictions.[133] Additionally, the advantages conferred upon Hong Kong, as a part of the GBA and the world's largest offshore renminbi business centre, allow it to bridge the gap between China, the Middle East and, in general, the rest of the world. Consequently, Hong Kong could act as a springboard for Middle Eastern investors to invest in China.[134] This is particularly important because investors in the Middle East are increasingly looking to diversify their investments beyond the region.[135] As Hong Kong seeks to transform itself into a regional green finance hub in Asia,[136] many opportunities in this area will also exist and Middle Eastern investors can leverage them. Since Hong Kong, the UAE and Saudi Arabia are BRI members, Hong Kong could also help to create capital and provide the necessary expert services that are required for the materialisation of BRI projects located in both countries.[137]

The enhanced bilateral relationship and collaboration promised by the Middle East trip would also be beneficial to businesses in Hong Kong, Saudi Arabia and the UAE. Through the trip, both the Hong Kong delegation and their counterparts in Saudi Arabia and the UAE were able to understand each of the respective places' business environments. The signing of MOUs would also lead to greater exchanges between Hong Kong, Saudi Arabia and the UAE in various industries. Particularly, the Dubai Chamber has identified that Hong Kong had attractive trade potential in certain industries, such as perfume and jewellery, for UAE investors and traders to explore.[138] Thus, the Dubai Chamber office's establishment in Hong Kong would make it easier for them to do so. In the long run, once the IPPA between Hong Kong and Saudi Arabia comes into effect, it would lead to greater investor protection and confidence for investors to invest

www.scmp.com/economy/china-economy/article/3039610/hong-kongs-status-trade-hub-based-political-stability-eu, accessed 2 February 2024.

[133] Sarah Zheng, 'Hong Kong's Economy Records Worst Contraction Since 2020' (*Bloomberg*, 31 October 2022). Available at: www.bloomberg.com/news/articles/2022-10-31/hong-kong-s-economy-records-worst-contraction-since-2020#xj4y7vzkg, accessed 2 February 2024.

[134] Natalie Wong, 'Hong Kong must Seize Opportunities with Middle Eastern Investors Eyeing Mainland China Market, Top Banker Says' (*South China Morning Post*, 14 February 2023) Available at: www.scmp.com/news/hong-kong/hong-kong-economy/article/3210089/middle-eastern-investors-keen-put-more-assets-mainland-china-lack-awareness-conduits-hong-kong, accessed 2 February 2024.

[135] Financial Secretary, 'Duty Visit to Saudi Arabia and Bahrain' (*Financial Secretary, Deputy Financial Secretary, The Government of the Hong Kong Special Administrative Region*, 30 October 2022). Available at: www.fso.gov.hk/eng/blog/blog20221030.htm, accessed 2 February 2024.

[136] Sheryl Tian Tong Lee and others, 'Hong Kong and Singapore Spar for Green Finance Supremacy in Asia' (*Bloomberg*, 8 December 2022). Available at: www.bloomberg.com/news/articles/2022-12-08/hong-kong-singapore-spar-for-the-green-finance-crown-in-asia?leadSource=uverify%20wall, accessed 2 February 2024.

[137] John Lee Ka-chiu, 'Middle East Visit Heralds Better Times for Hong Kong's Economy and People' (*South China Morning Post*, 13 February 2023). Available at: www.scmp.com/comment/opinion/article/3209941/middle-east-visit-heralds-better-times-hong-kongs-economy-and-people, accessed 2 February 2024.

[138] Government of Dubai Media Office, 'Dubai Chamber Launches Online Tool to Identify Export Gaps in Promising Markets' (*Government of Dubai*, 9 August 2021). Available at: www.mediaoffice.ae/en/news/2021/August/09-08/Dubai-Chamber, accessed 2 February 2024.

in both places. These would also contribute to potential bilateral investment and trade flows.

Two further implications should also be noted. First, the deepening relationship between Hong Kong, Saudi Arabia and the UAE will affect not only business but also areas such as culture and sport. During his Policy Address in 2022, John Lee pledged that his administration would further develop sports as an industry and continue to promote Hong Kong as an international sports events hub.[139] Consequently, the Aramco Team Series, the largest professional woman's team tournament in the world, will be held in Hong Kong in October 2023.[140] Second, a potential secondary listing of Aramco, the world's largest petroleum exporter and one of the world's most valuable companies, on the Hong Kong Stock Exchange would further elevate the territory's reputation as a prime international financial hub,[141] whilst acting as symbolic evidence that Hong Kong has reopened to the rest of the world.

V. RCEP AND THE FUTURE OF HONG KONG'S TRADE POLICY

As the agreement that created the world's largest FTA and which encapsulates one-third of the world's economy and population,[142] the RCEP Agreement has been a long time coming. Negotiations started in 2012;[143] the agreement was eventually signed on 15 November 2020[144] and first entered into force for 10 of its members, who had deposited a ratification instrument to the ASEAN Secretariat.[145] Currently, its membership centres around those who have an FTA with ASEAN,[146] a political and economic organisation consisting of 10

[139] Office of the Chief Executive, 'The Chief Executive's 2022 Policy Address – 2022.10.19' para 91.

[140] Local, 'Aramco Team Series to be Held at Fanling Golf Course in October' (*The Standard*, 7 February 2023). Available at: www.thestandard.com.hk/breaking-news/section/4/200045/Aramco-Team-Series-to-be-held-at-Fanling-golf-course-in-October, accessed 2 February 2024.

[141] Harry Clynch, 'Saudi Arabia's Aramco IPO: The Mega-Deal Hong Kong Needs?' (*Disruption Banking*, 2 March 2023). Available at: www.disruptionbanking.com/2023/03/02/saudi-arabias-aramco-ipo-the-mega-deal-hong-kong-needs/, accessed 2 February 2024.

[142] Andrew Mullen, 'Explainer | What is RCEP, the World's Largest Free Trade Deal that is Under Way?' (*South China Morning Post*, 1 January 2022). Available at: www.scmp.com/economy/global-economy/article/3161707/what-rcep-worlds-largest-free-trade-deal-under-way, accessed 2 February 2024.

[143] Grace Ho, 'A Trade Pact Nearly 10 Years in the Making: 5 Things to Know about RCEP' (*The Straits Times*, 15 November 2020). Available at: www.straitstimes.com/asia/a-trade-pact-nearly-10-years-in-the-making-5-things-to-know-about-rcep, accessed 2 February 2024.

[144] ASEAN, 'ASEAN Hits Historic Milestone with Signing of RCEP' (*ASEAN*, 15 November 2020). Available at: www.asean.org/asean-hits-historic-milestone-with-signing-of-rcep/, accessed 9 January 2024.

[145] ADB, 'RCEP Agreement to Enter into Force on 1 January 2022' (*ADB SEADS*, 11 November 2021) Available at: www.seads.adb.org/news/rcep-agreement-enter-force-1-january-2022/, accessed 2 February 2024.

[146] Peter A Petri and Ali Abdul-Raheem, 'Can RCEP and the TPP be Pathways to FTAAP?' in *State of the Region, 2014–2015* (Pacific Economic Cooperation Council 2014) 1, 10.

Southeast Asian countries. There are currently 15 members of the RCEP. At the time of writing, the RCEP Agreement has already entered into force in 13 countries.[147] The RCEP aims to create an economic relationship that is extensive and mutually advantageous and which would make it easier to increase trade and investment regionally and support the global economy's growth and development.[148] It also aims to complement the WTO Agreements, while using the latter's provisions as a blueprint for the expansion of areas where the RCEP Parties had agreed to do so.[149]

A. The RCEP: Objectives and Provisions

The RCEP Agreement consists of 20 chapters and covers a wide range of topics, including trade in goods and services, IPR, government procurement and sanitary and phytosanitary measures.[150] Instead of being 'WTO-plus', the RCEP Agreement is described as being 'WTO-consistent',[151] given its primary focal point is trade in goods rather than other non-tariff issues.[152] For example, in trade in goods, over 90 per cent of tariffs covering over 65 per cent of goods traded are to be eliminated within a 20-year period.[153] Similarly, in the chapter on trade in services, where national treatment,[154] market access,[155] most-favoured-nation treatment and local presence are covered, all RCEP members are subjected to a Schedule of Commitments. However, parties have the option to commit themselves to a negative or a positive list of service commitments.[156]

[147] Australian Border Force, 'Regional Comprehensive Economic Partnership Agreement' (*Australian Border Force*, 15 December 2022). Available at: abf.gov.au/free-trade-agreements/Pages/regional-comprehensive-economic-partnership-agreement.aspx, accessed 2 February 2024.

[148] Ministry of Foreign Affairs of Japan, 'Summary of the Regional Comprehensive Economic Partnership Agreement' (*Ministry of Foreign Affairs of Japan*) 1 Available at: www.mofa.go.jp/mofaj/files/100114908.pdf, accessed 2 February 2024.

[149] The ASEAN Secretariat, 'Summary of the Regional Comprehensive Economic Partnership Agreement' (*RCEP*) 1. Available at: www.rcepsec.org/wp-content/uploads/2020/11/Summary-of-the-RCEP-Agreement.pdf, accessed 9 January 2024.

[150] The ASEAN Secretariat, 'Regional Comprehensive Economic Partnership' (*RCEP*, 2019). Available at: www.rcepsec.org/legal-text/, accessed 2 February 2024

[151] Jeffrey D Wilson, 'Mega Regional Trade Deals in the Asia-Pacific: Choosing Between the TPP and RCEP?' (2015) 45 *Journal of Contemporary Asia* 345, 350.

[152] Yifei Xiao, 'Competitive Mega-regional Trade Agreements: Regional Comprehensive Economic Partnership (RCEP) vs. Trans-Pacific Partnership (TPP)' (2015) *College Undergraduate Research Electronic Journal* 5, 36.

[153] Congressional Research Service, 'Regional Comprehensive Economic Partnership (RCEP)' (*Congressional Research Service*, 17 October 2022) 1. Available at: www.crsreports.congress.gov/product/pdf/IF/IF11891, accessed 2 February 2024.

[154] Regional Comprehensive Economic Partnership Agreement, art 8.4.

[155] Ibid art 8.5.

[156] Directorate-General for External Policies, Policy Department, 'Short Overview of the Regional Comprehensive Economic Partnership' (*European Parliament*, February 2021) 1, 10. Available at: www.europarl.europa.eu/RegData/etudes/BRIE/2021/653625/EXPO_BRI(2021)653625_EN.pdf, accessed 2 February 2024.

Additionally, the RCEP members, in the chapter on electronic commerce, are prohibited from introducing customs duties on electronic transmissions. Under Articles 12.7(2) and 12.8(1) of the RCEP Agreement respectively, they are also obliged to introduce or preserve legislation designed to protect online consumers from fraud and misleading practices, as well as a scheme for the protection of online personal information. Nonetheless, given that the levels of development between the RCEP members are drastically different – Japan and South Korea are among the world's largest economies and developed countries, while Myanmar and Cambodia are classified as least-developed countries,[157] the RCEP, under its Guiding Principles, offers certain flexibilities and special and differential treatment to those who require such treatments.[158] Subsequently, there is a five-year period whereby Cambodia, Laos and Myanmar are not required to comply with certain provisions in the electronic commerce chapter – these include the Article 12.7(2) and 12.8(1) requirements.

However, while there is an investment chapter in the RCEP Agreement, which contains provisions on investment protection, no provisions on an investor-state dispute settlement mechanism are included. Instead, under art. 10.18 of the RCEP Agreement, the RCEP parties have agreed to commence negotiations for an investment dispute settlement mechanism within two years after the agreement had entered into force. Additionally, a working programme was set up to facilitate economic and technical cooperation and the effective implementation of the RCEP Agreement.[159] Finally, it should also be noted that a mechanism has been put in place to review emerging issues and update the text of the RCEP Agreement – this is done through meetings of the RCEP Ministers, the RCEP Joint Committee and its four subcommittees.

B. Hong Kong's Accession to RCEP

There are several reasons why the RCEP is important to Hong Kong. The RCEP presents Hong Kong with opportunities, both old and new. There are various countries which are parties to the RCEP, but with which Hong Kong does not have an FTA. Thus, being a party to the RCEP would allow Hong Kong to take advantage of major business prospects with these countries,[160] and vice versa.

[157] The World Bank, 'Least Developed Countries: UN Classification' (*The World Bank | Data*). Available at: www.data.worldbank.org/country/XL, accessed 9 January 2024.

[158] Shintaro Hamanaka, 'TPP versus RCEP: Control of Membership and Agenda Setting' (2014) 18 *Journal of East Asian Economic Integration* 163, 177; RCEP, 'Guiding Principles and Objectives for Negotiating the Regional Comprehensive Economic Partnership' (*RCEP*) 1. Available at: www.rcepsec.org/wp-content/uploads/2019/10/RCEP-Guiding-Principles-public-copy.pdf, accessed 2 February 2024.

[159] ibid art 15.5.

[160] Julien Chaisse, 'Hong Kong's Case for RCEP membership' (*East Asia Forum*, 7 May 2022). Available at: www.eastasiaforum.org/2022/05/07/hong-kongs-case-for-rcep-membership/, accessed 2 February 2024.

The RCEP also enables Hong Kong to leverage its existing strengths as a focal point for re-export and trade,[161] and to transform the territory into both a centre for professional services, such as arbitration and education, as well as a Renminbi settlement and offshore trading hub in the East-Asian region.[162]

Joining the RCEP would also allow Hong Kong businesses to take advantage of the preferential treatments conferred by the RCEP Agreement, such as tariff reductions and the subsequent benefits, including a reduction in businesses' operational costs[163] and the harmonisation of industrial chains in the Asia-Pacific region.[164] This will have knock-on effects on Hong Kong's economy and employment level.

Finally, participating in the world's largest free trade area would allow Hong Kong to further strengthen its ties with its trading and investment partners located in the Asia-Pacific region. This would help Hong Kong businesses to expand their operations.[165] The RCEP imposes strict entrance requirements and behaves as a fairly exclusive club. Out of the ten largest economies in the world, only four are eligible to join the RCEP, three of which have since become parties to the RCEP Agreement.[166] Consequently, participating in the RCEP could also strengthen Hong Kong's status and competitiveness in the international arena. It should also be noted that Hong Kong implements a free-trade policy and the government is also extending the territory's FTA network; it already has an FTA with the ASEAN countries. Thus, acceding to the RCEP would be a natural next step to take.

In this regard, since 2018, the Hong Kong government has indicated that it is interested in joining the RCEP as a member. This intimation was received in a positive light, particularly during the ASEAN Economic Ministers – Hong Kong Consultations in September 2022.[167] Upon the RCEP Agreement's

[161] HKTDC Research, 'ASIA: Hong Kong Makes Official Application to Join the RCEP' (*HKTDC Research*, 8 March 2022). Available at: www.research.hktdc.com/en/article/MTAwNDI3NzY4OA, accessed 2 February 2024.

[162] CGCC, 'Wing Chu: RCEP Likely to Help Hong Kong Establish Status as Hub for Re-exports' (2022) CGCC Vision 1. Available at: www.cgcc.org.hk/files/file/1666080744_f2.pdf, accessed 2 February 2024.

[163] The Hong Kong Special Administrative Region of the People's Republic of China, 'Policy Address – International Trade Centre' (*The Hong Kong Special Administrative Region of the People's Republic of China, The Chief Executive's 2022 Policy Address*, October 2022). Available at: www.policyaddress.gov.hk/2022/en/p44.html, accessed 2 February 2024.

[164] Julien Chaisse, 'The Case for Hong Kong Joining RCEP' (*East Asia Forum*, 2 September 2021). Available at: www.eastasiaforum.org/2021/09/02/the-case-for-hong-kong-joining-rcep/, accessed 2 February 2024.

[165] Cissy Zhou, Frank Tang, Orange Wang, 'China Backs Hong Kong to Join RCEP Trade Deal in Potential Boost to Territory's Flagging Logistics Sector' (*South China Morning Post*, 25 June 2021). Available at: www.scmp.com/economy/china-economy/article/3138789/china-backs-hong-kong-join-rcep-trade-deal-potential-boost, accessed 2 February 2024.

[166] Although India had previously participated in RCEP negotiations, it eventually withdrew. Thus, out of the ten largest economies in the world, only China, Japan and South Korea are parties to the RCEP Agreement.

[167] Commerce and Economic Development Bureau, 'Legislative Council Panel on Commerce, Industry, Innovation and Technology, 2022 Policy Address – Policy Initiatives of Commerce and Economic

entry into force on 1 January 2022, the Secretary for Commerce and Economic Development, on behalf of Hong Kong, wrote to the Depositary of the RCEP Agreement regarding the territory's formal accession to the RCEP.[168] The Depositary responded on 31 January that the RCEP members had been notified regarding Hong Kong's accession application.[169] It should be noted that under Article 20.9(5), the procedures for accession, which are to be approved by the RCEP Joint Committee, would have to be complied with throughout Hong Kong's accession to the RCEP.[170]

Given that Hong Kong, as a member of an FTA with ASEAN, is currently seeking to be one of the earliest non-RCEP negotiating original countries to accede to the free trade area, the next stage for Hong Kong would be to commence negotiations. After these negotiations conclude and all 15 members of the RCEP approve Hong Kong's accession, the Hong Kong Executive Council and the Chief Executive will meet. Subsequently, an order regarding the endorsement of the negotiations' results and the signature of the RCEP Agreement will be issued. Through a gazette notice, the Secretary for Commerce and Economic Development will then insert the new RCEP Agreement into Schedule 1 of the Trade Descriptions Ordinance,[171] thus allowing the agreement to enter into force in Hong Kong.

However, whilst Hong Kong can apply for accession, participation and accession to the RCEP are actually not open to all. Under Principle 6 of the RCEP Guiding Principles any country which is a party to an FTA with ASEAN and which did not join the initial RCEP negotiations would be able to apply for accession to the agreement. In other words, the prerequisite for joining the RCEP is that a party must have already signed an FTA with ASEAN – those who do not have an FTA with ASEAN will not be allowed to join the RCEP negotiations.

Development Bureau' (*Legislative Council of the Hong Kong Special Administrative Region of the People's Republic of China*, October 2022) LC Paper No CB(1)718/2022(03) 1, 7. Available at: www.legco.gov.hk/yr2022/english/panels/ci/papers/ci20221107cb1-718-3-e.pdf, accessed 2 February 2024.

[168] Legislative Council, 'Special FC Meeting on 12 April 2022 – Speaking Notes for Secretary for Commerce and Economic Development' (*Legislative Council of the Hong Kong Special Administrative Region of the People's Republic of China*, 12 April 2022) 1, 6. Available at: www.legco.gov.hk/yr2022/english/fc/fc/sp_note/session11-cedb-cit-e.pdf, accessed 2 February 2024.

[169] Commerce and Economic Development Bureau, 'Legislative Council Panel on Commerce, Industry, Innovation and Technology, 2021 Policy Address – Policy Initiatives of Commerce, Industry and Tourism Branch, Commerce and Economic Development Bureau' (*Legislative Council of the Hong Kong Special Administrative Region of the People's Republic of China*, February 2022) LC Paper No CB(1)50/2022(01) 1, 6. Available at: www.legco.gov.hk/yr2022/english/panels/ci/papers/ci20220211cb1-50-1-e.pdf, accessed 2 February 2024.

[170] Regional Comprehensive Economic Partnership Agreement, art 20.9(5).

[171] See, eg, Trade and Industry Department, 'Legislative Council Brief – Free Trade Agreement between Hong Kong and Australia (*Trade and Industry Department, The Government of the Hong Kong Special Administrative Region*, 28 June 2018) CR WT 324/9/2/2. Available at: www.tid.gov.hk/english/ita/fta/hkaufta/files/legco20190326_e.pdf, accessed 8 January 2024. All eight of Hong Kong's existing FTAs have been included in Schedule 1 of the Trade Descriptions Ordinance.

Furthermore, pursuant to Article 20.9(1) of the RCEP Agreement, any jurisdiction can apply to join the RCEP, provided that 18 months from the date that the agreement entered into force has passed.[172] Since Hong Kong had applied for an early accession to the RCEP Agreement in mid-January, the earliest that the territory could become a member of the RCEP would be in mid-July 2023, on expiry of this 18-month period. As an accession application has already been submitted, the next stage would be for the negotiations to be launched. In this sense, the Hong Kong government is planning to take part or play host to 60-odd discussions or gatherings with relevant RCEP countries and other participants in 2023.[173] It has also increased its lobbying efforts and maintained its contact with the RCEP countries so as to launch the negotiation process regarding Hong Kong's accession – these are to ensure that Hong Kong's accession to the RCEP is progressed as soon as possible with the approval of the RCEP members.[174]

C. Assessing the Impact of RCEP on Hong Kong

Being a member of RCEP will have certain implications. For one, the numerous and overlapping FTAs between ASEAN and its trading partners have led to the fragmentation of preferential policies and other trade rules.[175] This is known as the 'spaghetti bowl' effect.[176] Particularly, the application of preferential tariff regimes requires compliance with rules of origin under the respective FTAs. However, the complexity, fragmentation and overlapping of these rules increase the costs relating to administration and compliance.[177] This, therefore,

[172] Regional Comprehensive Economic Partnership Agreement, art 20.9(1).

[173] The Hong Kong Special Administrative Region of the People's Republic of China, 'The Chief Executive's 2022 Policy Address' (*Legislative Council of the Hong Kong Special Administrative Region of the People's Republic of China*, 19 October 2022) 1, 72. Available at: www.legco.gov.hk/yr2022/english/panels/20221019-policy-e.pdf, accessed 8 January 2024.

[174] Commerce and Economic Development Bureau, Commerce and Economic Development Bureau, 'Legislative Council Panel on Commerce, Industry, Innovation and Technology, 2022 Policy Address – Policy Initiatives of Commerce and Economic Development Bureau' (*Legislative Council of the Hong Kong Special Administrative Region of the People's Republic of China*, October 2022) LC Paper No CB(1)718/2022(03) 7. Available at: www.legco.gov.hk/yr2022/english/panels/ci/papers/ci20221107cb1-718-3-e.pdf, accessed 2 February 2024.

[175] Monan Zhang, 'RCEP Developing Toward Asia-Pacific Economic Integration' (*China-US Focus*, 20 November 2019). Available at: www.chinausfocus.com/finance-economy/rcep-developing-toward-asia-pacific-economic-integration, accessed 2 February 2024.

[176] Chunding Li and Donglin Li, 'When Regional Comprehensive Economic Partnership Agreement (RCEP) Meets Comprehensive and Progressive Trans-Pacific Partnership Agreement (CPTPP): Considering the 'Spaghetti Bowl' Effect' (2022) 58 *Emerging Markets Finance and Trade* 1988, 1993.

[177] Economic Analysis Division, Economic Analysis and Business Facilitation Unit, Financial Secretary's Office, Government of the Hong Kong Special Administrative Region, 'Third Quarter Economic Report 2016' (*Government of the Hong Kong Special Administrative Region*, November 2016) 1, 38. Available at: www.hkeconomy.gov.hk/en/pdf/er_16q3.pdf, accessed 8 January 2024.

reduces the actual benefits conferred by the FTAs[178] and undermines the overall economic integration process in the region. However, through the new RCEP Agreement, the overlapping trade rules are harmonised and all the existing ASEAN FTAs are consolidated into one.[179] These should reduce red tape[180] and maximise the RCEP's effects on trade promotion and regional economic integration. Additionally, as mentioned previously, while Hong Kong is a party to an FTA with some of the largest economies in Asia, it does not have one with either Japan or South Korea,[181] the third- and tenth-largest global economies respectively in 2021.[182] Thus, given that both countries are members of the RCEP, Hong Kong's accession to this free trade area would allow it to close this FTA gap, whilst enabling all three parties to mutually benefit from new business and trade opportunities.

In the context of trade, the elimination of most import tariffs decreases existing trade barriers in the RCEP region.[183] Given that trade rules and policies are integrated between RCEP parties,[184] this will deepen the economic relationships between these countries. Consequently, the free trade area will act as a crucial tool for economies to recover from the effects of the Covid-19 pandemic,[185] with reports estimating that $109 billion would be injected into global incomes each year. Although the RCEP's actual effect on both regional and international trade remains to be seen, reports have projected the RCEP's results to varying degrees. For example, the Chinese government has estimated that regional exports and imports would cumulatively increase by 18.30 per cent and 9.63 per cent respectively within 13 years of the RCEP's entry into force, whilst international

[178] ibid.

[179] Innwon Park, 'Comparison of the Regional Comprehensive Economic Partnership (RCEP) and Other Free Trade Agreements (FTAs)' (August 2022) ERIA Discussion Paper Series No 439, 1, 3. Available at: www.eria.org/uploads/media/discussion-papers/FY22/Comparison-of-the-Regional-Comprehensive-Economic-Partnership-(RCEP)-and-Other-Free-Trade-Agreements-(FTAs).pdf, accessed 2 February 2024.

[180] Office of the Government Economist, Financial Secretary's Office, Government of the Hong Kong Special Administrative Region, 'Box 3.2 RCEP and its Possible Impacts on Hong Kong' (*Government of the Hong Kong Special Administrative Region*, February 2021). Available at: www.hkeconomy.gov.hk/en/pdf/box-20q4-3-2.pdf, accessed 2 February 2024.

[181] Simon Lester, 'Professor Julien Chaisse Discusses Hong Kong's Application to Join RCEP' (*China Trade Monitor*, 8 March 2022). Available at: www.chinatrademonitor.com/professor-julien-chaisse-discusses-hong-kongs-application-to-join-rcep/, accessed 2 February 2024.

[182] WorldData.info, 'The 50 Largest Economies in the World' (*WorldData.info*). Available at: www.worlddata.info/largest-economies.php, accessed 14 May 2024.

[183] Office of the Government Economist, Financial Secretary's Office, Government of the Hong Kong Special Administrative Region.

[184] International Finance Business Desk, 'RCEP and its Impact on Global Trade' (*International Finance*, 21 March 2022). Available at: www.internationalfinance.com/rcep-impact-global-trade/, accessed 9 January 2024.

[185] Xin Wang, 'No Second-Rate Trade Deal: What RCEP Means for the Global Economy' (*Asian Global Online*, 30 June 2022). Available at: www.asiaglobalonline.hku.hk/not-second-rate-trade-deal-what-rcep-means-global-economy/, accessed 2 February 2024.

trade would grow cumulatively by 2.91 per cent[186] Correspondingly, in 2021, the United Nations Conference on Trade and Development projected that the RCEP's preferential tariff treatments would inject US$42 billion or almost 2 per cent into regional RCEP trade.[187] Furthermore, the Peterson Institute for International Economics has estimated that, by 2030, exports would rise by US$519 billion.[188] It should be noted, however, that non-RCEP members will be losing out as a consequence of the RCEP, due to the trade diversion effect.[189] Given RCEP's preferential tariff rates, this would make trading with RCEP countries more attractive.

This chapter first outlined the trends of FTAs in Asia and their relationship with the WTO, before analysing Hong Kong's need for FTAs and providing general observations from the list of Hong Kong's existing FTAs. It then analysed Hong Kong's eight FTAs individually, prior to examining the RCEP and its implications for international trade and existing FTAs in Hong Kong. Although FTAs are helpful tools for trade liberalisation, they also run counter to the existing order as established by the WTO. Their actual trade effects will also depend on the trade creation and trade diversion effects. Nevertheless, as a free trade proponent, Hong Kong still needs FTAs and is actively looking to further its trade connections as shown by the commencement of negotiations for new FTAs and its application to accede to the RCEP. Finally, in the context of the RCEP, based on existing models, the agreement poses significant implications for international trade and existing FTAs. Nonetheless, as it only entered into force a year ago, the reduction and elimination of trade barriers will take place gradually. Therefore, there will be time lags in the materialisation of the actual effect on both regional and international trade, as well as on the global and the RCEP members' economies. The RCEP is also considered as a living document and thus is subject to potential updates and upgrades in the future. As more quantitative data on the free trade area becomes available and the RCEP Agreement undergoes revisions in the future, further research will have to be done to reevaluate the effectiveness of the free trade area.

[186] 'RCEP to Benefit China and the World' (*The State Council, The People's Republic of China*, 21 March 2022). Available at: www.gov.cn/news/videos/202201/01/content_WS61cfc871c6d-09c94e48a304d.html, accessed 2 February 2024.

[187] UNCTAD, 'A New Centre of Gravity: The Regional Comprehensive Economic Partnership and its Trade Effects' (*UNCTAD*, 2021) 1, 12. Available at: www.unctad.org/system/files/official-document/ditcinf2021d5_en_0.pdf, accessed 9 January 2024.

[188] Xin Wang (n 185).

[189] Lisandra Flach and others, 'The Regional Comprehensive Economic Partnership Agreement and Its Expected Effects on World Trade' (2021) 56 *Inter-economic Review of European Economic Policy* 92.

6

Investing in Partnerships: The Role of Bilateral Investment Treaties in Hong Kong's Economic Policy

THIS CHAPTER DISCUSSES the intricate relationship between Hong Kong's economic policy and the territory's extensive network of international investment agreements (IIAs).[1] As a global financial hub and a strategic gateway to Mainland China, Hong Kong has long recognised the importance of fostering a stable and attractive investment environment. This chapter aims to explore the centrality of investment treaties to Hong Kong's economy and assess how these agreements have contributed to the territory's economic development.

The history of bilateral investment treaties (BITs) may be traced back to the late nineteenth century when nations started entering into treaties to safeguard the property and commercial interests of their citizens who were resident in other nations. Although the first modern BIT was signed in 1959 between Germany and Pakistan, it was not until the 1960s and 1970s that BITs started to achieve general acceptability as a mechanism for attracting foreign investment. The first modern BIT was inked in 1959 between Germany and Pakistan. During this time, many developing nations came to the realisation that economic growth and development might potentially benefit from the involvement of foreign capital, so they started to implement policies designed to attract international investors. In the 1980s and 1990s, there was a significant rise in the number of IIAs signed, notably in Latin America and Asia. This was due partly to the liberalisation of trade and investment policy in many countries and partly to increasing competitiveness among nations to attract foreign investment.

In recent years, IIAs have been subjected to a substantial amount of modification. Provisions on sustainable development, the protection of human rights and the environment and the use of international arbitration as a way to settle conflicts have become more common in legal documents drafted in

[1] Generally speaking, international investment agreements (IIAs) also known as Bilateral Investment Treaties (BITs) and chapters on foreign investment in Preferential Trade Agreements (PTAs), provide a variety of safeguards to foreign investors. These agreements are referred to collectively as 'IIAs'.

the twenty-first century. In addition, concern has grown during the past decade about the potential negative impact that foreign investment could have on developing countries. This concern has specifically been raised in relation to issues such as the grabbing of land, the degradation of the environment and the displacement of local communities. As a direct result, a number of nations began to renegotiate or terminate existing IIAs and to adopt new investment agreements that include stricter provisions on sustainable development and the protection of human rights.

This chapter begins by examining the crucial role that investment treaties play in Hong Kong's economy and highlights their significance in attracting foreign direct investment (FDI) and strengthening economic ties with partner countries. It also discusses the territory's strategic approach to negotiating these agreements, which aims to bolster investor confidence and safeguard Hong Kong's position as a leading global financial centre. It goes on to consider Hong Kong's practice of negotiating and implementing IIAs. It scrutinises the territory's approach to these agreements, paying particular attention to the principles and objectives that have guided Hong Kong's IIA policy over the years. This analysis aims to offer valuable insights into the territory's strategy for leveraging investment treaties to advance its economic goals. The chapter then proceeds to identify and discuss the three generations of Hong Kong's international investment agreements, charting the evolution of the territory's investment treaty landscape. By categorising Hong Kong's IIAs into distinct groups, the chapter aims to shed light on the strategic shifts in the territory's approach to investment treaties and explore how these changes have impacted its overall economic policy. In sum, Chapter 6 provides a comprehensive examination of the role of bilateral investment treaties in Hong Kong's economic policy. By analysing the territory's IIA practice, the legal framework governing these agreements and the evolution of Hong Kong's investment treaty landscape, the chapter seeks to deepen our understanding of the pivotal role that investment treaties play in shaping Hong Kong's economy and its position in the global financial arena.

I. THE CENTRALITY OF INVESTMENT TREATIES TO HONG KONG'S ECONOMY

International investment treaties are essential to Hong Kong's standing as a global financial centre. Hong Kong is one of Asia's most active IIA negotiators despite having a relatively limited treaty network.[2] Prior to the handover on 1 July 1997, Chinese laws and regulations governing foreign investment were applied analogously to the mainland-based businesses that were partially or

[2] Julien Chaisse, 'Assessing the Exposure of Asian States to Investment Claims' (2013) 6 *Contemporary Asia Arbitration Journal* 187, 195.

entirely financed by investors from Hong Kong.[3] Further, the United Kingdom handled Hong Kong's international relations until 1997 and several of the UK's investment treaties were extended to Hong Kong by means of an Exchange of Notes.[4]

Hong Kong was a major financial hub at the time of the handover and continued to grow following the 1997 Asian financial crisis. There were concerns, nevertheless, that in order to keep this position, Hong Kong would have to formally promise that it was one of two systems operating under a single nation. The 1984 Joint Declaration between China and the United Kingdom on the Question of Hong Kong, in instance, says that Hong Kong 'will retain the status of an international financial centre, and its markets for foreign exchange, gold, securities and futures will continue. There will be free flow of capital. The Hong Kong dollar will continue to circulate and remain freely convertible'.[5] The Joint Declaration further states that '[p]rivate property, ownership of enterprises, legitimate right of inheritance and foreign investment will be protected by law'.[6] While it was theoretically possible for China's IIAs to be applied to Hong Kong after 1997, this was not possible owing to the competing economic interests of the two countries.[7] A special network of investment treaties was crucial for preserving investor trust after 1997, since Hong Kong's economic advantage depended on its position as a major global commercial and financial hub.[8]

Hong Kong has retained its position as a Special Administrative Region since 1 July 1997, operating under the 'one nation, two systems' principle and enjoying a high degree of autonomy authorised by the Basic Law. The following pertinent provisions are part of the Basic Law of the Hong Kong Special Administrative Region of the People's Republic of China, which was approved in 1990 at the Third Session of the Seventh National People's Congress:

- Assures that 'the ownership of businesses and investments from outside the Region shall be safeguarded by law'.[9]
- Hong Kong must maintain an acceptable economic and legal environment to ensure the continuation of Hong Kong's role as a global financial centre.[10]

[3] Jianming Shen, 'Cross-Strait Trade and Investment and the Role of Hong Kong' (1997) 16 *Wisconsin International Law Journal* 661, 665.

[4] Exchange of Notes Between the UK and Sri Lanka Concerning the Extension to Hong Kong of the Agreement for the Promotion and Protection of Investments (14 January 1981); UK-Jordan BIT (1979) entered in force in 1980, Extended to Hong Kong entered into force on 14 May 1986; Rudolf Dolzer and Margrete Stevens, *Bilateral Investment Treaties* (Leiden, Martinus Nijhoff Publishers, 1995) 25.

[5] The Joint Declaration on the Question of Hong Kong (signed 19 December 1984) 1399 UNTS, art 3(7).

[6] ibid art 3(5).

[7] Eileen Denza and Shelagh Brooks, 'Investment Protection Treaties: United Kingdom Experience' (1987) 36 *International & Comparative Law Quarterly* 908, 918.

[8] Nancy C Jackson, 'The Legal Regime of Hong Kong after 1997: An Examination of the Joint Declaration of the United Kingdom and the People's Republic of China' (1987) 5 *International Tax & Business Lawyer* 377, 410.

[9] Joint Declaration on the Question of Hong Kong (19 December 1984) 1399 UNTS, art 105.

[10] ibid art 109.

- Monetary and financial systems must protect the free functioning of financial businesses and financial markets, as well as regulate and monitor them in accordance with the law.
- Hong Kong will maintain unrestricted capital movement within, into and out of the Region.
- Hong Kong will create an economic and legal climate that promotes investment.

These provisions demonstrate the significance of foreign investment and finance in preserving Hong Kong's autonomy. The negotiation of IIAs is not expressly authorised by the Basic Law. because the Central People's Government is in charge of agreements on the protection and promotion of investment, which falls under the purview of foreign affairs. Nevertheless, Hong Kong is permitted to use any additional powers provided to it by the Central People's Government, the Standing Committee of the National People's Congress, or the National People's Congress, according to Article 20 of the Basic Law. Accordingly, Hong Kong may also negotiate and reach similar agreements with foreign States and territories with the Central People's Government's express permission.[11]

II. HONG KONG'S INTERNATIONAL INVESTMENT AGREEMENTS PRACTICE

Hong Kong's engagement with International Investment Agreements (IIAs) offers a unique perspective on the evolution and implementation of these legal instruments in fostering a conducive environment for foreign investment. As a Special Administrative Region with a distinct legal framework and a strong history of international trade and investment, Hong Kong's IIAs practice provides valuable insights into the negotiation, drafting and effectiveness of these agreements in attracting foreign investment and safeguarding investor rights.

The analysis of IIAs is fascinating from a legal point of view for several different reasons. In the first place, it makes it possible to comprehend both the similarities and the variations between the various IIAs with regard to the legal safeguards and duties that are offered to foreign investors. In terms of the protection and promotion of investments, this may be helpful in identifying best practices as well as areas in need of development.

Secondly, doing a comparison of different IIAs may shed light on the process of negotiating and writing these types of agreements, as well as how other nations and regions address the issue of investment protection and promotion.

[11] Wan Pun Lung, 'Application and Conclusion of Treaties in the Hong Kong Special Administrative Region of the People's Republic of China: Sixteen Years of Practice' (2013) 12 *Chinese Journal of International Law* 589, 603.

The negotiation of prospective future IIAs may be informed by this knowledge, which can also help to prevent potential problems.

Thirdly, contrasting different types of IIAs may help shed light on the efficiency of these types of agreements in terms of attracting foreign investment and safeguarding the legal rights of foreign investors. When debating whether to put money into a certain nation, governments and corporations may use this information to help guide their decisions. Comparing different IIAs may also provide a better grasp of the consistency and coherence of international investment law, in addition to its development over the course of time. This information may be used to guide the formation of future IIAs as well as the negotiation of multilateral investment agreements. When it comes to settling disputes between investors and governments, comparing IIAs may be helpful in identifying possible discrepancies and conflicts between various agreements. This is something that can be crucial when trying to find a solution. In conclusion, comparing IIAs is interesting from a legal perspective because it enables a deeper understanding of the legal framework for foreign investment; it can inform the negotiation and drafting of future agreements; and it can help to identify potential conflicts and inconsistencies in international investment law.

Hong Kong has demonstrated its commitment to safeguarding the interests of foreign investors through the execution of 21 bilateral investment treaties (BITs) and the endorsement of nine Free Trade Agreements (FTAs) that incorporate dedicated chapters on investment. Notably, among these FTAs is the seminal Investment Agreement under the framework of the Mainland and Hong Kong Closer Economic Partnership Agreement, commonly referred to as the China–Hong Kong CEPA Investment Agreement (2017). Together, these agreements establish Hong Kong's network of IIAs with 31 distinct foreign economies, demonstrating the region's strategic intent to secure its position as a global nexus for trade and investment.

Leveraging its robust economic foundations, Hong Kong actively pursues integration into the Regional Comprehensive Economic Partnership (RCEP), understanding the agreement's significant potential to drive foreign investment throughout the Asia-Pacific region.[12] As the RCEP covers a substantial market, accounting for a third of global GDP, it offers a coherent framework conducive to trade and investment, which aligns with Hong Kong's strategic interests.[13] With its formal application in January 2022, Hong Kong seeks to utilise the trade facilitation and integrated supply chains that the RCEP promotes. This move is a calculated step towards achieving membership by the close of 2024,

[12] Cannix Yau, 'Hong Kong Could Join World's Biggest Trading Bloc Next Year, With Most Members Backing City's Inclusion', *South China Morning Post*, 16 September 2023. Available at: www.scmp.com/news/hong-kong/hong-kong-economy/article/3234804/hong-kong-could-join-worlds-biggest-trading-bloc-next-year-after-most-members-back-citys-inclusion.

[13] Office of the Government Economist, '2020 Economic Background and 2021 Prospects' (Financial Secretary's Office, Government of the Hong Kong Special Administrative Region February 2021) at 51–66.

with the goal of enhancing its central role in the region's economic landscape.[14] By targeting economies that have robust trade ties with Hong Kong, possess untapped market potential, or hold strategic geographic positions – and by aligning with trading partners that uphold comparable trading principles – Hong Kong endeavours to broaden the horizon for its business and investment sectors. The ultimate goal is to not only enhance Hong Kong's standing as a preeminent international trade and investment hub but also to weave a more intricate and far-reaching fabric of economic and trade partnerships in Asia Pacific.

In a discourse delivered in November 2023, the Chief Executive of Hong Kong, Mr. John Lee, delineated Hong Kong's strategic intent to fortify its economic resilience while remaining an exemplar of an open economy that steadfastly promotes the principles of free trade and multilateralism.[15] Substantiating this commitment, Hong Kong has embarked on negotiations to establish an FTA with Peru, a venture that notably includes the formulation of a comprehensive investment chapter. Concurrently, the SAR is engaged in substantive negotiations with Bahrain, Bangladesh and Saudi Arabia regarding BITs. These deliberations underscore Hong Kong's pursuit of fortified bilateral relations. Importantly, the prospective BITs with Bahrain, Bangladesh and Saudi Arabia, each at varying stages of negotiation, are emblematic of Hong Kong's endeavour to weave a more diversified network of investment treaties. This approach aligns with the broader strategic vision of securing economic interests through a framework that provides legal certainty and protection for cross-border investments. In the case of Bahrain and Saudi Arabia, the BIT negotiations are reflective of Hong Kong's keen interest in deepening ties with economies within the Gulf Cooperation Council (GCC), a region burgeoning with investment potential and economic opportunities, particularly in areas such as financial services, infrastructure and innovation. As for Bangladesh, the BIT represents a significant move towards engaging with emerging markets in South Asia, recognising the region's escalating role in global economic dynamics and the consequential investment prospects. The strategic diversification of Hong Kong's economic partnerships through these BITs and FTAs is indicative of an adaptive policy stance.

In conclusion, Hong Kong's approach to IIAs demonstrates the importance of establishing a robust legal framework for foreign investment and the

[14] See also John Lee thanks Singapore's prime minister for support of Hong Kong's participation in RCEP, The Standard, 24 July 2023. Available at: www.thestandard.com.hk/breaking-news/section/4/206296/John-Lee-thanks-Singapore's-prime-minister-for-support-of-Hong-Kong's-participation-in-RCEP; CE expresses optimism about joining RCEP, RTHK, 28 July 2023. Available at: https://news.rthk.hk/rthk/en/component/k2/1711080-20230728.htm.

[15] Chief Executive John Lee, Speech at International Forum on 'Leading in a Time of Transition', Hong Kong Government Press Releases, 2 November 2023. Available at: www.info.gov.hk/gia/general/202311/02/P2023110200265p.htm. See also 'SAR to boost cooperation with RCEP members: Chief Executive John Lee', RTHK, 2 November 2023. Available at: https://news.rthk.hk/rthk/en/component/k2/1726142-20231102.htm.

ongoing development of such agreements. By actively signing IIAs and engaging in negotiations with key trading partners, Hong Kong attests its dedication to protecting foreign investors and strengthening its position as an international trade and investment hub. Furthermore, the continuity of Hong Kong's pre-1997 IIAs with the Chinese Government's endorsement highlights the significance of maintaining and enhancing the legal framework for foreign investment in the region and beyond.

III. THE THREE GENERATIONS OF HONG KONG INTERNATIONAL INVESTMENT AGREEMENTS

The development and transformation of Hong Kong's IIAs can be studied over three successive generations, each reflecting the territory's changing economic and political landscape as well as its strategic approach towards foreign investment. From its initial BITs signed prior to 1997 to the more recent IIAs reflecting diverse treaty partners and updated provisions, Hong Kong's IIA practice showcases its adaptability and commitment to fostering a conducive environment for investment. In this section, we will explore the three generations of Hong Kong's IIAs, highlighting their key features, the context in which they were signed and their implications for Hong Kong's position as an international financial centre.

The first BIT of Hong Kong was signed with the United Kingdom in 1998, immediately following the handover. A Hong Kong–US BIT was expected to come into effect from 30 June 1997, but negotiations were never concluded. Between 1998 and 2005, Hong Kong did not sign any BITs. The most recent IIAs signed by Hong Kong were with ASEAN (2017), Australia, Mexico and the United Arab Emirates. Three categories may be used to classify these IIAs (see Table 6.1: those signed before 1997, those inked between 1998 and 2010 and those signed after 2016 to the present.

Table 6.1 presents a classification of Hong Kong's IIAs into three distinct groups, which provide a comprehensive overview of the evolution and geographical distribution of Hong Kong's investment treaty network.

As evident from the Table 6.1, Group 1 consists of Hong Kong's early IIAs, signed between 1992 and 1997, primarily with developed countries in Europe, Asia and Australasia. These agreements involve prominent trading partners such as Japan, Korea, Austria, the Belgium-Luxembourg Economic Union (BLEU), Germany, France, Italy, New Zealand, Switzerland, Sweden, Denmark, Australia and the Netherlands. These initial IIAs were instrumental in establishing Hong Kong's reputation as a trustworthy and appealing destination for foreign investments, laying the groundwork for its IIA framework.

Group 2 represents a transitional period in Hong Kong's IIA strategy. The agreements signed between 2009 and 2010 encompassed a more geographically diverse array of countries. This group includes the Hong Kong–Finland Bilateral Investment Treaty (BIT) and the Hong Kong–Thailand BIT, highlighting Hong

Table 6.1 The three groups of Hong Kong's IIAs

Group 1	*Group 2*	*Group 3*
• Hong Kong– Korea, Republic of BIT (1997) • Hong Kong–Japan BIT (1997) • Hong Kong–Austria BIT (1996) • Hong Kong–BLEU (Belgium-Luxembourg Economic Union) – BIT (1996) • Hong Kong–Germany – BIT (1996) • Hong Kong–France – BIT (1995) • Hong Kong–Italy BIT (1995) • Hong Kong–New Zealand BIT (1995) • Hong Kong–Switzerland BIT (1994) • Hong Kong–Sweden BIT (1994) • Hong Kong–Denmark BIT (1994) • Hong Kong–Australia BIT (1993) • Hong Kong–Netherlands BIT (1992)	• Hong Kong– Finland BIT (2009) • Hong Kong–Thailand (BIT) 2005 • Hong Kong–United Kingdom (BIT) (1998)	• Hong Kong–Mexico BIT (2020) • Hong Kong–United Arab Emirates BIT (2019) • Hong Kong–Australia – Investment Agreement (2019) • Hong Kong–ASEAN • Investment Agreement (2017) • Hong Kong–China – CEPA Investment Agreement (2017) • Hong Kong–Chile BIT (2016) • Hong Kong–Canada BIT (2016) • Hong Kong–Kuwait BIT (2010)

Source: Elaborated by the author from various public sources (UNCTAD, Hong Kong Government and Investor-State Law Guide).

Kong's growing focus on European and Southeast Asian markets. These agreements indicate Hong Kong's determination to diversify its investment treaty network and forge new partnerships with countries beyond its traditional sphere of influence.

Group 3 showcases Hong Kong's most recent IIAs, signed between 2010 and 2020, incorporating both developed and developing countries across Asia, North and South America and the Middle East. Noteworthy agreements in this group comprise the Hong Kong–Mexico BIT, Hong Kong–United Arab Emirates BIT, Hong Kong–Australia Investment Agreement, Hong Kong–ASEAN Investment Agreement, Hong Kong–China CEPA Investment Agreement, Hong Kong–Chile

BIT, Hong Kong–Canada BIT and Hong Kong–Kuwait BIT. This group demonstrates Hong Kong's ongoing efforts to fortify and diversify its investment treaty network while also enhancing its integration with regional partners, particularly within the ASEAN region and Mainland China.

In summary, the three groups of Hong Kong's IIAs exhibit a strategic evolution in its investment treaty landscape. This classification highlights the territory's progression from primarily partnering with developed countries to broadening its network to include a more diverse range of nations, reflecting Hong Kong's unwavering commitment to fostering a robust and varied investment environment.

Prior to 1 July 1997, all agreements were strictly governed by the Hong Kong Model Agreement. The inaugural treaty that Hong Kong signed with Netherlands marked a significant departure from standard treaty models of the time.[16] It was pioneering in instituting explicit temporal boundaries within the arbitration process, thereby injecting a degree of predictability and efficiency into proceedings that was uncommon at the time. Notably, it eschewed the incorporation of reciprocal arrangements concerning most-favoured-nation (MFN) and national treatment clauses, delineating a bold approach to the bilateral investment treaty framework. Moreover, the Hong Kong – Netherlands BIT (1992) introduced an innovative methodology for calculating compensation in the event of expropriation, transcending traditional market-based assessments. This method integrated equitable principles that accounted for a spectrum of economic factors, including the initial capital investment, accumulated depreciation, any profits already repatriated, the replacement value of the investment, prevailing currency exchange rates, and other relevant economic indicators. This comprehensive valuation paradigm set a precedent for ensuring compensation that reflected the genuine economic value of the investment, rather than just its market price at a specific point in time. The first IIA that Hong Kong signed was with the Netherlands in 1992 and it was seen as exceptional since it was the first BIT to include specific time restrictions for the conduct of arbitral proceedings and because it removed reciprocal agreements with other nations from most-favourable-nation treatment (MFN) and national treatment. Additionally, it presented a fresh idea for determining compensation: equitable principles taking into account the capital invested, depreciation, capital previously repatriated, replacement value, currency exchange rates and other important considerations.[17] Additionally, it presented a fresh idea for determining compensation: equitable principles taking into account the capital invested, depreciation, capital previously repatriated, replacement value, currency exchange rates and other important considerations.

[16] Agreement on the Encouragement and Protection of Investments Between the Government of Hong Kong and the Government of the Kingdom of the Netherlands (signed 19 November 1992).

[17] Elihu Lauterpacht, 'International Law and Private Foreign Investment' (1997) 4 *Indiana Journal of Global Legal Studies* 259, 269.

The model used for the first eleven BITs that Hong Kong signed is largely consistent. The preambles of these agreements declare that the BIT is concluded under the authority of the sovereign government, which oversees its foreign affairs, signalling Hong Kong's move towards sovereignty.[18] These agreements define 'investments' broadly based on assets,[19] designate investors as residents of Hong Kong[20] and usually adhere to European models for conventional treatment and protection norms. In its BITs, Hong Kong often refers itself to an 'area' rather than a 'territory'. The ISDS clauses, in contrast to the large majority of IIAs signed by governments, stipulate that the investor is allowed to make an arbitration claim in accordance with UNCITRAL arbitration procedures 'if parties are not able to agree upon a dispute forum within 6 months'.[21] The majority of these agreements have a 15- or 20-year term.[22]

Post-1997, BITs involving Hong Kong, starting with the Hong Kong–UK BIT of 1998, required explicit approval from China and necessitated signature by the HKSAR Government.[23] These initial agreements, spanning from 1998 to 2005, exhibit only subtle departures from the Hong Kong Model Agreement. Notably, the Hong Kong–UK BIT (1998) expressly excludes individuals with dual citizenship from its application. Additionally, there is a consistent preference for UNCITRAL arbitration across these treaties, coupled with a three-month cooling-off period.[24] In essence, the early phase of treaty negotiations post-handover is characterised by a cautious and traditional adherence to the established BIT model, underscoring a conservative approach in Hong Kong's investment treaty strategy.

In recent years, Hong Kong has recalibrated its approach to international investment agreements, transitioning from its traditional BIT model to embrace

[18] Hong Kong–Netherlands (1992) BIT; Hong Kong–Denmark (1994) BIT; Hong Kong Sweden BIT (1994); Hong Kong–New Zealand BIT (1995).

[19] Hong Kong–Sweden BIT (1994), art 1(3).

[20] Hong Kong–Denmark BIT, art 1(2); Hong Kong–Sweden BIT (1994), art 1(2).

[21] Hong Kong–Netherlands BIT (1992), art 10; Hong Kong–Sweden BIT (1994), art 9; Hong Kong Italy BIT (1995), art 10; Hong Kong–Korea BIT (1996), art 9(3); Hong Kong Thailand BIT (2005), art 8.

[22] Hong Kong–France BIT (1995), art 14(1); Hong Kong–Kuwait BIT (2010), art 12.

[23] Agreement between the Government of the Hong Kong Special Administrative Region of the People's Republic of China and the Government of the United Kingdom of Great Britain and Northern Ireland for the Promotion and Protection of Investments (signed 30 July 1998).

[24] As an illustrative example, the Hong Kong–Korea BIT (1997) embodies Hong Kong's procedural preferences within its international investment agreements. Specifically, Article 9(3) of this treaty highlights a structured approach to dispute resolution, mandating recourse to UNCITRAL arbitration if disputes are not amicably settled within a six-month period after the written notification of the dispute. This period emphasises the initial pursuit of a negotiated settlement before arbitration is considered. If no alternative dispute resolution mechanism is agreed upon within this timeframe, the parties are compelled to engage in arbitration under the prevailing UNCITRAL Rules. This approach, which is a consistent feature in Hong Kong's treaties, underlines a procedural framework designed to foster dialogue before formal arbitration and to ensure that the resulting arbitration awards are final and binding, as affirmed by Article 9(4), thus upholding the principles of finality and enforceability in international investment law. See Agreement between the Government of Hong Kong and the Government of the Republic of Korea for the Promotion and Protection of Investments (signed 30 June 1997).

more contemporary practices that reflect a keen sensitivity to the changing dynamics of global trade and investment. This shift, while indicative of an adaptation to the multifaceted needs of Hong Kong's diverse array of treaty partners, continues to uphold the distinct legal character that has long been a hallmark of the region's investment landscape.

A critical aspect of these adaptations is the definition of Hong Kong investors as permanent residents.[25] This legal characterisation has significant implications for the scope of protection afforded under the IIAs. It potentially widens the field of who can claim investor status, thus offering a broader protective net for individuals domiciled in Hong Kong, who might not otherwise qualify under the corporate-centric definitions prevalent in many BITs.

The evolution of the definition of 'investment' in these treaties, underscored by the inclusion of the 'Salini test', not only reflects a deliberate alignment with the prevailing standards of investment treaty regimes but also signifies Hong Kong's intent to prioritise investments with substantive economic contributions over purely financial claims.[26] The exclusion of mere monetary claims from the definition of investments curtails the propensity for speculative and non-substantive claims to clutter the dispute resolution process, thus sharpening the focus on genuine, value-adding economic activities.

At the vanguard of legal innovation in international investment law is the Hong Kong–Canada BIT (2016), which boldly expands the notion of investment to encompass financial instruments such as loans and debt securities.[27] By setting forth a clear delineation of what constitutes a financial institution, Hong Kong not only bridges the traditional divide between finance and investment law

[25] For instance, Agreement between the Government of the Hong Kong Special Administrative Region of the People's Republic of China and the Government of the United Mexican States for the Promotion and Reciprocal Protection of Investments (23 January 2020). In this treaty, '"investor" means: (a) in respect of the HKSAR: (i) a natural person of the HKSAR; or (ii) an enterprise constituted or organised under the laws and regulations of the HKSAR and engaged in substantive business operations in the area of the HKSAR.'

[26] The definition of investment in the Hong Kong – United Arab Emirates (UAE) BIT (2019) encompasses a broad spectrum of assets, resonating with the substantial capital contribution aspect of the Salini test. (See Agreement between the Government of the Hong Kong Special Administrative Region of the People's Republic of China and the Government of the United Arab Emirates for the Promotion and Reciprocal Protection of Investments (signed 16 June 2019). The Hong Kong–UAE BIT specifies various forms of investment, from tangible property to intellectual rights and business concessions, underscoring the diverse nature of assets that entail economic commitment, akin to the Salini criterion on the substantiality and duration of the investment. Claims to money or performance with a financial value associated with an investment align with the Salini risk element, indicating a requisite financial exposure inherent in the assets. By excluding certain claims related to commercial transactions and trade financing, the definition tacitly differentiates between regular commercial operations and substantial investments, paralleling the Salini emphasis on investments that contribute beyond mere financial transactions. Lastly, while not explicit, the requirement for investments to comply with local laws suggests a contribution to the host state's economic order, indirectly nodding to the Salini test's economic development factor.

[27] Agreement Between the Government of Canada and the Government of the Hong Kong Special Administrative Region of the People's Republic of China for the Promotion and Protection of Investments (signed 10 February 2016) art 1.

but also anticipates the increasingly pivotal role that financial services are poised to play in investment flows.

The recalibration of compensation standards, mandating the reflection of the "real value" in cases of expropriation, is a testament to Hong Kong's commitment to maintaining an equitable investment climate.[28] This approach prioritises a comprehensive and equitable assessment, including factors such as invested capital, depreciation, and market conditions, to ascertain the true financial loss to the investor. Moreover, it affords investors legal recourse for review of the valuation, embedding a layer of protection and due process within the investment framework.

The deliberate exclusion of ISDS from MFN clauses in these recent treaties represents a nuanced understanding of the intricate balance between investor protection and sovereign autonomy.[29] By circumscribing the application of MFN to ISDS, Hong Kong is seen to be responding prudently to the growing international apprehension about the expansive interpretation of MFN clauses, which have previously led to unintended extensions of treaty obligations.

The Hong Kong–Australia Investment Agreement (2019) emerges as a paradigmatic shift in investment treaty design, decisively adopting stringent FET standards that resist the trend towards expansive investor rights as it conspicuously recalibrates the framework of investor protection by embedding a constrained interpretation of FET standards, consciously aligned with the customary international law minimum standard of treatment of aliens.[30] This circumscribed application delineates the FET provision to avert any extension beyond the baseline of international law, effectively circumscribing the proliferation of investor rights that has been prevalent in contemporary investment treaty practice. By tethering the FET obligation to the well-established tenets of customary international law and eschewing any supplementary or augmented

[28] See, eg, Hong Kong–United Arab Emirates (UAE) BIT (2019) art 6: 'Such compensation shall amount to the real value of the expropriated investment immediately before the expropriation or before the impending expropriation became public knowledge whichever is the earlier. Where the real value cannot be readily ascertained, the compensation shall be determined in accordance with generally recognised principles of valuation and equitable principles taking into account the capital invested, depreciation, capital already repatriated, replacement value, currency exchange rate movements and other relevant factors. Compensation shall include interest at a normal commercial rate from the date of expropriation until the date of payment, shall be made without undue delay, be effectively realisable and be freely convertible. The investor affected shall have a right, under the law of the Contracting Party making the expropriation, to prompt review by a judicial or other independent authority of that Contracting Party, of the investor's case and of the valuation of the investment in accordance with the principles set out in this paragraph.'

[29] See, eg, Investment Agreement between the Government of the Hong Kong Special Administrative Region of the People's Republic of China and the Government of the Republic of Chile (signed 18 November 2016) art 5(3): 'For greater certainty, the treatment referred to in this Article does not encompass any dispute resolution mechanisms, such as those in Section C (Settlement of Disputes between an Investor and the Host Party).'

[30] Investment Agreement between the Government of Australia and the Government of the Hong Kong Special Administrative Region of the People's Republic of China (signed 26 March 2019) art 8.

entitlements, the agreement enshrines a stringent threshold for state liability. This approach signals a deliberate pivot from prior expansive interpretations that often-left regulatory authorities in a straitjacket of legal uncertainty. The agreement's articulation of the 'due process' principle as a constituent of FET and the requirement of 'police protection' as part of the full protection and security obligation underscore a commitment to due process and the rule of law, all the while preserving the state's sovereign right to regulate. Moreover, the stipulation that inconsistencies with an investor's expectations do not inherently constitute a treaty breach underlines a resistance to the subjective interpretative trends that have, in other contexts, led to expansive readings of investment protections.

With respect to dispute resolution, Hong Kong's preference for UNCITRAL arbitration over ICSID manifests a strategic maneuver towards procedural adaptability and more expansive enforcement under the auspices of the New York Convention.[31] This calculated move, likely influenced by the relative procedural autonomy offered by UNCITRAL rules, positions Hong Kong favourably within the international arbitration community, ensuring that the enforcement of awards remains robust and universally respected.

Finally, the incorporation of 'fork-in-the-road' provisions, which compel investors to choose between domestic remedies and international arbitration irreversibly, is a strategic insertion that aims to mitigate the risk of parallel proceedings and reinforces the primacy of domestic legal remedies. The Hong Kong–Mexico BIT (2020) exhibits a strategic approach to treaty crafting, exemplified by its condition that investors must forgo (not 'waive' in the sense of giving up a known right, but rather 'agree not to pursue') the initiation or continuation of domestic legal proceedings if opting for arbitration. This 'fork-in-the-road' provision obliges an irrevocable decision to pursue either domestic remedies or international arbitration, thus preventing concurrent proceedings on the same matter and safeguarding against the risks of conflicting judgments.[32]

The recent updates to Hong Kong's IIAs showcase a nuanced approach to international investment law. Procedurally, they lean towards a more adaptable arbitration system, preferring UNCITRAL rules to the more rigid ICSID, enhancing enforcement under the New York Convention. Substantively, they refine the scope of investment and investor status, aligning fair and equitable

[31] Article 16 of Hong Kong–Mexico BIT (2019) explicitly offers investors the option to submit claims under the UNCITRAL Arbitration Rules, underscoring Hong Kong's commitment to procedural flexibility and the enforcement benefits that stem from adherence to the New York Convention. The inclusion of alternative arbitration rules, subject to the agreement of disputing parties as per Article 16(3)(b), further accentuates this flexibility, while the stipulation that the chosen rules govern the arbitration, except as modified by the agreement itself in art 16(4), allows for tailored dispute resolution mechanisms.

[32] This not only preserves the integrity of the domestic judicial system by preventing forum shopping but also upholds the principle of finality and respects the parties' commitment to the chosen dispute resolution mechanism, as per art18(4), which requires a written and delivered consent to the dispute settlement process.

treatment with international norms. The introduction of 'fork-in-the-road' provisions represents a commitment to decisiveness in dispute resolution, deterring duplicative proceedings and upholding the primacy of chosen legal forums. Collectively, these innovations demonstrate Hong Kong's forward-looking strategy in balancing robust investment protection with respect for the regulatory framework within its unique constitutional setup.

To bridge the historical context with the contemporary landscape, it is instructive to analyse the transformative trajectory of Hong Kong's IIAs. This evolution reflects a strategic adaptation from its pre-1997 position as a British colony, where it laid the groundwork for a novel approach to treaty practice, to its current status under 'One Country, Two Systems'. It was suggested ten years ago that Hong Kong's IIA practice was a notable accomplishment in external autonomy and a crucial turning point in the history of BITs and international law.[33] This argument's foundation was that, in a unique historical setting, Hong Kong had established what was thought to be a novel and successful model of treaty practice, setting the stage for state succession to IIAs.[34] In fact, the shift in Hong Kong's treaty practice is not merely a chronological progression but a response to its burgeoning role as a global financial hub. The emphasis on aligning IIAs with international finance norms speaks volumes about Hong Kong's proactive measures in external autonomy and indicates a sophisticated calibration of its legal and economic instruments. This calibration ensures that its IIAs not only align with, but also actively shape, the contours of modern international investment law, reinforcing Hong Kong's position in the global financial order.

Furthermore, the past decade has brought into sharp focus the efficacy of Hong Kong's IIA framework amidst changing geopolitical and economic conditions. The litmus test for Hong Kong's innovative treaty practice is its application in resolving investment disputes. The next chapter will scrutinise Hong Kong's IIAs within the crucible of these disputes, discussing further the success and adaptability of its treaty practice over time.

[33] Sally Lord Ellis and Laura Shea, 'Foreign Commercial Dispute Settlement in the People's Republic of China' (1980) 6 *International Trade Law Journal* 155, 172.

[34] Kun Fan, 'Mediation of Investor–State Disputes: A Treaty Survey' (2020) 2 *Journal of Dispute Resolution* 327.

7

Navigating Bilateral Tax Relations: Hong Kong's Tax Treaty Landscape

Hong Kong, as a thriving international financial centre, occupies a unique position in the global economy. The territory's economic success can be attributed to its strategic geographical location, openness to trade and robust legal framework, including its tax system. A key aspect of Hong Kong's tax policy is the negotiation and implementation of bilateral tax treaties, which play a pivotal role in fostering cross-border investment and trade. This chapter discusses the intricacies of Hong Kong's tax treaty landscape and its implications for the territory's bilateral tax relations.

For several reasons, Hong Kong's bilateral tax policy is of paramount importance in the broader context of trade and investment bilateral relations. Firstly, as an international financial hub, Hong Kong plays a critical role in facilitating cross-border transactions, which necessitates a stable and transparent tax environment. By negotiating and implementing bilateral tax treaties, Hong Kong not only mitigates the risk of double taxation for businesses and investors, but also fosters a climate of legal certainty and predictability which, in turn, enhances its attractiveness as a destination for global investment and commerce.

Secondly, Hong Kong's unique position as a Special Administrative Region (SAR) of China gives it a high degree of autonomy in formulating its tax policies. Consequently, the territory can maintain a separate tax treaty network from Mainland China, which enables it to cater to the specific needs of its economy and investors, while also complementing China's broader tax treaty objectives. This distinctive tax policy landscape amplifies Hong Kong's strategic importance in the global arena; not only does it serve as a bridge between Mainland China and the rest of the world, but it also reinforces the territory's role as a key player in the international economic system.

Finally, Hong Kong's bilateral tax policy is unique and significant from a global perspective, as it reflects the territory's commitment to upholding international tax standards, such as those proposed by the Organization for Economic Cooperation and Development (OECD) and the G20. By actively participating in global tax initiatives and incorporating key provisions in its tax treaties, Hong Kong demonstrates its dedication to fostering a fair, transparent and cooperative global tax environment, which, in turn, bolsters its reputation as a responsible and trusted international financial centre.

The primary objective of this chapter is to provide a comprehensive overview of Hong Kong's bilateral tax relations through the lens of its tax treaty network. In doing so, the chapter aims to illuminate the various ways in which tax treaties contribute to the territory's economic policy and international relations and assesses the challenges and opportunities that may arise in this context. This analysis is situated within the broader framework of the book, which seeks to explore Hong Kong's engagement in international economic matters, including trade, investment and taxation.

The chapter is structured as follows. Firstly, it provides an overview of the fundamental principles and rationale behind double taxation avoidance agreements (DTAAs), emphasising their significance for Hong Kong's economic policy and international relations. Secondly, it presents a detailed analysis of Hong Kong's tax treaty network, discussing both comprehensive and limited scope agreements and highlighting the distinctive features of these treaties. Thirdly, it evaluates the impact of Hong Kong's tax treaty network on the territory's investment and trade, as well as the potential consequences for its tax revenues and fiscal autonomy. The chapter concludes with a forward-looking assessment of Hong Kong's tax treaty landscape, identifying potential areas for growth and improvement and noting the future challenges that the territory may face in navigating the complex web of bilateral tax relations.

I. TAXATION AS A PILLAR OF HONG KONG'S INTERNATIONAL ECONOMIC POLICY

Double Taxation Avoidance Agreements (DTAAs) are international treaties between two countries designed to prevent the occurrence of double taxation on the same income, profits, or gains. Double taxation arises when the same income, profits, or gains are subject to tax in both the taxpayer's jurisdiction of residence and the source country where the income, profits, or gains are generated. DTAAs play a vital role in promoting international trade and investment by minimising the tax burden and providing certainty for taxpayers.

The primary objectives of DTAAs are threefold:

- *Allocation of taxing rights*: DTAAs establish rules to determine which jurisdiction has the right to tax specific types of income, profits, or gains. Generally, taxing rights are allocated based on the residence of the taxpayer, the source of income, or a combination of both. The agreements typically allocate exclusive taxing rights to one jurisdiction or provide for a limited right to tax in the source country, with the taxpayer's country of residence granting a tax credit or exemption to prevent double taxation.
- *Reduction of withholding tax rates*: DTAAs often provide for reduced withholding tax rates on dividends, interest and royalties paid by a resident of one jurisdiction to a resident of the other jurisdiction. These reduced

rates facilitate cross-border investment and minimise the tax burden on investors.

- *Exchange of information and assistance in tax collection*: DTAAs facilitate cooperation between tax authorities of the contracting countries by providing for the exchange of information relevant to the enforcement of domestic tax laws. This cooperation helps combat tax evasion and improve tax compliance. Additionally, some DTAAs include provisions for mutual assistance in tax collection, allowing one jurisdiction to request assistance from the other in collecting tax debts.

DTAAs are based on internationally recognised principles and models, such as the Organisation for Economic Co-operation and Development (OECD) Model Tax Convention and the United Nations Model Double Taxation Convention. These models serve as a basis for negotiation and provide guidance on the allocation of taxing rights, methods for eliminating double taxation and other key aspects of tax treaties.

In summary, DTAAs play a crucial role in fostering international trade and investment by eliminating or reducing the tax burden associated with cross-border transactions. They allocate taxing rights between countries, reduce withholding tax rates and facilitate cooperation between tax authorities, ensuring a more predictable and transparent tax environment for businesses and individuals engaged in international economic activities.

Hong Kong concluded its first DTAA with Mainland China in 1998.[1] Since then it has concluded a total of 55.[2] Each DTAA can vary based on certain aspects such as the contracting party's state of development and various protocols.[3] The Double Taxation Avoidance Agreement (DTAA) refers to the tax treaty signed by two or more nations to avoid paying double taxes by the taxpayers on the same income. When a person lives in one jurisdiction but earns their living in another, a DTAA is applicable.

These agreements play a crucial role in empowering trade and commerce in a globalised world.[4] They reduce uncertainty in taxation regimes by providing

[1] Julien Chaisse and Xueliang Ji, 'Rethinking Hong Kong's Tax Agreements: Challenges of Transparency, Harmonisation and Global Tax Reform' (2021) 51 *Hong Kong Law Journal* 405.

[2] The prime intent behind DTAAs seems to attract investors and make a nation a favourite destination for investors. DTAAs can provide relief in two ways: Bilateral treaties and unilateral relief. Under bilateral treaties, relief can be granted by either taxation method where income is taxed only in one country, or by providing tax credit in which an individual is required to pay taxes in both countries but the country of which the taxpayer is a resident, provides some sort of relief. Under unilateral relief, where there is no mutual agreement between nations, the relaxation is provided by the home nation.

[3] Julien Chaisse and Xueliang Ji, 'Rethinking Hong Kong's Tax Agreements: Challenges of Transparency, Harmonisation and Global Tax Reform' (2021) 51 *Hong Kong Law Journal* 405.

[4] 'The rapid expansion of Hong Kong's double tax agreement network is likely to create tax planning opportunities for global corporations with operations across Asia. Hong Kong is now a signatory of 17 DTAs, the most recent being the November finalisation of a DTA with Japan and the December finalisation of one with New Zealand. Although Singapore, with an extensive

clear and specific regulations. DTAAs can be comprehensive and tax income from all sources, or they can be specific and tax only revenue from select sources, eg shipping, inheritance and air travel. DTAAs are advantageous to taxpayers and establish a sound ground for economic development. They enable people to expand their income sources without worrying about being taxed more than once.

II. HONG KONG'S TAX TREATY NETWORK: A LEGAL OVERVIEW

This section provides an overview of domestic tax policy, referring to national concepts and policies that are used as a starting point for negotiating tax treaties. It includes brief and general comments on the specified issues, as well as a full description of developments on each OECD Model Convention item.

Hong Kong did not participate in any DTAs prior to 1998, but the number of DTAs it has signed has increased significantly since 2010.[5] Initially, information disclosure was prohibited in the DTA.[6] However, in 2009, the OECD Exchange of Information Article was allowed to be incorporated in HK DTA negotiations.[7]

The HK tax system is based on UK tax legislation, therefore HK only taxes income that 'arises or generated from Hong Kong'.[8] Some states' eagerness to negotiate DTAs with Hong Kong may be influenced by different national ideas and policies. In certain nations, such as Australia, tax income accounts for a larger share of the gross domestic product (GDP).[9]

The evolving conditions of various Contracting States may have an impact on DTA clauses. Mandatory binding arbitration, for example, is only incorporated in a few Hong Kong DTAs.[10] 'If the beneficial owner of the royalties is a resident

network of more than 60 treaties, is generally considered the most desirable holding company jurisdiction in Asia, Hong Kong is quickly mounting a serious challenge to Singapore's pre-eminence in this regard', P Previtera, B Boyle and M Kent, 'Optimizing Asian Operations through Hong Kong's Double Tax Agreement Network' (2011) 61 *Tax Notes International* 859.

[5] Nolan Cormac Sharkey and Kathrin Bain, 'An Australia–Hong Kong Double Tax Agreement: Assessing the Costs and Benefits' (2011) 9 *eJournal of Tax Research* 269.

[6] ibid.

[7] John Tsang, *Budget Speech by the Financial Secretary* (Speech delivered to the Legislative Council, Hong Kong). Available at: www.info.gov.hk/gia/general/200902/25/P200902250108.htm, accessed 28 September 2023

[8] Ayesha MacPherson and Garry Laird, *Hong Kong Taxation Law and Practice* (Hong Kong, The Chinese University of Hong Kong Press, 2010), p 13. See Inland Revenue Ordinance 1947 (No 20 of 1947) ss 5 (Property Tax), 8 (Salaries Tax) and 14 (Profits Tax).

[9] The Heritage Foundation, '2011 Index of Economic Freedom – Hong Kong', Available at: www.heritage.org/index/Country/HongKong, accessed 28 September 2023.

[10] See Julien Chaisse 'Making Tax Dispute Resolution Mechanisms More Effective – The Base Erosion and Profit Shifting Project and Beyond' (2017) 10 Contemporary Asia Arbitration Journal 1; Xueliang Ji, 'The Changing Paradigm of International Tax Dispute Settlement: What Are the Promises and Challenges of Mandatory Arbitration for China?' (2020) 21 *Oregon Review of International Law* 134.

of the other Contracting Party, the tax shall not exceed a certain percentage of the gross amount of the royalties.'[11] In comparison to Mexico, the figure is 10 per cent, whereas in comparison to the UK, it is 3 per cent.[12] Mandatory binding arbitration is only included in few Hong Kong DTAs.[13] The distinction between 'developed' and 'developing' may not be totally relevant in understanding the causes of variances in Hong Kong DTAs. Protocols have altered the article over the years.[14] For example, Hong Kong signed a DTA with Austria in 2010 and a new protocol in 2014.[15]

Protocols have been used to make additional changes to the DTA agreed between Hong Kong and New Zealand.[16] The agreement states that Article 8 of the Agreement will apply to international air traffic on the day the Agreement enters into force.[17] The second paragraph clearly defines the scope of competent authority while the third paragraph defines implementation of pension benefit clause. In relation to paragraph 4, automatic information exchange is not necessary. With regard to Article 24, the New Zealand competent authority may provide material to the Office of the Ombudsman in the investigation of complaints against the New Zealand Inland Revenue Department's administrative activities.[18] Further it states that protocol is integral part and stipulates when enters into force.

As of 2023, the DTA signed between Hong Kong and Mainland China has already gone through five protocols. The phrase 'penalty or interest' in paragraph 2 of Article 3 of the First Protocol has been clarified in Article 1 of the First Protocol.[19] The phrases 'assets' and 'primarily' of paragraph 4 of Article 13 are defined in full in Article 2 of the First Protocol.[20] Article 3 of the First

[11] The number is based on the specific requirement in different DTAs.

[12] HK–Mexico double tax agreement (2012), art 12, para 2; HK–UK double tax agreement (2010), art 12, para 2.

[13] HK–Italy double tax agreement (2013), art 24, para 5; HK–Jersey double tax agreement (2013), art 23, para 5; HK–Liechtenstein double tax agreement (2011), art 24, para 5; HK–Canada double tax agreement (2013), art 23, para 6; HK–Netherlands double tax agreement (2010), art 24, para 5; HK–Guernsey double tax agreement (2013), art 23, para 5; HK–Switzerland double tax agreement (2012), art 24, para 5; HK–Japan double tax agreement (2015), art 24, para 5; HK–Pakistan double tax agreement (2017), art 25, para 5.

[14] HK–Pakistan double tax agreement (2017), art 25, para 5; HK–Canada double tax agreement (2013), art 23, para 6.

[15] HK–Austria double tax agreement (2010); HK–Austria double tax agreement (Second Protocol) (2014).

[16] Paragraphs 1 to 4 of the Protocol to the Agreement between the Government of the Hong Kong Special Administrative Region of the People's Republic of China and the Government of New Zealand for the Avoidance of Double Taxation and the Prevention of Fiscal Evasion with Respect to Taxes on Income.

[17] ibid para 1 of the Protocol to the Agreement.

[18] HK–New Zealand double tax agreement (Second Protocol) (2017), para 1.

[19] Paragraph 1 of the Protocol to the Arrangement between the Mainland of China and the Hong Kong Special Administrative Region for the Avoidance of Double Taxation and the Prevention of Fiscal Evasion with Respect to Taxes on Income; HK–Mainland China double tax arrangement (2006), art 3, para 2.

[20] Paragraph 2 of the Protocol to the Arrangement between the Mainland of China and the Hong Kong Special Administrative Region for the Avoidance of Double Taxation and the Prevention

Protocol refers to consent of the parties exchanging information[21] and of the Second Protocol, '6 months' in subparagraph (2) to paragraph 3 of Article 5 of the Arrangement has been replaced with '183 days'.[22] The previous phrase defining 'foreign investment enterprises income tax' has been replaced by 'enterprise income tax'.[23] The 'place of establishment' in Article 2 of the Second Protocol has replaced the 'place of head office' in sub-paragraph (1) of paragraph 1 of Article 4 of the prior Arrangement.[24] According to Article 4 of the Second Protocol, 'not less than 50% of the assets of the company must consist of immovable property at any time within the three years prior to the alienation of the shares of the company by the holder of the shares' while applying paragraph 4 of Article 13 of the Arrangement.[25]

In Article 5 of the Second Protocol, paragraph 5 of Article 13 of the Arrangement has been replaced by the following sentence:

> Gains obtained by a resident of One Side from the marginalisation of shares, other than the shares referred to in paragraph 4, or other rights in the capital of a company that is a resident of the Other Side may be taxed in that Other Side if the recipient of the gains had a participation, directly or indirectly, in not less than 25% of the capital of the company at any time within the 12 months preceding the alienation.[26]

In Article 1 of the Third Protocol, Article 24 of the Arrangement has been substituted and changed as Article 1 does not now prohibit one side from communicating with the other side on taxes covered by this Arrangement. Any information collected under paragraph 1 by One Side shall be treated as confidential in the same manner as information gained under that side's domestic legislation. Information will only be shared with persons or authorities (including courts and administrative bodies) involved in the assessment or collection of, enforcement or prosecution of, or resolution of appeals concerning the taxes mentioned in paragraph 1. In no event shall the provisions of paragraphs 1 and 2 be understood to impose the responsibility on One Side.

The limits of paragraph 3 apply to the requirement stated in the preceding sentence. No information shall be withheld by One Side solely because it is held by a bank, another financial institution, nominee, or person acting in a fiduciary capacity, or because it relates to ownership interests in a person, under any circumstances shall such limitations be construed as allowing One Side to

of Fiscal Evasion with Respect to Taxes on Income; HK–Mainland China double tax arrangement (2006), art 13, para 4.

[21] Paragraph 3 of the Protocol to the Arrangement between the Mainland of China and the Hong Kong Special Administrative Region for the Avoidance of Double Taxation and the Prevention of Fiscal Evasion with Respect to Taxes on Income; HK–Mainland China double tax arrangement (2006), art 24, para 1

[22] HK–Mainland China double tax arrangement (2006), art 5, para 3, sub-para (2); HK–Mainland China double tax arrangement (Second Protocol) (2008), art 3.

[23] ibid art 2, para 3, sub-para (1)(ii); ibid art 1.

[24] ibid art 4, para 1, sub-para (1); ibid, art 2.

[25] HK–Mainland China double tax arrangement (Second Protocol) (2008), art 4.

[26] ibid art 5.

withhold such information.[27] In Article 1 of the Fourth Protocol, paragraph 1 of Article 8 of the Arrangement has been replaced with the following sentence: 'Income and profits derived by an enterprise of One Side from the operation of ships, aircraft or land transport vehicles in shipping, air and land transport in the Other Side shall be exempt from tax (including value added tax and other similar taxes in the Mainland of China) in that Other Side.'[28]

The tax imposed in paragraph 2 of Article 12 of the Agreement has been described in further detail in connection to Article 1 of the Fourth Protocol. The tax levied 'must not exceed 7% of the gross amount of the royalties', while the tax charged for an aircraft and ship leasing firm 'shall not exceed 5% of the gross amount of the royalties'.[29] The basic need regulated in paragraph 6 of Article 13 of the Arrangement has been replaced with more comprehensive regulation based on Article 3 of the Fourth Protocol, which is primarily concerned with the alienation of stock market shares.[30] A person whose main purpose is to utilise the article by 'the creation or disposition of the interests acquired' should be excluded.[31] With respect to Article 5 more taxes have been added to the scope of information to be transmitted in accordance with Article 5.[32]

The residency of 'a person other than an individual' should be defined by both sides of the Contracting States,[33] according to Article 2 of the Fifth Protocol. If no mutual agreement is reached, 'such individual shall be ineligible for any tax reduction or exemption offered by this Arrangement.'[34] In Article 3 of the Fifth Protocol, paragraphs 5 and 6 of Article 5 of the Arrangement have been substituted in the updated protocol clearly defines the scope of contracts required by this article.[35]

Paragraph 6 of the Agreement has been replaced by the following sentence:

> 'Paragraph 5 is not applicable where the person conducts business in One Side as an independent agent and acts in that One Side in the ordinary course of that business on behalf of an enterprise of the Other Side.[...] Where, on the other hand, a person operates entirely or nearly exclusively on behalf of one or more enterprises to which he or she is closely associated, that person is not considered an independent agent within the meaning of this paragraph with respect to any such enterprise.'[36]

A new paragraph has also been inserted in Article 5 of the Agreement to establish if a person is 'closely tied to an enterprise'.[37] The ensuing expression has

[27] HK–Mainland China double tax arrangement (Third Protocol) (2010), art 1.
[28] HK–Mainland China double tax arrangement (Fourth Protocol) (2015), art 1.
[29] ibid art 2; HK–Mainland China double tax arrangement (2006), art 12, para 2.
[30] HK–Mainland China double tax arrangement (Fourth Protocol) (2015), art 3; HK–Mainland China double tax arrangement (2006), art 13, para 6.
[31] HK–Mainland China double tax arrangement (Fourth Protocol) (2015), art 4.
[32] ibid art 5.
[33] HK–Mainland China double tax arrangement (Fifth Protocol) (2019), art 2.
[34] ibid.
[35] ibid art 3; HK–Mainland China double tax arrangement (2006), art 5, para 5.
[36] HK–Mainland China double tax arrangement (Fifth Protocol) (2019), art 3.
[37] ibid.

been replaced in Article 3 of the Fifth Protocol, paragraph 4 of Article 13 of the Arrangement, Paragraph 2 of the Protocol to the Arrangement and Article 4 of the Second Protocol to the Arrangement: Profits obtained by a resident of One Side through the disposal of shares or similar interests, such as partnership or trust interests, can be subjected to tax in the Other Side if, at any point in the three years preceding the disposal, these shares or similar interests derived more than 50 per cent of their value directly or indirectly from immovable property, as outlined in Article 6, located in that Other Side. Article 14 now features three new provisions addressing tutors and researchers. As per Article 5 of the Fifth Protocol to the Arrangement, remuneration provided by the source state is exempt from taxation in the host state for three years and related income is tax-exempt in both countries. Article 4 of the Fourth Protocol has been eliminated and the Agreement now features 'Article 24A: Eligibility for Benefits'.

In conclusion, the examination of Hong Kong's Double Tax Agreements reveals a nuanced framework, balancing local fiscal interests and compliance with international standards, while also catering to the particular requirements of each contracting party. The distinct variations seen in the Agreements, especially when compared to the OECD Model Convention, showcase the flexibility of Hong Kong's DTAs in responding to global tax dynamics. These discrepancies highlight the evolving nature of international tax regulations and the need for further research and analysis to fully comprehend the implications of such variations. The continued adaption of these Agreements to reflect changing economic and legislative landscapes ensures they remain effective instruments in preventing fiscal evasion, fostering economic cooperation and facilitating cross-border commerce.

III. DISCREPANCIES AND DEVELOPMENTS IN HONG KONG'S DOUBLE TAX AGREEMENTS: A COMPARATIVE ANALYSIS WITH THE OECD MODEL CONVENTION

Despite being largely regarded as a model for tax agreements, the OECD Model Convention is not always followed by Hong Kong's DTAs. Each HK DTA has a unique content due to numerous Contracting Parties and varying signature dates. In addition to examining the HK agreement's compliance with the OECD Model Convention's rules, this section intends to draw attention to specific HK agreement discrepancies.

A. Differential Taxation Policies: Comparative Analysis between the OECD Model Convention and Hong Kong's Double Tax Agreements (DTAs)

The extent of taxes differs from the OECD Model Convention since some HK DTAs do not include penalties or interest levied in accordance with the laws of either Contracting Party.[38] Some of Hong Kong DTAs, like paragraph 4 of Article 2 of the HK–Austria double tax agreement, also place emphasis on taxes that the Contracting Parties may implement in the future.[39]

According to Hong Kong's DTAs, a person may be considered a permanent establishment (PE) of an enterprise if certain criteria are met. If a person acting on behalf of an enterprise does not have independent standing, that person may be considered a PE if they meet the following criteria: (a) routinely keeps a stock of items for the benefit of the business;[40] and (b) routinely obtains orders for the business or its partners.[41]

According to the OECD Model Convention, the income that a resident of a Contracting Party derives from immovable property located in another Contracting Party (including income from agriculture or forestry) is not subject

[38] HK–Czech double tax agreement (2012), art 2, para 5; HK–India double tax agreement (2018), art 2, para 5; HK–New Zealand double tax agreement (2017), art 2, para 5.

[39] HK–Ireland double tax agreement (2010), art 2, para 4; HK–Russia double tax agreement (2016), art 2, para 4; HK–South Africa double tax agreement (2015), art 2, para 4; HK–Korea double tax agreement (2014), art 2, para 4; HK–Netherlands double tax agreement (2010), art 2, para 4; HK–France double tax agreement (2011), art 2, para 4; HK–Luxembourg double tax agreement (2011), art 2, para 4; HK–Japan double tax agreement (2015), art 2, para 4; HK–Switzerland double tax agreement (2012), art 2, para 4; HK–Saudi Arabia double tax agreement (2018), art 2, para 4; HK–Thailand double tax agreement (2005), art 2, para 4; HK–Brunei Darussalam double tax agreement (2010), art 2, para 4; HK–Spain double tax agreement (2012), art 2, para 4; HK–Kuwait double tax agreement (2012), art 2, para 4; HK–Qatar double tax agreement (2013), art 2, para 4; HK–Latvia double tax agreement (2017), art 2, para 4; HK–Liechtenstein double tax agreement (2011), art 2, para 4; HK–Vietnam double tax agreement (2014), art 2, para 4; HK–Jersey double tax agreement (2013), art 2, para 4; HK–Indonesia double tax agreement (2010), art 2, para 4; HK–India double tax agreement (2018), art 2, para 4; HK–Italy double tax agreement (2013), art 2, para 4; HK–Hungary double tax agreement (2010), art 2, para 4; HK–Portugal double tax agreement (2012), art 2, para 4; HK–Pakistan double tax agreement (2017), art 2, para 4; HK–Malaysia double tax agreement (2012), art 2, para 4; HK–Mexico double tax agreement (2012), art 2, para 4; HK–UK double tax agreement (2010), art 2, para 4; HK–Mainland China double tax arrangement (2006), art 2, para 4; HK–Guernsey double tax agreement (2013), art 2, para 4; HK–Arab Emirates double tax agreement (2015), art 2, para 4; HK–Romania double tax agreement (2016), art 2, para 4; HK–Malta double tax agreement (2012), art 2, para 4; HK–Finland double tax agreement (2018), art 2, para 4; HK–Austria double tax agreement (2010), art 2, para 4; HK–New Zealand double tax agreement (2017), art 2, para 4; HK–Georgia double tax agreement (2020), art 2, para 4; HK–Macao double tax arrangement (2020), art 2, para 4.

[40] HK–Arab Emirates double tax agreement (2015), art 5, para 5(b); HK–Indonesia double tax agreement (2010), art 5, para 5(b); HK–Vietnam double tax agreement (2014), art 5, para 5(b); HK–Saudi Arabia double tax agreement (2018), art 5, para 5(b); HK–Brunei Darussalam double tax agreement (2010), art 5, para 5(b); HK–Malaysia double tax agreement (2012), art 5, para 5(b); HK–Mexico double tax agreement (2012), art 5, para 5(b); HK–Portugal double tax agreement (2012), art 5, para 5(b); HK–Cambodia double tax agreement (2019), art 5, para 5(b); HK–Czech double tax agreement (2012), art 5, para 5(b); HK–Kuwait double tax agreement (2012), art 5, para 5(b); HK–Luxembourg double tax agreement (2011), art 5, para 5(b); HK–South Africa double tax agreement (2015), art 5, para 5(b); HK–Romania double tax agreement (2016), art 5, para 5(b); HK–Pakistan double tax agreement (2017), art 5, para 6(b); HK–Belgium double tax agreement (2004), art 5, para 5(b); HK–Russia double tax agreement (2016), art 5, para 5(b); HK–India double tax agreement (2018), art 5, para 5(b); HK–Thailand double tax agreement (2005), art 5, para 5(b); HK–New Zealand double tax agreement (2017), art 5, para 8(b).

[41] HK–India double tax agreement (2018), art 5, para 5(c); HK–Thailand double tax agreement (2005), art 5, para 5(c).

to exclusive taxation by the source state. The HK–Liechtenstein double tax agreement is an exception to this practice.[42]

In several of Hong Kong's DTAs, the residence state enjoys exclusive taxation rights, in contrast to the OECD Model Convention where the state of residence and source state share taxation powers. Only the resident's state of residence should apply for taxation of dividends paid by a firm to a resident of another Contracting Party.[43] 'Shall' is replaced with 'may' in the OECD Model Convention 2017.[44]

According to several of Hong Kong's DTAs, if a resident of the other Contracting Party receives interest from a Contracting Party and is the beneficial owner of the interest, the interest shall only be taxable in the owner's state of residence. Interest accruing in a Contracting State may also be taxed in the source state in accordance with that state's legislation if the beneficial owner of the interest is a resident of that state, but the tax so imposed must not exceed a specific percentage of the gross amount of the interest.[45]

Residents' royalties owned by a resident of the other Contracting State are solely subject to taxation in their home state.[46] According to the Hong Kong's DTAs, royalties earned in a Contracting State and paid to a resident of another Contracting Party 'may' be taxed there.[47] When it feels there is a gap in the Article, Hong Kong reserves the authority to add a clause clarifying the source of royalties to paragraph 12.[48] There may be additional types of copyrights in the future due to the growth of the digital economy.[49]

From my perspective, Hong Kong DTAs' royalty regulations are more stringent than those of the OECD Model Convention. According to several

[42] OECD Model Convention 2017, art 6, para 1; HK–Liechtenstein double tax agreement (2011), art 6, para 1.

[43] HK–Liechtenstein double tax agreement (2011), art 10, para 1; HK–Jersey double tax agreement (2013), art 10, para 1; HK–Brunei Darussalam double tax agreement (2010), art 10, para 1; HK–Mexico double tax agreement (2012), art 10, para 1; HK–Malta double tax agreement (2012), art 10, para 1.

[44] OECD Model Convention 2017, art 10, para 1.

[45] According to the HK–Saudi Arabia double tax agreement (2018), art 11, para 2; HK–Belarus double tax agreement (2017), art 11, para 2; HK–Kuwait double tax agreement (2012), art 11, para 2; HK–Brunei Darussalam double tax agreement (2010), art 11, para 2(a); HK–Spain double tax agreement (2012), art 11, para 2; HK–New Zealand double tax agreement (2017), art 11, para 2; HK–Hungary double tax agreement (2010), art 11, para 2; HK–Macao double tax arrangement (2020), art 11, para 2; HK–Georgia double tax agreement (2020), art 11, para 2, the amount is 5 per cent. Based on HK–Estonia double tax agreement (2019), art 11, para 2(a); HK–Latvia double tax agreement (2017), art 11, para 2(a); HK–Romania double tax agreement (2016), art 11, para 3, it is zero per cent. Referring to HK–Romania double tax agreement (2016), art 11, para 2, it is 3 per cent. In relation to the HK–Italy double tax agreement (2013), art 11, para 2, it is 12.5 per cent. Based on HK–Mainland China double tax arrangement (2006), art 11, para 2, it is 7 per cent. Referring to HK–Thailand double tax agreement (2005), art 11, para 2(c), it is 15 per cent.

[46] OECD Model Convention 2017, art 12, para 1.

[47] HKSAR DTAs share this clause in their respective art 12 (Royalties), para 1.

[48] OECD Model Convention 2017 (Changes to the Positions of Non-Member Economies), para 284.

[49] ibid para 287.

Hong Kong DTAs, 'royalties' refer to 'the use of, or the right to use, industrial, commercial, or scientific equipment'. The term 'royalties' is also used in the HK–Mexico Double Tax Agreement to refer to 'the reception of, or the right to receive, visual images or sounds or both, for transmission by (1) satellite; (2) cable, optic fibre or similar technology;[50] or the use of, or the right to use, in connection with television or radio broadcasting, visual images or sounds or both, for transmission to the public by (1) satellite; (2) cable, optic fibre or similar technology'. Transport vehicles are referred to as 'commercial equipment' in the HK-Belarus double tax agreement.[51] The term 'royalties' also includes 'gains generated from the alienation of any such right or property which are contingent on the productivity, use, or disposition'.[52] The term 'royalties' as used in the HK–Canada double tax agreement excludes income covered by Article 8 (Shipping and Air Transport).[53] According to a review of certain of Hong Kong's DTAs, 'fees for technical services' refers to payments made to anybody other than the recipient's employee for technical, management, or consulting services.[54]

The word 'royalties' refers to the privilege of using industrial, commercial, or scientific apparatus. Payments made to anyone fall under the category of 'fees for technical services', with the exception of the payer's own employee.[55]

Some Hong Kong DTAs have the only right to tax earnings from entertainment or sports-related activities that take place in a host state.[56] The residency state of the athletes or artists must tax the linked income if the activities represent 'a plan of cultural exchange between the Governments of both Contracting Parties'.[57]

[50] HK–Mexico double tax agreement (2012), art 12, para 3(e)(f).

[51] HK–Belarus double tax agreement (2017), art 12, para 3.

[52] HK–Mexico double tax agreement (2012), art 12, para 3.

[53] HK–Canada double tax agreement (2013), art 12, para 3.

[54] HK–Pakistan double tax agreement (2017), art 13, para 3; HK–Cambodia double tax agreement (2019), art 13, para 3; HK–Malaysia double tax agreement (2012), art 13, para 3; HK–Brunei Darussalam double tax agreement (2010), art 13, para 3; HK–New Zealand double tax agreement (2017), art 12, para 3(d).

[55] HK–Estonia double tax agreement (2019), art 16, para 3; HK–Malaysia double tax agreement (2012), art 18, para 3; HK–India double tax agreement (2018), art 18, para 3; HK–Indonesia double tax agreement (2010), art 17, para 3; HK–Macao double tax arrangement (2020), art 17, para 3; HK–Georgia double tax agreement (2020), art 16, para 3.

[56] HK–Netherlands double tax agreement (2010), art 16, para 3; HK–Thailand double tax agreement (2005), art 17, para 3; HK–Hungary double tax agreement (2010), art 16, para 3.

[57] HK–Indonesia double tax agreement (2010), art 17, para 3; HK–India double tax agreement (2018), art 18, para 3; HK–Hungary double tax agreement (2010), art 16, para 3; HK–Thailand double tax agreement (2005), art 17, para 3; HK–Malaysia double tax agreement (2012), art 18, para 3; HK–Netherlands double tax agreement (2010), art 16, para 3; HK–Switzerland double tax agreement (2012), art 17, para 3; HK–Canada double tax agreement (2013), art 16, para 3; HK–Qatar double tax agreement (2013), art 17, para 3; HK–Korea double tax agreement (2014), art 16, para 3; HK–Macao double tax arrangement (2020), art 17, para 3; HK–Georgia double tax agreement (2020), art 16, para 3.

In accordance with the non-OECD economies' positions on the personnel of diplomatic missions and consular posts under the OECD Model 2010,[58] Hong Kong (HK) has registered a special provision on Article 28, paragraph 1. Since Hong Kong is not a sovereign state, it reserves the right to substitute 'government missions' for 'diplomatic missions'.[59]

The OECD Model Convention and Hong Kong's DTAs interpret source state taxing rights differently when it comes to pensions. According to Hong Kong's DTAs, any pension (apart from a lump-sum payment) given to a person in exchange for services done to a Contracting Party by the government of that party or paid from funds established by or donated by that government, 'may' be subject to taxation in that party.[60] However, according to the OECD Model Convention, that party 'must' tax the corresponding tax.[61]

In several DTAs, alimony or other maintenance payments made by a resident of one Contracting Party to a resident of the other Contracting Party are taxed solely in the Contracting Party in which they were made, to the extent they are not deductible by the payer in the first-mentioned Party.[62] The extent is not necessary in paragraph 1 of article 21 (Other Income) of the OECD Model Convention and the residence state has the sole authority to tax all income.[63] The United Nations (UN) Model Convention refers to alimony even though it is not included under the OECD Model.[64]

Income that has already been subject to taxation by the source state is 'allowed as a credit against HONG KONG tax payable in respect of that income'.[65] Despite having a territorial taxation system, Hong Kong allows for the deduction of income where 'it is incurred in the development of taxable profits'.[66]

Despite the non-discrimination clause being given such a high priority in the OECD Model Convention, one Hong Kong agreement still does not have

[58] OECD Model Tax Convention on Income and on Capital: Condensed Version (22 July 2010) 462.

[59] ibid.

[60] HK–New Zealand double tax agreement (2017), art 18, para 2(a).

[61] OECD Model Convention 2017, art 19, para 2(a).

[62] HK–Ireland double tax agreement (2010), art 20, para 3; HK–Guernsey double tax agreement (2013), art 20, para 3; HK–Malta double tax agreement (2012), art 20, para 3; HK–Spain double tax agreement (2012), art 20, para 3; HK–Hungary double tax agreement (2010), art 20, para 3; HK–Indonesia double tax agreement (2010), art 21, para 3; HK–Jersey double tax agreement (2013), art 20, para 3; HK–Canada double tax agreement (2013), art 20, para 4; HK–UK double tax agreement (2010), art 20, para 4; HK–Luxembourg double tax agreement (2011), art 17, para 3; HK–Kuwait double tax agreement (2012), art 17, para 3.

[63] OECD Model Convention 2017, art 21, para 1.

[64] ibid; UN Model Convention 2017, art 21, para 2.

[65] The HKSAR DTAs share this clause in the respective art 22 (Elimination of Double Taxation).

[66] Ying Zhang, '*HK – Corporate Taxation*' s. 1.4.4. Available at: https://research.ibfd.org/#/doc?url=/linkresolver/static/cta_hk_auth&refresh=1590284728927#cta_hk_auth, accessed 28 September 2023.

one.[67] 'Every kind and description' of taxes are addressed by the OECD Model Convention.[68] However, in accordance with the DTAs of Hong Kong, the provisions of the article pertaining to covered taxes are only to be applied to taxes that are covered by Article 2 of the DTAs of Hong Kong (taxes covered)[69] or the subject of this Agreement.[70]

B. Assessment of Hong Kong's Tax Agreements: Compliance, Evolution and Exceptions

Since Hong Kong is not a sovereign state, it has reserved the ability to change what 'resident' means in its tax agreements.[71] The OECD Model Convention 2010 and 2017 introduced the functional distinct entity concept, often known as the Authorised OECD Approach (AOA).[72] There are two processes in determining the profit attribution to the PEs based on the AOA. A functional and factual analysis of the PE must be done as a first step, along with the assignment of major human functions, assets and hazards.[73] The arm's-length concept should be followed in the second phase when determining the fraudulent dealings between the PE and the parent business.[74] Only two of HK's post-2010 DTAs adhere to AOA, while the majority only follow the arm's-length principle, according to a review of those agreements.[75] Agreement pre-2010 follows the arm's-length principle which was regulated by OECD Model Conventions.[76]

The state with the authority to tax the profits produced by a firm through 'the operation of ships or aircraft in international commerce' is the state where the enterprise has its primary place of business.[77] This provision is in accordance

[67] OECD Model Convention 2017, art 24; HK–Saudi Arabia double tax agreement (2018) does not have this clause.

[68] OECD Model Convention 2017, art 24, para 6.

[69] HK–Belarus double tax agreement (2017), art 23, para 5; HK–Pakistan double tax agreement (2017), art 24, para 6; HK–Canada double tax agreement (2013), art 22, para 6; HK–Cambodia double tax agreement (2019), art 24, para 5; HK–Romania double tax agreement (2016), art 22, para 5; HK–Georgia double tax agreement (2020), art 23, para 6.

[70] HK–Kuwait double tax agreement (2012), art 22, para 6; HK–Qatar double tax agreement (2013), art 23, para 6; HK–Indonesia double tax agreement (2010), art 23, para 6; HK–Brunei Darussalam double tax agreement (2010), art 23, para 6; HK–Thailand double tax agreement (2005), art 23, para 6.

[71] OECD Model Convention 2010, positions on art 4, para 2.1.

[72] OECD Model Convention 2010, art 7, para 2; OECD Model Convention 2017, art 7, para 2.

[73] OECD Model Convention 2010, art 7, para 2.

[74] ibid.

[75] Only HK–Estonia double tax agreement (2019), art 7, para 2; HK–Italy double tax agreement (2013), art 7, para 2 comply with AOA.

[76] OECD Model Convention 2008, art 7, para 2; OECD Model Convention 2005, art 7, para 2; HK–Belgium double tax agreement (2004), art 7, para 2; HK–Thailand double tax agreement (2005), art 7, para 2; HK–Mainland China double tax arrangement (2006), art 7, para 2.

[77] The HKSAR DTAs share this clause in their respective art 8, para. 1.

with the 2017 OECD Model Convention.[78] If the major goal of any individual involved with the development or assignment of the debt-claim is to take advantage of the provision, no remedy shall be provided under Article 11 in some DTAs.[79] The implicit source rule in the OECD Model states that dividends are sourced in the state where the distributing corporation has its headquarters.[80] According to Section 26 of the Inland Revenue Ordinance, dividends received from a business that has to pay profits tax are exempt.[81] Dividends originating in Hong Kong are free under the local rule, because profits tax is one of the territory's main taxes.

Mandatory binding arbitration is not a dispute resolution method that every DTA has adopted.[82] Despite being a developing nation, Pakistan's DTA includes the same required binding arbitration clause as Canada's.[83] Hong Kong has expressed a reservation regarding Article 25(5) of the OECD Model and reserves the right to exclude it from their DTAs.[84] Only a few Hong Kong DTAs incorporate a mandatory binding arbitration clause for resolving tax-related disputes in accordance with paragraph 5 of Article 25 of the OECD Model Convention on MAPs.[85] When Hong Kong does add an arbitration clause in its agreements,

[78] OECD Model Convention 2017, art 8, para 1.

[79] HK–UK double tax agreement (2010), art 11, para 7; HK–Indonesia double tax agreement (2010), art 11, para 8; HK–Qatar double tax agreement (2013), art 11, para 5; HK–Russia double tax agreement (2016), art 11, para 6; HK–South Africa double tax agreement (2015), art 11, para 8; HK–Brunei Darussalam double tax agreement (2010), art 11, para 8; HK–France double tax agreement (2011), art 11, para 8; HK–India double tax agreement (2018), art 11, para 8; HK–Romania double tax agreement (2016), art 11, para 9; HK–Italy double tax agreement (2013), art 11, para 8; HK–Switzerland double tax agreement (2012), art 11, para 10; HK–Canada double tax agreement (2013), art 11, para 9.

[80] IBFD Global Tax Treaty Commentaries, chapter on art 10, s 3.3.1.

[81] Stefano Mariani, 'The Source of Dividends in HK Tax Law' [2015] 21 *Asia Pacific Tax Bulletin* 1.

[82] Only HK–Italy double tax agreement (2013), art 24, para 5; HK–Jersey double tax agreement (2013), art 23, para 5; HK–Liechtenstein double tax agreement (2011), art 24, para 5; HK–Canada double tax agreement (2013), art 23, para 6; HK–Netherlands double tax agreement (2010), art 24, para 5; HK–Guernsey double tax agreement (2013), art 23, para 5; HK–Switzerland double tax agreement (2012), art 24, para 5; HK–Japan double tax agreement (2015), art 24, para 5; HK–Pakistan double tax agreement (2017), art 25, para 5 contain a mandatory binding arbitration clause. State sovereignty is the main reason why some countries tend not to include mandatory arbitration in their double tax treaties. See Xueliang Ji, 'The Changing Paradigm of International Tax Dispute Settlement: What Are the Promises and Challenges of Mandatory Arbitration for China?' (2020) 21 *Oregon Review of International Law* 135. See also Julien Chaisse, 'Investor-State Arbitration in International Tax Dispute Resolution-- A Cut above Dedicated Tax Dispute Resolution?' (2016) 41 *Virginia Tax Review* 149.

[83] HK–Pakistan double tax agreement (2017), art 25, para 5; HK–Canada double tax agreement (2013), art 23, para 6.

[84] 2017 Update to the OECD Model Tax Convention, para 300.

[85] OECD Model Convention 2017, art 25, para 5; HK–Italy double tax agreement (2013), art 24, para 5; HK–Jersey double tax agreement (2013), art 23, para 5; HK–Liechtenstein double tax agreement (2011), art 24, para 5; HK–Canada double tax agreement (2013), art 23, para 6; HK–Netherlands double tax agreement (2010), art 24, para 5; HK–Guernsey double tax agreement (2013), art 23, para 5; HK–Switzerland double tax agreement (2012), art 24, para 5; HK–Japan double tax agreement (2015), art 24, para 5; HK–Pakistan double tax agreement (2017), art 25, para 5 contain this clause.

the clause is to be based on the OECD, according to footnote 156 and the related text of the GTTC chapter on A 25.[86]

Due to domestic law, Hong Kong did not comply with the standards of the OECD Model Exchange of Information Article in the early DTAs it signed. However, in 2009, its Financial Secretary announced that the OECD Exchange of Information Article would be included for Hong Kong to negotiate the following DTAs.[87] This stance, which is supported by domestic legislation, asserts that Hong Kong would only share information about taxable periods after the agreement entered into force.[88]

The OECD Model Convention is a good starting point for understanding Hong Kong's DTAs, but the unique circumstances influencing the drafting of these agreements has resulted in a few key differences that merit additional consideration. Exclusion of collection assistance clauses[89] is one example where Hong Kong DTAs do not mirror the Convention.[90] In a few unique cases, Hong Kong DTAs are exceptions to the rule, such as one agreement with an entitlement to benefits clause[91] and one agreement without the standard non-discrimination clause.[92] When it comes to students, some Hong Kong DTAs diverge from OECD Model Convention art 20 by focusing on the taxation of teachers and researchers.[93] In addition, only a proportion of Hong Kong DTAs follow Convention regulatory guidance on capital taxation in Article 22.[94] When it comes to the treatment of MAPs outlined in paragraph 5 of Article 25 of the

[86] HK can be an example. See, eg, the Guernsey–HK Income Tax Agreement (2013) and the Canada–HK Income Tax Agreement (2012).

[87] John Tsang, 'Budget Speech by the Financial Secretary' (*The Government of the Hong Kong Special Administrative Region Press Releases*, 25 February 2009). Available at: www.info.gov.hk/gia/general/200902/25/P200902250108.htm, accessed 2 November 2023.

[88] OECD Model Tax Convention on Income and on Capital: Condensed Version (22 July 2010) 462. As per the revisions laid out in the Inland Revenue (Amendment) (No 3) Bill 2009, the Inland Revenue Department of Hong Kong now possesses the authority to 'gather and disseminate information pertinent to any case that could potentially impact any liability, duty, or obligation of an individual under the laws of a jurisdiction beyond Hong Kong'. The Commissioner of the Inland Revenue has been vested with the power to issue search warrants to facilitate this data collection. Moreover, it has become unlawful for a taxpayer to furnish deceptive information concerning tax affairs external to Hong Kong.

[89] OECD Model Convention 2017, art 27.

[90] OECD Model Convention 2017, art 29; HK–Finland double tax agreement (2018), art 21.

[91] OECD Model Convention 2017, art 29; HK–Finland double tax agreement (2018), art 21.

[92] OECD Model Convention 2017, art 24; HK–Saudi Arabia double tax agreement (2018) does not have this clause.

[93] OECD Model Convention 2017, art 20; Only the HK–Saudi Arabia double tax agreement (2018), art 21, HK–Mainland China double tax arrangement, Fifth Protocol (2019) and HK–Macao double tax arrangement (2020) have clauses related to teachers and researchers.

[94] OECD Model Convention 2017, art 22; Only the HK–Austria double tax agreement (2010), art 21; HK–Luxembourg double tax agreement (2011), art 21; HK–Belarus double tax agreement (2017), art 21; HK–Belgium double tax agreement (2004), art 21; HK–France double tax agreement (2011), art 21; HK–Liechtenstein double tax agreement (2010), art 21; HK–Georgia double tax agreement (2020), art 21 contain this article.

Convention, mandatory binding arbitration clauses only appear in some Hong Kong DTAs.[95]

These divergences should not be viewed in an altogether negative light, as any negotiated agreement between multiple parties must necessarily reflect considerations relevant to those parties. Those considerations can be related to the development conditions of the Contracting Parties, as well as other features of their respective political economies. One mechanism providing flexibility to states on these matters is provided by the Multilateral Convention to Implement Tax Treaty Related Measures to Prevent Base Erosion and Profit Shifting ('Multilateral Instrument' or 'MLI').[96] An example of making use of provisions such as paragraph 5 of Article 16 (MAP) can be found in the HK–New Zealand DTA, which does not precisely mirror the OECD Model Convention while providing benefits to both parties.[97] These benefits include the facilitation of trade and investment between both jurisdictions while also leaving room for profits to accrue to Mainland China.[98] Cases such as these highlight the importance of measuring deviations from the OECD Model Convention in the light of broader aims pursued by Contracting Parties.

Tax revenue is a critical component of a nation's GDP[99] and HK must keep up with pervasive international competition to maintain its status as a global financial centre and an attractive destination for foreign investment. While lowering withholding taxes may seem counterintuitive at first, these reductions can be paired with enhanced relief measures to ultimately drive more benefits[100] and maintain leadership in treaty development standards.[101] Promoting international tax regime development also provides crucial inbound and outbound investment support for the Belt and Road Initiative (BRI) and China's broader

[95] OECD Model Convention 2017, art 25, para 5; HK–Italy double tax agreement (2013), art 24, para 5; HK–Jersey double tax agreement (2013), art 23, para 5; HK–Liechtenstein double tax agreement (2011), art 24, para 5; HK–Canada double tax agreement (2013), art 23, para 6; HK–Netherlands double tax agreement (2010), art 24, para 5; HK–Guernsey double tax agreement (2013), art 23, para 5; HK–Switzerland double tax agreement (2012), art 24, para 5; HK–Japan double tax agreement (2015), art 24, para 5; HK–Pakistan double tax agreement (2017), art 25, para 5 contain this clause.

[96] Adrian Sawyer, 'Hong Kong Special Administrative Region's Developing Double Tax Agreement Regime: A Case Study of The Hong Kong Special Administrative Region-New Zealand Double Tax Agreement' (2011) *Asian Institute of International Financial Law Working Paper No 7* 14.

[97] Adrian Sawyer, 'Hong Kong Special Administrative Region's Developing Double Tax Agreement Regime: A Case Study of The Hong Kong Special Administrative Region-New Zealand Double Tax Agreement' (2011) *Asian Institute of International Financial Law Working Paper No 7* 14.

[98] ibid.

[99] Oren Penn et al., 'Session 5: Tax Regimes in Other High GDP Countries' (2008) *Tax Magazine* 87.

[100] ibid 592.

[101] K. Petkova et al., 'On the Relevance of Double Tax Treaties' (2020) 27 *International Tax and Public Finance* 590.

development goals.[102] For this reason, Hong Kong DTAs should aim to exempt foreign dividends and prioritise bilateral tax agreements with BRI partner states. Because of fundamental linkages between tax policies and local and international governance, these perspectives should be top of mind when reviewing and developing Hong Kong's DTAs.

PART II CONCLUSION

The main findings of Part II – Bilateral Endeavours: Strengthening Hong Kong's Economic Relations shed light on Hong Kong's efforts to forge strong economic ties with other countries through bilateral agreements and initiatives. The analysis highlights the territory's strategic approach in enhancing its global economic relations and the implications of these efforts for its broader economic goals.

- Hong Kong has actively pursued and participated in FTAs and Investment Promotion and Protection Agreements (IPPAs) to bolster its economic connections with key trading partners. These agreements facilitate market access, reduce trade barriers and provide a stable environment for investments.
- Double Taxation Agreements (DTAs) form an essential part of Hong Kong's bilateral tax cooperation efforts. By eliminating double taxation and enhancing tax transparency, these agreements promote cross-border trade and investment and contribute to a more predictable business environment.
- Hong Kong's robust bilateral economic relations enable the territory to leverage its unique position as a gateway between mainland China and the rest of the world, fostering growth and driving regional integration.

As highlighted in Part I, the overall implications of the analysis indicate that Hong Kong's bilateral endeavours complement its strong unilateral foundations. These concerted efforts in forging economic ties with other countries contribute to its status as a leading financial centre and improve its ability to navigate the challenges and opportunities in the global economic landscape. Linking these findings to the main lessons of Part I, it is evident that Hong Kong's success in maintaining a vibrant domestic economy is inextricably tied to its strategic engagement in bilateral economic relations. By effectively balancing its unilateral policies with bilateral endeavours, the territory has reinforced its position as an essential player in the global economy.

[102] The Belt and Road Initiative (BRI) was proposed by president Xi Jinping in 2013 and its aim is to accelerate 'the economic integration of countries along the route of the historic Silk Road'. Available at: www.beltroad-initiative.com/belt-and-road/, accessed 23 March 2021. See Julien Chaisse and Mitsuo Matsushita 'China's "Belt and Road" Initiative – Mapping the World Trade Normative and Strategic Implications' (2018) 52 *Journal of World Trade* 163; Julien Chaisse and Jamieson Kirkwood 'Chinese Puzzle: Anatomy of the (Invisible) Belt and Road Investment Treaty' (2020) 23 *Journal of International Economic Law* 245.

As we transition to Part III, the focus shifts to exploring Hong Kong's involvement in international economic organisations and its commitment to multilateralism. By examining the territory's contributions to these institutions and the impact of its participation on its domestic policies and global economic standing, we can gain a comprehensive understanding of Hong Kong's role in shaping the world economy and identify potential strategies for further enhancing its multilateral engagement.

Part III

Multilateral Engagement: Hong Kong's Role in Global Economic Institutions

IN PART III, we consider the multilateral economic regime, which encompasses international economic interactions and agreements established and maintained by multiple countries. Adopting the constructivist theoretical framework, Part III investigates Hong Kong's role within these institutions and how the territory contributes to and reaps benefits from the multilateral economic system. Constructivism contends that norms, ideas and social processes influence state behaviour in the international system. Within the context of international economic law, the emergence, interpretation and evolution of legal norms rely on the actors' intersubjective understanding and shared values. The multilateral economic regime is supported by three primary pillars: the World Trade Organisation (WTO), international investment treaties and international tax legislation. Collectively, these pillars aim to foster cooperation, stability and growth among nations by ensuring fair competition, safeguarding investors' rights and combating tax evasion. Hong Kong's multilateral engagement is crucial, drawing significant support from the WTO, the International Centre for Settlement of Investment Disputes (ICSID) and international tax law. In this section, we explore Hong Kong's involvement in these multilateral institutions, emphasising the territory's dedication to free trade and open markets through active participation in the WTO (Chapter 9). As a founding member, Hong Kong highly appreciates the guidelines and standards developed by the WTO, which guarantee predictability and stability in the global trading system. The WTO agreements offer a framework for trade policies that cover products, services and intellectual property, all of which are vitally important to Hong Kong's open, small and trade-dependent economy. Moreover, this section discusses the significance of the ICSID Convention for protecting foreign investments in Hong Kong (Chapter 10). As a signatory to the ICSID Convention, Hong Kong is committed to creating a fair and open environment for foreign investors and resolving disputes promptly and effectively. The ICSID serves as an impartial and efficient platform for settling disputes between investors and countries, contributing to a stable and predictable investment climate and attracting foreign investment. Lastly, this section discusses the importance of international tax law for Hong Kong (Chapter 11), particularly in addressing tax evasion and avoidance. By adhering to international tax regulations, such as the Organisation for Economic Co-operation and Development (OECD) Base Erosion and Profit Shifting (BEPS) initiative, Hong Kong sustains its reputation as a trustworthy and transparent financial centre. Implementing the Common Reporting Standard (CRS) for the automatic exchange of financial account information exemplifies Hong Kong's commitment to preventing tax evasion and ensuring compliance with international tax norms.

8

World Trade on the Horizon: Hong Kong's Engagement with the WTO

TRADE AND FINANCIAL services are important economic drivers for Hong Kong and are crucial to maintaining its status as a prominent international hub for both. Hong Kong is a distinct customs territory.[1] It participates in organisations that uphold international economic law and commercial agreements under the name 'Hong Kong, China'. In 1986, Hong Kong signed on as a contracting party to the GATT of 1947, the forerunner of the WTO and took part in the Uruguay Round of multilateral trade discussions, which began in 1986. Since the Marrakesh Agreement Establishing the World Trade Organisation was successfully finalised in 1994, it has been a founding member and participant in the multilateral trading system based on rules. Hong Kong actively supports and promotes a global trading system that is free, open and stable. It has continued to be a distinct WTO member under the name 'Hong Kong, China' since the handover in 1997.

Since its establishment as a British colony in 1843, the focus on international trade has transformed Hong Kong's economy and allowed it to grow and flourish,[2] for more than 170 years. Despite its small size relative to other economies, the territory has often been regarded as one of the world's leading international financial centres[3] and trading nations.[4] As a World Trade Organisation ('WTO') member since its inception, Hong Kong has derived its trade policy from its

[1] The legal authority for Hong Kong's membership in the World Trade Organisation (WTO) is entrenched in Article 116 which provides that: 'The Hong Kong Special Administrative Region shall be a separate customs territory. The Hong Kong Special Administrative Region may, using the name "Hong Kong, China", participate in relevant international organizations and international trade agreements (including preferential trade arrangements), such as the General Agreement on Tariffs and Trade and arrangements regarding international trade in textiles. Export quotas, tariff preferences and other similar arrangements, which are obtained or made by the Hong Kong Special Administrative Region or which were obtained or made and remain valid, shall be enjoyed exclusively by the Region.'

[2] Jiming Ha, Kelvin Fan and Chang Shu, 'Export Performance in Hong Kong Offshore Trade and Re-Exports' (2003) *Hong Kong Monetary Authority Quarterly Bulletin* 5, 6.

[3] Z/Yen, 'GFCI 32 Rank' (*Z/Yen*, 22 September 2022). Available at: www.longfinance.net/programmes/financial-centre-futures/global-financial-centres-index/gfci-32-explore-the-data/gfci-32-rank/, accessed 13 November 2022.

[4] UNCTAD, 'Evolution of the World's 25 Top Trading Nations' (*UNCTAD*, 6 April 2021). Available at: unctad.org/topic/trade-analysis/chart-10-may-2021, accessed 13 November 2022.

intention to pursue free trade and apply no barriers to trade.[5] Consequently, these policies have generally been applauded by other countries.[6] However, they are also not without flaws. Additionally, Hong Kong has both ratified plurilateral agreements and participated in negotiations on these types of agreements. This chapter attempts to shed a better light on Hong Kong's trade policy and its evolution. It first explains Hong Kong's membership with the WTO before giving an overview of Hong Kong's trade in goods and trade in services regimes in light of the General Agreement on Tariffs and Trade ('GATT') and General Agreement on Trade in Services ('GATS'). It will then summarise Hong Kong's past Trade Policy Reviews ('TPRs') before examining the rationales for it to ratify plurilateral agreements and outlining its ongoing negotiations regarding this type of treaty.

I. EMBRACING GLOBAL TRADE: HONG KONG'S WTO MEMBERSHIP JOURNEY

Article XII:1 of the Marrakesh Agreement permits a separate customs territory with full sovereignty over its trade policy to join the WTO.[7] Consequently, although it is not a jurisdiction, Hong Kong has been a member of the WTO since 1 January 1995. Before the WTO was established, it had also been a member of the General Agreement on Tariffs and Trade since 23 April 1986.[8] In this regard, as a WTO member, Hong Kong is subject to the Marrakesh Agreement, as well as the other multilateral trade agreements annexed thereto.[9] It should also be noted that even though it is the sixth largest trading economy in goods[10] and ranks as the 38th biggest economy in the world,[11] Hong Kong still defines itself as a developing economy within the WTO system.[12] Thus, theoretically, it is entitled to special and differential treatment.[13]

[5] Trade and Industry Department, 'Hong Kong's Trade Policy' (*Trade and Industry Department, The Government of the Hong Kong Special Administrative Region*, 20 July 2022). Available at: www.tid.gov.hk/english/trade_relations/trade_policy/trpolicy.html, accessed 13 November 2022.

[6] See, eg, HKSAR Government, 'WTO Members Commend Hong Kong, China for its Free Trade Regime (With Photos)' (The Government of the Hong Kong Special Administrative Region Press Releases, 29 November 2018). Available at: www.info.gov.hk/gia/general/201811/29/P2018112900153.htm, accessed 13 November 2022.

[7] Marrakesh Agreement Establishing the World Trade Organisation (15 April 1994) LT/UR/A/2 art XII:1. Available at: http://docsonline.wto.org.

[8] World Trade Organisation, 'Hong Kong, China and the WTO' (*World Trade Organisation*). Available at: www.wto.org/english/thewto_e/countries_e/Hong_Kong_china_e.htm, accessed 13 November 2022.

[9] Marrakesh Agreement Establishing the World Trade Organisation (n 7) art XII:1.

[10] Cherry Yeung, 'Economic and Trade Information on Hong Kong' (*HKTDC Research*, 27 October 2022). Available at: research.hktdc.com/en/Article/MzIwNjkzNTY5, accessed 13 November 2022.

[11] WorldData.info, 'Indicators of Economy in Hong Kong' (*WorldData.info*). Available at: www.worlddata.info/asia/Hong-Kong/economy.php, accessed 13 November 2022.

[12] World Trade Organisation, 'Groups in the Negotiations by WTO Member' (*World Trade Organisation*, 12 April 2021). Available at: www.wto.org/english/tratop_e/dda_e/groups_by_country_e.htm, accessed 13 November 2022.

[13] Hong Kong has, however, not requested the granting of special and differential treatment for a number of years. There are also calls for it to renounce its entitlement to such treatment or to reassess

Hong Kong has played an active role within the WTO. It hosted the Sixth WTO Ministerial Conference in mid-December 2005 and has supplied vice-chairs and chairs to various committees and bodies.[14] Nonetheless, unlike Member States, such as the United States and the European Union,[15] who have made use of the WTO dispute settlement mechanism as both disputing parties and third parties, Hong Kong has rarely participated in a WTO dispute as a disputing party but rather as a third party.

The task of orchestrating trade agreements in Hong Kong is managed by the Trade and Industry Department ('TID'). The mandate to commence these discussions lies in the hands of the Chief Executive, while the Executive Council provides strategic counsel on FTA negotiations. Primarily, the TID shoulders the responsibility for fostering trade relations between Hong Kong and its global counterparts, while simultaneously upholding Hong Kong's rights and economic interests. The TID also synchronises the drafting and negotiation of both regional and bilateral trade agreements, which encompass the agreements between China, Hong Kong and other international economies. It is also accountable for strategising bilateral accords with commercial associates to both stimulate and safeguard investments. The department further plays a crucial role in facilitating Hong Kong's proactive engagement in WTO activities and in the implementation of trade agreements and policies. The department also offers comprehensive support services to the industrial sector and small and medium enterprises (SMEs). This includes the issue of certificates of origin, export and import licences and accreditations of Hong Kong service providers.[16]

Since the CEPA was signed in June 2003, it has been the responsibility of the Customs and Excise Department to maintain the necessary control mechanisms to ensure that goods exported under the agreement conform to the necessary requirements. The World Trade Organisation (WTO) and the OECD Trade Committee, including the annual OECD Ministerial Council Meeting's Trade and Investment Session, are both attended by the Hong Kong Economic and Trade Office (HKC) based in Geneva. Since 1994 and 1995, respectively, HKC has participated in the OECD's Committee on Financial Markets and Committee on Trade. The current Permanent Representative of Hong Kong, China to the WTO is Mr Lo Chi Hong, Laurie. Lo is a member of HKETO-Geneva, the Commerce, Industry and Tourism Branch and the Bureau of Commerce and Economic Development.[17]

its classification as a developing country. See Trade Policy Review Body – 26 and 28 November 2018 – Trade Policy Review – Hong Kong, China – Minutes of the meeting (6 March 2019) WT/TPR/M/380 paras 4.61 and 5.38. Available at: http://docsonline.wto.org.

[14] Trade and Industry Department, 'World Trade Organisation (WTO)' (*Trade and Industry Department, The Government of the Hong Kong Special Administrative Region*, 11 November 2022). Available at: www.tid.gov.hk/english/ito/wto/wto_overview.html, accessed 29 January 2024.

[15] World Trade Organisation, 'Disputes by Members' (*World Trade Organisation*). Available at: www.wto.org/english/tratop_e/dispu_e/dispu_by_country_e.htm, accessed 29 January 2024.

[16] Final report Hong Kong, China – Chile joint study group on the feasibility of a Free Trade Agreement (July 2009).

[17] Hong Kong Economic and Trade Office in Geneva, 'About Us' (*Hong Kong Economic and Trade Office in Geneva*). Available at: www.hketogeneva.gov.hk/en/about/index.html, accessed 29 January 2024.

On the subject of the Hong Kong government's authority, the Hong Kong delegation seeks consultations. If a member state considers that an action adopted by another member state has prevented it from receiving a benefit given by one of the covered agreements, it may seek further deliberations.[18] If discussions fail to resolve the conflict within 60 days after receiving the request for consultations, the complaining state may request the formation of a panel. The respondent state cannot prevent or postpone the formation of a panel unless the DSB decides otherwise by consensus.[19] Private parties are not authorised to attend the confidential sessions or make submissions other than those of the state in issue, even if they are directly implicated.

Since its accession to the GATT and thereafter the WTO, Hong Kong has only acted as a complainant in two disputes, 26 years apart. The first was launched during the GATT era in 1996 and concerned Turkey's imposition of quantitative restrictions on Hong Kong's textile and clothing exports from 1 January 1996,[20] in light of its customs union with the European Union. Hong Kong took the view that these measures were a violation of Turkey's obligations under GATT 1994 and were not justified under Article XXIV, GATT 1994.[21] The second dispute stemmed from the United States' revocation of Hong Kong's Special Trading Status on 14 July 2020 which, among other consequences, led to a change in the origin labelling requirements of Hong Kong-manufactured exports from 'Made in Hong Kong' to 'Made in China'.[22] The revocation of the special status and, by extension, the regulatory change, were made as a result of what the United States perceived as a threat to the jurisdiction's national security by the situation in Hong Kong.[23] Nonetheless, this prompted Hong Kong to challenge this labelling regime change at the WTO level.[24] Hong Kong has never acted as a respondent in a WTO dispute. However, certain aspects of its trade policies have been subject to scrutiny; these will be addressed in section IV on Hong Kong's past TPRs. In terms of its participation in WTO disputes Hong Kong has acted as as a third party, in 22 cases.[25] concerning a wide range of topics, including anti-dumping measures and tariff treatment on information and technological products. More recently, Hong Kong was involved as a third party in a series of cases concerning the implementation by the US of tariffs on steel and aluminium imports based on national security concerns.[26]

[18] Andreas F Lowenfeld, *International Economic Law* (Oxford, Oxford University Press, 2008) 152.

[19] DSU, art 6.1.

[20] Request for consultations by Hong Kong, China, *Turkey – Restrictions on Imports of Textile and Clothing Products* (15 February 1996) WT/DS29/1, G/L/64. Available at: http://docsonline.wto.org.

[21] ibid.

[22] Country of Origin Marking of Products of Hong Kong, 85 Fed Reg 48551 (11 August 2020).

[23] *United States: Origin Marking Requirement- Communication from the United States* (13 November 2020) WT/DS597/2. Available at: http://docsonline.wto.org.

[24] *United States: Origin Marking Requirement – Request for Consultation by Hong Kong China* (3 November 2020) WT/DS597/1, G/L/1365, G/RO/D/8, G/TBT/D/53. Available at: http://docsonline.wto.org.

[25] World Trade Organisation, 'Disputes by Members' (n 15).

[26] See, eg, United States: Certain Measures on Steel and Aluminium Products – Communications from the United States (28 August 2020) WT/DS564/2. Available at: http://docsonline.wto.org.

II. COMMITMENTS AND CONTRIBUTIONS: HONG KONG'S GATT AND GATS OBLIGATIONS

As mentioned previously, as a member of the WTO, Hong Kong is bound by the Marrakesh Agreement and the multilateral trade agreements under its annexes.[27] As such, it will have to comply with key WTO principles, such as the provision of equal treatment to all foreign parties (ie, the Most-Favoured Nation ('MFN') principle) and between domestic and foreign actors (ie, the National Treatment ('NT') principle) and the reduction and elimination of customs duties, tariffs and quantitative restrictions.[28] This section aims to provide an overview of Hong Kong's trade in goods and trade in services regimes, which will be addressed in turn.

A. Facilitating Trade in Goods: GATT Commitments

The GATT governs the trade in goods and imposes certain general obligations upon the WTO member states; thus, Hong Kong will have to comply with these undertakings. Nonetheless, as a WTO member state pursuing a free trade policy, Hong Kong does not impose tariffs on imports and exports or trade barriers.[29] However, four commodities are subjected to excise duties: liquor, tobacco, hydrocarbon oil and methyl alcohol.[30] While the level of excise duties for tobacco and hydrocarbons depends on their sub-type – for example, cigars are charged at a rate of HK$2,455 per kilogramme, while the rate for Chinese-prepared tobacco is HK$468 per kilogramme – the excise duty for liquor and methyl alcohol is dependent on their alcohol by volume ('ABV'). Particularly, amongst the three types of liquors: wine, liquor with an ABV of no more than 30% and liquor with an ABV of more than 30%, only the last type is subject to a 100% excise duty. Additionally, depending on their type, commodities may also be subject to technical standards and sanitary and phytosanitary measures,[31] which are designed to satisfy the need for public health, safety and security protection or to comply with Hong Kong's international obligations.[32] These measures include import

[27] Marrakesh Agreement Establishing the World Trade Organisation (n 7), art XII:1.

[28] World Trade Organisation, 'Principles of the Trading System' (*World Trade Organisation*). Available at: www.wto.org/english/thewto_e/whatis_e/tif_e/fact2_e.htm, accessed 29 January 2024.

[29] Trade and Industry Department, 'Hong Kong's Trade Policy' (n 4).

[30] Customs and Excise Department, 'Types and Duty Rates' (*Customs and Excise Department, The Government of the Hong Kong Special Administrative Region*, 24 February 2016). Available at: www.tid.gov.hk/english/ito/wto/wto_overview.html, accessed 1 October 2023.

[31] International Trade Administration, 'Standards for Trade – Hong Kong & Macau' (*International Trade Administration*, 12 March 2021). Available at: www.trade.gov/country-commercial-guides/standards-trade-Hong-Kong-macau, accessed 1 October 2023.

[32] HKTDC Research, 'Hong Kong's Trade Policy' (*HKTDC Research*). Available at: www.research.hktdc.com/en/Article/MzM0NDk2NTI4, accessed 29 January 2024.

and export licences, health certificates[33] and labelling requirements.[34] For example, Hong Kong requires food products to be labelled with a list of allergens and information to substantiate their claimed nutritional value.[35]

B. Fostering Trade in Services: GATS Commitments

The GATS governs trade in services with four modes: cross-border supply, consumption abroad, commercial presence and movement of natural persons. It introduces obligations similar to those under the GATT with which WTO member states must comply.[36] Member states are also able to make commitments not to restrict access and operations in their specific sectoral markets and register restrictions in relation to specific sectors and services.[37] These can be found in the relevant Schedule of Specific Commitments.[38]

Regarding Hong Kong's commitment to the GATS, to date, some form of commitment exists in 68 out of 155 service sectors.[39] Currently, Hong Kong has no horizontal restrictions on all four modes of supply of service, while the presence of natural persons is subject to certain conditions.[40] Commitments to recognise the NT principle and allow for market access have also been granted to certain modes of supply of services in various sectors. For example, specific commitments in the soundtrack recording service sector ensure unimpeded market access for cross-border supply, consumption abroad and commercial presence, with respect for the NT principle in commercial

[33] Centre for Food Safety, 'Import Control – Imported Food Control' (*Centre for Food Safety, The Government of the Hong Kong Special Administrative Region*, 26 October 2022). Available at: www.cfs.gov.hk/english/import/import_ifc.html, accessed 1 October 2023.

[34] International Trade Administration, 'Standards for Trade – Hong Kong & Macau' (n 31).

[35] Centre for Food Safety, 'Nutrition Labelling – FAQ for General Public' (*Centre for Food Safety, The Government of the Hong Kong Special Administrative Region*, 1 February 2021). Available at: www.cfs.gov.hk/english/faq/faq_14.html, accessed 1 October 2023.

[36] DG Trade, 'What does "Mode of Supply" for Services Mean?' (*European Commission | DG Trade*). Available at: www.trade.ec.europa.eu/access-to-markets/en/faqs/what-does-mode-supply-services-mean, accessed 1 October 2023. See also General Agreement on Trade in Services (15 April 1994) LT/UR/A-1B/S/1, art I.

[37] World Trade Organisation, 'Guide to Reading the GATS Schedules of Specific Commitments and the List of Article II (MFN) Exemptions' (*World Trade Organisation*). Available at: www.wto.org/english/tratop_e/serv_e/guide1_e.htm, accessed 1 October 2023.

[38] World Trade Organisation, 'Schedules of Specific Commitments and Lists of Article II Exemptions' (*World Trade Organisation*). Available at: www.wto.org/english/tratop_e/serv_e/serv_commitments_e.htm, accessed 1 October 2023.

[39] Committee on Regional Trade Agreements – Factual presentation – Free Trade Agreement between Hong Kong, China and Australia – Goods and services – Report by the Secretariat – Revision (16 December 2020) WT/REG400/1/Rev.1 para 4.24. Available at: http://docsonline.wto.org.

[40] Trade and Industry Department Multilateral Division, 'Hong Kong, China's Services Commitments under the World Trade Organisation (WTO) General Agreement on Trade in Services (GATS)' (*Trade and Industry Department, The Government of the Hong Kong Special Administrative Region*, January 2015). Available at: www.tid.gov.hk/english/trade_relations/tradefora/files/HKC_Services_Commitments.pdf 1, 2, accessed 29 January 2024.

presence.[41] Contrastingly, there are no limitations on market access for the modes of consumption abroad and commercial presence and no restrictions on NT for the mode of commercial presence in the hotel service sector. Notably, Hong Kong has chosen not to grant specific commitments in certain sectors such as education and healthcare services.[42]

III. ASSESSING PROGRESS: HONG KONG'S TRADE POLICY REVIEW HISTORY

Amongst other objectives under Annex 3 of the Marrakesh Agreement, the Trade Policy Review Mechanism aims to make the trade policies of WTO member states more transparent, to aid in the smooth operation of the multilateral trading system.[43] It thus subjects WTO members to a periodic assessment of their trade policies. The TPR, which is the final written product, provides recommendations to the recipient members on how their trade policy can be enhanced, while opportunities are given to answer any concerns that other members may have about the TPR recipient member's trade policies during review meetings.

To date, Hong Kong has had six TPRs conducted since 1990. Two were held in the GATT era and four after the WTO's establishment. For 26 years in a row, Hong Kong has been regarded as the freest economy in the world.[44] Thus, the response to its trade policy, both during its TPRs and their corresponding review meetings, has generally been positive. However, Hong Kong's trade policy is not without its flaws, with several recurring issues brought forth by other member states during Hong Kong's TPR review meetings.

For example, one of the most significant issues has been Hong Kong's IPR regime. Although the 1998 TPR acknowledged that IPRs were more rigorously enforced in Hong Kong,[45] they have still been a primary concern of many WTO members, from both developed and developing countries. Predominantly, WTO members were concerned about IPR infringements, particularly in the quantity of imported pirated and counterfeit goods that were being sold in or transiting through Hong Kong to markets abroad. This concern was raised during the

[41] Hong Kong – Schedule of Specific Commitments (15 April 1994) GATS/SC/39 1, 12. Available at: http://docsonline.wto.org.

[42] Committee on Regional Trade Agreements – Factual presentation – Free Trade Agreement between Hong Kong, China and Australia – Goods and services – Report by the Secretariat – Revision, para 4.24.

[43] Julien Chaisse and Mitsuo Matsushita, 'Maintaining the WTO's Supremacy in the International Trade Order: A Proposal to Refine and Revise the Role of the Trade Policy Review Mechanism' (2013) 16 *Journal of International Economic Law* 9, 13.

[44] Stuti Mishra, 'Hong Kong Ranked the World's Freest Economy by Canadian Think Tank for the 26th Time in a Row' (Independent, 9 September 2022). Available at: www.independent.co.uk/asia/east-asia/Hong-Kong-free-economy-fraser-institute-b2163710.html, accessed 29 January 2024.

[45] World Trade Organisation, 'Hong Kong, China: December 1998' (*World Trade Organisation*). Available at: www.wto.org/english/tratop_e/tpr_e/tp095_e.htm, accessed 29 January 2024.

meeting to discuss Hong Kong's 2002 TPR[46] and continued to feature throughout Hong Kong's subsequent five TPRs, as the issue now covers both physical and digital goods.[47] Countries were also concerned about the unauthorised third-party registration of well-known companies' trademarks in Hong Kong.[48] In response, Hong Kong detailed the actions that the government and its Customs and Excise Department were undertaking to resolve these two sub-issues.

Similarly, during Hong Kong's TPR review meetings, members raised the issue of excise duties on wine and spirits several times. Countries were concerned that raising the excise duty on wine from 60% to 80% would have a negative impact on domestic wineries and limit Hong Kong consumers' access to a variety of wine.[49] Although excise duties on wine were eventually abolished, those on liquors with more than 30% ABV were not; this thus affected tequila, whose ABV exceeded the threshold. Consequently, members took issue with this discriminatory discrepancy,[50] particularly because of the competitive and replaceable nature of liquor with different ABV percentages. Nonetheless, noting that public health concerns had to be considered on this matter,[51] Hong Kong responded that there were no plans to re-evaluate excise duties on spirits.[52]

Finally, apprehensions were expressed concerning the absence of an official consolidation of competitive conduct in Hong Kong. The worry was that this could obstruct equal competition and unrestricted commerce, whilst also limiting 'the discernment of anti-competitive behaviours'. In response, Hong Kong indicated that initiatives were in progress to broaden its competitive framework, culminating in the implementation of the Competition Ordinance in 2015. Further concerns surfaced about the restricted range of merger regulations, applicable exclusively to the telecommunications industry. Addressing this issue, Hong Kong did not dismiss the possibility of extending the ambit of merger control in the future.[53]

[46] Trade Policy Review Body – 16 and 18 December 2002 – Trade Policy Review – Hong Kong, China – Minutes of the meeting (17 February 2003) WT/TPR/M/109 paras 47, 86 and 91. Available at: http://docsonline.wto.org.

[47] Trade Policy Review Body – 26 and 28 November 2018 – Trade Policy Review – Hong Kong, China – Minutes of the meeting, paras 4.46–4.47.

[48] See, eg, Trade Policy Review Body – 13 and 15 December 2006 – Trade Policy Review – Hong Kong, China – Minutes of the meeting – Addendum (16 February 2007) WT/TPR/M/173/Add.1 1, 21. Available at: http://docsonline.wto.org.

[49] Trade Policy Review Body – 16 and 18 December 2002 – Trade Policy Review – Hong Kong, China – Minutes of the meeting, para 63.

[50] Trade Policy Review Body – 1 and 3 December 2010 – Trade Policy Review – Hong Kong, China – Minutes of the meeting (26 January 2011) WT/TPR/M/241 paras 56–57. Available at: http://docsonline.wto.org.

[51] Trade Policy Review Body – 26 and 28 November 2018 – Trade Policy Review – Hong Kong, China – Minutes of the meeting (6 March 2019) WT/TPR/M/380/Add.1 1, 53. Available at: http://docsonline.wto.org.

[52] Trade Policy Review Body – 19 and 21 November 2014 – Trade Policy Review – Hong Kong, China – Minutes of the meeting (19 January 2015) WT/TPR/M/306 para 5.16. Available at: http://docsonline.wto.org.

[53] ibid para 5.6.

IV. EXPANDING THE TRADE HORIZON: HONG KONG'S INVOLVEMENT IN PLURILATERAL AGREEMENTS AND NEGOTIATIONS

There are many reasons why countries may wish to accede to plurilateral agreements. For Hong Kong, one that has led to the ratification of such agreements is the protracted WTO multilateral negotiation process.[54] Within the WTO sphere, multilateral agreements are concluded as long as consensus has been reached (ie, no opposition to the decision is manifested).[55] Due to the large number of WTO member states involved in trade agreement negotiations, it is often difficult to satisfy all parties, especially on contentious issues. Consequently, unless members are prepared to compromise and accept trade-offs, reaching a consensus is extremely difficult.[56] Moreover, the increasing formation of coalitions in WTO negotiation rounds has led to enhanced bargaining power amongst the members.[57] Subsequently, due to the prerequisite for consensus, coalitions that are against a negotiated text or decision can derail an agenda relatively easily, instead of moving towards an agreement that is acceptable to all parties.[58] In the Doha Round, any disagreement, no matter how small, prevented the conclusion of an agreement.[59] Thus, despite negotiations being launched in 2001, very little had been achieved, with many regarding them as 'defunct' by 2015.[60] This demonstrates the drawn-out process of WTO multilateral negotiations and that they are not guaranteed.

Plurilateral agreements, in theory, create a more level playing field between signatories and, therefore, more jobs and business opportunities.[61] For Hong Kong, ratifying plurilateral agreements is also a way to rectify the free-rider problem because Hong Kong's exports are subject to the relevant customs and tariffs imposed by its trading partners, whilst imports from these partners can benefit from Hong Kong's free-trade policy. In fact, these formed part of the rationale

[54] Trevor T W Wan and others (eds), 'An Interview with Mr. Stuart Harbinson – Trump, Covid-10 and 'Free-Riding': Where Is the World Trade Organisation Headed' [2020] *Public Jurist* 14, 16.

[55] Amadou-Mahtar M'Bow, 'The Practice of Consensus in International Organisation' (1978) 30 *International Social Science Journal* 893, 897.

[56] Bernard Hoekman and David Vines, 'Multilateral Trade Cooperation: What Next?' (2007) 23 *Oxford Review of Economic Policy* 311, 323.

[57] Mateo Diego-Fernández, 'Trade Negotiations Make Strange Bedfellows' (2008) 7 *World Trade Review* 423, 426, 434–5.

[58] Kent Jones, 'Impediments to Doha Round Consensus and the Search for WTO Solutions' in Kent Jones, *Reconstructing the World Trade Organisation for the 21st Century: An Institutional Approach* (New York, Oxford University Press 2014) 83, 95.

[59] Meredith Kolsky Lewis, 'The Prisoners' Dilemma Posed by Free Trade Agreements: Can Open Access Provide an Escape?' (2010) 11 *Chicago Journal of International Law* 631, 640.

[60] Financial Times, 'The Doha Round Finally Dies a Merciful Death' (*Financial Times*, 21 December 2015). Available at: www.ft.com/content/9cb1ab9e a7c2-11e5-955c-1e1d6de94879, accessed 1 October 2023.

[61] Legislative Council Secretariat Research and Library Services Division, 'Information Note – Government Procurement Agreement of the World Trade Organisation' (30 April 2003) IN23/02-03 1, 19.

for Hong Kong's ratification of the Agreement on Government Procurement ('GPA'). Accessing the agreement helps Hong Kong achieve its government procurement goals of obtaining optimal value for money and promoting fair competition.[62] Therefore, ratifying the GPA was a compatible move for Hong Kong's free-trade and equitable competition policies.[63]

As of the time of writing, Hong Kong has signed eight free trade agreements ('FTAs') with countries, such as the member states of the European Free Trade Association, with the most recent one being with Australia.[64] Currently, there are 22 investment promotion and protection agreements ('IPPAs') in place in Hong Kong, one of which was signed with the Association of Southeast Asian Nations ('ASEAN').[65]

On top of these concluded agreements, Hong Kong also has multiple treaty negotiations ongoing. Pending the agreements' entry into force, Hong Kong has concluded negotiations for three additional IPPAs. It is also in IPPA negotiations with Russia, Iran and Turkey. Additionally, after ratifying the FTA with ASEAN, the Hong Kong government has sought formally to accede to the Regional Comprehensive Economic Partnership; a formal application was submitted on 1 January 2022.[66]

Hong Kong has at present ratified two plurilateral trade agreements, namely the GPA and the Information Technology Agreement.[67] Although there are currently no ongoing FTA negotiations,[68] Hong Kong has been participating in negotiations aiming to create agreements that would facilitate trade and investment. These agreements include an agreement developed by members of the

[62] Financial Services and the Treasury Bureau, 'Guide to Procurement' (*Financial Services and the Treasury Bureau, The Government of the Hong Kong Special Administrative Region*). Available at: www.fstb.gov.hk/en/treasury/gov_procurement/guide-to-procurement.htm#topic-2, accessed 14 November 2022.

[63] Paper on Doha Development Agenda and Plurilateral Agreements Relevant to Hong Kong under the World Trade Organisation. Prepared by the Legislative Council Secretariat (background brief) (17 November 2015) CB (1)148/15-16(06) 1, 6.

[64] Trade and Industry Department, 'Hong Kong's Free Trade Agreements (FTAs)' (*Trade and Industry Department, The Government of the Hong Kong Special Administrative Region*, 10 November 2022). Available at: www.tid.gov.hk/english/ita/fta/index.html, accessed 14 November 2022.

[65] Trade and Industry Department, 'Hong Kong's Investment Promotion and Protection Agreements' (*Trade and Industry Department, The Government of the Hong Kong Special Administrative Region*, 8 November 2022). Available at: www.tid.gov.hk/english/ita/ippa/index.html, accessed 1 October 2023.

[66] HKSAR Government, 'LCQ4: Regional Comprehensive Economic Partnership' (*The Government of the Hong Kong Special Administrative Region Press Releases*, 1 June 2022). Available at: www.info.gov.hk/gia/general/202206/01/P2022060100534.htm, accessed 14 November 2022.

[67] Trade and Industry Department, 'Hong Kong's Participation in Plurilateral Trade Agreements' (*Trade and Industry Department, The Government of the Hong Kong Special Administrative Region*, 20 July 2022). Available at: www.tid.gov.hk/english/trade_relations/tradefora/plurilateral_trade_agreements.html, accessed 1 October 2023.

[68] Trade and Industry Department, 'Consultation Papers' (*Trade and Industry Department, The Government of the Hong Kong Special Administrative Region*, 20 July 2022). Available at: www.tid.gov.hk/english/aboutus/noticeboard/consultpaper.html, accessed 1 October 2023.

Joint Initiative on Investment Facilitation, the Environmental Goods Agreement ('EGA') and the Trade in Services Agreement ('TISA').

The Joint Initiative on Investment Facilitation was launched in 2017 with the aim of establishing a plurilateral agreement on investment for development.[69] Negotiations on this agreement commenced in September 2020[70] and, so far, 112 WTO members, including Hong Kong, are participating.[71] The new agreement aims to facilitate investment and covers topics such as reducing bureaucracy, improving transparency and assisting developing countries.

Regarding TISA, Hong Kong has been participating in the 23-nation negotiation process since 2013, believing that being a participant in this agreement would improve opportunities for service-based companies.[72] The TISA negotiations build upon the provisions of the GATS, with the aim of creating an agreement that enhances market access to services and the liberalisation of trade in services through the strengthening of regulations. In doing so, the text that is being negotiated aims to tackle the regulatory practices that may act as a market access barrier to trade in services, whilst providing a greater level of certainty in the investment environment for services. Although there have been 21 rounds of negotiations (the most recent being held in December 2016), an end date for negotiations has not been set.

Regarding EGA, negotiations between Hong Kong and 13 other WTO members[73] started in July 2014[74] with the aim of reducing tariffs on environmental goods. No tariffs are imposed on environmental goods or, in general, imported goods to Hong Kong. Nevertheless, since the aim of negotiating NEGA was to reduce tariffs on environmental goods, the Hong Kong government took the position that a reciprocal reduction and/or elimination of tariffs on environmental goods by its trading partners would be advantageous to its export trade and business sectors. Moreover, the cost reduction of environmental goods because of a reduction or elimination of tariffs could lead to their

[69] World Trade Organisation, 'Investment Facilitation for Development' (*World Trade Organisation*). Available at: www.wto.org/english/tratop_e/invfac_public_e/invfac_e.htm, accessed 14 November 2022.

[70] Global Affairs Canada, 'World Trade Organisation Joint Statement Initiative on Investment Facilitation for Development' (*Government of Canada | Gouvernement du Canada*, 3 June 2021). Available at: www.international.gc.ca/world-monde/international_relations-relations_internationales/wto-omc/investment-facilitation-investissements.aspx?lang=eng, accessed 1 October 2023.

[71] ibid.

[72] Trade and Industry Department, 'Trade in Services Agreement (under negotiation)' (*Trade and Industry Department, The Government of the Hong Kong Special Administrative Region*, 11 November 2022). Available at: www.tid.gov.hk/english/trade_relations/tradefora/wto_TISA.html, accessed 1 October 2023.

[73] As of the time of writing, the number of WTO members participating in EGA negotiations has increased to 18.

[74] Trade and Industry Department, 'Environmental Goods Agreement (under negotiation)' (*Trade and Industry Department, The Government of the Hong Kong Special Administrative Region*, 20 July 2022). Available at: www.tid.gov.hk/english/trade_relations/ega/index.html, accessed 1 October 2023.

increased usage, thereby protecting the environment. These factors formed the rationale for Hong Kong to participate in the negotiations. So far, 18 rounds of negotiations have been held, with differences on various issues still remaining and no signs of a negotiated text being produced. Regardless, it has been agreed that only when a sufficient number of WTO members have joined the EGA; its benefits will be accorded to non-participating member states.

Although Hong Kong has made progress in addressing and rectifying the concerns that have been raised by other WTO member states regarding its trade policy, as well as engaging in plurilateral agreement negotiations, its more-than-two-decades-old reputation as the world's freest economy has never been more precarious. Recent events, particularly those of the 2019–2020 protests and China's subsequent intervention in the territory, are a real cause for concern. There are fears that Hong Kong will lose its traditional status as the epitome of a free market economy.[75] Nonetheless, how big the impact will be and the extent to which these recent developments in the territory will affect trade policy in Hong Kong and its economic freedom standing remain to be seen. Further research will have to be done once they manifest in the future.

In conclusion, Hong Kong's decision to ratify plurilateral agreements stems from various considerations, one being the lengthy and complex WTO multilateral negotiation process. Multilateral agreements within the WTO require consensus, a state of affairs rarely achieved when so many member states, all with different concerns, are involved. Complex issues often require compromise and trade-offs and the increasing formation of coalitions can exacerbate the difficulty of reaching a consensus. This led to protracted negotiations such as the Doha Round, launched in 2001 and which was still perceived as inconclusive by 2015. Moreover, plurilateral agreements are perceived to create a more balanced competitive landscape among the signatories, promoting job creation and business opportunities. Hong Kong, in particular, has also used such agreements to address the free-rider problem arising from its free-trade policy. This was part of the rationale behind Hong Kong's ratification of the Agreement on Government Procurement (GPA), which aligns with its policy objectives of optimal value for money and supporting fair and transparent competition.

[75] James Gwartney and others, *Economic Freedom of the World: 2021 Annual Report* (Fraser Institute 2021) 1, 7.

9

Cross-Border Investments: Hong Kong and the Multilateral Investment Framework

As a global financial hub, Hong Kong plays a pivotal role in facilitating cross-border investments and shaping the multilateral investment framework. As a Special Administrative Region of China and with its well-established legal system, Hong Kong is an attractive destination for investors seeking a stable and reliable environment for their investments. Chapter 9 considers the various aspects of Hong Kong's engagement with multilateral investment frameworks, including its involvement with the International Centre for Settlement of Investment Disputes (ICSID), the New York Convention, the Multilateral Investment Guarantee Agency (MIGA), the United Nations Commission on International Trade Law (UNCITRAL) Working Group III and the World Trade Organisation's (WTO) investment facilitation initiatives. By examining Hong Kong's participation in these frameworks and its role in shaping global investment norms, this chapter aims to provide a comprehensive understanding of how the territory navigates the complex landscape of cross-border investments and contributes to the development of international investment policy.

The importance of an overarching framework for foreign investment protection has been recognised since the 1920s. A number of bilateral investment treaties (BITs) emerged after the Second World War, the first of which was signed between West Germany and Pakistan in 1959.[1] However, a significant milestone was reached when negotiations for the Multilateral Agreement on Investment (MAI) commenced in May 1995 at the Organisation for Economic Co-operation and Development (OECD) level.[2] The proposed MAI was envisaged as an overarching international investment agreement that was to be accessible to non-OECD countries,[3] whereby, amongst other protection

[1] Rudolf Dolzer and Margrete Stevens, *Bilateral Investment Treaties* (Leiden, Martinus Nijhoff Publishers 1995) 1.

[2] OECD, 'Multilateral Agreement on Investment' (*OECD*). Available at: www.oecd.org/investment/internationalinvestmentagreements/multilateralagreementoninvestment.htm, accessed 9 October 2023.

[3] ibid.

standards, the non-discriminatory principles – national treatment and most-favoured-nation and all sectors – would be encompassed.[4] However, for various reasons, the negotiations were abandoned. Thus, what now remains is a series of procedural framework conventions which aim to provide investors with grievance redressal avenues.

Until the handover in 1997, the United Kingdom (UK) acceded to and extended conventions and treaties to Hong Kong as a Crown territory of the UK.[5] The 1965 International Convention for the Settlement of Investment Disputes (ICSID Convention) between States and Nationals of Other States was signed by the UK in 1965.[6] The UK also ratified the New York Convention (NYC) on the Recognition and Enforcement of Foreign Arbitral Awards of 1958 in 1975 and made a 'reciprocity reservation'[7] under its Article I.3. In April 1977, the applicability and coverage of the NYC and ICSID Conventions were extended to Hong Kong. If Hong Kong becomes involved in more investment disputes, the ICSID Convention and NYC are important and will play very significant roles in the recognition and enforcement of investment arbitration awards.

Section I provides further details on the ICSID and analyses Hong Kong's role as a disputing party and its designation as a constituent subdivision or agency. Section II discusses the NYC and how it comes into play for investment disputes stemming from the Belt and Road Initiative (BRI). Section III considers the role that the Multilateral Investment Guarantee Agency (MIGA) plays and its relevance to China (specifically the BRI) and Hong Kong. Section IV provides updates on the United Nations Commission on International Trade Law (UNCITRAL) Working Group III's work whilst comparing the stances of Hong Kong and China in investor-state dispute settlement (ISDS) reforms. Section V outlines the progress that the World Trade Organisation (WTO) has made on investment facilitation and discusses Hong Kong's perspective on this area.

I. ENGAGING WITH THE ICSID CONVENTION: HONG KONG'S MEMBERSHIP AND PRACTICE

In 1962, the World Bank facilitated the signature of the ICSID Convention to enable global investment[8] and establish a mechanism for the apolitical settlement

[4] William H Witherell, 'The OECD Multilateral Agreement on Investment' (1995) 1, 7. Available at: https://unctad.org/system/files/official-document/iteiitv4n2a2_en.pdf, accessed 9 October 2023.

[5] Stephen D Mau, 'Hong Kong's Experience with the New York Convention: An Introduction' (1996) 9 *Global Business & Development Law Journal* 393, 405.

[6] Convention on the Settlement of Investment Disputes between States and Nationals of Other States (adopted 18 March 1965, entered into force 14 October 1966) 575 UNTS 159 (ICSID Convention).

[7] See Albert Jan van den Berg, *The New York Convention of 1958: Towards a Uniform Judicial Interpretation* (Boston, Kluwer Law and Taxation 1981) 416.

[8] Bruno Zeller and Richard Lightfoot, 'Good Faith: An ICSID Convention Requirement' (2018) 8 *Victoria University Law & Justice Journal* 19.

of investment disputes.[9] Currently, there are 165 State parties to the ICSID Convention.[10] By establishing an autonomous system for conciliation and arbitration, the ICSID provides an effective ISDS mechanism for foreign private investors and host states. Through this mechanism, foreign investors can have access to what is considered a more depoliticised dispute resolution regime and host states can safeguard their national interests better by avoiding participation in other (or even multiple) forums of international litigation.[11] Foreign investors can bring claims directly against host States, instead of depending on their home States to secure remedies on their behalf.[12] However, they retain the right and can choose to file a suit in a domestic court of the host state if they so desire.[13] The structural flexibility provided by the ICSID Convention is often seen as valuable by foreign investors.[14]

A. Accession, Membership and Dispute Resolution

Hong Kong is not a direct signatory to the ICSID Convention. After the 1997 handover, however, the ICSID Convention became applicable to Hong Kong via China's membership. The ICSID Convention applies to all territories for whose international relations a member state is responsible.[15] However, for the ICSID Convention to apply, a jurisdiction must first become a member of ICSID. Under Article 67 of the ICSID Convention, only members of the International Bank for Reconstruction and Development[16] (IBRD) and those that are parties to the Statute of the International Court of Justice and whose invitation to accede has been approved by two-thirds of the ICSID Administrative Council can sign the ICSID Convention.

The accession process begins with the jurisdiction notifying the ICSID Secretary-General that it plans to become a member of ICSID by signing the

[9] Wenhua Shan, 'EU Enlargement and the Legal Framework of EU–China Investment Relations' (2005) 6 *Journal World Investment and Trade* 237, 245.

[10] ICSID, 'List of Contracting States and Other Signatories of the Convention (as of 25 October 2022)' (*ICSID*, 2022) 1. Available at: https://icsid.worldbank.org/sites/default/files/ICSID%203/ICSID-3--ENG.pdf, accessed 9 October 2023.

[11] Christoph H Schreuer, *The ICSID Convention: A Commentary* (1st edn, Cambridge, Cambridge University Press, 2001) xi

[12] Ibironke T Odumosu, 'The Antinomies of the (Continued) Relevance of ICSID to the Third World' (2007) 8 *San Diego International Law Journal* 345, 358.

[13] Kate M Supnik, 'Making Amends: Amending the ICSID Convention to Reconcile Competing Interests in International Investment Law' (2009) 59 *Duke Law Journal* 343, 351.

[14] Eric Gottwald, 'Leveling the Playing Field: Is It Time for a Legal Assistance Centre for Developing Nations in Investment Treaty Arbitration?' (2007) 22 *American University International Law Review* 237, 248–49.

[15] ICSID Convention, art 70.

[16] Under Article II, section 1 of the IBRD Articles of Agreement, memberships to the IBRD are open to countries who are members of the International Monetary Fund.

ICSID Convention;[17] the convention is then signed at the World Bank.[18] Under Article 73 of the ICSID Convention, the state must then deliver an instrument that ratifies, accepts or approves the ICSID Convention to the IBRD. Finally, under Article 68(2), 30 days after the ratification, acceptance or approval instrument has been deposited, the convention will then enter into force and the state becomes a contracting state of ICSID.[19]

Currently, the ICSID Convention has entered into force in 158 contracting states, with seven countries as signatory states.[20] The United Nations (UN) has 193 member states, 2 UN General Assembly non-member observer states and 11 other states. In this sense, ICSID is said to have quasi-universal membership. However, this does not mean that the ICSID Convention may not be denounced by its contracting states. Article 71 of the ICSID Convention permits the withdrawal from the convention through a written notice to the depositary, with the act being effective six months after it has been delivered and there has been a receipt of acknowledgement. Until these six months have passed, the denunciating country's ICSID responsibilities and rights are still in effect.[21] Currently, Bolivia and Venezuela have denounced the ICSID Convention;[22] although Ecuador followed suit in July 2009.[23] Despite Bolivia's denunciation on 2 May 2007, it re-joined the convention on 3 September 2021.[24]

An ICSID arbitration proceeding is triggered when a foreign investor, or the claimant, submits a Request for Arbitration, which is subsequently screened and registered.[25] Under Article 25(1) of the ICSID Convention, three requirements must be met for an ICSID tribunal to have jurisdiction: (i) the responding jurisdiction must be a contracting state of ICSID, (ii) the dispute stemmed from investment; and (iii) both the responding party and the investor have consented in writing to submit the dispute to arbitration. A tribunal is then constituted, with members appointed under the requirements of Article 37 of

[17] ICSID, 'Joining ICSID' (*ICSID*). Available at: icsid.worldbank.org/about/member-states/joining-icsid, accessed 9 October 2023.

[18] IBRD, 'Memorandum on Signature and Ratification, Acceptance or Approval of the Convention on the Settlement of Investment Disputes between States and Nationals of Other States' para 3.

[19] ICSID, 'Guide to Membership in the ICSID Convention' (*ICSID*, 2020) 1, 5. Available at: https://icsid.worldbank.org/sites/default/files/Guide_to_Membership_in_the_ICSID_Convention_2020.pdf, accessed 9 October 2023.

[20] ICSID, 'List of Contracting States and Other Signatories of the Convention (as of 25 October 2022)' (n 12).

[21] ICSID Convention, art 72.

[22] José Carlos Bernal Rivera and Mauricio Viscarra Azuga, 'Life after ICSID: 10th Anniversary of Bolivia's Withdrawal from ICSID' (*Kluwer Arbitration Blog*, 12 August 2017). Available at: www.arbitrationblog.kluwerarbitration.com/2017/08/12/life-icsid-10th-anniversary-bolivias-withdrawal-icsid/, accessed 9 October 2023.

[23] Nicolas Boeglin, 'ICSID and Latin America: Criticisms, Withdrawals and Regional Alternatives' (June 2013). Available at: www.bilaterals.org/?icsid-and-latin-america-criticisms&lang=fr, accessed 9 October 2023.

[24] ICSID, 'List of Contracting States and Other Signatories of the Convention (as of 25 May 2023)' 2.

[25] ICSID, 'Practice Notes for Respondents in ICSID Arbitration' (*ICSID*, 2015) 1, 15. Available at: https://icsid.worldbank.org/sites/default/files/publications/Practice%20Notes%20for%20Respondents%20-%20Final.pdf, accessed 9 October 2023.

the ICSID Convention. Afterwards, the tribunal holds a pre-hearing organisational meeting,[26] which is followed by a hearing, with the disputing parties also submitting written pleadings. Finally, a written award, which may be subjected to a subsequent interpretation, revision or annulment,[27] is issued. The award legally binds the disputing parties while the lack of an appellate mechanism means that there is no right of appeal.[28] ICSID contracting states are expected to recognise and uphold ICSID awards by treating them as though their courts had issued them.[29] Thus, if the award is not honoured, a party may pursue it using their own legal system.[30]

B. Hong Kong's Role in Arbitrator Appointments

In recent years, Hong Kong has emerged as a significant player in international arbitration, particularly in the realm of investment disputes. As a Special Administrative Region of China, Hong Kong's involvement in the International Centre for Settlement of Investment Disputes (ICSID) arbitrator appointments demonstrates its growing influence and recognition in this field. This section examines Hong Kong's role in the appointment of arbitrators and conciliators within the ICSID framework and the contribution of Hong Kong permanent residents to the ICSID Database of Arbitrators, Conciliators and Ad Hoc Committee Members. Understanding Hong Kong's participation in this process provides valuable insight into the territory's broader engagement with international investment dispute resolution mechanisms.

A typical arbitral tribunal established under the ICSID Convention is composed of three arbitrators: each disputing party appoints one and the two-party-appointed arbitrators appoint the third arbitrator.[31] Generally, arbitrators are familiar with the areas related to the dispute.[32] ICSID tribunals apply governing rules that were previously agreed upon between the disputing parties.[33] Arbitral proceedings are available publicly in part and arbitral awards can be enforced widely.[34]

[26] ibid 26.

[27] ICSID Convention, arts 50–52.

[28] ibid art 53(1).

[29] ibid art 54(1).

[30] ibid art 54(2).

[31] ICSID, 'Number of Arbitrators and Method of Appointment – ICSID Convention (2006 Rules)' (*ICSID*) Available at: icsid.worldbank.org/procedures/arbitration/convention/process/appointment/2006, accessed 9 October 2023.

[32] David R Sedlak, 'ICSID's Resurgence in International Investment Arbitration: Can the Momentum Hold' (2004) 23 *Penn State International Law Review* 147, 152.

[33] ICSID Convention, art 42(1).

[34] ibid Preamble; Christopher F Dugan and others, *Investor State Arbitration* (New York, Oxford University Press, 2008) 182; Campbell McLachlan and others, *International Investment Arbitration: Substantive Principles* (Oxford, Oxford University Press, 2007) 83.

China appoints Hong Kong permanent residents who are Chinese citizens to its ICSID list of arbitrators and conciliators. Under Articles 13 and 14, both member states and the Chairman of the ICSID Administrative Council are permitted to appoint a number of individuals to the Panels of Arbitrators and Conciliators.[35] Such designations are made, subject to numerous factors, including the candidates' qualifications and moral character.[36]

Although Member states are free to designate individuals of a different nationality to the two panels, most have nevertheless appointed their own nationals as arbitrators and conciliators to ICSID,[37] with each term lasting for six years and subject to renewal.[38]

Currently, two Hong Kong permanent residents are on the ICSID Database of Arbitrators, Conciliators and Ad Hoc Committee Members: Anthony Neoh and Teresa Cheng. Neoh was designated by China from 2010 to 2016 as a conciliator,[39] and Cheng was appointed to the database by the Chairman of the ICSID Administrative Council in 2011 as an arbitrator.[40] When her term expired in 2017, she was then reappointed by China, with her term of appointment due to expire in 2023.

In conclusion, Hong Kong's involvement in the appointment of arbitrators and conciliators for ICSID showcases the territory's growing prominence in the international arbitration landscape. The participation of Hong Kong permanent residents, such as Anthony Neoh and Teresa Cheng, in the ICSID Database of Arbitrators, Conciliators and Ad Hoc Committee Members highlights the territory's commitment to fostering expertise and contributing to the development of international investment dispute resolution mechanisms. It is expected that Hong Kong will continue to play an increasingly important role in the field of investment arbitration, as the territory further strengthens its position as a global financial and legal hub.

C. Hong Kong as an ICSID Disputing Party

Even though Hong Kong has not been actively involved as a respondent in investment arbitration disputes, it is interesting to note that most disputes involving Hong Kong nationals have been instituted under the ICSID Convention. This

[35] ICSID Convention, arts 13 and 14. In each of the panels, ICSID member states can appoint four persons, whilst the Chairman can appoint six persons.

[36] Ibid art 14.

[37] See ICSID, 'Members of the Panels of Conciliators and of Arbitrators' (*ICSID*). Available at: www.icsid.worldbank.org/sites/default/files/ICSID%2010/ICSID-10.pdf, accessed 9 October 2023.

[38] ICSID Convention, art 15.

[39] ICSID, 'Dr. Anthony Neoh' (*ICSID*). Available at: www.icsid.worldbank.org/resources/databases/arbitrators-conciliators-ad-hoc-committee-members/profile?cvid=55, accessed 9 October 2023.

[40] ICSID, 'Ms. Teresa Cheng' (*ICSID*). Available at: www.icsid.worldbank.org/resources/databases/arbitrators-conciliators-ad-hoc-committee-members/profile?cvid=602, accessed 9 October 2023.

may be because of Hong Kong's position as a financial hub, which attracts companies from other jurisdictions.

Additionally, several reasons may explain why Hong Kong has not been a respondent to any publicly known ISDS, namely (i) the few BITs that Hong Kong has signed with their limited options for dispute resolution;[41] and (ii) Hong Kong's favourable investment climate.

Currently, Hong Kong has signed 22 BITs, or investment promotion and protection agreements (IPPAs), with third countries. However, most of them only allow the use of arbitration under the UNCITRAL Arbitration Rules for dispute resolution, although greater ISDS options, such as the option to opt for arbitral rules that have been mutually agreed upon by disputing parties, have appeared in subsequent BITs.[42] Additionally, Hong Kong's BIT and IPPA network is still relatively small. As far as the total number of BITs and the total number of treaties with investment provisions are concerned, it is currently ranked 105th and 122nd respectively out of 235 economies,.[43] Hong Kong would, therefore, have a significantly lower chance of becoming a respondent in an ICSID action than a nation with a large BIT network and more ISDS choices.

Hong Kong is also an appealing foreign direct investment (FDI) destination due to its favourable investment environment. This has been attributed to many factors, such as Hong Kong's reputation as an economy with a free trade policy[44] and the low crime and corruption levels,[45] which have been ensured by the existence of an independent judiciary and respect for the rule of law.[46] Correspondingly, the transparency of public administration, such as a consultation period required before any amendments or introduction of legislation,[47] the free flow of information[48] and adequate minority investor protection[49] also contribute to the fostering of foreign investors' confidence. Crucially, the

[41] Julien Chaisse, Kehinde Olaoye, 'Hong Kong, SAR China's New Approach to Investment Treaty Arbitration' (*Kluwer Arbitration Blog*, 10 July 2021). Available at: ww.arbitrationblog.kluwerarbitration.com/2021/07/10/Hong-Kong-sar-chinas-new-approach-to-investment-treaty-arbitration/, accessed 9 October 2023.

[42] ibid.

[43] UNCTAD Investment Policy Hub, 'International Investment Agreements Navigator' (*UNCTAD | Investment Policy Hub*). Available at: www.investmentpolicy.unctad.org/international-investment-agreements/by-economy, accessed 9 October 2023.

[44] Shuyong Liu, 'Hong Kong: A Survey of Its Political and Economic Development over the Past 150 Years' (1997) 151 *The China Quarterly* 583, 591.

[45] European Commission, 'Joint Report to the European Parliament and the Council – Hong Kong Special Administrative Region: Annual Report 2017' JOIN(2018) 7 final 1, 1.

[46] ibid 1–2.

[47] Bureau of Economic and Business Affairs, '2022 Investment Climate Statements: Hong Kong' (*US Department of State*, 29 July 2022). Available at: www.state.gov/reports/2022-investment-climate-statements/Hong-Kong/, accessed 9 October 2023.

[48] Ibid.

[49] IFC, 'Hong Kong Ranked as the Third Most Business-Friendly Economy in the World' (*IFC*, 29 October 2014). Available at: www.pressroom.ifc.org/all/pages/PressDetail.aspx?ID=24957, accessed 9 October 2023.

Hong Kong government imposes very few regulations on businesses,[50] and commercial businesses are conducted based on non-discrimination between domestic and foreign enterprises. For example, both Hong Kong and foreign-owned companies are taxed at the same corporate profit tax rate[51] and regulations are unambiguous and kept to a minimum.[52] Consequently, the territory has frequently topped or been near the top of the World Bank's list of economies on ease of doing business since 2005.[53]

Nevertheless, since 26 August 2022, Hong Kong has been encapsulated by the ICSID jurisdiction, having been designated a constituent subdivision or agency of China.[54]

For the ICSID jurisdiction to be extended to constituent subdivisions or agencies, two conditions have to be complied with.[55] Under Article 25(1) of the ICSID Convention, a subdivision or agency of a contracting state may consent to ICSID arbitration and for which ICSID jurisdiction would extend to it, ie, the subdivision or agency can then become disputing parties to an ICSID dispute,[56] provided that the particular contracting state has designated the concerned subdivision or agency as its constituent part. A further requirement is provided in Article 25(3), whereby the contracting state must approve its constituent subdivision's or agency's consent unless such approval is waived.

In light of China's designation, Hong Kong can participate in ICSID proceedings under their names and must perform any required procedural actions themselves and not by China, the contracting state.[57] This confers procedural autonomy on Hong Kong and crucially, subjects it to the jurisdiction of ICSID.[58]

[50] IBRD, 'Doing Business in 2004: Understanding Regulations' (*IBRD*, September 2003) 1, xiv, 89. Available at: https://archive.doingbusiness.org/content/dam/doingBusiness/media/Annual-Reports/English/DB04-FullReport.pdf, accessed 9 October 2023.

[51] Bureau of Economic and Business Affairs, '2021 Investment Climate Statements: Hong Kong' (*US Department of State*, 22 July 2021). Available at: www.state.gov/reports/2021-investment-climate-statements/Hong-Kong/, accessed 9 October 2023.

[52] Bureau of Economic and Business Affairs, '2022 Investment Climate Statements: Hong Kong' (n 48).

[53] IBRD, 'Doing Business in 2005: Understanding Regulations' (*IDRB*, September 2004) 1, 2. Available at: https://archive.doingbusiness.org/content/dam/doingBusiness/media/Annual-Reports/English/DB05-FullReport.pdf, accessed 9 October 2023.

[54] The ICSID Secretariat also publishes a list of constituent subdivisions or agencies that have been designated by their respective contracting states.

[55] Hanno Wehland, Jurisdiction and Admissibility in Proceedings under the ICSID Convention and ICSID Additional Facility Rules. in Crina Baltag (ed), ICSID Convention after 50 Years: Unsettled Issues: Unsettled Issues (Kluwer Law International 2017) para 8.04[A][2].

[56] William Rand and others, 'ICSID's Emerging Jurisprudence: The Scope of ICSID's Jurisdiction' (1986–1987) 19 *NYU Journal of International Law and Politics* 33, 43.

[57] Christoph H Schreuer and others, *The ICSID Convention: A Commentary* (2nd edn, Cambridge, Cambridge University Press, 2009) 916.

[58] ibid.

II. HARNESSING THE NEW YORK CONVENTION FOR INVESTMENT DISPUTES

In the realm of international commercial arbitration, the New York Convention (NYC) has played a vital role in streamlining the enforcement process of arbitral awards across borders. This section will examine the core principles and provisions of the NYC, its applicability to investment disputes and its relevance in today's global economic landscape.

The NYC has established a uniform structure related to the enforcement stage of international commercial arbitration.[59] The convention was adopted in 1958 and is still open for accession by the members of the UN.[60] With Timor-Leste's 2023 ratification, a total of 172 states and territories have ratified the Convention.[61] The primary goal of the NYC is to recognise and/or enforce the arbitral tribunal's awards. Contracting states must treat both international and domestic arbitration awards equally. The Convention shall apply to any 'agreement in writing'.[62] During the arbitral procedure, the parties' agreement is paramount. According to Article I, arbitral awards include those issued by permanent arbitral institutions and ad hoc arbitral tribunals.[63] The law of the forum can be applied if there is no party agreement. When an award is rendered by the arbitral tribunal, it can be enforced more easily than a foreign court judgment in ratifying countries.

A. The New York Convention and the 'Belt and Road' Initiative

Many have proposed the use of arbitral institutions in the resolution of investment disputes stemming from the BRI.[64] However, the enforceability of any arbitral awards rendered will be crucial in ensuring that they are effective.[65] In this

[59] See generally, Arbitration Ordinance (2011) (Cap 341) (H.K.) and Convention on the Recognition and Convention on the Recognition and Enforcement of Foreign Arbitral Awards (adopted 10 June 1958, entered into force 7 June 1959) 330 UNTS 3 (1958 New York Convention).

[60] See KW Patchett, The New York Convention on the Recognition and Enforcement of Foreign Arbitral Awards. Explanatory Documentation Prepared for Commonwealth Jurisdictions, (Commonwealth Secretariat 1981) 3. Available at: https://uncitral.un.org/sites/uncitral.un.org/files/media-documents/uncitral/en/new york convention-commonwealth.pdf, accessed 9 October 2023.

[61] See New York Arbitration Convention, 'Contracting States' (*New York Arbitration Convention*). Available at: www.newyorkconvention.org/countries, accessed 9 October 2023.

[62] 1958 New York Convention (n 67) arts II, IV.

[63] ibid art I.

[64] See, eg, Jiaxiang Hu and Jie (Jeanne) Huang, 'Dispute Resolution Mechanisms and Organizations in the Implementation of "One Belt, One Road" Initiative: Whence and Whither' (2018) 52 *Journal of World Trade* 815.

[65] Guiguo Wang, 'The Belt and Road Initiative in Quest for a Dispute Resolution Mechanism' (2017) 25 *Asia Pacific Law Review* 1, 4.

sense, as the most significant mechanism for an arbitral award's enforcement,[66] the NYC will be extremely relevant.

Currently, China is an NYC member state. Arbitral awards rendered in a jurisdiction that is also a signatory to the NYC will generally be enforced by Chinese domestic courts. However, there are some issues with China's reciprocity and commercial reservations for NYC. With regard to the former, the NYC only applies to awards issued by a jurisdiction that is also a party to the convention.[67] With the latter, the NYC only applies to disputes that arose from a legal commercial relationship, the determination of which is to be determined by the domestic law of the jurisdiction making this reservation[68] –in this case, China.

Although the majority of Asian BRI member states have acceded to the NYC, some have yet to do so, including the Solomon Islands. Thus, under China's reciprocity reservation, any investors looking to enforce an arbitral award that is rendered in these countries will be unable to rely on the NYC in a Chinese domestic court. Rather, under Article 283 of China's Civil Procedure Law, foreign investors could rely either on the principle of reciprocity or on a relevant international agreement to which both the non-NYC signatory party and China are contracting states instead.[69] More significantly, the area of investment does not fall within the ambit of China's commercial reservation. Therefore, the NYC will not apply to any investment arbitral awards that are to be enforced in China.[70]

B. Positioning Hong Kong as an Investment Structuring Hub

On 1 July 1997, in a significant move, China extended the application of the New York Convention (NYC) to include Hong Kong.[71] This development cemented Hong Kong's position as a prominent player in the arbitration field, particularly

[66] ibid; 1958 New York Convention Guide, 'Introduction' (*1958 New York Convention Guide*). Available at: www.newyorkconvention1958.org/index.php?lvl=cmspage&pageid=10&menu=674&opac_view=-1, accessed 9 October 2023.

[67] 1958 New York Convention Guide, 'Article I' (*1958 New York Convention Guide*). Available at: www.newyorkconvention1958.org/index.php?lvl=cmspage&pageid=10&menu=617&opac_view=-1, accessed 9 October 2023.

[68] ibid.

[69] John Choong and Xin Liu, 'Enforcing Arbitration Awards in China' (*Thomson Reuters Practical Law*, February 2023). Available at: www.ca.practicallaw.thomsonreuters.com/6-381-9839?transitionType=Default&contextData=(sc.Default)&firstPage=true, accessed 9 October 2023.

[70] Jingzhou Tao and Mariana Zhong, 'The Changing Rules of International Dispute Resolution in China's Belt and Road Initiative' in Zhang and others (eds), *China's Belt and Road Initiative – Changing the Rules of Globalization* (London, Palgrave Macmillan, 2018) 318.

However, in an opinion released on 16 June 2015, the Supreme People's Court of the People's Republic of China commented that reciprocal recognition and enforcement of arbitral awards which had been rendered in a BRI country, which was not an NYC signatory, should be encouraged.

[71] 1958 New York Convention Guide, 'Hong Kong' (*1958 New York Convention Guide*). Available at: www.newyorkconvention1958.org/index.php?lvl=cmspage&pageid=11&menu=579&opac_view=-1, accessed 9 October 2023.

within the thriving economic region of the Greater Bay Area, encompassing Guangdong, Hong Kong and Macao. The sophisticated arbitration system in place in Hong Kong is well-equipped to handle a broad array of dispute types, not least those related to investment. This offers substantial assurances to businesses operating in the region, facilitating an environment that is conducive to trade, investment and economic cooperation. It underscores the importance of Hong Kong in maintaining harmonious business relationships in this economically significant region, thereby contributing to the overall prosperity of the Greater Bay Area.

Investment structuring, which is generally permitted under investment law, is an action in which the control and corporate framework of foreign investment are structured in such a way that the availability of substantive and procedural protections accorded by investment treaties is taken into account. This is to ensure that foreign investments in a host jurisdiction are significantly protected by an investment treaty and that the option to engage in ISDS is available, which would otherwise not be protected or accessible to foreign investors. This enhances foreign investors' protection in a host jurisdiction. To give an example, if both the host and investor jurisdiction do not have an investment treaty with each other, through investment structuring, a national of the investor jurisdiction can be accorded investment protection if the project is structured in a way that it would be covered by a BIT between a third jurisdiction and the investor jurisdiction.[72]

The NYC also applies to non-ICSID investment arbitral awards.[73] In the above example, if the BIT between the third jurisdiction and the investor jurisdiction provides for the resolution of investment disputes via non-ICSID arbitration, the NYC would apply to any subsequent arbitral award that is rendered in a signatory state of the convention. Should the investor wish to enforce the award in an NYC signatory's court, they could then rely on the convention to aid their case.

Hong Kong has long been considered an investment structuring centre, with many law firms providing such a legal service.[74] Thus, for investors seeking to structure their foreign investments in such a way that will ensure they can rely on the NYC for any potential enforcement of investment arbitral awards, Hong Kong would be a desirable location for structuring investments.

In conclusion, the New York Convention has been instrumental in shaping the international arbitration landscape by providing a robust and uniform enforcement mechanism for arbitral awards. Its broad ratification and application to various types of disputes, including investment disputes, underscore its

[72] See Julien Chaisse, 'The Treaty Shopping Practice: Corporate Structuring and Restructuring to Gain Access to Investment Treaties and Arbitration' (2015) 11 *Hastings Business Law Journal* 225, 247.

[73] Emmanuel Gaillard and Ilija Mitrev Penushliski, 'State Compliance with Investment Awards' (2021) 35 *ICSID Review – Foreign Investment Law Journal* 540, 544.

[74] See The Legal 500, 'Investment Funds' (*The Legal 500*). Available at: www.legal500.com/c/Hong-Kong/investment-funds/, accessed 9 October 2023.

significance in the global economy. As the world becomes increasingly interconnected, the NYC's role in facilitating the resolution of cross-border disputes will continue to be crucial. The Convention's adaptability and responsiveness to the evolving needs of the international community highlight its enduring relevance, ensuring that it remains a cornerstone of the global dispute resolution framework. The principles of the NYC will undoubtedly influence future developments in international commercial arbitration and its ability to cap territory to accommodate emerging trends and challenges will be critical to its continued success.

III. EXPLORING CHINA'S RELATIONSHIP WITH THE MULTILATERAL INVESTMENT GUARANTEE AGENCY

The Multilateral Investment Guarantee Agency (MIGA) is a critical institution within the global investment landscape, offering political risk insurance and credit enhancement to facilitate foreign direct investment (FDI) in emerging economies. Established under the World Bank Group, MIGA plays a pivotal role in promoting economic growth, reducing poverty and fostering sustainable development.[75] As a Special Administrative Region of China, Hong Kong's engagement with multilateral economic norms and its position as an international financial hub necessitate an in-depth examination of China's relationship with MIGA. This section aims to provide a comprehensive analysis of China's interaction with MIGA, its role in the agency and the relevance of MIGA to both China and Hong Kong.

The section will begin by offering an overview of MIGA, its primary functions and its significance in the global investment environment. It will then proceed to examine China's involvement with MIGA, highlighting key aspects of their relationship, including China's membership, contributions and the impact of Chinese investments on MIGA's operations. Subsequently, the section will discuss the relevance of MIGA to Hong Kong, exploring how the agency's activities intersect with Hong Kong's role as a financial centre and its broader engagement with multilateral economic norms. In so doing, the section seeks to provide valuable insights into the dynamics of China's relationship with MIGA and its implications for Hong Kong's position within the global investment landscape.

[75] Formed under the umbrella of the World Bank and with all member states of the IBRD allowed to become its members (Convention Establishing the Multilateral Investment Guarantee Agency (adopted 11 October 1985, entered into force 23 June 1988) 1508 UNTS 99 ('MIGA Convention') art 4), MIGA is the world's biggest body on investment risk insurance (Quiting Wang, 'The Perfection of Subrogation System in Overseas Investment Insurance System' (2022) 6 *Journal of Humanities, Arts and Social Science* 479, 480).

A. MIGA's Function and Impact

The Multilateral Investment Guarantee Agency (MIGA), a pivotal entity under the World Bank Group, offers a range of invaluable services to facilitate and safeguard foreign direct investments. Notably, its good office services play a crucial role in mediating potential disputes between foreign investors and host jurisdictions, ensuring that conflicts are resolved amicably and fostering project continuity. The host jurisdiction benefits from continued development, while investors receive substantial returns on their investment. Moreover, MIGA imposes a set of environmental and social performance standards on all projects it guarantees. By advising guarantee holders and investors on how to adhere to these standards, MIGA actively promotes responsible and sustainable investment practices, thereby contributing to the overall goal of enhancing quality of life and combating poverty. China's endorsement of the MIGA Convention reflects its recognition of the critical need for such an international system to protect its foreign investments. This necessity is particularly pronounced in the context of China's ambitious 'Belt and Road' Initiative (BRI), which involves substantial investment activities in numerous developing and least-developed countries. These nations inherently present higher political risk, thus amplifying the importance of MIGA's investment guarantees. Projects within the China-Indochina Peninsula Economic Corridor, for instance, encompass participation from several such countries, necessitating a considerable volume of investment guarantees. As such, MIGA's role is integral to the successful execution of the BRI, providing much-needed insurance against potential risks and thereby boosting investor confidence. Consequently, China's interaction with MIGA underscores the agency's significant influence on the global investment landscape and China's commitment to sustainable and secure investment practices.

Under Article 2 of the Convention establishing the Multilateral Investment Guarantee Agency (MIGA Convention), MIGA aims to complement the work of the IBRD, the International Finance Corporation and other international development financial organisations by facilitating investment flows between its member states, particularly between developing countries. In doing so, the agency aims to encourage FDI in developing countries by offering eligible investors and lenders political risk insurance and credit improvement assurances,[76] which would then assist their economic growth, combat poverty and enhance the quality of life for their populations.[77] Such political risk coverages include currency inconvertibility and transfer restriction, expropriation, war and civil

[76] MIGA, 'About Us' (*MIGA*). Available at: www.miga.org/about-us, accessed 9 October 2023.

[77] World Bank, 'MIGA (Multilateral Investment Guarantee Agency)' (*World Bank*, September 2012. Available at: www.web.worldbank.org/archive/website01363/WEB/0__CO-83.HTM, accessed 9 October 2023.

disturbance, breach of contract by the host jurisdiction's government and the non-honouring of financial obligations.[78]

The work that MIGA does on political risk assurance is also supplemented by its other services. For example, MIGA provides good office services to help resolve investment disputes between foreign investors and the host jurisdiction amicably, which helps promote project continuity.[79] This is mutually beneficial for both disputing parties, as the project would facilitate the host economy's development, whilst the success of the project could yield foreign investors significant returns on investment. Similarly, MIGA-guaranteed projects are also subjected to a series of social and environmental performance standards.[80] The organisation, therefore, advises guarantee holders, which finance the projects and hold a guarantee as issued by MIGA,[81] and investors on how the standards are to be observed through its expertise in these areas.[82]

B. MIGA's Significance for China and Hong Kong

As an investment insurance agency, MIGA plays an important role in protecting Chinese and Hong Kong guarantee holders and investors from risks that stem from foreign investments and, thus, financial losses. China's acceptance of the MIGA Convention suggests that it recognises the necessity of such a system for foreign investment insurance.[83] This is particularly important because, more often than not, the materialisation of the BRI involves investing in significant numbers of developing and least-developed countries, which have a higher political risk. For example, the China-Indochina Peninsula Economic Corridor involves the participation of Vietnam, Thailand, Laos, Cambodia, Myanmar and Malaysia.[84] Thus, significant numbers of investment guarantees are required.[85] China is also a host jurisdiction for 43 MIGA-guaranteed projects and an investor country for 28 projects, while lenders from China are involved in more than 20 projects.[86]

[78] MIGA Convention (n 76) art 11.

[79] MIGA, 'Dispute Resolution' (*MIGA*). Available at: www.miga.org/dispute-resolution, accessed 9 October 2023.

[80] World Bank Group, *The World Bank Group A to Z* (Washington DC, World Bank Publications 2014) 107–108.

[81] MIGA, 'Operational Regulations (as amended by the Board of Directors through August 27, 2022)' (*MIGA*) xiv. Available at: www.docs.pca-cpa.org/2016/02/Operational-Regulations-of-the-Multilateral-Investment-Guarantee-Agency-as-amended-through-Aug.-27-2002.pdf, accessed 9 October 2023.

[82] MIGA, 'What We Do' (*MIGA*). Available at: www.miga.org/what-we-do, accessed 9 October 2023.

[83] Yushu Feng, 'China and the Multilateral Investment Guarantee Agency' (1999) *Policy Research Working Paper 1763* 1, 12.

[84] OECD, *OECD Business and Finance Outlook 2018* (Paris, OECD Publishing 2018) 69.

[85] Songling Yang, 'Investment Dispute Settlement Mechanism in the Context of the Belt and Road Initiative' (2022) 126 *Journal of Law, Policy and Globalization* 29, 34.

[86] MIGA, 'Projects' (*MIGA*). Available at: www.miga.org/projects?project_status=All&env_category=All&project_type=All&covid_19=All&board_date%5Bmin%5D=&board_

Hong Kong was a part of the British delegation at the World Bank before the handover on 1 July 1997 and then a part of China's delegation afterwards.[87] The MIGA Convention is also currently in force in Hong Kong,[88] having been applicable since 9 April 1986.[89] It has been an investor economy in five projects,[90] with banks from Hong Kong acting as guarantee holders for eight projects.[91]

MIGA comes into play in two main ways. Investing in developing countries poses a higher risk than investing in developed countries. Thus, MIGA can instil greater investor confidence by offering better investment protections and securities to Chinese and Hong Kong investors and the numerous lenders in Hong Kong and China that are financing the projects. This is especially true where force majeure risks are involved, as they are often not covered by commercial lenders and export credit organisations.[92] MIGA's involvement eases any worries that the guarantee-holders and foreign investors from China and Hong Kong may have about the concerned project in the host economy. For China as a host economy, MIGA also creates a more favourable investment climate there, as it reduces the risk of investment. This ensures that foreign investors' confidence remains in the economy and potentially incentivises potential foreign investors to invest, thus encouraging further FDI flow into China.

date%5Bmax%5D=&title=&guarantee_holder%5B2816%5D=2816&guarantee_holder%5B2821%5D=2821&guarantee_holder%5B2826%5D=2826&guarantee_holder%5B781%5D=781&guarantee_holder%5B782%5D=782&guarantee_holder%5B783%5D=783&guarantee_holder%5B616%5D=616&guarantee_holder%5B950%5D=950&guarantee_holder%5B951%5D=951&guarantee_holder%5B959%5D=959&guarantee_holder%5B2406%5D=2406&project_id=&slp_type=All&page=0, accessed 9 October 2023.

[87] Hong Kong Monetary Authority, 'Guide to Hong Kong Monetary, Banking and Financial Terms' (*Hong Kong Monetary Authority*, 23 July 2021). Available at: www.hkma.gov.hk/eng/data-publications-and-research/guide-to-monetary-banking-and-financial-terms/world_bank_group/, accessed 9 October 2023.

[88] Department of Justice, 'Multilateral Agreements' (*Department of Justice, The Government of the Hong Kong Special Administrative Region*, 9 January 2023). Available at: www.doj.gov.hk/en/external/treaties.html, accessed 21 January 2023.

[89] Legislative Council Panel on Constitutional Affairs, 'Constitutional Affairs (Papers) 16 Dec 96' (*Legislative Council of the Hong Kong Special Administrative Region of the People's Republic of China*). Available at: www.legco.gov.hk/yr96-97/english/panels/ca/papers/xx1612x3.htm#E16E2, accessed 9 October 2023. The Sino-British Joint Liaison Group also approved the continual application of the MIGA Convention after 30 June 1997.

[90] MIGA, 'Projects' (MIGA). Available at: www.miga.org/projects?project_status=All&env_category=All&project_type=All&covid_19=All&board_date%5Bmin%5D=&board_date%5Bmax%5D=&title=&investor_country%5B%5D=402&project_id=, accessed 9 October 2023.

[91] MIGA, 'Projects' (*MIGA*). Available at: www.miga.org/projects?project_status=All&env_category=All&project_type=All&covid_19=All&board_date%5Bmin%5D=&board_date%5Bmax%5D=&title=&guarantee_holder%5B%5D=3031&guarantee_holder%5B%5D=2506&guarantee_holder%5B%5D=725&guarantee_holder%5B%5D=853&guarantee_holder%5B%5D=980&project_id=, accessed 9 October 2023.

[92] Shi Hua and Yuanzheng Cai, 'On the Role and Limitation of the MIGA in BOT Investment Mode for the Belt and Road Initiative' (2019) 9 *Journal of WTO and China* 88, 97.

IV. HONG KONG'S INVOLVEMENT IN UNCITRAL WORKING GROUP III

In recent years, there has been a growing global consensus on the need to reform the investor-state dispute settlement (ISDS) system, addressing concerns related to transparency, consistency and the overall legitimacy of the arbitration process. As a response, the United Nations Commission on International Trade Law (UNCITRAL) initiated Working Group III, focusing on ISDS reform. Hong Kong, as a Special Administrative Region of China with a well-established legal infrastructure, plays a significant role in these reform efforts. This section will contextualise Hong Kong's involvement in UNCITRAL Working Group III, examine its contributions to the ongoing discussions and assess the impact of ISDS reforms on Hong Kong as a hub for international arbitration and investment.[93] By exploring the territory's engagement with the Working Group,[94] this section aims to highlight Hong Kong's commitment to shaping the future of global investment policy and dispute resolution mechanisms. Regular meetings have been held by the Working Group and all stakeholders have contributed their expertise to the deliberations.[95] During the ISDS reform process, the interests and obligations of countries and investors should be carefully dealt with.[96] UNCITRAL does not merely act as a venue for international law-making, but also as an actor that has navigated a complex series of relationships in hopes of forging a salient role for the organisation in the reforms process'. Over the last two Working Group III sessions, 108 UNCITRAL member states and observer states, 17 international governmental organisations and 58 non-governmental organisations attended and were involved in the meetings.[97] This demonstrates the scale of Working Group III meetings, as well as the importance that countries, international governmental organisations and non-governmental organisations place on ISDS reforms.

[93] Due to many problems existing in the current ISDS mechanism, such as the absence of an appeal mechanism and inconsistent arbitral awards, the UNCITRAL Working Group III was authorised in 2017 during its 50th session to discuss possible reforms of investment treaty arbitration. UNCITRAL Working Group III, 'Possible Reform of Investor-State Dispute Settlement (ISDS) – Submission from the Government of China – Note by the Secretariat' (19 July 2019) UN Doc A/CN.9/WG.III/WP.177; UNGA, 'Report of the United Nations Commission on International Trade Law' UNCITRAL 50th Session Supp No 17 UN Doc A/72/17 para 264.

[94] The three-step agenda of Working Group III was to '(a) first, identify and consider concerns regarding investor-State dispute settlement; (b) second, consider whether reform was desirable in the light of any identified concerns; and (c) third, if the Working Group were to conclude that reform was desirable, develop any relevant solutions to be recommended to the Commission'. UNGA ibid.

[95] UNCITRAL Working Group III, 'Possible Reform of Investor-State Dispute Settlement (ISDS) – Note by the Secretariat' (18 September 2017) UN Doc A/CN.9/WG.III/WP.142 2.

[96] UNGA para 258.

[97] The numbers were obtained through a comparison of the list of attendees for the 43rd and 44th Sessions. The European Union has been grouped into the 'UNCITRAL member states and observer states' category.

A. UNCITRAL Working Group III's Mandate

The 44th session of the UNCITRAL Working Group III session was held in Vienna between 23–27 January 2023.[98] It was attended by 58 members of the Working Group, 34 observer states, observers from the European Union and various other international organisations.[99] The primary ISDS topics of the session were the draft codes of conduct and commentary for arbitrators and judges and an appellate mechanism within the ISDS framework.[100]

On the draft codes of conduct and commentary, the primary areas of discussion were the avoidance of conflicts of interest, the sanctions that could be imposed as a result of a non-compliance with the draft code and the provision that addresses the obligations to disclose information that could lead to a potential conflict of interests by candidate arbitrators and arbitrators.[101] Particularly on the obligation to disclose, there were sentiments that the provision: 'The fact of non-disclosure does not in itself establish [a lack of impartiality or independence] [a breach of Articles 3 to 6 of the Code]'[102] should not be interpreted as granting a discharge to candidate arbitrators and arbitrators from their duties to disclose.[103]

Discussions regarding the draft provisions on the functioning of an appellate mechanism were held.[104] Moreover, although widespread support for the existence of such a mechanism was observed, there were concerns regarding the potential extra time and pecuniary costs that disputing parties would incur from using such a system.[105] Suggestions were also made regarding the possible model of the appellate mechanism, in which the discussion scope should cover other mechanisms, rather than merely concentrating on a standing two-tier system.[106] In subsequent discussions, it was concluded that, considering the primary goals of an appellate mechanism, the benefits and drawbacks of the

[98] UNCITRAL, 'Working Group III: Investor-State Dispute Settlement Reform' (*United Nations | United Nations on International Trade Law*). Available at: www.uncitral.un.org/en/working_groups/3/investor-state, accessed 9 October 2023.

[99] UNCITRAL Working Group III, 'Report of Working Group III (Investor-State Dispute Settlement Reform) on the work of its forty-fourth session (Vienna, 23–27 January 2023)' (7 February 2023) UN Doc A/CN.9/1130 paras 4–7.

[100] ibid paras 9–11.

[101] Yarik Kryvoi, '44th session of the UNCITRAL Working Group III: Code of Conduct for Arbitrators, its Enforcement, Corruption Allegations in ISDS' (*British Institute of International and Comparative Law*, 3 February 2023). Available at: www.biicl.org/blog/53/44th-session-of-the-uncitral-working-group-iii-code-of-conduct-for-arbitrators-its-enforcement-corruption-allegations-in-isds?cookiesset=1&ts=1676204401, accessed 9 October 2023.

[102] UNCITRAL Working Group III, 'Possible Reform of Investor-State Dispute Settlement (ISDS) – Draft Codes of Conduct and Commentary – Note by the Secretariat' (23 November 2022) UN Doc A/CN.9/WG.III/WP.223 24.

[103] UNCITRAL Working Group III, 'Report of Working Group III (Investor-State Dispute Settlement Reform) on the Work of its forty-fourth session (Vienna, 23–27 January 2023)' (n 100) para 41.

[104] ibid paras 125–48.

[105] ibid para 123.

[106] ibid para 122.

various implementation models would require further investigation.[107] Finally, the interactions between the new appellate mechanism and the existing review mechanisms were addressed. Specifically, it was recommended that the new mechanism, should not mirror that of the existing mechanism.[108] However, contrasting views were also observed, as to whether the appellate mechanism should replace the existing review mechanisms.[109]

B. Hong Kong's Contribution to ISDS Reform

Hong Kong has provided a wide range of mechanisms for the resolution of investment disputes; an enforcement system also exists for disputing parties to enforce an arbitral award. Since 2017, the territory's Department of Justice (DoJ) has been a part of China's delegation at the UNCITRAL Working Group III meetings.[110] Additionally, the DoJ has partnered up with UNCITRAL and the Asian Academy of International Law (AAIL) and organised various workshops, conferences and discussion forums regarding ISDS reforms.

A common theme resolves around these events, namely the use of mediation in investment disputes. This is unsurprising, given Hong Kong's emphasis on mediation and its promotion of such a dispute resolution method.[111] For example, in her speech at a webinar organised by the AAIL on 26 February 2021, the then Secretary of Justice, Teresa Cheng, noted that a lot of effort was put into cultivating investment mediation in Hong Kong.[112]

In contrast, during the UNCITRAL Working Group III meetings regarding ISDS reform, China embraced the proposal for the establishment of a permanent appellate mechanism, in relation to the construction of an 'ad hoc or standing multilateral mechanism'.[113] Additionally, on the reform of the appointment and ethics of arbitrators, it was pointed out that the selection of arbitrators is

[107] ibid para 165.
[108] ibid para 153.
[109] ibid paras 151–52.
[110] Department of Justice, 'Legislative Council Panel on Administration of Justice and Legal Services – Professional Development for Legal Profession – International Organisation Secondment Programmes' (*Legislative Council of the Hong Kong Special Administrative Region of the People's Republic of China*, September 2021) LC Paper No CB(4)1549/20-21(03) 1, 5. Available at: www.doj.gov.hk/en/legco/pdf/ajls20210927e1.pdf, accessed 25 February 2024.
[111] Dini Sejko, 'UNCITRAL Working Group III on ISDS Reform Virtual Pre-Intersessional Meeting on the Use of Mediation in ISDS Background Paper for Session 3 – Hybrid Models of Arbitration and Mediation' (2020) 7. Available at: www.aail.org/wpcontent/uploads/2020/11/2020_UNCITRAL_WGIII_Background_Paper_Session_3.pdf, accessed 9 October 2023.
[112] HKSAR Government, 'Speech by SJ at Webinar 'Why Hong Kong is Irreplaceable' (English only) (with photos)' (*The Government of the Hong Kong Special Administrative Region Press Releases*, 26 February 2021). Available at: www.info.gov.hk/gia/general/202102/26/P2021022600789.htm, accessed 25 February 2024.
[113] UNCITRAL Working Group III, 'Possible Reform of Investor-State Dispute Settlement (ISDS) – Note by the Secretariat – Addendum' (30 July 2019) UN Doc A/CN.9/WG.III/WP.166/Add.1.

the basic right of parties and arbitrators should obey the code of conduct.[114] Referring to dispute prevention and mitigation, China recommends developing an alternative dispute resolution mechanism and adding a consultation process before the arbitration procedure.[115] Finally, China has also emphasised the importance of transparency in third-party funding.[116]

Hong Kong has long advocated mediation as a preferred mode of resolving investment disputes. Central to this drive is the region's robust policy framework, shaped by legislative and institutional supports that facilitate the use of mediation. One of the key legislative landmarks is the Mediation Ordinance, enacted in 2013, which provides a solid legal foundation for the mediation process and establishes a clear framework for its application.[117] Complementing these legislative supports are dedicated bodies that promote mediation, such as the Hong Kong Mediation Centre and the Hong Kong International Arbitration Centre (HKIAC), which offers a well-established framework for international mediation. They are instrumental in both training mediators and promoting Hong Kong as an ideal place for international dispute resolution. Moreover, Hong Kong has also embarked on several initiatives to popularise mediation. Among these is the 'Mediate First' campaign, launched by the DoJ, which encourages businesses to consider mediation as the first resort in resolving disputes. Furthermore, the Hong Kong Mediation Accreditation Association Limited (HKMAAL) was established to provide accreditation for mediators, thus ensuring a pool of highly skilled professionals. Success stories abound, showcasing the effectiveness of mediation in Hong Kong. One notable instance is the resolution of a substantial commercial dispute in 2020 where the parties reached an agreement through HKIAC's administered mediation within a matter of weeks, thereby avoiding a protracted and costly litigation process.

In the context of ISDS reforms, Hong Kong has remained steadfast in its promotion of mediation. Recognising the benefits of mediation in investment disputes, such as cost-efficiency, preservation of business relationships and the ability to design creative solutions, Hong Kong has actively endorsed the inclusion of mediation in international dispute resolution frameworks. The then Secretary of Justice Teresa Cheng, in her address at a webinar by the Asian Academy of International Law in 2021, underscored this commitment, highlighting Hong Kong's extensive efforts in cultivating the field of investment mediation. Overall, Hong Kong's focus on mediation demonstrates its proactive approach to ISDS reforms. By integrating mediation into its dispute resolution

[114] UNCITRAL Working Group III, 'Possible Reform of Investor-State Dispute Settlement (ISDS) – Submission from the Government of China – Note by the Secretariat' 5.

[115] ibid.

[116] ibid.

[117] HKSAR, Cap. 620 Mediation Ordinance. Available at: www.elegislation.gov.hk/hk/cap620?xpid= ID_1438403538278_003>.

strategy, Hong Kong is offering a more flexible and amicable approach to resolving investment disputes, aligning with global trends and reiterating its status as a leading hub for international dispute resolution.

From the above it can be seen that, even though the UNCITRAL reform process is still ongoing, different positions have been adopted by China (proposing a permanent appellate mechanism) and Hong Kong (supporting mediation). This also shows that Hong Kong still maintains some degree of autonomy in international economic dispute settlement, even though its political sovereignty appears to be diminishing.

The aim of this section was not only to discuss Hong Kong as a respondent or Hong Kong investors as claimants but also to demonstrate what actions Hong Kong has taken in the ISDS forum as a systemic stakeholder. In other words, this part is talking about the special status of Hong Kong in the ISDS forum. It can be seen that Hong Kong is actively participating in the ISDS forum. If there are investment disputes involving Hong Kong or its investors as parties, Hong Kong has provided a comprehensive system to resolve related disputes and enforce the awards. This improves its attractiveness to foreign investors. Domestic investors can also enjoy this better protection.

V. ADVANCING INVESTMENT FACILITATION AT THE WTO

The World Trade Organisation (WTO) has long been recognised as a key institution in the global trade regime, facilitating the negotiation and enforcement of trade rules and fostering international cooperation. In recent years, the scope of the WTO's activities has expanded to address the growing importance of investment facilitation in promoting sustainable development, economic growth and global economic integration. As an active member of the WTO and a major international financial hub, Hong Kong's engagement in the investment facilitation agenda is of critical significance.

After the collapse of the Fifth Ministerial Conference in Cancún in 2003, as a result of a failure to reach a consensus in the negotiations on Singaporean issues,[118] including investment, this area was also removed from the WTO negotiation tables in 2004.[119] Nevertheless, in early 2017, two separate partnerships, MIKTA and Friends of Investment Facilitation for Development (FIFD), began organising informal talks and workshops, which gradually evolved into a discussion on whether the WTO was an appropriate venue to negotiate an

[118] Robert E Baldwin, 'Failure of the WTO Ministerial Conference at Cancun: Reasons and Remedies' (2006) 29 *The World Economy* 677, 684.

[119] WTO, 'Text of the 'July Package' – The General Council's Post-Cancún Decision' (*WTO*, 1 August 2004). Available at: www.wto.org/english/tratop_e/dda_e/draft_text_gc_dg_31july04_e.htm, accessed 9 October 2023.

agreement on investment facilitation.[120] The cumulative result was the launching of the Joint Initiative on Investment Facilitation for Development (JIIFD) in December of the same year.[121] As a member of the WTO, Hong Kong has been actively participating in various negotiations to achieve a multilateral result, including investment facilitation.

A. The Joint Initiative on Investment Facilitation for Development

On 13 December 2017, a Joint Statement Initiative on Investment Facilitation for Development was signed by 70 WTO member states, which served as an announcement for the creation of the JIIFD.[122] Negotiations for the agreement were formally launched on 25 September 2020, after structured discussions were completed.[123] During the subsequent rounds of discussions, various issues were covered, including the non-discrimination principles[124] and special and differential treatment.[125] Alongside the negotiation rounds, various inter-sessional meetings, small group discussion groups and workshops were also held. For example, on 10 July 2017, the FIFD held a workshop to enable exchanges between relevant stakeholders on various investment facilitation topics.[126] Currently, 113 member states are participating in the negotiations. A new consolidated text that resulted from the negotiations since April 2021, has also been circulated[127]

[120] Sofia Baliño and others, 'Investment Facilitation: History and the Latest Developments in the Structured Discussions' (*IISD*, 31 January 2020) 1, 7. Available at: www.iisd.org/publications/report/investment-facilitation-history-and-latest-developments-structured-discussions, accessed 19 February 2024. ICSID, 'Guide to Membership in the ICSID Convention' (*ICSID*, 2020) 1, 5. Available at: www.icsid.worldbank.org/sites/default/files/Guide_to_Membership_in_the_ICSID_Convention_2020.pdf, accessed 9 October 2023.

[121] Sofia Baliño and Nathalie Bernasconi Osterwalder, 'Investment Facilitation at the WTO: An Attempt to Bring a Controversial Issue into an Organisation in Crisis' (*Investment Treaty News*, 27 June 2019). Available at: www.iisd.org/itn/en/2019/06/27/investment-facilitation-at-the-wto-an-attempt-to-bring-a-controversial-issue-into-an-organization-in-crisis-sofia-balino-nathalie-osterwalder/, accessed 9 October 2023.

[122] Ministerial Conference – Eleventh Session – Buenos Aires, 10-13 December 2017 – Joint Ministerial Statement on Investment Facilitation for Development (13 December 2017) WT/MIN(17)/59. Available at: www.docsonline.wto.org.

[123] WTO, 'Structured Discussions on Investment Facilitation for Development Move into Negotiating Mode' (*WTO*, 25 September 2020). Available at: www.wto.org/english/news_e/news20_e/infac_25sep20_e.htm, accessed 9 October 2023.

[124] WTO, 'Investment Facilitation Negotiators Confirm Aim of Finalizing Text-based Talks by End-2022' (*WTO*, 8 July 2022). Available at: www.wto.org/english/news_e/news22_e/infac_08jul22_e.htm, accessed 9 October 2023.

[125] WTO, 'Investment Facilitation Agreement Negotiators Wrap Up Productive Year' (*WTO*, 8 December 2020). Available at: www.wto.org/english/news_e/news20_e/infac_08dec20_e.htm, accessed 9 October 2023.

[126] WTO, 'Workshop on Investment Facilitation for Development' (*WTO*, 10 July 2017). Available at: www.wto.org/english/tratop_e/invest_e/workshopinvestjuly17_e.htm, accessed 9 October 2023.

[127] WTO, 'Circulation of Draft Agreement Marks Major Milestone in Investment Facilitation Talks' (*WTO*, 16 December 2022). Available at: www.wto.org/english/news_e/news22_e/infac_16dec22_e.htm, accessed 9 October 2023.

and would be a reference point to guide the next stages of the negotiations.[128] It is anticipated that the draft agreement will be concluded in late 2023 or 2024.[129]

B. Hong Kong's Stance on Investment Facilitation within the WTO

Consistently, Hong Kong has positioned itself as a pro-investment protection and facilitation territory. This can also be seen at the WTO-level, of which the territory has been a part since 1 January 1995.

During the General Council Meeting held on 27–28 February and April 2017, the representative of Hong Kong acknowledged that investment facilitation was an area where more could be done and hoped that the understanding of such a topic would be yielded from further discussions.[130] Crucially, in subsequent meetings, Hong Kong has often highlighted the need for the member states' engagement and cooperation in the investment facilitation work that was to be conducted at the WTO, in light of the difficulties that it was facing at that time,[131] and expressed its hopes for the formalisation of debates on this matter at WTO-level.[132]

Hong Kong's position on investment facilitation, after the JIIFD's launch, has remained consistent. During various General Council meetings, Hong Kong urged member states which had yet to join the initiative to do so,[133] especially as it would preserve the viability of the WTO system. As negotiations for a multilateral agreement on investment facilitation got underway, Hong Kong noted that it was actively participating in the process[134] and firmly supporting the work that was being done.[135] It also reinforced its position that the JIIFD and other joint initiatives would assist in the process of modernising the WTO system and its rules[136] such that they would be more adapted to addressing new

[128] WTO, 'Investment Facilitation Talks Intensify to Conclude Draft Agreement in First Half of 2023' (*WTO*, 1 February 2023). Available at: www.wto.org/english/news_e/news23_e/infac_02feb23_e.htm, accessed 9 October 2023.

[129] ibid.

[130] General Council – Held in the Centre William Rappard on 27–28 February 2017 and Reconvened on 7 April 2017 – Minutes of Meeting (3 May 2017) WT/GC/M/166 para 11.27. Available at: www.docsonline.wto.org.

[131] General Council – Held in the Centre William Rappard on 10 and 18 May 2017 – Minutes of Meeting (21 July 2017) WT/GC/M/167 73. Available at: www.docsonline.wto.org.

[132] Trade Negotiations Committee – Held in the Centre William Rappard on 28 November 2017 – Minutes of Meeting (8 February 2018) TN/C/M/38 para 4.393. Available at: www.docsonline.wto.org.

[133] General Council – Held in the Centre William Rappard on 18 October 2018 – Minutes of Meeting (20 November 2018) WT/GC/M/174 62. Available at: www.docsonline.wto.org.

[134] General Council – Held in the Centre William Rappard on 3 March 2020 – Minutes of Meeting (16 April 2020) WT/GC/M/182 110. Available at: www.docsonline.wto.org.

[135] General Council – Held in the Centre William Rappard on 28 February 2019 – Minutes of Meeting (15 April 2019) WT/GC/M/176 118. Available at: www.docsonline.wto.org.

[136] General Council – Held in Virtual Format on 1–2 and 4 March 2021 – Minutes of Meeting (23 April 2021) WT/GC/M/190 para 10.67. Available at: www.docsonline.wto.org.

and emerging topics.[137] During the meeting to discuss its latest Trade Policy Review report in 2018, the representative for Hong Kong reaffirmed the territory's commitment to cooperate with its fellow member states in the furtherance of investment facilitation and the work that was being performed to achieve a multilateral solution in the future.[138]

This chapter offers a comprehensive examination of Hong Kong's engagement with essential multilateral investment frameworks and its influential role in shaping international investment policy. It discusses Hong Kong's relevance and interaction with various multilateral investment norms, highlighting the territory's active participation in the development of these rules, albeit to varying degrees. Hong Kong has adopted a collegial approach towards investor-state dispute settlement (ISDS) reforms, as demonstrated by its focus on mediation and emphasis on cooperation within the World Trade Organisation (WTO). It is crucial to note that, besides multilateral investment rule-making, Hong Kong has also been progressively expanding its investment treaties network, with several agreements currently under negotiation. Substantial work remains around ISDS reforms, particularly concerning the Joint Initiative on Investment Facilitation for Development (JIIFD) and the United Nations Commission on International Trade Law (UNCITRAL) Working Group III. Upon achieving substantive tangible deliverables, it will be necessary to assess their adequacy.

The primary findings of the chapter can be outlined as follows: Hong Kong's engagement with the International Centre for Settlement of Investment Disputes (ICSID) demonstrates its commitment to offering a stable and reliable environment for investors while simultaneously bolstering its reputation as an international dispute resolution centre. The territory's accession to the New York Convention and its involvement in facilitating investment disputes not only fortify its position as a hub for investment structuring but also support the BRI by providing a dependable arbitration framework. Hong Kong's association with the Multilateral Investment Guarantee Agency (MIGA) showcases the territory's strategic alignment with China's economic interests, given that MIGA offers risk mitigation and investment guarantees for cross-border investments. The territory's proactive involvement in the UNCITRAL Working Group III highlights its dedication to enhancing the ISDS system and contributing to its reform endeavours. Lastly, Hong Kong's commitment to the WTO's investment facilitation initiatives, including the JIIFD, signifies its resolve to encourage international cooperation and advance investment facilitation in harmony with global economic development objectives. The analysis presented in Chapter 9 bears substantial legal implications for both Hong Kong and international economic law. As a prominent financial

[137] General Council – Held in Virtual Format on 27–28 July 2021 – Minutes of Meeting (4 October 2021) WT/GC/M/192 para 14.58. Available at: www.docsonline.wto.org.

[138] Trade Policy Review Body – 26 and 28 November 2018 – Trade Policy Review – Hong Kong, China – Minutes of the Meeting (6 March 2019) WT/TPR/M/380 para 2.9. Available at: www.docsonline.wto.org.

hub, Hong Kong's active participation in these multilateral investment frameworks elevates its role in moulding global investment norms and contributes to the overall stability and coherence of international economic law. Moreover, the territory's devotion to these frameworks signals its commitment to fostering a rules-based international investment regime, which enhances investor confidence and promotes sustainable cross-border investment.

10

Hong Kong and the Evolution of International Taxation: Aligning with Global Tax Norms

THE AREA OF international tax law is one that is both intricate and ever developing. It also has a long and illustrious history. The notion of double taxation is one of the oldest types of international tax legislation. It emerged in the late nineteenth and early twentieth centuries as nations started to industrialise and worldwide commerce developed. When a single source of income is subject to taxes in two or more nations, this practice is known as 'double taxation'. It may result in higher compliance costs and decreased economic efficiency. As a solution to this issue, governments started signing bilateral tax treaties with one another to eliminate the possibility of double taxation and provide provisions for the interchange of tax information on both sides. The League of Nations and the World Economic Conference both made attempts to solve international tax concerns in the 1920s and 1930s. However, these efforts were mostly unsuccessful owing to the outbreak of the Second World War. After the war, the United Nations (UN) and the Organisation for Economic Co-operation and Development (OECD) started looking at ways to work together on international tax issues. In the 1960s and 1970s, increased attention to international tax concerns resulted from a growing tendency towards globalisation as well as an increase in the mobility of both money and people. In fact, international tax law has a lengthy history that has been moulded by advancements in economics and politics. It continues to develop in response to new problems and possibilities, with a primary emphasis on cooperative endeavours, openness and equitable treatment of all parties.

Hong Kong's foreign economic policy includes international tax legislation for several reasons. First, foreign commerce and investment drive Hong Kong's economy. The territory's sophisticated financial industry and strategic position at Asia's crossroads make it a worldwide financial and commercial centre. International tax law creates a predictable and stable tax environment, making Hong Kong an appealing trade and investment location. Second, Hong Kong has a free-trade economy with minimal taxes. International tax law ensures that Hong Kong's tax system does not discriminate against international enterprises and investors, helping it to retain this competitive edge. This keeps Hong Kong competitive for commerce and investment. Third, international tax law may handle globalisation and digital economy issues such as the multilateralisation of international tax law. For example, the Base Erosion and Profit Shifting (BEPS) project and the Multilateral Instrument (MLI) ensure that multinational corporations pay their fair share of taxes in Hong Kong, levelling the playing field for domestic and foreign businesses and promoting fair competition in international trade and investment. Fourth, Hong Kong has always supported international tax cooperation, and has signedmany bilateral tax treaties and ratifying the Multilateral Convention to Implement Tax Treaty Related Measures to Prevent Base Erosion and Profit Shifting (MLI). The Common Reporting Standard (CRS) and Multilateral Competent Authority Agreement for the Automatic Share of Financial Account Information require Hong Kong to automatically exchange tax information (MCAA). This increases openness and reduces tax evasion, producing a more stable and predictable international tax environment for commerce and investment. In conclusion, international tax law is an important part of Hong Kong's international economic policy because it creates a predictable and stable tax environment, maintains a competitive advantage, addresses globalisation and the digital economy and commits to international tax cooperation, making Hong Kong an attractive destination for trade and investment.

I. THE MULTILATERALISATION OF INTERNATIONAL TAX LAW AND ITS DRIVING FORCES

The transition away from the previous system of bilateral tax treaties and towards a global tax system that is more coordinated and unified is referred to as the multilateralisation of international tax law. This refers to the method through which this transition is taking place. This process is being driven by the recognition that the existing system of bilateral tax treaties is becoming increasingly inadequate to address the challenges of globalisation and the digital economy, such as base erosion and profit shifting (BEPS) by multinational corporations[1] Base Erosion and Profit Shifting (BEPS) refers to tax-motivated income-shifting within multinational firms.[2] The multilateralisation of international tax law intends to enhance the coherence and consistency of the worldwide tax system, minimise the costs of complying with international tax laws and raise the efficacy of international tax cooperation. The Base Erosion and Profit Shifting (BEPS) project was initiated by the Organisation for Economic Co-operation and Development (OECD) in 2013 and it has since become one of the most important initiatives in this domain.

[1] Yariv Brauner, 'What the BEPS?' (2014) 16 *Florida Tax Review* 55.

[2] Luzius U Cavelti, Christian Jaag and Tobias F Rohner, 'Why Corporate Taxation Should Mean Source Taxation: A Response to the OECD's Actions against Base Erosion and Profit Shifting' (2017) 2017 *World Tax Journal* 352.

A. The Base Erosion and Profit Shifting (BEPS) Project

The BEPS project attempted to identify and solve gaps and mismatches in the existing international tax system to build a coordinated international response to tax evasion by multinational firms. This was accomplished by analysing the current international tax system. The project resulted in the adoption of 15 actions aimed at addressing BEPS, including measures to improve transparency and the exchange of information, strengthening rules for the allocation of profits and preventing the artificial avoidance of permanent establishment status. These actions were all adopted as a result of the project.

B. The Multilateral Instrument (MLI)

Another significant effort that has been implemented is the Multilateral Instrument (MLI), which was established by the OECD to allow nations to change their existing bilateral tax treaties to adopt the BEPS measures.[3] The MLI's provision of a model for governments to use when incorporating BEPS provisions into existing bilateral tax treaties significantly reduced the need for previous treaties to be renegotiated. By 2021, more than 100 countries had signed the MLI, of which around 50 had completed the ratification process.

The multilateralisation of international tax law has emerged as a critical response to the challenges posed by globalisation and the digital economy. This process, motivated by the need to address issues such as BEPS, aims to create a more coordinated and unified international tax system. Hong Kong plays an important role in shaping the evolving landscape of international tax law as an actor in the realm of international economic law with limited domestic tax rules and policies. Hong Kong contributes to fostering a rules-based international tax regime, ensuring a stable environment for cross-border trade and investment, while maintaining its status as a global financial hub by actively participating in multilateral initiatives and adopting tax policies aligned with global standards.

II. MULTILATERAL INITIATIVES AND PROGRESS IN INTERNATIONAL TAX LAW

In recent years, numerous multilateral initiatives have emerged to address the complexities and challenges of the global tax landscape, seeking to provide more cohesive and consistent approaches to international taxation.[4] This section

[3] Yariv Brauner, 'Treaties in the Aftermath of BEPS' (2016) 41 *Brooklyn Journal of International Law* 973.

[4] Andres Baez Moreno and Yariv Brauner, 'Taxing the Digital Economy Post BEPS. Seriously' (2019) 58 *Columbia Journal of Transnational Law* 121.

considers the key multilateral initiatives that have played a significant role in shaping the international tax law landscape. We will discuss the Common Reporting Standard (CRS), which mandates the automatic exchange of financial account information among countries to enhance transparency and reduce tax evasion. Furthermore, we will examine the United Nations' efforts, including their treaties and models, which aim to provide a fair and effective framework for international taxation. We will also explore the Inclusive Framework on BEPS, which brings together over 130 countries and jurisdictions to collaboratively implement BEPS measures and tackle the tax challenges posed by the digital economy. Lastly, we will evaluate the challenges and criticisms faced by the multilateralisation process, highlighting the areas where improvements are needed to achieve the desired outcomes in international tax law.

A. The Common Reporting Standard (CRS)

The Common Reporting Standard (CRS), developed by the OECD and adopted by the G20 in 2014, is an effort related to this topic.[5] The Common Reporting Standard (CRS) requires nations to share information about their financial accounts with one another on a yearly basis in order to improve transparency and reduce tax evasion.[6] Over 100 nations are already using the CRS and in 2017 the first information exchanges were carried out using the system.

B. United Nations' Efforts and Treaties

The United Nations (UN) plays a significant part in the process of multilateralising international tax law. The United Nations General Assembly in 2019 ratified the Treaty on the Elimination of Double Taxation in Connection with the Adjustment of Profits of Associated Enterprises (Treaty on the Elimination of Double Taxation in connection with the Adjustment of Profits of Associated Enterprises), which aims to improve the coherence and consistency of the international tax system by eliminating double taxation. In addition, there have been a variety of additional multilateral efforts aimed at tackling particular problems in the system of international taxes.

The OECD's Inclusive Framework on BEPS, which was established in 2016, brings together over 130 countries and jurisdictions to collaborate on the implementation of the BEPS measures and to address the unique tax challenges posed

[5] Steven Yeo and Soren Seitz, 'Common Reporting Standards' (2016) 9 *International In-House Counsel Journal* 1.

[6] Paolo Piantavigna, 'Tax Abuse and Aggressive Tax Planning in the BEPS Era: How EU Law and the OECD are Establishing a Unifying Conceptual Framework in International Tax Law, Despite Linguistic Discrepancies' (2017) 2017 *World Tax Journal* 47.

by the digital economy. The multilateralisation of international tax law is a process that is still continuing and there are still many difficulties that need to be solved. For instance, the BEPS initiative has been criticised both for being too complicated and for not going far enough in terms of tackling the tax difficulties presented by the digital economy. Concerns have also been raised over the possibility of existing bilateral tax treaties coming into conflict with the Multilateral Investment Treaty (MLI).

The multilateralisation of international tax law is viewed as an essential step towards a more coherent, uniform and successful worldwide tax system, notwithstanding the problems that it faces. It is expected that this procedure will continue to develop in the face of new problems and possibilities, with an emphasis on collaboration, openness and justice as its guiding principles.[7] Multilateral initiatives include the Multilateral Convention to Implement Tax Treaty Related Measures to Prevent Base Erosion and Profit Shifting (MLI), the Common Reporting Standard (CRS), the Global Forum on Transparency and Exchange of Information for Tax Purposes, the Inclusive Framework on BEPS, the United Nations Model Double Taxation Convention between Developed and Developing Countries and the United Nations Model Double Taxation Convention between Developed and Developing Countries.

C. Challenges and Criticisms of the Multilateralisation Process

The multilateralisation of international tax law provides support for the multilateral trade and investment regimes that are already in place. This support comes in the form of assistance in the development of an international tax system that is more coherent and consistent and is better equipped to deal with the challenges posed by globalisation and the digital economy. This serves to establish a more stable and predictable international tax climate that is more hospitable to trade and investment which, in turn, has a positive impact on those activities. One of the most important ways in which the multilateralisation of international tax law can support the established multilateral regimes for trade and investment is by lowering the compliance costs and administrative burdens associated with the current system of bilateral tax treaties.

The multilateralisation of international tax law, in particular through the utilisation of the Multilateral Instrument (MLI) and the Common Reporting Standard (CRS), enables countries to modify their existing bilateral tax treaties and to automatically exchange tax information. This reduces the need for the renegotiation of existing treaties and increases transparency. In addition, countries are able to modify their existing bilateral tax treaties. This helps to establish

[7] Luzius U Cavelti, Christian Jaag and Tobias F Rohner, 'Why Corporate Taxation Should Mean Source Taxation: A Response to the OECD's Actions against Base Erosion and Profit Shifting' (2017) 2017 *World Tax Journal* 352.

a more predictable and uniform international tax climate that is more friendly to commerce and investment, which in turn helps to make the world a better place for business.

Furthermore, multilateralisation of international tax law contributes to the strengthening of already established multilateral trade and investment regimes by helping to solve the BEPS problems caused by multinational corporations. The goal of the BEPS project, launched by the OECD in 2013 and an important initiative in the multilateralisation of international tax law, is to develop a coordinated international response to multinational corporation tax avoidance. This will be accomplished by identifying and correcting gaps and misalignments in the current international tax system. Furthermore, the BEPS project aims to create a global standard for reporting tax evasion. This helps to guarantee that multinational enterprises pay their fair share of taxes, so establishing a more level playing field for both local and international businesses and supporting fair competition in international commerce and investment. In addition, current multilateral trade and investment regimes are supported by the multilateralisation of international tax law since it increases transparency and collaboration among nations.

The Common Reporting Standard (CRS) and the Inclusive Framework on BEPS, for example, call for the automatic exchange of financial account information and the participation of more than 130 countries and jurisdictions respectively.[8] In addition, the CRS calls for the automatic exchange of financial account information. This serves to promote transparency and prevent tax evasion, producing an international tax climate that is more stable and predictable, which is more favourable to commerce and investment. In conclusion, the multilateralisation of international tax law provides support for pre-existing multilateral trade and investment regimes by producing an international tax system that is more coherent and consistent. This system is better equipped to deal with the challenges that are posed by globalisation and the digital economy. It helps to decrease compliance costs and administrative burdens, address base erosion and profit shifting, promote transparency and collaboration across nations and address base erosion and profit shifting. All these variables work together to make the international tax environment more stable and predictable, making it more favourable to international commerce and investment.

III. HONG KONG'S ECONOMIC MULTILATERALISM IN TAXATION

The concept of 'economic multilateralism in taxation' effectively captures Hong Kong's strategic positioning as a pivotal hub of global trade and investment, concurrently highlighting its adherence to and advocacy for a set of international

[8] Steven Yeo and Soren Seitz, 'Common Reporting Standards' (2016) 9 *International In-House Counsel Journal* 1.

tax standards and cooperative accords. This term conveys the multifaceted role of Hong Kong in fortifying its status as a global nexus of trade, commerce, finance, and communications. In alignment with its strategic objectives, Hong Kong engages in various international and regional economic and trade organisations. Underpinning this international outreach is the Basic Law, which empowers the HKSAR to independently establish, nurture relations, and enter into as well as execute agreements with pertinent global entities in the economic and trade arenas, among others.

The Trade and Industry Department of the HKSAR orchestrates its participation in key global economic forums, including WTO, the Asia-Pacific Economic Cooperation, and the Pacific Economic Cooperation Council. Crucially, in the realm of international taxation, the HKSAR's involvement with the Organisation for Economic Co-operation and Development (OECD) is of paramount importance. Within the OECD framework, Hong Kong plays an instrumental role as a Participant in both the Trade Committee and the Committee on Financial Markets. This engagement, initiated in 1994 and 1995 respectively, has been maintained beyond the significant political transition of 1 July 1997, with Hong Kong continuing its involvement under the designation 'Hong Kong, China'. This sustained participation underscores the HKSAR's commitment to shaping and adhering to international taxation policies and practices, reflecting its pivotal role in global economic governance.

Delving deeper into the roles of the Trade Committee and the Committee on Financial Markets, it is crucial to understand their influence and implications in the sphere of international taxation, a domain where Hong Kong has demonstrated its steadfast commitment. The Trade Committee primarily focuses on formulating policies that foster free and fair trade among nations. It plays a pivotal role in shaping trade regulations that have far-reaching tax implications, such as setting standards for customs duties and addressing tax-related barriers to international commerce. This committee's work directly influences the nature of cross-border trade taxation, an area where Hong Kong's participation is both strategic and impactful. On the other hand, the Committee on Financial Markets is instrumental in shaping policies that govern international financial markets and their operation. This committee's work encompasses a broad spectrum of financial policies, including those related to taxation of financial instruments and transactions. It delves into areas like the harmonization of international tax rules for financial products, combating tax evasion in financial markets, and addressing issues related to the taxation of cross-border financial services. Hong Kong's involvement in this committee enables it to contribute to, and align with, international standards on the taxation of financial markets, thereby reinforcing its position as a compliant and forward-thinking participant in the global financial landscape.

Through these committees, Hong Kong plays a critical role in shaping and adhering to the policies that impact international taxation in trade and financial markets. This involvement not only illustrates Hong Kong's commitment to global economic cooperation but also highlights its significant influence in moulding the policies that underpin the international tax architecture. This interaction extends beyond committee meetings, reflecting in Hong Kong's bilateral agreements aimed at facilitating tax information exchange and averting the risks of double taxation. Furthermore, Hong Kong's concerted efforts in combating tax evasion and addressing harmful tax practices underscore its commitment to promoting a transparent and equitable international tax environment.

A. Hong Kong's Participation in Organisation for Economic Co-operation and Development Tax-Related Working Groups

Hong Kong is a member of a large number of committees and working groups under the Organisation for Economic Co-operation and Development (OECD). The OECD's BEPS project, which aims to address this issue, is currently in the process of developing new international tax rules and guidelines. These are intended to ensure that profits are taxed in the same locations as the economic activities that generate those profits where value is created. The OECD/G20 Inclusive Framework on BEPS was an initiative launched by the OECD and the G-20 in 2013. It outlines 15 Actions to 'tackle tax avoidance, improve the coherence of international tax rules, ensure a more transparent tax environment and address the tax challenges arising from the digitalisation of the economy'.[9] These 15 Actions can be distilled into four categories: minimum standards; international standards; best practices; and analytical reports.[10] In order to put measures in place to join the Inclusive Framework on BEPS, Hong Kong published a consultation paper in 2016.[11]

Hong Kong has taken a number of steps to address the concerns raised by the OECD's BEPS initiative. These steps include the implementation of a three-tiered profit attribution rule, which will be used to determine the tax liability of multinational corporations operating in Hong Kong and the amendment of tax treaties in order to incorporate the Multilateral Instrument (MLI) provisions. The three-tiered profit attribution rule, which applies to businesses that conduct operations in Hong Kong through a related entity, ensures that profits are attributed to the Hong Kong entity based on its economic activities and functions. This rule applies to businesses that carry on business in Hong Kong. This regulation ensures that earnings are allocated to the Hong Kong company in a way that reflects the economic content of the activities that it engages in. The aim of

[9] OECD, 'International collaboration to end tax avoidance' (*OECD*). Available at: www.oecd.org/tax/beps/, accessed 10 October 2023.

[10] *GovHK*, 'Consultation Paper on measures to counter Base Erosion & Profit Shifting' (*GovHK*). Available at: www.gov.hk/en/residents/government/publication/consultation/docs/2016/BEPS.pdf, accessed 10 October 2023.

[11] ibid.

this rule is to stop multinational corporations from unfairly moving profits out of Hong Kong.

The issue of multinational corporations unfairly moving earnings to low or no-tax countries by using aggressive tax planning tactics is one of the main focuses of the BEPS project and one of the primary aims of the initiative is to solve this problem. Transfer pricing is a significant area of attention in the BEPS project because it is often used as a way of moving earnings to subsidiaries situated in low-tax countries. This is why transfer pricing is a key area of focus in the project. The Organisation for Economic Cooperation and Development (OECD) has developed a set of guidelines for transfer pricing that are known as the OECD Transfer Pricing Guidelines. These guidelines offer a framework for determining the price that would be paid by parties who are not related to one another in a transaction. Pursuant to the Inland Revenue (Amendment) (No.6) Ordinance, Hong Kong put into practice the transfer pricing principles that were issued and codified as the minimum criteria of the BEPS package in 2018. As per the OECD 2015 Report on Action 5 of the BEPS Project[12] that pertains to preferential tax treatments that facilitate BEPS, Hong Kong does not patent boxes a special head under the corporate tax that are 'output-related tax incentives that apply reduced rates to income earned from exploiting IP'.[13]

HK conforms with the OECD standards which provide for a 'Profits tax concession for carried interest' framework.[14] In fact, many jurisdictions, including those that are members of the OECD, use these principles as the foundation for the transfer pricing policies and regulations in their respective countries. The OECD has also developed the Action Plan on BEPS, which includes 15 actions to address BEPS issues, several of which are focused on transfer pricing. This plan was developed in response to the OECD's concerns regarding the erosion of tax bases and the shifting of profits.

Furthermore, the BEPS project includes the development of new transfer pricing rules and guidelines. One such example is Country-by-Country (CbC) reporting, which mandates that multinational corporations report specific information on their global allocation of income and taxes paid, in addition to specific indicators of economic activity among the countries in which they conduct business. This will give tax authorities a better knowledge of where multinational corporations are producing profits and will assist in the detection of high-risk transactions and structures that may be utilised for tax evasion.

[12] OECD, 'Countering Harmful Tax Practises More Effectively, Taking into Account Transparency and Substance – Action 5: 2015 Final Report' (*OECD*, 2015). Available at: www.oecd-ilibrary.org/docserver/9789264241190-en.pdf?expires=1654515968&id=id&accname=guest&checksum=1A9F63CCAF309028752DC034C5253C29, accessed 10 October 2023.

[13] Annette Alstadsæter, Salvador Barrios, Gaetan Nicodeme, Agnieszka Maria Skonieczna, Antonio Vezzani, 'Patent Boxes Design, Patents Location and Local R&D' (2018) 33 *Economic Policy* 131.

[14] OECD, 'Harmful Tax Practises– Peer Review Results' (*OECD*, January 2022). Available at: www.oecd.org/tax/beps/harmful-tax-practices-consolidated-peer-review-results-on-preferential-regimes.pdf, accessed 10 October 2023.

The concepts of transfer pricing have a tight connection to the OECD's BEPS initiative as transfer pricing is often utilised as a method of shifting profits to subsidiaries situated in low-tax nations. The OECD has developed transfer pricing guidelines; the BEPS project includes actions and new rules to address transfer pricing issues and ensure that transfer pricing outcomes are in line with value creation. Both initiatives were undertaken to address and resolve concerns regarding transfer pricing.

OECD and the Council of Europe formulated the Multilateral Convention on Mutual Administrative Assistance in Tax Matters which came into effect in 1995 and underwent a Protocol amendment in 2010. The underlying objective is to promote global cooperation to combat tax avoidance.[15] The Convention was signed by the People's Republic of China in 2013 and was extended to Hong Kong on 1 September 2018.[16]

In addition, Hong Kong has signed and approved the Multilateral Convention to Implement Tax Treaty Related Measures to Avoid Base Erosion and Profit Shifting ('MLI Convention'), which amends existing tax treaties to prevent treaty misuse and enhance dispute settlement. After several rounds of negotiations between 100 countries across the globe, the MLI Convention was concluded in 2016.[17] On 7 June 2017 Hong Kong also signed the Multilateral Convention to the MLI Convention which came into effect in Hong Kong in 2022.[18]

This is an OECD convention which forms a part of the OECD Inclusive Framework on BEPS to curb tax evasion by lowering BEPS by multinational firms. The MLI provisions include steps to discourage people from shopping around for better treaties, to tighten processes for mutual agreement and to improve dispute settlement. This will assist Hong Kong to improve the efficiency of its tax treaty network and better align its tax treaties with the BEPS principles.

B. Country-by-Country Reporting and Other Tax Initiatives

In addition, Hong Kong is in the process of implementing Country-by-Country (CbC) reporting, which requires multinational corporations to report specific information on their global allocation of income and taxes paid, in addition

[15] OECD, 'Convention on Mutual Administrative Assistance in Tax Matters' (*OECD*). Available at: www.oecd.org/tax/exchange-of-tax-information/convention-on-mutual-administrative-assistance-in-tax-matters.htm, accessed 10 October 2023.

[16] OECD, 'Jurisdictions Participating in the Convention on Mutual Administrative Assistance in Tax Matters' (*OECD*, May 2022). Available at: www.oecd.org/ctp/exchange-of-tax-information/Status_of_convention.pdf, accessed 10 October 2023.

[17] OECD, 'Multilateral Convention to Implement Tax Treaty Related Measures to Prevent BEPS' (*OECD*). Available at: www.oecd.org/tax/treaties/multilateral-convention-to-implement-tax-treaty-related-measures-to-prevent-beps.htm, accessed 10 October 2023.

[18] OECD, 'Signatories and Parties to the Multilateral Convention to Implement Tax Treaty Related Measures to Prevent Base Erosion and Profit Shifting' (*OECD*). Available at: www.oecd.org/tax/treaties/beps-mli-signatories-and-parties.pdf, accessed 10 October 2023.

to certain indicators of economic activity among the countries in which they conduct business.[19] This will assist in the detection of high-risk transactions and structures that may be utilised for tax evasion and give tax authorities a clearer picture of where multinational corporations (MNEs) are making profits.

The Global Forum on Transparency and Exchange of Information for Tax Purposes is another event in which Hong Kong participates. The Forum encourages the application of international standards for tax purposes that call for openness and the sharing of information with other governments. Because of this, Hong Kong will be able to increase its interchange of information with other jurisdictions, which is an essential component in the battle against tax evasion and aggressive tax planning. In addition, Hong Kong has increased its enforcement measures to fight tax avoidance and evasion and it has also formed a specialised team to monitor and investigate BEPS instances. This team monitors and investigates cases. This includes the implementation of a new law that gives the territory's Inland Revenue Department (IRD) the authority to impose penalties on taxpayers who engage in tax avoidance and evasion, as well as the appointment of additional staff to the IRD to enhance its capabilities of enforcement.

Hong Kong is contributing significantly to the BEPS initiative and has already put in place several countermeasures to deal with BEPS-related problems. These include the implementation of the three-tiered profit attribution rule, the amendment of tax treaties to include the MLI provisions, the implementation of CbC reporting, participation in the Global Forum on Transparency and Exchange of Information for Tax Purposes and strengthening its enforcement measures to combat tax avoidance and evasion. This demonstrates Hong Kong's dedication to resolving the challenges posed by BEPS, ensuring that earnings are taxed in the same jurisdiction as the economic activities that generate those profits and the location where value is generated.

IV. THE ROAD TOWARDS A GLOBAL MINIMUM CORPORATE TAX

The idea of a global corporate minimum tax is an ongoing attempt by countries, international organisations and other stakeholders to set a minimum amount of tax that multinational firms are required to pay on their worldwide profits. The purpose of this measure is to stop businesses from moving their earnings to countries with lower tax rates to avoid paying higher taxes in other nations. In general, governments and other groups which are in support of a worldwide corporate minimum tax claim that it would help establish a fair playing field for all firms and discourage tax dodging. In addition, they believe that it will help

[19] Andrew P Morriss, 'Forward down the Road to Serfdom: International Tax Law as a Means of Central Planning' (2022) 17 *Journal of Law, Economics & Policy* 454.

generate jobs.[20] They also claim that it has the potential to bring in enormous amounts of cash for governments, which could then be used to support public services and infrastructure. On the other hand, some businesses and business groups are opposed to the idea of a worldwide corporate minimum tax on the grounds that it might raise the amount of tax liability they are already required to carry and make them less competitive in the international market. They further claim that a worldwide minimum tax on corporations might discourage foreign investment in particular nations and impede economic progress in certain areas. By making it more difficult for businesses to operate without incurring tax liability, a global corporate minimum tax, if enacted, has the potential to drastically alter the manner in which commerce is carried out all over the globe. It is also possible that this may result in higher income for governments, which they can then put toward funding public services and infrastructure. On the other hand, it may make it more challenging for certain businesses to compete in the global economy and may discourage foreign investment in some nations.

A. Challenges and Progress in Implementing the Global Corporate Minimum Tax: Hong Kong's Involvement and Impact

A number of different projects and suggestions have been made in recent years with the goal of establishing a Global Corporate Minimum Tax. The objective of the Base Erosion and Profit Shifting (BEPS) initiative, which is being directed by the Organisation for Economic Co-operation and Development (OECD), is to create a new framework for international tax that would include a global minimum tax that would apply to multinational firms. Over 130 different nations and administrative divisions are participating in the initiative as supporters. In 2021, the USA made public its own plan for a global minimum tax on businesses and recommended a minimum tax rate of 21 per cent to be applied to the overseas profits of multinational firms.

Over 130 nations reached an agreement in November 2021 on a worldwide minimum corporation tax rate of 15 per cent. A two-tier solution was accepted by the OECD/G20 Inclusive Framework on BEPS whereby the first tier sought to enhance the distribution of taxation and taxation rights among countries,[21] and the second tier instituted a minimum effective corporate tax rate of 15 per cent for multinational corporations with revenue exceeding €750 million.[22] In 2021

[20] Paige McHugh, 'The Case for a Global Excess Profits Tax: A Response to Dr Tarcisio Diniz Magalhaes & Professor Allison Christians' (2022) 29 *Indiana Journal of Global Legal Studies* 231.

[21] OECD, 'Two-Pillar Solution to Address the Tax Challenges Arising from the Digitalisation of the Economy' (*OECD*, October 2021). Available at: www.oecd.org/tax/beps/brochure-two-pillar-solution-to-address-the-tax-challenges-arising-from-the-digitalisation-of-the-economy-october-2021.pdf, accessed 10 October 2023.

[22] OECD, 'OECD releases Pillar Two model rules for domestic implementation of 15% global minimum tax' (*OECD*, December 2021). Available at: www.oecd.org/tax/beps/oecd-releases-pillar-

Hong Kong became a part of this statement.[23] There are several exemptions and incentives that come with Hong Kong's corporate tax rate which is 16.5 per cent that can potentially bring down the effective tax rate below 15 per cent levying additional taxes on MNEs doing business there.[24]

This agreement has the potential to improve international corporate taxation by assisting governments to reduce the incidence of tax avoidance and evasion committed by corporations. However, since its inception, governments have been confronted with considerable challenges when attempting to implement the tax. In addition to concerns pertaining to public policy, there has also been significant political pressure exerted against the implementation of a worldwide minimum corporation tax.

Some companies have pushed against the tax and governments have been cautious to apply it first for fear that their companies may suffer a competitive disadvantage if other nations do not swiftly follow suit. Because of this, a worldwide minimum corporation tax was left out of the Inflation Reduction Act (IRA) that was passed in the United States. The International Revenue Agency (IRA) did establish a minimum corporation tax of 15 per cent on accounting book revenue, but this tax is distinct in a number of ways and does not correspond to the worldwide agreement. It is important to note that the IRA minimum tax does not assess taxable income on a Country-by-Country basis like other taxes do. It has been difficult for the European Union (EU), which was another pioneer in the formation of the accord, to make progress with the implementation. Due to the procedural restrictions, it is very difficult to impose the tax throughout the whole of the European Union (EU) unless all 27 nations of the bloc agree to do so unanimously. At present 26 members that have signed off on it, but Hungary is against it. Due to the complexity of these issues, the OECD has said that the official standards will not be finalised until 2024.

B. Achieving Global Corporate Minimum Tax Reform: The Importance of Critical Mass and the Domino Effect

Despite the significant progress made in the discussions led by the OECD, there is a growing concern that nations will ultimately lose interest in the efforts to

two model-rules-for-domestic-implementation-of-15-percent-global-minimum-tax.htm, accessed 10 October 2023.

[23] OECD, 'Members of the OECD/G20 Inclusive Framework on BEPS joining the October 2021 'Statement on a Two-Pillar Solution to Address the Tax Challenges Arising from the Digitalisation of the Economy' (*OECD*, November 2021). Available at: www.oecd.org/tax/beps/oecd-g20-inclusive-framework-members-joining-statement-on-two-pillar-solution-to address-tax-challenges-arising-from digitalisation-october-2021.pdf, accessed 10 October 2023.

[24] John Timpany and Lewis Lu, 'Hong Kong SAR: The impact of the OECD's BEPS 2.0 proposals' (*International Tax Review*, 24 August 2021). Available at: www.internationaltaxreview.com/Article/b1t8h4gpjyynn4/Hong-Kong-sar-the-impact-of-the-oecds-beps-20-proposals, accessed 10 October 2023.

reform the international corporation tax system. This loss of interest could lead to the demise of a worldwide minimum corporation tax, even though the road ahead is far from easy.

However, it is important to note that the discussions have achieved notable advancements in finalising the implementation regulations for key aspects of the agreement, such as the 'undertaxed earnings rule'. Under this rule, if a multinational corporation (MNC) generates profits in a jurisdiction with a corporate tax rate below the agreed minimum of 15 per cent, participating nations have the authority to 'top up' the tax rate applied to the MNC's earnings.

The inclusion of this enforcement mechanism creates significant financial incentives for non-participating nations that house MNCs. These countries are encouraged to join the agreement and collect additional corporation tax revenue because they stand to benefit financially from doing so.

Therefore, while concerns persist about the long-term sustainability of the worldwide minimum corporation tax, the ongoing discussions, led by the OECD, have yielded tangible progress in shaping the implementation regulations. These developments highlight the potential benefits for both participating and non-participating nations, thereby creating incentives for broader participation and cooperation in the pursuit of international tax reform.

For instance, suppose that the corporation tax rate in Country A is 25 per cent, whereas the rate in Country B is 10 per cent and the rate in Country C is 9 per cent. The rate of 15 per cent is considered the worldwide minimum tax rate. Company X generates revenue in Country B, where it also maintains its operations, but Country C is home to the company's headquarters. Additional tax income would be collected from Company X's reported earnings in Country B by Country A, which would 'top-up' the taxes already paid on those profits by 5 per cent (the worldwide minimum of 15 per cent less Country B's rate of 10 per cent). Because Company X's home nation, Country C, is not participating in the agreement and does not top up the tax rate on Company X's revenue in Country B, the agreement authorises Country A to do this as a participating country. This is because Country C is Company X's home country. This scenario showcases the concept of a worldwide minimum tax rate and its implications for multinational corporations operating in different countries. It highlights the role of participating countries in collecting additional taxes from companies that have operations in lower-tax jurisdictions. Overall, the concept of a worldwide minimum tax rate represents a significant development in international tax policy, aiming to address tax avoidance and create a more equitable global tax framework. It emphasises the importance of collaboration among countries to ensure that corporations contribute their fair share of taxes, regardless of the jurisdictions in which they operate.

The requirement for a critical mass of nations to implement the Global Corporate Minimum Tax is the pivotal aspect of this regulation. Once a major economy has successfully implemented the tax and begins generating increased revenue, it becomes more likely that other countries will follow suit. MNCs operating in non-participating countries would still be subject to higher taxes and those nations would strive to retain the income being sent out by their MNCs. This initial implementation acts as the catalyst, triggering a chain reaction of adoption.

In conclusion, the successful implementation of the Global Corporate Minimum Tax relies heavily on a critical mass of nations adopting the new framework, which in turn could create a domino effect among the remaining countries. Hong Kong, as a key actor in international economic law and an influential financial hub, could play a significant role in promoting the adoption of the tax reforms. If Hong Kong embraces the tax reform, it would not only encourage other nations to follow suit but also reinforce the principles of transparency and fairness in the global tax landscape. By participating in the OECD-led discussions and implementing the Global Corporate Minimum Tax, Hong Kong could contribute to a more equitable and effective international tax system, which would ultimately benefit all participating countries, their economies and the global community as a whole.

PART III CONCLUSION

Part III provides a comprehensive overview of Hong Kong's active participation in and contributions to international economic organisations, as well as the implications of its multilateral engagement on its domestic policies and global standing.

A key observation is that Hong Kong has consistently demonstrated a strong commitment to multilateralism by actively participating in prominent global economic institutions such as the WTO, the IMF and the World Bank. Through its involvement in these organisations, Hong Kong can contribute to the shaping of global economic policies and standards. This active engagement enhances Hong Kong's regulatory framework and policy environment, benefiting its domestic economy in the process.

Moreover, Hong Kong's participation in multilateral institutions allows for collaboration and the establishment of partnerships with other economies. This further strengthens its position as a significant global financial centre, solidifying its influence and reputation in the international arena.

However, it is important to consider some objective criticism regarding Hong Kong's multilateral engagement. One critique revolves around Hong Kong's status as a Special Administrative Region (SAR) of China. As such, Hong Kong's decision making and policy implementation could be influenced or limited by the central Chinese government. This could potentially hinder Hong Kong's full leveraging of its participation in multilateral institutions and its independent shaping of global economic policies. Another concern regards the effectiveness of Hong Kong's representation in these global economic organisations. As a non-sovereign entity, Hong Kong's voice and voting power within these institutions may not hold the same weight as that of sovereign nations. This raises questions about the extent to which Hong Kong can genuinely influence policy outcomes and advocate for its specific interests on an equal footing with other participating members. Critics also argue that Hong Kong's multilateral engagement may prioritise its own economic interests, potentially at the expense of broader social and environmental considerations. This perspective raises concerns about Hong Kong's active contribution to global economic policies addressing significant global challenges such as inequality, sustainability and social development.

In conclusion, the analysis suggests that Hong Kong's multilateral engagement complements its unilateral foundations and bilateral efforts, allowing the territory to maintain a strong and thriving domestic economy while leveraging its global influence to promote its economic interests.

By examining the mechanisms and processes through which Hong Kong addresses and resolves economic disputes in its international relations, Part IV *Resolving Economic Conflicts: Dispute Settlement in Hong Kong's International Relations* explores how Hong Kong manages potential conflicts and ensures stability in its economic relationships. This focus on dispute settlement provides valuable insights into Hong Kong's resilience and adaptability in the face of global challenges.

Part IV

Resolving Economic Conflicts: Dispute Settlement in Hong Kong's International Relations

AS AN INFLUENTIAL global financial hub, Hong Kong plays a significant role in international economic law. Its position as a Special Administrative Region of China provides it with both opportunities and challenges when navigating the complex world of multilateralism, bilateralism and unilateralism. In this context, Part IV discusses Hong Kong's approach to resolving economic conflicts and its participation in dispute settlement mechanisms within the realm of international relations. It should be noted that Hong Kong's international dispute resolution practice is restricted to trade, tax and investment-related disputes and that it therefore solely engages in 'economic' international dispute settlement.[1] This being the case, this part does not address Hong Kong's participation in other, equally significant international dispute settlement ('IDS') despite the fact that Hong Kong is a signatory to other international dispute settlement treaties mechanisms like the International Court of Justice ('ICJ') and International Tribunal for the Law of the Sea.[2]

The discussion in Part IV is also rooted in the evolving dynamics of global trade and investment, with an increasing number of disputes arising between countries due to divergent economic policies, interests and legal frameworks. Lately, Hong Kong has suffered the consequences of the worsening economic, diplomatic and geopolitical relations between China and the United States of America. The National People's Congress of China authorised its Standing

[1] The Department of Justice (DoJ) aims to 'commit to the development and promotion of Hong Kong as a leading international legal and dispute resolution services centre in the Asia Pacific region, which objective complements Hong Kong's position as an international business and financial centre'. See the Government of Hong Kong Special Administrative Region, 'LCQ14: Hong Kong as an International Arbitration Hub', (*The Government of Hong Kong Special Administrative Region*, 18 December 2019). Available at: www.info.gov.hk/gia/general/201912/18/P2019121800402.htm, accessed 28 March 2024.

[2] Kathleen Claussen, 'Sovereignty's Accommodations: Quasi-States as International Lawmakers' in Karen N Scott, et al (eds), *Changing Actors in International Law* (Leiden, Brill Nijhoff, 2020) 27, 45. Other than international economic law, there are fewer examples of international dispute settlement raised by and against quasi-states.

Committee in May 2020 to pass legislation outlawing actions in Hong Kong that endanger China's national security.[3] The US Secretary of State produced a report citing this subsequent weakening of Hong Kong's jurisdiction, which concluded that the region's revised status no longer merited special protection under US law.[4] The Hong Kong administration, for its part, promptly expressed its determination to seek recourse against the US measures by calling for the establishment of a WTO Panel in October 2020[5] through the WTO's dispute resolution mechanism.[6] The legal standing of Hong Kong before international courts and tribunals has taken on new theoretical and practical significance, which Part IV evaluates against the backdrop of the swift changes in the legal structure as well as the evident spillover of the US–China trade war.

Hong Kong, as an open economy with extensive trade and investment links worldwide, is inevitably affected by such disputes and must find effective means to address them. This part not only highlights Hong Kong's involvement in the settlement of international economic disputes but also evaluates its effectiveness and the implications of its strategies on the wider IEL landscape. Part IV has three main aims. First, it seeks to provide a comprehensive understanding of Hong Kong's involvement in international dispute resolution mechanisms, such as the WTO's Dispute Settlement Body and investor-state dispute settlement ('ISDS') under bilateral investment treaties. Second, it seeks to analyse the impact of Hong Kong's participation in these mechanisms on its international relations and economic policy. Finally, it aims to identify the challenges and opportunities that Hong Kong faces in the evolving landscape of dispute resolution and offer insights into the potential paths for its future engagement in IEL.

[3] Chris Buckley, et al, 'New Security Law Gives China Sweeping Powers Over Hong Kong', (*New York Times*, 29 June 2020). Available at: www.nytimes.com/2020/06/29/world/asia/china-hong-kong-security-law-rules.html, accessed 28 March 2024.

[4] Bureau of East Asian and Pacific Affairs, '2020 Hong Kong Policy Act Report' (*US Department of State*, 28 May 2020). Available at: www.state.gov/2020-hong-kong-policy-act-report/, accessed 28 March 2024. This development was later formalised through an Executive Order dated 14 July 2020 (hereinafter Order), Executive Order No 13936, 85 CFR 138 (14 July 2020) (Apart from the several modifications in the export control regime applicable to the Hong Kong Special Administrative Region (hereinafter HKSAR), the Order also imposes sanctions on persons engaged in, inter alia, 'human rights abuse' and policies which may impair Hong Kong's security or autonomy. It also extends these sanctions to 'all property and interests in property [of such persons] that are in the United States, that hereafter come within the United States (hereinafter US), or that are or hereafter come within the possession or control of any United States person'. See also Mao-Wei Lo and Chien-Huei Wu, 'From USHKPA to HKHRDA and HKAA: The Turnings of U.S.–China Policy and the End of Hong Kong's Full Autonomy' (2021) 25(2) *UCLA J Intl L and Foreign Affairs* 93, 93.

[5] Hong Kong has formally requested consultations with the US about its 'made in China' marking requirement. HKTDC Research, 'Hong Kong Files WTO Case Against U.S. "Made in China" Marking Requirement' (*HKTDC Research*, 3 November 2020). Available at: www.research.hktdc.com/en/article/NTgwODY0OTUz, accessed 28 March 2024.

[6] Finbarr Bermingham, 'Hong Kong warned WTO challenge to potential US trade sanctions could be "counterproductive"' (*South China Morning Post*, 29 May 2020). Available at: www.www.scmp.com/economy/china-economy/article/3086713/hong-kong-warned-wto-challengepotential-us-trade-sanctions, accessed 28 March 2024.

Part IV is organised into several chapters, each focusing on a different aspect of Hong Kong's approach to resolving economic conflicts. It begins with an examination of Hong Kong's participation in multilateral dispute settlement mechanisms, such as the WTO and its role in shaping the rules and norms of international trade (Chapter 11). It goes on to explore Hong Kong's bilateral engagements in dispute resolution, including its approach to negotiating and implementing investment treaties with provisions on ISDS (Chapter 12). Finally, it discusses Hong Kong's unilateral measures in addressing economic conflicts, such as its domestic legal and regulatory framework and evaluates the effectiveness of these measures in safeguarding Hong Kong's interests while maintaining its position as a leading global financial centre (Chapter 13).

11

Steering Through Disputes: Hong Kong's Engagement in WTO Dispute Settlement

THE DISPUTE RESOLUTION mechanism provided by the World Trade Organisation ('WTO') is significant because it gives member nations a way to resolve trade disputes in a manner that is both fair and effective. The WTO has a dispute settlement system that is designed to ensure that trade relations between member nations are conducted in accordance with the organisation's rules and principles. This mechanism is an essential part of the WTO system.

The WTO system for the settlement of conflicts encompasses a variety of different methods for the resolution of disputes. These procedures include consultation, mediation and panel hearings. These methods are intended to give a methodical approach to resolving conflicts, with the objective of reaching a solution acceptable to all parties involved. In the event that the parties involved in the dispute are unable to come to an agreement over how to resolve it, the procedures before the Panel will result in a decision that is final and legally binding. The Appellate Body, another essential component of the conflict resolution procedure from a legal standpoint, is a standing body of seven individuals who consider appeals from the panel report. The Appellate Body offers a mechanism for reviewing the judgements made by the panels and it also helps to verify whether the decisions made by the panels are compatible with the rules and principles established by the WTO. The WTO Understanding on Rules and Procedures Governing the Settlement of Disputes ('DSU') lays out the processes to be followed to resolve disputes within the context of the WTO dispute settlement system. It is a legally obligatory provision for all members of the WTO since it is an essential component of the WTO Agreement. The DSU makes provision for a variety of mechanisms for the settlement of disputes. These mechanisms include consultation, mediation, panel proceedings and appeals.

In this chapter, Hong Kong's involvement in the DSU and its effect on Hong Kong's economic sovereignty are examined. Members are the primary subjects of WTO rights and duties (there are 164 members at the time of writing).[1]

[1] World Trade Organisation, 'Members and Observers' (*World Trade Organisation*). Available at: www.www.wto.org/english/thewto_e/whatis_e/tif_e/org6_e.htm, accessed 28 March 2024.

The members include customs territories in addition to sovereign states (such territories include both trade giants such as the European Union ('EU') and small territories such as the Macao Special Administrative Region ('SAR') of China. Further, the WTO differs from other international organisations like the United Nations ('UN') in that it allows distinct custom territories with an independent trade policy to be WTO members, pursuant to Article XII of the WTO Agreement.[2] Hong Kong, being a founding and full member of the WTO, has adopted the corresponding rights and duties of the Uruguay Round negotiations and has accepted the single undertaking of all the WTO agreements, including the WTO DSU.[3]

I. EMBRACING THE WTO DISPUTE SETTLEMENT BODY: HONG KONG'S ACTIVE PARTICIPATION

The WTO agreements grant members a wide range of rights and impose several obligations on how they should conduct international trade. Thereby, the major point of contention is how members of the WTO system assess and enforce these underlying rights and obligations. An efficient dispute resolution system that assists in settling disputes over underlying rules is essential to any enforcement process. A system like this is necessary to encourage and ensure the observance of the rules. Article XXIII of the General Agreement on Tariffs and Trade ('GATT') 1994 and the DSU both clearly outline the fundamental institutional and jurisdictional limits of WTO dispute settlement.[4] For disputes resulting from all covered agreements made under the WTO's purview, the DSU has developed a uniform and compulsory dispute settlement procedure. It fully codifies the applicable procedural rules and guidelines. All agreements and disputes are governed by the same fundamental principles (however, certain covered agreements may provide for special or additional rules which are applicable as *lex specialis*[5] to disputes arising under that agreement). The DSU's

[2] World Trade Organisation, 'Accession: Explanation, How to Become a Member of the WTO' (*World Trade Organisation*). Available at: www.wto.org/english/thewto_e/acc_e/acces_e.htm, accessed 28 March 2024.

[3] Trade and Industry Department, 'International Trade Organizations: World Trade Organization' (*Trade and Industry Department, The Government of the HKSAR*). Available at: www.tid.gov.hk/english/ito/wto/wto_overview.html, accessed 28 March 2024; World Trade Organisation, 'Hong Kong, China and the WTO' (*World Trade Organization*). Available at: www.wto.org/english/thewto_e/countries_e/hong_kong_china_e.htm, accessed 29 June 2024 (Hong Kong, China and the WTO).

[4] See generally Rüdiger Wolfrum and Peter-Tobias Stoll, 'General Agreement on Tariffs and Trade 1994', in Rüdiger Wolfrum et al (eds) 2 *Max Planck Comment. On World Trade Law, WTO-Institutions and Dispute Settlement* (Leiden, Brill Nijhoff, 2006) 193; UNCTAD, 'Dispute Settlement: World Trade Organisation' (2003), UN Doc UNCTAD/EDM/Misc.232/Add.11, 41.

[5] WTO, 'WTO Analytical Index GATT 1994 – General (DS Reports)' (December 2022) 6 (WTO Analytical Index GATT 1994). See generally William J Davey, 'The WTO and Rules-Based Dispute Settlement: Historical Evolution, Operational Success and Future Challenges' (2014) 17 *Journal of International Economic Law* 679.

rule-based framework guarantees that members in the multilateral trading system may do so in a secure and predictable manner.[14]

However, the Appellate Body of the WTO became defunct in 2020. In light of this Appellate Body crisis, 19 countries, including Australia, Brazil, Canada and China, along with the EU, led an initiative to arbitrate trade disputes in the interim through the so-called Multi-Party Interim Agreement ('MPIA').[6] The MPIA system also includes Hong Kong as a participating member.[7] A replica arbitration system can be established to address the Appellate Body crisis since Article 25 of the DSU permits arbitration of WTO disputes as an alternative to the Panel and Appellate Body procedures.[8] The primary issue with this system is whether it can produce decisions that have legal force.

Nevertheless, Hong Kong's tribulations extend far beyond the dysfunctional state of the WTO's Appellate Body. Hong Kong is a pawn in a complex geopolitical struggle between China and the USA and may well be affected by further US sanctions aimed at China.[9] In June 2020, following the enactment of China's National Security Law,[10] the US Department of Commerce revoked Hong Kong's unique status, a move that could dramatically shift the trade dynamics.[11] However, this measure by the US arguably contradicts its commitments under the WTO agreements, as the distinctive status of Hong Kong is an establishment recognised by the entirety of the WTO membership. As a countermeasure, in October 2020, Hong Kong elected to challenge certain US actions via the WTO's dispute resolution mechanism.

II. HONG KONG ON THE FRONTLINES: ACTING AS COMPLAINANT AND RESPONDENT IN WTO DISPUTE SETTLEMENT

The WTO only allows its members direct access to its meetings and work. This also applies to dispute resolution procedures, in which only members

[6] Alessandra Mignolli, 'The European Union Faces the Crisis of the WTO Dispute Settlement System: Tensions Between Multilateralism and Unilateralism in International Trade Law' (2020) 3 *International Legal Order and Human Rights* 485, 495.

[7] Participating members are Australia; Brazil; Canada; China; Chile; Colombia; Costa Rica; the European Union; Guatemala; Hong Kong, China; Iceland; Mexico; New Zealand; Norway; Pakistan; Singapore; Switzerland; Ukraine and Uruguay.

[8] WTO, 'Multi-party Interim Appeal Arbitration Arrangement pursuant to Article 25 of the DSU' (30 April 2020) pmbl, WTO Doc JOB/DSB/1/Add.12. Available at: www.hketogeneva.gov.hk/doc/1A12.pdf, accessed 28 March 2024.

[9] Ernst-Ulrich Petersmann, 'Neo-liberal, State-Capitalist and Ordo-Liberal Conceptions of World Trade: The Rise and Fall of the WTO Dispute Settlement System' (2020) EUI Department of Law Research Paper No. 2020/16, 3. Available at: ssrn.com/abstract=3727995, accessed 28 March 2024.

[10] Finbarr Bermingham, 'Hong Kong warned WTO challenge to potential US trade sanctions could be "counterproductive"' (*South China Morning Post*, 29 May 2020). Available at: www.scmp.com/economy/china-economy/article/3086713/hong-kong-warned-wto-challenge-potential-us-trade-sanctions, accessed 28 March 2024.

[11] US Department of Commerce, 'Statement from U.S. Secretary of Commerce Wilbur Ross on Revocation of Hong Kong Special Status' (*US Department of Commerce*, 29 June 2020). Available at: www.2017–2021.commerce.gov/news/press-releases/2020/06/statement-us-secretary-commerce-wilbur-ross-revocation-hong-kong.html, accessed 28 March 2024.

may formally participate.[12] Industries, consumers and Non-governmental Organisations ('NGOs') are examples of private players and persons that are forbidden from initiating formal dispute resolution proceedings. They have no rights before WTO panels or the Appellate Body.[13] The choice to submit a complaint with the WTO dispute settlement mechanism is taken unilaterally by governments. This system operates in accordance with accepted principles of public international law, according to which the rights of individuals – both natural and legal – derive only from those of nation states.[14] The practice of diplomatic protection has traditionally been driven by political expediency.

To date, Hong Kong has initiated 22 cases as a third party and two cases as a complainant under the DSU.[15] On 12 February 1996, Hong Kong submitted its first complaint, seeking consultations after Turkey placed quantitative import restrictions on Hong Kong's textile and garment items on 1 January 1996. According to Hong Kong, these actions were unjustified under Article XXIV of the GATT 1994 and in violation of Turkey's commitments under Articles XI and XIII. The case *DS597 United States–Origin Marking Requirement*, the second complaint brought by Hong Kong, is focused on the special trade status that the US had granted Hong Kong until 2020.[16] This decision is further analysed in the next section.

Hong Kong has not actively participated in the WTO dispute settlement process until recently. However, given the hostility between China and the US, Hong Kong may rely more on the WTO's dispute settlement process to settle future disputes. Future adoption of this mechanism might strengthen Hong Kong's position in the ongoing trade war between the US and China.

III. ANALYSING THE UNITED STATES–ORIGIN MARKING REQUIREMENT DISPUTE: HONG KONG'S STANCE AND STRATEGY

In December 2022, the WTO Dispute Settlement Panel issued a landmark ruling in the case of the *US–Origin Marking Requirement*.[17] The Panel ruled against the product labelling requirement introduced by the US, which mandated that all goods from Hong Kong be marked 'China' as their country of origin. This ruling resulted in an adjudicative outcome favouring Hong Kong.

[12] WTO, 'Dispute Settlement System Training Module: Chapter 1 Introduction to the WTO Dispute Settlement System' (*WTO*). Available at: www.wto.org/english/tratop_e/dispu_e/disp_settlement_cbt_e/c1s4p1_e.htm, accessed 28 March 2024.

[13] ibid.

[14] Zubeida Mustafa, 'The Principle of Self-Determination in International Law' (1971) 5 *International Lawyer* 479, 479.

[15] See, eg, *Turkey: Restrictions on Imports of Textile and Clothing Products – Request for Consultations by Hong Kong* (15 February 1996) WT/DS29/1 and G/L/64.

[16] *United States: Origin Marking Requirement- Communication from the Panel* (27 October 2022) WT/DS597/7.

[17] WTO, 'Panel Report on US Duties on Turkish Pipe and Tube Products' (*WTO*, 27 January 2022). Available at: www.wto.org/english/news_e/news22_e/597r_e.htm, accessed 6 April 2024.

The US imposed a labelling requirement in response to China's actions that undermined Hong Kong's autonomy, including the enactment of the National Security Law. The US argued that this measure was justified on national security grounds, invoking Article XXI(b) of the GATT 1994.[18]

The Panel, however, disagreed with the American argument that the Article XXI(b) clause was 'self-judging' and believed that it was open to objective determination. The Panel concluded that the US had failed to prove the existence of an emergency in international relations and, therefore, could not justify the origin-marking requirement under Article XXI(b). The ruling found the US measure to be in breach of Article I:1 of the GATT 1994, Articles 2(c) and 2(d) of the Agreement on Rules of Origin[19] and Article 2.1 of the Agreement on Technical Barriers to Trade ('TBT Agreement').[20]

This ruling is significant for Hong Kong and the WTO because it not only addresses discriminatory trade practices against Hong Kong but also sets a precedent for the interpretation and application of 'self-judging' clauses in various international treaties beyond the multilateral trade regime.[21] The Panel's extensive reasoning on this matter may have broader implications for future disputes involving such clauses.

Despite the importance of this ruling, the Office of the US Trade Representative has rejected the Panel's report, citing 'flawed interpretation and conclusions' and arguing that the ruling 'underscores the need for fundamental WTO reform'. This highlights the ongoing tension between the US and the WTO, as well as the challenges the organisation faces in balancing member states' interests and enforcing international trade rules.

A. US–Hong Kong Trade Ties: An Historical Overview and Legal Consequences

The year 2020 can be viewed as an immediate precursor to the current dispute. In accordance with the US–Hong Kong Policy Act 1992, the Hong Kong Human Rights Act, the Hong Kong Autonomy Act 2020, the International Emergency Economic Powers Act and the National Emergencies Act, President Trump issued an executive order on 14 July 2020, entitled 'Executive Order on

[18] WTO, 'General Agreement on Tariffs and Trade 1947' (*WTO*, 30 October 1947). Available at: www.wto.org/english/docs_e/legal_e/gatt47_02_e.htm, accessed 6 April 2024.

[19] WTO, 'Agreement on Rules of Origin' (WTO, 15 April 1994). Available at: www.wto.org/english/docs_e/legal_e/22-roo_e.htm, accessed 6 April 2024.

[20] WTO, 'Agreement on Technical Barriers to Trade' (WTO, 15 April 1994). Available at: www.wto.org/english/docs_e/legal_e/17-tbt.pdf, accessed 6 April 2024.

[21] Robert Howse and Joanna Langille, 'Continuity and Change in the World Trade Organization: Pluralism Past, Present and Future' (2023) 117 *American Journal of International Law* 1; Mona Pinchis-Paulsen, 'Let's Agree to Disagree: A Strategy for Trade-Security' (2022) 25 *Journal of International Economic Law* 527.

Hong Kong Normalisation'. This order aims to establish a standard relationship between the US and Hong Kong. By exercising his executive authority, President Trump suspended the application of Section 201(a) of the US-Hong Kong Policy Act 1992 based on the determination that Hong Kong no longer possessed sufficient autonomy to warrant differential treatment compared to China. Consequently, the US Customs and Border Protection announced in the Federal Register on 11 August 2020 the implementation of a new requirement for labelling the jurisdiction of origin on imported goods produced in Hong Kong. Under this regulation, which took effect on 9 November 2020, foreign products manufactured in Hong Kong could no longer bear a label indicating 'Hong Kong' as their origin. Instead, the items were required to be marked as originating from 'China'.

The principal rationale for the Executive Order was the enactment of the National Security Law in Hong Kong. The US government argued that recent developments in Hong Kong constituted a breach of the 1984 Joint Declaration between the Government of the United Kingdom of Great Britain and Northern Ireland and the Government of the People's Republic of China (PRC) on the question of Hong Kong.[22] This declaration addressed the issue of jurisdiction over Hong Kong (Sino-British Joint Declaration 1984).

To fully comprehend the origins of this dispute, it is crucial to examine its broader historical context. On 5 June 1997, shortly before the handover on 1 July, the US Customs Service published a notice in the Federal Register stating that goods produced in Hong Kong should continue to be marked as originating from 'Hong Kong'. According to Section 304 of the Tariff Act 1930,[23] all foreign-origin items imported into the US must bear a conspicuous mark with the English name of the jurisdiction of origin, unless specifically exempted.

On 1 July 1997, the US acknowledged that China had resumed its sovereignty over Hong Kong in line with the Sino-British Joint Declaration on the Question of Hong Kong 1984. In this context, the US–Hong Kong Policy Act 1992 was enacted to guide the US government's approach to Hong Kong's status, both before and after 1997. This Act required the US Secretary of State to report on Hong Kong's situation to the appropriate heads of two congressional bodies in the US in 1993, 1995, 1997, 1998, 1999 and 2000. The US–Hong Kong Policy Act 1992 was updated by the Hong Kong Human Rights and Democracy Act 2019, which took effect in 2019. This Act aimed to ensure the implementation of specific measures outlined in the Sino-British Joint Declaration 1984 and sought guarantees for their execution. Prior to the 1997 handover, the primary concern was maintaining Hong Kong's economic stability. After a century of British rule, China and Britain agreed to transfer sovereignty over Hong Kong to China in 1984. This agreement was formalised with the signing of the Sino-British Joint Declaration 1984.

[22] UK Parliament, *Hong Kong: Recent Developments and the UK Response*, (CBP-8616, 2021).
[23] Tariff Act 1930, s 304: Marking of imported articles and containers.

From a legal perspective, in October 2020, Hong Kong opted to challenge the US' specific revocation measures. As an authoritative figure in law, it is noteworthy that Hong Kong's decision to contest these measures stems from the perceived discriminatory treatment arising from US-imposed regulations, which have significant implications for trade and international relations between the two territories.[24] The consultations that Hong Kong sought on 30 October 2020 will exclusively address the 'Made in China' labelling issue in this ongoing conflict.[25]

The US–Hong Kong Policy Act 1992 emerged from the recognition of Hong Kong's status as a highly autonomous region within China, possessing its own distinct legal and economic systems. This Act served as the foundation for the present conflict by enabling the US to distinguish Hong Kong from mainland China in terms of trade and commercial relations.

The Act was enacted in response to the Sino-British Joint Declaration 1984 which facilitated the transfer of Hong Kong's sovereignty to mainland China in 1997 while preserving certain rights for the territory. The Act authorised the continued application of international agreements between the US and Hong Kong, as well as the enforcement of existing US laws in Hong Kong, in the same manner as before 1 July 1997. In alignment with this Act, the US Department of Commerce and US Customs and Border Protection formulated regulations that allowed for the acknowledgement of Hong Kong as a separate customs territory, akin to its administration under British rule. Notably, the US–Hong Kong Policy Act 1992 granted the US President the power to rescind Hong Kong's special treatment through an executive order if the President determined that Hong Kong lacked sufficient autonomy to justify such treatment.[26]

In response to the enactment of the National Security Law by China, President Trump specifically took this action against Hong Kong.[27] As Hong Kong's special treatment has been terminated, the trade constraints, tariffs and regulations applicable to US-China commerce now also extend to Hong Kong. Considering the ongoing trade tensions between the US and China and the multitude of sanctions imposed by the US on both imports from and exports to China, these conditions are undeniably more burdensome than the favourable trade terms Hong Kong had enjoyed.[28]

[24] WTO, 'Hong Kong, China Initiates Dispute Complaint Against US Origin Marking Requirements' (WTO, 3 November 2020). Available at: www.wto.org/english/news_e/news20_e/ds597rfc_03nov20_e.htm, accessed 28 March 2024.

[25] HKTDC Research, 'Hong Kong Files WTO Case Against US "Made in China" Marking Requirement' (*HKTDC Research*, 3 November 2020)). Available at: www.research.hktdc.com/en/article/NTgwODY0OTUz, accessed 28 March 2024. See also US Code, ch 66, s 5713.

[26] ibid s 5722.

[27] Zhaoyin Feng, 'Trump Targets China over Hong Kong Security Law' (*BBC News*, 30 May 2020). Available at: www.bbc.com/news/world-us-canada-52856876, accessed 28 March 2024.

[28] Dorcas Wong and Alexander Chipman Koty, 'The US-China Trade War: A Timeline' (*China Briefing*, 25 August 2020). Available at: www.chinabriefing.com/news/the-us-china-trade-war-a-timeline/, accessed 28 March 2024.

Thus, the removal of Hong Kong's special treatment has two major impacts: first, it requires future shipments of goods made in Hong Kong to the US to possess the 'Made in China' label;[29] and second, it raises the threat and likelihood that the additional customs duties already levied on exports from China may also be levied on exports from Hong Kong because of the trade war.

In conclusion, trade relations between the US and Hong Kong have been shaped by a complex historical context and legal framework. The enactment of the US–Hong Kong Policy Act 1992 and the subsequent Hong Kong Human Rights and Democracy Act 2019 has served as the foundation for the current conflict between the two territories. The revocation of Hong Kong's special treatment by the US has significant implications for future trade relations between the two territories. This ongoing dispute highlights the need for transparency, accountability and respect for international law in trade relations between nations. It also serves as a reminder that national security concerns must be balanced against the fundamental principles of non-discrimination and transparency in WTO law.

B. Confronting US Trade Measures: Hong Kong's Challenges under WTO Agreements

Under Article III of the GATT, WTO members are entitled to national treatment. WTO members are prohibited by Article III:2 from imposing greater internal taxes on imported products in comparison to 'like' products.[30] It can be reasonably contended that the Act and potential revocation actions undertaken by the US might contravene GATT Article III when considered alongside the US's commitments to Hong Kong under the WTO framework. As previously noted, the revocation measures may adversely affect Hong Kong exports, subjecting them to higher taxes or levies compared to 'like' US domestic goods. Consequently, these actions appear to have breached Article III of the GATT.

Moreover, additional GATT provisions may also be implicated. First, the GATT generally prohibits export restrictions and bans. Pursuant to GATT Article XI:1, the overall elimination of quantitative restrictions apply not only to the importation of goods but also to measures constraining their exportation.[31] Second, Article IX:4 GATT stipulates that domestic rules and regulations on

[29] Eric Lam, 'US to Label Hong Kong's Goods as "Made in China" in Blow to Territory' (*Bloomberg*, 11 August 2020). Available at: www.bloomberg.com/news/articles/2020-08-11/u-s-to-label-hong-kong-s-goods-as-made-in-china-in-blow-to-territory, accessed 28 March 2024.

[30] Ministry of Economy, Trade and Industry, 'Part II Chapter 2 National Treatment Principle' in 2008 Report on Compliance by Major Trading Partners with Trade Agreements – WTO, FTA/EPA, BIT (2008) 265, 266.

[31] Stephen A Broome, 'Conflicting Obligations for Oil Exporting Nations?: Satisfying Membership Requirements of both OPEC and the WTO' (2006) 38 *George Washington International Law Review* 409, 415.

labelling ('Made in China') must facilitate compliance without actually injuring the goods, significantly lowering their worth, or unnecessarily raising their cost.[32] Third, the US is required to amend its WTO schedules in line with the procedures of Article XXVIII read with the XXIV:6 GATT if the additional customs duties previously imposed on Chinese exports are also imposed on exports from Hong Kong.

The consultations that Hong Kong sought on 30 October 2020, were limited to the issue of labelling.[33] Hong Kong has restricted its claim to labelling, apparently in an effort to reduce the possibility that the US will successfully invoke national security. Articles I:1, IX:1 and X:3(a) of the GATT 1994, Article 2(c)(d)(e) of the Agreement on Rules of Origin and Article 2.1 of the TBT Agreement serve as the legal foundation for the present complaint.[34]

The most-favourable nation (hereinafter 'MFN') principle is embodied in Article 2.1 of the TBT Agreement. To successfully argue that the contested measures violate Article 2.1 of the TBT Agreement, three conditions must be satisfied. Firstly, the disputed measure must qualify as a technical regulation (as stipulated by Annex 1.1 of the TBT Agreement); secondly, the imported product must be deemed 'like' in relation to domestically produced goods and goods originating from other countries; and finally, it must be subjected to less favourable treatment compared to 'like' goods from other nations.[35] In this particular case, the US labelling requirements fall within the scope of technical regulations, as defined by the TBT Agreement. Nevertheless, Hong Kong imports are accorded less favourable treatment than 'like' imports from other countries, thereby contravening Article 2.1 of the Agreement.[36]

The US used the national security exception under Article XXI of the GATT to defend its measures.[37] According to the US, the essential security measures under the TBT Agreement should not be reviewed.[38] This clarification can be found in the 2019 panel report *DS512: Russia – Measures Concerning Traffic in Transit*.[39] In this case, the Panel scrutinised the exception carefully, offering valuable insights into its interpretation and application in the context of

[32] WTO Analytical Index GATT 1994 (n 11) 4, art IX.

[33] *US–Origin Marking Requirement* (n 30).

[34] *United States: Origin Marking Requirement – Request for Consultation by Hong Kong China* (3 November 2020) WT/DS597/1, G/L/1365, G/RO/D/8, G/TBT/D/53.

[35] *United States: Origin Marking Requirement – First Written Submission of the United States of America* (2 July 2021) WT/DS597, para 304.

[36] *Request for Consultation by Hong Kong China* 2; *United States: Measures Concerning the Importation, Marketing and Sale of Tuna and Tuna Products – Appellate Body Report* (13 June 2012) WT/DS381/AB/R, para 202.

[37] See generally Brandon J Murrill, 'The "National Security Exception" and the World Trade Organisation' (*Congressional Research Service*, 28 November 2018). Available at: www.fas.org/sgp/crs/row/LSB10223.pdf, accessed 28 March 2024; *United States: Origin Marking Requirement – Communication from the United States* (13 November 2020) WT/DS597/2.

[38] *First Written Submission of the United States of America* (n 41) 98.

[39] *Russia: Measures Concerning Traffic in Transit – Report of the Panel* (26 April 2019) WT/DS512/R, appendix.

international trade disputes.[40] The Panel observed that a member state cannot unilaterally decide that a measure is justified for national security reasons without any possibility of review by the WTO. Certain objective criteria that must be satisfied for a member state to invoke the national security exception under Article XXI. This report serves as a crucial reference point for understanding the boundaries and conditions under which such an exception may be legitimately employed by a member state such as the US. The Panel concluded in its report that Russia's actions fell within the ambit of the national security exception.[41]

In conclusion, US trade actions against Hong Kong have raised concerns over potential violations of the WTO agreements. The Act and potential revocation actions may contravene Article III of the GATT, which prohibits imposing greater internal taxes on imported products in comparison to domestic goods. GATT provisions on export restrictions and labelling requirements may also be implicated. The use of the national security exception under Article XXI of the GATT to defend measures has been scrutinised in the Russian case, providing insights into its interpretation and application in international trade disputes. The limited consultations sought by Hong Kong on the issue of labelling have reduced the possibility of the US successfully invoking national security. However, challenges to trade actions remain under the WTO agreements. It is crucial to uphold the principles of non-discrimination and transparency in international trade as well as to ensure that national security exceptions do not undermine the fundamental principles of WTO law.

C. Decoding the Impact of the US-Origin Marking Requirement Decision: Security Exceptions and WTO Jurisprudence

For seven-and-a-half decades, the dispute resolution mechanisms of the WTO and the GATT 1947 did not address the exceptions stipulated in

[40] Regarding the national security exception rule, the Russia–Ukraine decision provided two significant clarifications that have direct bearing on the ongoing dispute between Hong Kong and the US.

Justiciability: The panel determined that the national security exception under GATT Article XXI is not completely 'self-judging' and that the WTO Dispute Settlement Body has the authority to review whether the conditions for invoking the exception are met. This means that a member state cannot unilaterally decide that a measure is justified for national security reasons without any possibility of review by the WTO.

Objective criteria: The panel clarified that there are certain objective criteria that must be satisfied for a member state to invoke the national security exception under Article XXI. The panel identified three conditions: (a) the challenged measure must be taken in the context of an 'emergency in international relations' involving a threat to the essential security interests of the member state; (b) the measure must be related to the interests protected under Article XXI (such as fissionable materials, arms and ammunition); and (c) the measure must not be applied in a manner that would constitute arbitrary or unjustifiable discrimination or a disguised restriction on international trade. This framework establishes a clearer understanding of when the national security exception can be applied, preventing its misuse in trade disputes.

[41] Chao Wang, 'Invocation of National Security Exceptions Under GATT Article XXI: Jurisdiction to Review and Standard of Review' (2019) 18 *Chinese Journal of International Law* 695, 707.

Article XXI (b).[42] The *United States – Origin Marking Requirement* dispute[43] represents a significant addition to the relatively scarce yet growing body of WTO jurisprudence concerning security exceptions.[44]

The recent ruling in the *United States-Origin Marking Requirement*, is a landmark decision with far-reaching implications for the interpretation and application of national security exemptions in international trade law. The ruling provides a comprehensive and detailed analysis of the 'self-judging' clause, which allows WTO members to unilaterally determine whether their measures are necessary to safeguard their essential security interests and has been the subject of much interpretive debate and controversy.

National security exemptions are a crucial tool for enabling nations to protect their security interests without violating their WTO obligations.[45] However, this exemption is subject to strict conditions and must not be used as a pretext for protectionism or discrimination. The *United States–Origin Marking Requirement* ruling reaffirms the importance of transparency and accountability in the exercise of exemption and underscores the need to balance national security concerns with the principles of non-discrimination and transparency in international trade.

This ruling is particularly significant in the context of the ongoing trade war between the US and China and the fraught relationship between Hong Kong and the US. Hong Kong's invocation of the WTO dispute settlement mechanism for only the second time in its history highlights the importance of its unique legal status as a separate customs territory and member of the WTO.[46] The ruling is also notable for being the only panel report where Hong Kong is a disputing party, given that in the other dispute, Turkey discontinued its restrictions on imports of textile and clothing products.[47]

In conclusion, the *United States–Origin Marking Requirement* ruling represents a milestone in the development of WTO jurisprudence on national

[42] Stephanie Switzer, 'The World Trade Organisation Dispute Settlement Mechanism' in Edgardo Sobenes, Sarah Mead, Benjamin Samson (eds), *The Environment Through the Lens of International Courts and Tribunals* (Hague, TMC Asser Press, 2022) 121–58.

[43] (Hong Kong, China) (World Trade Organization (WTO) December 2022 Panel Report in the United States Origin Marking Requirement).

[44] HKSAR Government, 'Hong Kong's Response to Written Questions from the United States on Hong Kong's Implementation of the World Trade Organisation Agreement on Subsidies and Countervailing Measures' (February 2022).

[45] Saverio Di Benedetto, 'The National Security Clauses in International Economic Agreements: A Loophole for States to Escape Their Obligations?' in Maria R Mauro and Federico Pernazza (ed), *State and Enterprise: Legal Issues in the Global Market* (Cham, Springer International Publishing, 2023) 53–72.

[46] Julien Chaisse and Xueliang Ji, 'Hong Kong's Participation in International Dispute Settlement: Deviations from Conventional Sovereignty' (2022) 17 *Asian Journal of WTO and International Health Law and Policy* 287.

[47] James Crawford and Freya Baetens, 'The Influence of International Trade Law on International Law' in Daniel Bethlehem, Donald McRae, Rodney Neufeld and Isabelle Van Damme (eds), *The Oxford Handbook of International Trade Law* (2nd edn, New York, Oxford University Press 2022) 160.

security exemptions and underscores the importance of upholding the rule of law in international trade. The ruling clarifies the legal framework for invoking the national security exemption under WTO law and sets important limits on its scope and application. The ruling's broader implications for the interpretation and application of self-judging provisions in other international treaties beyond the multilateral trade framework, as well as its significance for the trade relationship between the US and Hong Kong, make a crucial and timely contribution to the ongoing debate on the role of national security in international trade law.[48] As such, the ruling reaffirms the importance of upholding the rule of law in international trade and promoting transparency and accountability in exercising national security exemptions.

D. International Emergencies and the 'One Country, Two Systems' Principle: Key Insights from the WTO Panel Report

The WTO Panel determined that the US' origin marking requirement violated Article I:1 of the GATT 1994, as it subjected Hong Kong's goods to less favourable treatment than those from other countries. Additionally, the Panel concluded that the US failed to establish that the situation in Hong Kong constituted an emergency within the sphere of international relations, rendering its actions unjustifiable under Article XXI(b)(iii).[49] Similar to previous reports in *Russia – Measures Concerning Traffic in Transit (Russia – Traffic in Transit)* and *Qatar – Certain Measures Concerning Goods from the United Arab Emirates*, the primary legal issue in this dispute centred around the national security exception under Article XXI(b)(iii) of the GATT 1994. It is crucial to note that the WTO Panel reiterated the earlier Panel's findings and confirmed that the US invocation of Article XXI contravened the WTO rules.[50]

In light of the broader context of these disputes and the recently published trade reports on steel and aluminium,[51] the *United States–Origin Marking Requirement* warrants close examination because of its particular history and broader implications for US–China trade relations in the post-Trump era. The consequences of designating products as 'Made in China', the 'One Country, Two Systems' principle within the WTO's legal framework and the definition

[48] WTO, 'DS597: United States – Countervailing Measures on Certain Pipe and Tube Products from Turkey' (*WTO*). Available at: www.wto.org/english/tratop_e/dispu_e/cases_e/ds597_e.htm, accessed 28 March 2024.

[49] Giorgio Sacerdoti and Leonardo Borlini, 'Systemic Changes in the Politicisation of the International Trade Relations and the Decline of the Multilateral Trading System' (2023) 24 *German Law Journal* 17.

[50] Yaoyuan Zhang, 'The Revival of Spectre: Voluntary Import Expansions and the WTO Compatibility' (2023) 18 *Asian Journal of WTO and International Health Law and Policy* 231.

[51] Sophie-Katharina Perl, *The Protection of National Security in International Economic Law–US policy on Steel and Aluminium in the Light of WTO Law* (Beiträge zum Transnationalen Wirtschaftsrecht, 2022).

of emergency in the realm of international relations, are three key points that merit emphasis.

Pursuant to Articles 1 and 4 of the Understanding on Rules and Procedures Governing the Settlement of Disputes, Article XXII:1 of the GATT 1994, Article 7 of the Agreement on Rules of Origin and Article 14.1 of the TBT Agreement, Hong Kong initiated a request for consultations with the US on 30 October 2020. Hong Kong contended that the origin marking requirements conflicted with the US' obligations under Article I:1, Article IX:1 and Article X:3(a) of the GATT 1994, as well as Articles 2(c), (d) and (e) of the Agreement on Rules of Origin and Article 2.1 of the TBT Agreement.[52] Furthermore, Hong Kong maintained that these requirements breached GATT 1994. In response, the US asserted that measures were taken in response to a situation in Hong Kong that posed a threat to its vital security interests. The US also argued that Article XXI(b) of the GATT 1994 was self-judging in nature and that the Panel in *Russia–Traffic in Transit*, had erred in asserting its authority to review a responding party's invocation of Article XXI of the GATT 1994.[53] The US contended that this constituted an error since Article XXI(b) of the GATT 1994 was designed as a self-judging provision.[54]

Initially, the Panel established the appropriate sequence for its examination, stating that it deemed it suitable to commence its analysis with Hong Kong's claim of discriminatory most-favoured-nation (MFN) treatment concerning origin markings under Article IX:1 of the GATT 1994 (paragraph 7.15). Subsequently, the Panel shifted its attention to assessing whether Article XXI(b) was self-judging in nature, thereby precluding it from scrutinising the measures in question (paragraph 7.3). The Panel then conducted a grammatical analysis of the relative clause in the Chapeau to Article XXI(b) (para 7.47), followed by a comparative examination of the English, French and Spanish versions of the text (paragraph 7.70). In accordance with the first paragraph of Article 31 of the Vienna Convention on the Law of Treaties (1969), the Panel proceeded to analyse the textual context and negotiation history of Article XXI. Upon reaching its final determination and considering all the evidence presented, the Panel concluded that the American origin marking requirement was not justifiable under Article XXI(b)(iii) of the GATT 1994.

Notably, the Panel posited that an emergency in international relations need not exclusively stem from bilateral relations within a member's territory; rather, it could encompass a broader scope involving multiple WTO members. The Panel examined the contemporary global landscape, recognising the

[52] WTO Agreement on Technical Barriers to Trade (adopted 15 April 1994, entered into force 1 January 1995) 1867 UNTS 120.

[53] Understanding on the Interpretation of Article XXI of the GATT 1994 (11 December 2019). Available at: www.directdoc.aspx (wto.org).

[54] Oliver Hailes, 'Lithium in International Law: Trade, Investment and the Pursuit of Supply Chain Justice' (2022) 25 *Journal of International Economic Law* 148.

numerous political, economic, social and environmental conflicts and disparities that shape today's world. However, the Panel emphasised that despite these ideological differences among members, trade connections continue to be sustained.[55]

The Panel arrived at its conclusions by drawing factual analogies with the decision in *Russia–Traffic in Transit*.[56] It emphasised that the UN General Assembly recognised the situation between Ukraine and Russia as one of armed conflict and that multiple countries had imposed sanctions on Russia. Severed diplomatic, consular and economic ties with Qatar served as another point of comparison in this analysis. In relation to the situation in Hong Kong, the US has attempted to rely on the views of other nations. The Panel's factual comparison may be interpreted as implying that, for the US to successfully assert a security exception, it needed to present evidence of comparable gravity to the Russia–Traffic in Transit dispute.

The Panel emphasised that the findings in *Russia–Traffic in Transit* would significantly influence its analysis due to the comprehensive submissions and reliance of all parties on the conclusions. This was despite the Panel's awareness that the contexts of relations between Russia and Ukraine and China and the US are different (paragraph 7.33).

In their analysis and evaluation of the evidence, the Panel appeared to favour the US in terms of providing sufficient proof. However, the US attempted to rely heavily on domestic instruments, reports and statements by US officials regarding Hong Kong's situation, as well as news articles and comments from other nations and members. Although there were ample reasons for concern about the human rights situation in Hong Kong, the Panel concluded that there was no complete breakdown of ties between the two jurisdictions. There was no evidence of measures taken against China; measures against Hong Kong targeted only specific areas; relations between the US and Hong Kong did not undergo a significant change; tariff treatment remained comparable before the imposition of the origin marking requirement; and there was no evidence that the US or other WTO members had severed diplomatic, consular or economic relations with China or Hong Kong. These considerations inform the assessment.[57] Consequently, the question arises as to whether the US could have provided more candid explanations about the circumstances, potentially leading to a more favourable decision for the US. This also highlights the limited economic and legal impact of a proxy war, which may be overstated in newspaper headlines,

[55] Joel Slawotsky, 'The Weaponisation of Human Rights in US–China Trade Policy: Impacts and Risks' (2022) 56 *Journal of World Trade* 547.

[56] Anhand S Miglani, 'A Contemporary Contextualization of Security Under Article XXI of the GATT' (2022) 17 *Global Trade and Customs Journal* 485.

[57] Weihuan Zhou, Huiqin Jiang and Zhe Chen, 'Trade vs. Security: Recent Developments of Global Trade Rules and China's Policy and Regulatory Responses from Defensive to Proactive' (2022) 22 *World Trade Review* 193.

as well as the continued interdependence of economic relations between the US and China, despite their conflicting stances on Hong Kong and Taiwan.[58]

In conclusion, the WTO panel report on the *United States Origin Marking Requirement* sheds light on the concepts of emergency in international relations and the principle of One Country, Two Systems. The Panel highlighted that an emergency in international relations need not solely stem from bilateral relations within a member's territory and could encompass a broader scope involving multiple WTO members. Moreover, the panel report raises significant legal issues concerning the relationship between the 'One Country, Two Systems' principle and WTO law. The ruling emphasises that WTO members, including special administrative regions such as Hong Kong, are subject to the fundamental principle of non-discrimination in international trade law. The panel report highlights the importance of upholding the rule of law and ensuring that national security exceptions do not undermine the fundamental principles of non-discrimination and transparency in WTO law. It serves as a timely reminder that national security measures must be justified and that WTO members must exercise caution to avoid conflating trade measures with protectionist policies.

E. National Security and Proxy Trade Conflicts: A Multilateral View on the US-Origin Marking Requirement Case

Hong Kong's legal standing within the multilateral trading system framework emerged as a critical issue in the panel report. One of the most significant points raised by Hong Kong was that, although it is an integral part of China, its fundamental legislation asserts that it is a separate customs territory and a member of the WTO.[59] This marks the first time that the implications of China's 'One Country, Two Systems' policy have been scrutinised in a panel report. Although China joined the WTO in December 2001, the Hong Kong Special Administrative Region has maintained its status as a separate member, continuing to operate under the name 'Hong Kong, China'. China's accession to the WTO in 2001 was, for better or worse, a momentous event in international trade history, with far-reaching consequences.[60] Additionally, the Macao SAR has been a member of both the GATT 1947 and the WTO since

[58] Daniel Wilcox, 'Convergence and Hegemony: The United States and China in the 21st Century' (*Union College*, 2022). Available at: www.digitalworks.union.edu/cgi/viewcontent.cgi?article=3721&context=theses, accessed 28 March 2024.

[59] Richard J. Hunter Jr, Héctor R Lozada and John H Shannon, 'The Debate on Reforms of the WTO Appellate Process: A Proxy for a More Serious Discussion of the Future of the WTO' (2023) 6 *Education Quarterly Reviews* 86.

[60] Xaliq Rüstəmov and Khalig Rustamov, 'Contemporary Trends in China's Foreign Trade' (2022) 135 *Scientific Collection «InterConf»* 37.

11 January 1991 and 1 January 1995, respectively. On 1 January 2002, Taiwan joined the WTO under the formal names of the Separate Customs Territory of Taiwan, Penghu, Kinmen and Matsu. The Panel reiterated that the dispute's complexity arose from Hong Kong's dual status as both a separate customs territory and an inalienable part of China. This status was connected to the US assessment that 'Hong Kong … is no longer sufficiently autonomous to justify differential treatment in relation to the People's Republic of China'.[61] However, the Panel noted that there were no diverging opinions regarding Hong Kong and that China's participation in the WTO and its geographic boundaries were separate issues.[62]

The decision reached, in this case, opens the door for Hong Kong and Macao to use the WTO dispute resolution system, given the special circumstances of China's membership of the WTO and the consequences of discriminatory labelling requirements.[63] This outcome also sets the stage for future jurisprudence on the matter of proxy trade disputes, encompassing interests at bilateral, regional and international levels. Hong Kong and Macao are the only non-state territories that are members of the WTO, creating a precedent that might allow other smaller territories to employ the WTO to protect their interests.[64]

In its third-party submission, China contended that the National Security Law had been enacted in accordance with Hong Kong's constitutional Basic Law and the 'One Country, Two Systems' policy. Furthermore, China emphasised that these measures had not altered Hong Kong's status as a separate customs territory, nor had its qualifications or status as a WTO member been affected in any manner by these developments. This case highlights the potential for non-state territories to assert their rights and interests within the framework of the WTO dispute resolution system, paving the way for further exploration of this unique legal territory in international trade law.

The *United States–Origin Marking Requirement* panel report raises important questions regarding the interpretation of national security in the context of the WTO.[65] While the WTO has had a limited impact on how questions of national security are interpreted, the rise of national security legislation and policies has brought these issues to the forefront of state challenges to

[61] Justine Yu, 'The United States' Ineffective Response Towards Hong Kong's National Security Law' (2022) 73 *Hastings Law Journal* 161.

[62] Gregory T Chin, 'Geopolitics and Hong Kong as International Financial Centre: A Dynamic IPE Perspective' (2022) 28 *Asia Pacific Business Review* 660.

[63] Giorgio Sacerdoti, 'The WTO and its Dispute Settlement System in 2022: From the First Appellate Arbitrations to the Unsuccessful Invocation of the Security Exception' (2023) Bocconi Legal Studies Research Paper No 4369702). Available at: www.papers.ssrn.com/sol3/papers.cfm?abstract_id=4369702, accessed 28 March 2024.

[64] Xinhua Gu, Zhaotong Lian, Lei Peng and Qingbin Zhao, 'A Comparative Study of Bank Efficiency in Three Chinese Regions: Mainland China, Hong Kong and Macao' (2023) 46 *Journal of Financial Research* 547.

[65] Clara Weinhardt and Till Schöfer, 'Differential Treatment for Developing Countries in the WTO: The Unmaking of the North–South Distinction in a Multipolar World' (2022) 43 *Third World Quarterly* 74.

the rules-based multilateral system. In this context, the *United States–Origin Marking Requirement* decision highlights the challenges faced by the WTO in a multipolar world where national security is a central focus.

The panel report emphasises that measures taken by WTO members in the name of national security must meet the requirements established by the WTO to be legal. This underscores the importance of WTO law in ensuring the predictability and safety of the multilateral trading system. However, the report also acknowledges that the use and non-use of trade-related actions must be maintained within certain boundaries.[66]

The *United States–Origin Marking Requirement* decision has wider implications for geo-economics and the legitimacy of proxy trade conflicts, which go beyond the MFN non-discrimination standards currently in place. The report also raises concerns about the limited economic and legal impacts of proxy trade wars, which may be overstated in news headlines. It also highlights the continued interdependency of economic relations between the US and China, despite their conflicting positions regarding Hong Kong and Taiwan.[67]

The panel report further notes that Hong Kong's status as a separate customs territory and an inalienable part of China presents a complex problem within the multilateral trade system. This issue is related but separate from the issues of discriminatory treatment and the labelling of products as 'Made in China'. While the WTO Panel recognised the significance of Hong Kong's position, it stressed that measures must comply with WTO jurisprudence.

The US has criticised the Panel's recommendations, arguing that matters of national security should be outside the scope of WTO dispute resolution. The decision in the *United States–Origin Marking Requirement* underscores the need for careful consideration of national security issues within the framework of the multilateral trade system and raises questions about the balance between national security interests and WTO obligations.

In conclusion, the WTO Panel Report on the *United States–Origin Marking Requirement* case has shed light on the complexities of national security issues and their relationship with the multilateral trading system. The ruling has important implications for non-state territories, such as Hong Kong and Macao, in asserting their rights and interests within the framework of the WTO dispute resolution system. The decision also highlights the challenges of reconciling national security interests with WTO law and underscores the importance of transparency and accountability in the use of national security exceptions. Moreover, the ruling raised concerns about the legitimacy of proxy trade conflicts and their impact on the MFN non-discrimination standards currently in place. This is a timely reminder of the need for careful consideration

[66] AI Ukpe, *Differentiated Differentiation: Using Progressive Regulation as a Framework for Special and Differential Treatment in the WTO* (Wageningen, Wageningen University, 2022).

[67] Peter Lindsay, 'The Ambiguity of GATT Article XXI: Subtle Success or Rampant Failure' (2002) 52 *Duke Law Journal* 1277.

of national security issues within the framework of the multilateral trade system and the importance of upholding the rule of law in international trade.

F. Lessons Learned: Implications for Hong Kong's Future in International Dispute Settlement

In conclusion, the recent ruling in the *United States – The Origin Marking Requirement* case is a significant milestone in Hong Kong's involvement in the international dispute settlement (IDS) mechanism. The ruling serves as a reminder that the fundamental principle of non-discrimination in international trade law applies to all WTO members, including special administrative regions such as Hong Kong. The decision also highlights the difficulties of reconciling national security interests with WTO law and the challenges of ensuring that national security exceptions are not abused.

This ruling has significant implications for the trade relationship between the US and Hong Kong. With the discontinuation of Hong Kong's special treatment, trade restrictions, taxes and regulations that apply to US–China trade will also apply to Hong Kong. This means that the trade conditions in Hong Kong are likely to become more onerous than before. The ruling also raises broader issues regarding the use of national security as a justification for trade measures and highlights the importance of transparency and accountability in the exercise of such measures.

Moreover, this case highlights the importance of Hong Kong's unique legal status in the WTO. As a separate customs territory and member of the WTO, Hong Kong has the right to bring trade disputes to the multilateral dispute settlement mechanism. This case demonstrates that Hong Kong can assert its rights under WTO law and seek redress for alleged violations of trade rights.

Overall, the ruling is an important reminder of the importance of upholding the rule of law in international trade and the need to ensure that national security exceptions do not undermine the fundamental principles of non-discrimination and transparency in WTO law. This is a milestone for Hong Kong's involvement in international dispute settlement and reaffirms the importance of the WTO in promoting and enforcing the principles of free and fair trade.

IV. SUPPORTING FROM THE SIDELINES: HONG KONG'S ROLE AS A THIRD PARTY IN WTO DISPUTE SETTLEMENT

WTO members can take part in processes started by other members as third parties in addition to making direct requests for consultation. Article 10 of the DSU states that in order to be granted the opportunity to take part in proceedings, the interested member state must show 'substantial interest' in the issue before a panel. The third parties are required to disclose their interests to the

Dispute Settlement Body (DSB). This covers the right to a single hearing before the panel, the opportunity to make written statements and the right to be provided with the arguments put forth by opposing parties during the initial panel meeting.[68]

Third parties involved in disputes may additionally assert 'enhanced' third-party rights in addition to 'regular' third-party rights.[69] Third parties can benefit from enhanced third-party rights in order to better safeguard their interests. The WTO Panel granted enhanced third-party rights to 16 out of 21 parties in the *EC–Bananas III* dispute.[70] Third parties may observe the second substantive meeting of the panel with the parties and make a brief statement at a suitable time during that meeting. WTO jurisprudence demonstrates that the existence of a member's interest in a specific dispute is not usually called into doubt.[71] However, large delegations with substantial resources often take the role of third parties due to systemic interests and the precedential implications of reports published and adopted by the Panel and Appellate Body.[72]

Table 11.1 Hong Kong, China's Participation as a Third Party in WTO Disputes

Hong Kong, China as a Third Party	*WTO Agreement involved (as cited in panel request)*
DS21: Australia – Measures Affecting the Importation of Salmonids	GATT 1994, Art XI
DS34: Turkey – Restrictions on Imports of Textile and Clothing Products	GATT 1994, Arts XI, XIII,
DS58: United States – Import Prohibition of Certain Shrimp and Shrimp Products	GATT 1994, Arts I, XI, XIII, XX
DS152: United States – Sections 301–310 of the Trade Act 1974	GATT 1994, Arts I, II, III, VIII, XI
DS217: United States – Continued Dumping and Subsidy Offset Act of 2000	GATT 1994, Arts X:3, VI:3, VI:2
DS234: United States – Continued Dumping and Subsidy Offset Act of 2000	GATT 1994, Arts VI, X

(continued)

[68] Understanding on Rules and Procedures Governing the Settlement of Disputes (adopted 15 April 1994) art 10, App 3, Marrakesh Agreement Establishing the World Trade Organization (adopted 15 April 1994, entry into force 1 January 1995) 1869 UNTS 401, annex 2.

[69] Takemasa Sekine, 'Enhanced Third Party Rights Under the WTO Dispute Settlement System' (2018) 15 *Manchester Journal of International Economic Law* 354, 357.

[70] *European Communities: Regime for the Importation, Sale and Distribution of Bananas Report of the Panel* (22 May 1997) WT/DS27/R/USA, paras 7.4, 7.8. The term 'enhanced third party' was not used in this case; Sekine (n 75) 358.

[71] *Korea: Definitive Safeguard Measure on Imports of Certain Dairy Products – Report of the Panel* (12 January 2000) WT/DS98/R, para 7.13.

[72] Krzysztof J Pelc, 'Twenty Years of Third-Party Participation at the WTO: What Have We Learned?' in Manfred Elsig, Bernard Hoekman and Joost Pauwelyn (eds), *Assessing the World Trade Organization: Fit for Purpose?* (New York, Cambridge University Press, 2017) 203, 209.

Table 11.1 *(Continued)*

Hong Kong, China as a Third Party	*WTO Agreement involved (as cited in panel request)*
DS294: United States – Laws, Regulations and Methodology for Calculating Dumping Margins (Zeroing)	GATT 1994, Art VI
DS315: European Communities – Selected Customs Matters	GATT 1994, Arts X:3, X:1
DS322: United States – Measures Relating to Zeroing and Sunset Reviews	GATT 1994, Art VI
DS337: European Communities – Anti-Dumping Measure on Farmed Salmon from Norway	GATT 1994, Arts VI:1, VI
DS375: European Communities and its Member States – Tariff Treatment of Certain Information Technology Products	GATT 1994, Arts II:1, X:1, X:2, XXIII
DS376: European Communities and its Member States – Tariff Treatment of Certain Information Technology Products	GATT 1994, Arts II:1, X:1, X:2, XXIII
DS377: European Communities and its Member States – Tariff Treatment of Certain Information Technology Products	GATT 1994, Arts II:1, X:1, X:2, XXIII
DS544: United States – Certain Measures on Steel and Aluminium Products	GATT 1994, Arts II:1(a), II:1(b), I:1, X:3(a), XIX:1, XIX:2
DS547: United States – Certain Measures on Steel and Aluminium Products	GATT 1994, Arts I:1, II:1(a), II:1(b), X:3, XI:1, XIX, XIX:1, XIX:2
DS548: United States – Certain Measures on Steel and Aluminium Products	GATT 1994, Arts I:1, II:1(a), II:1(b), X:3(a), XI:1, XIX:1, XIX:2
DS550: United States – Certain Measures on Steel and Aluminium Products	GATT 1994, Arts I:1, II:1, II:1(a), II:1(b), X:3(a), XI:1, XIX:1, XIX:2 (as cited in request for consultations)
DS551: United States – Certain Measures on Steel and Aluminium Products	GATT 1994, Arts I:1, II:1(a), II:1(b), XI:1, XIX:1, XIX:2
DS552: United States – Certain Measures on Steel and Aluminium Products	GATT 1994, Arts I:1, II:1(a), II:1(b), X:3(a), XI:1, XIX:1, XIX:2
DS554: United States – Certain Measures on Steel and Aluminium Products	GATT 1994, Arts I:1, II:1(a), II:1(b), X:3(a), XI:1, XIX:1, XIX:2
DS556: United States – Certain Measures on Steel and Aluminium Products	GATT 1994, Arts I:1, II:1(a), II:1(b), X:3(a), XI:1, XIX
DS564: United States – Certain Measures on Steel and Aluminium Products	GATT 1994, Arts I:1, II:1(a), X:3(a), XI:1, XIII:1, XIX:1, XIX:2

Source: Compiled by the author from WTO, Disputes by member as of June 2023.[73]

[73] Available at: www.wto.org/english/tratop_e/dispu_e/dispu_by_countr y_e.htm.

The 22 instances listed in the table above all involved GATT interpretation. Hong Kong's involvement in lawsuits as a third party has been restricted to trade-in goods. At first glance, this restriction may appear odd, given that Hong Kong's economy is based on services. However, the trade-in goods are directly impacted by services (such as shipping, financing and insurance). Furthermore, perhaps most significantly, Hong Kong's economic strength is heavily reliant on retaining its status as a centre for Chinese exports to the rest of the globe. In this regard, Hong Kong's participation as a third party in WTO disputes might be interpreted as a sign of the critical necessity to preserve a free market for goods, which is one of the criteria for the territory's economic sovereignty.

In conclusion, Hong Kong's active participation in the WTO's dispute settlement mechanism has proven to be essential for safeguarding its economic sovereignty and upholding its rights as a separate customs territory and a WTO member. The recent landmark ruling in the *United States–Origin Marking Requirement* case has shed light on the complexities of national security issues and their relationship with the multilateral trading system. It reaffirms the importance of upholding the rule of law, non-discrimination and transparency in international trade. Hong Kong's involvement as a third party in WTO disputes, particularly in trade-in goods, underscores its commitment to preserving a free market for goods and maintaining its position as a crucial hub for Chinese exports. Despite its predominantly service-based economy, the trade in goods directly impacts the services sector, highlighting the interconnectedness of Hong Kong's economic strength. The ruling has broader implications beyond Hong Kong, as it sets a precedent for the interpretation and application of 'self-judging' clauses in international treaties, emphasising the need for careful consideration of national security issues within the multilateral trade system. It also raises questions about the balance between national security interests and WTO obligations. Furthermore, Hong Kong's involvement in the WTO dispute settlement process may become increasingly significant as deteriorating US–China relations increase the probability of trade disputes. By utilising the WTO's mechanisms, Hong Kong can seek redress for alleged violations of trade rights and strengthen its position in the ongoing trade war. However, the challenges faced by the WTO, including the defunct Appellate Body and the need for fundamental reform, highlight the ongoing tension between member states' interests and the enforcement of international trade rules. The balance between national security considerations and the principles of the WTO remains an important area of debate and further exploration. Overall, Hong Kong's engagement in WTO dispute settlement reflects its commitment to the rules-based multilateral trading system, the protection of its economic interests and the pursuit of fair and effective resolution of trade disputes. It highlights the significance of the WTO in promoting and enforcing the principles of free and fair trade and underscores the importance of transparency, accountability and the rule of law in international trade.

12

Investor-State Dispute Settlement: Navigating Hong Kong's Role and Responsibilities

CHAPTER 12 DISCUSSES the complex world of Investor-State Dispute Settlement (ISDS) and examines Hong Kong's role and responsibilities within this framework. As a global financial hub, Hong Kong has a vested interest in navigating the intricacies of international investment disputes. This chapter seeks to provide a comprehensive overview of Hong Kong's involvement in ISDS, its investors' participation in investment arbitration and the implications of financial institutions' roles in recent investment disputes.

International investment agreements (IIAs), including bilateral investment treaties (BITs), preferential trade agreements with chapters on foreign investment[1] and sector-specific plurilateral agreements, such as the Energy Charter Treaty,[2] contain substantive and well-defined foreign investment obligations. More than 3,000 IIAs constitute a proliferated network of investment protection, with most of these IIAs normally containing the same or similar clauses which share the same purpose.[3] Foreign investors can sue the state hosting their investment directly under an ISDS mechanism for failure to perform their obligations under IIAs.[4] This mechanism also vests the disputing parties with the power to appoint their arbitrators.[5]

[1] See, eg, The North American Free Trade Agreement (US–Canada-Mexico) (signed on 17 December 1992, entered into force on January 1, 1994) 32 ILM 289 (NAFTA); Agreement Establishing the ASEAN–Australia–New Zealand Free Trade Area (ASEAN–Australia–New Zealand FTA) (27 February 2009) [2010] ATS 1.

[2] The Energy Charter Treaty (ECT) (17 December 1994) 2080 UNTS 95.

[3] Andrew D Mitchell and James Munro, 'Someone Else's Deal: Interpreting International Investment Agreements in the Light of Third-Party Agreements' (2017) 28 *European Journal of International Law* 669, 673.

[4] Marco Bronckers, 'Is Investor-State Dispute Settlements (ISDS) Superior to Litigation Before Domestic Courts? An EU View on Bilateral Trade Agreements' (2015) 18 *Journal of International Economic Law* 655, 655.

[5] Chi-Chung Kao, 'The Inclusion of Investment Court System into the EU–China BIT: Innovations, Prospects and Problems' in Julien Chaisse (ed), *China-European Union Investment Relationships: Towards a New Leadership in Global Investment Governance?* (Cheltenham, Edward Elgar Publishing, 2018) 247, 251–52.

The ISDS is an important legal mechanism because it enables investors to safeguard their interests and enforce the rights granted to them under investment agreements. These agreements often contain clauses that safeguard foreign capital from being expropriated, provide access to international arbitration for the settlement of disputes and ensure fair and equal treatment of foreign investments. ISDS makes it possible for investors to sue for compensation in the event that they incur losses or damages as a consequence of a violation of these commitments assured by a host state. ISDS also plays a systemic function in the context of international economic dispute resolution by encouraging stability and predictability in international investment relations. This is one of the ways in which ISDS contributes to the settlement of international economic disputes.

ISDS has the potential to gain considerable importance in Hong Kong's international dispute resolution strategy as a direct consequence of the trade war between the United States of America and China and China's enactment of the National Security Law. Pursuant to the several executive actions that have followed, Hong Kong has lost its special status under US law and consequently will no longer enjoy preferential treatment in trading with the US. In the past, part of this preferential treatment included access to certain export licence exceptions, which protected Hong Kong from becoming embroiled in the US–China trade war. Being treated equally with China in its trade relations with the US may curtail the economic activity in Hong Kong significantly –thereby affecting both domestic entities and foreign investors within its territory.

Sovereign acts can be reviewed by arbitral tribunals so constituted and public interests can be challenged consequently.[6] Hong Kong may strategically choose to use its BITs to challenge the erosion of the value of its investments in relation to the US through ISDS provisions in its BITs in the future. Hong Kong could have more BITs to diversify its foreign investments. For instance, getting BITs with Korea, Switzerland or Brazil would permit to orient more foreign direct investment (FDI) towards these jurisdictions and make Hong Kong less dependent on the US.

The chapter begins by introducing the mechanisms, trends and future prospects of ISDS in the context of Hong Kong. It highlights the importance of understanding the various dispute resolution processes and their implications for both Hong Kong-based investors and the wider international investment law landscape. Next, the chapter discusses the active participation of Hong Kong investors in investment arbitration. It outlines the firsts and trends in this area, with a particular focus on the financial services sector. This section emphasises the significance of Hong Kong's financial industry and its influence on investment arbitration practices. The chapter then discusses the role of

[6] See Luca Pantaleo, 'Lights and Shadows of the TTIP Investment Court System' in Luca Pantaleo et al (eds), *Tiptoeing to TTIP: What Kind of Agreement for What Kind of Partnership?* (CLEER Paper 2016) 77, 91.

financial institutions in recent investment disputes involving Hong Kong investors. It presents an overview of the trends and implications of these disputes for international investment law, offering insights into the unique challenges and opportunities presented by financial investment disputes. In the final section, the chapter explores the complexities of financial investment disputes in international investment law through a case study of Hong Kong. This section is subdivided into three parts: examining the jurisprudence of investment treaty claims by Hong Kong subsidiaries in relation to shareholding and investment structures; discussing indirect control issues in financial investments and investment arbitration, with lessons from Hong Kong and recent developments; and navigating the grey area between investment treaties and financial instruments in the global financial sector. By providing a detailed analysis of Hong Kong's role and responsibilities in ISDS, this chapter offers valuable insights into the dynamics of international investment law disputes and the challenges and opportunities Hong Kong faces as an actor in international economic law.

I. INVESTOR-STATE DISPUTE SETTLEMENT AND HONG KONG: MECHANISMS, TRENDS AND FUTURE PROSPECTS

In the context of international investment law, Hong Kong's BITs are uniquely referred to as Investment Promotion and Protection Agreements (IPPAs). This semantic distinction reflects Hong Kong's approach to promoting and protecting foreign investments while emphasising the territory's commitment to fostering a business-friendly environment. The term 'Investment Promotion and Protection Agreements' captures two key aspects of these agreements. First, the 'promotion' element highlights Hong Kong's proactive approach to encouraging foreign investment by providing investors with a stable and predictable legal framework. This is achieved through various means, such as ensuring fair and equitable treatment (FET), offering protection against discriminatory measures and providing guarantees on the free transfer of investments and returns. Second, the 'protection' aspect of IPPAs underscores Hong Kong's commitment to safeguarding the interests of foreign investors by establishing a clear set of rules and mechanisms for the resolution of investment disputes. This typically includes provisions for ISDS, which allows investors to seek recourse through international arbitration in case of disputes arising from alleged breaches of the IPPA. The use of the term IPPAs instead of the more common BITs reflects Hong Kong's unique status as a Special Administrative Region (SAR) of China, operating under the 'One Country, Two Systems' principle. By adopting the IPPA nomenclature, Hong Kong distinguishes its investment agreements from those signed by mainland China and emphasises its distinct legal system and regulatory framework. In conclusion, the semantic distinction between Hong Kong's IPPAs and BITs is not merely a matter of terminology. Rather, it underscores Hong Kong's unique approach to fostering a business-friendly environment, protecting foreign investors and maintaining its distinct legal and regulatory framework within the context of the 'One Country, Two Systems' principle.

To date, Hong Kong has signed 22 IPPAs to protect investors and to ensure some typical protection standards, like compensation for expropriation, are provided. In Hong Kong's investment treaties, the term 'area' instead of 'territory' is firstly applied, as the term 'territory' is usually used to describe the 'scope of sovereign States'.[7] In 2019, Hong Kong signed a free trade agreement with an associated investment agreement with Australia.[8] Compared with the 1993 Hong Kong–Australia BIT, the FET standard in the 2019 agreement is much narrower, which makes it largely unnecessary for Hong Kong to amend its domestic legislation. The application of Chinese treaties such as IIAs, to Hong Kong, is unsettled. The China–Russia investment treaty has expressly excepted Hong Kong from the scope of its application.[9] Like most IIAs, the ISDS provisions of these investment treaties require that when an investment dispute between an investor of one Contracting Party and the other Contracting Party to such a treaty arises, the parties should first endeavour to settle the same amicably.[10]

However, these investment treaties permit the submission of a claim to procedures agreed upon by both parties if the dispute cannot be amicably resolved after a period of time – three months,[11] six months[12] or 60 days[13] from written notification of the claim. When the disputing parties cannot reach an agreement

[7] Zeng Huaqun, 'Initiative and Implications of Hong Kong's Bilateral Investment Treaties', (2010) 11 *The Journal of World Investment & Trade* 669, 677; Agreement on the Encouragement and Protection of Investments between the Government of Hong Kong and the Government of the Kingdom of the Netherlands (HK–Netherlands) (19 November 1992) [1993] HKTBA 3, art 1.1.

[8] Brenda Horrigan and others, 'Australia and Hong Kong Sign New Trade Agreement Containing Investor-State Dispute Resolution Provisions' (*Herbert Smith Freehills*, 28 March 2019), Available at: https://hsfnotes.com/arbitration/2019/03/28/australia-and-hong-kong-sign-new-trade-agreement-containing-investor-state-dispute-resolution-provisions/, accessed 25 May 2024.

[9] Odysseas G Repousis, 'On Territoriality and International Investment Law: Applying China's Investment Treaties to Hong Kong and Macao' (2015) 37 *Michigan Journal of International Law* 113, 127.

[10] The Hong Kong Special Administrative Region bilateral investment treaties (hereinafter HKSAR BITs) share this clause.

[11] Agreement between the Government of the Hong Kong Special Administrative Region of the People's Republic of China and the Government of the United Kingdom of Great Britain and Northern Ireland for the Promotion and Protection of Investments (HK–United Kingdom) (30 July 1998) [1999] HKTBA 4, art 8 (HK–UK BIT(1998)); Agreement between the Government of Hong Kong and the Government of Australia for the Promotion and Protection of Investments (Australia–HK) (15 September 1993) [1993] HKTBA 5, art 10 (HK–Australia BIT (1993)); Agreement between the Government of the Hong Kong Special Administrative Region of the People's Republic of China and the Government of the Republic of Finland for the Promotion and Protection of Investments (Finland–HK) (2 July 2009) [2014] HKTBA 2, art 8(1) (HK–Finland BIT (2009)).

[12] Except HK–UK BIT (1998), HK–Australia BIT (1993), HK–Finland BIT (2009) and Agreement between the Government of the Hong Kong Special Administrative Region of the People's Republic of China and the Government of Canada for the Promotion and Protection of Investments (Canada–HK) (10 February 2016) [2016] HKTBA 8, art 21 para 1 (HK–Canada BIT (2016)), the other HKSAR BITs share this clause.

[13] HK–Canada BIT (2016).

following such procedures within a stipulated period, usually three[14] or six months,[15] they can resort to international arbitration to resolve the dispute. In particular, foreign investors can initiate arbitration proceedings on behalf of a company that is involved in the dispute and owned or controlled by them.[16] Even though arbitration of disputes remains the preferred dispute settlement mechanism, in the past few years Hong Kong has embraced mediation of Investor-State disputes.[17]

The great majority of Hong Kong's BITs provide for arbitration under the UNCITRAL Arbitration Rules and parties can choose to modify the non-mandatory provisions of these existing rules. Alternatively, disputes can also be submitted to the International Court of Arbitration of the International Chamber of Commerce (ICC) or the Arbitration Institute of the Stockholm Chamber of Commerce (SCC) for settlement by an arbitral tribunal.[18] The UNCITRAL rules applicable to the disputing parties should be the latest iteration of these rules.[19] Arbitral awards are binding on the disputing parties and should be enforced according to the relevant domestic law.[20] Alternatively, investors can also choose

[14] HK–UK BIT (1998); HK–Australia BIT (1993); HK–Finland BIT (2009).

[15] Except HK–UK BIT (1998), HK–Australia BIT (1993), HK–Finland BIT (2009), HK–Canada BIT (2016), the other HKSAR BITs share this clause.

[16] Agreement between the Government of Hong Kong and the Government of Japan for the Promotion and Protection of Investment (HK–Japan) (15 May 1997) [1997] HKTBA 8, art 9, para 4 (HK–Japan BIT (1997)); HK–Canada BIT (2016), art 20, para 2; Investment Agreement between the Government of the Hong Kong Special Administrative Region of the People's Republic of China and the Government of the Republic of Chile (Chile–HK) (18 November 2016) art 21, para 1(b). Available at: https://investmentpolicy.unctad.org/international-investment-agreements/treaty-files/5413/download (HK–Chile BIT (2016)).

[17] Kun Fan, 'Mediation of Investor-State Disputes: A Treaty Survey' (2020) 2 *Journal of Dispute Resolution* 327, 334; Guo Yvonne, 'From Conventions to Protocols: Conceptualizing Changes to the International Dispute Resolution Landscape' (2020) 11 *Journal of International Dispute Settlement* 217, 229.

[18] Agreement Between the Government of the Hong Kong Special Administrative Region of the People's Republic of China and the Government of the United Arab Emirates for the Promotion and Reciprocal Protection of Investments (HK–United Arab Emirates) (16 June 2019) art 8(5). Available at: https://investmentpolicy.unctad.org/international-investment-agreements/treaty-files/5865/download. (HK–Arab Emirates BIT (2019)).

[19] Agreement between the Government of Hong Kong and the Government of the Republic of Austria for the Promotion and Protection of Investments (Austria–HK) (11 October 1996) [1997] HKTBA 22, art 9 (HK–Austria BIT (1993)).

[20] Agreement between the Government of Hong Kong and the Government of the Federal Republic of Germany for the Encouragement and Reciprocal Protection of Investments (Germany–HK) (31 January 1996) [1998] HKTBA 5, art 10 (HK–Germany BIT (1996)); Agreement between the Government of Hong Kong and the Government of the Republic of France for the Reciprocal Promotion and Protection of Investments (French-HK) (30 November 1995) [1997] HKTBA 3, art 9 (HK–France BIT (1995)); HK–Finland BIT (2009) art 8(3); Agreement between the Government of the Hong Kong Special Administrative Region of the People's Republic of China and the Government of the State of Kuwait for the Promotion and Protection of Investments (HK–Kuwait) (13 May 2010) [2013] HKTBA 9, art 8, para 3 (HK–Kuwait BIT (2010)); Agreement between the Government of Hong Kong and the Government of the Republic of Korea for the Promotion and Protection of Investments (HK–South Korea) (30 June 1996) [1997] HKTBA 21, art 9(4) (HK–Korea BIT (1997)); HK–Arab Emirates BIT (2019) art 8 (7); HK–Chile BIT (2016) art 32.

administrative or judicial settlement mechanisms[21] or reference to the competent courts[22] of the other disputing party. Similarly, investors can seek an interim measure of protection from a court of the disputing party.[23] However, the same dispute cannot be submitted to an arbitral tribunal.[24] Hong Kong's rights under the BIT regime are dependent on individual treaties and their texts.[25]

Hong Kong has never been a respondent jurisdiction in any publicly known investment arbitration action. However, as a party to international dispute settlement conventions and treaties, it continues to be an active player in the international investment law regime. As a crown colony of the United Kingdom, Hong Kong was subject to the 1962 ICSID Convention and the New York Convention (NYC) until 1997. After 1997, Hong Kong joined these conventions through China's participation.

In the 166 states that have ratified the NYC, which was enacted in 1958, there is a consistent framework for the enforcement and acceptance of international arbitral awards. The most preferred institution for amicably settling disputes between foreign investors and nations continues to be the ICSID Convention. The majority of cases involving Hong Kong investors have been lodged under the ICSID Convention, despite the fact that Hong Kong's IIAs do not allow dispute settlement. The fact that Hong Kong is a financial centre may help to explain this trend. Additionally, Hong Kong is taking part in the current discussions of UNCITRAL Working Group III on Reforming Investor-State Dispute Settlement. The fact that Hong Kong and China have made distinct proposals for reforming ISDS during these talks implies that Hong Kong aims to maintain its independence on ISDS-related topics, even if the future of its political sovereignty is uncertain.

II. HONG KONG INVESTORS AS ACTIVE USERS OF INVESTMENT ARBITRATION: FIRSTS, TRENDS AND THE FINANCIAL SERVICES SECTOR

Hong Kong actively participates in the current ISDS regime. However, there is an inconsistency between its capital and economic status and numerous assumptions about state participation in the ISDS regime. According to a 2010 empirical study, it has been argued that more investment disputes in the financial services

[21] HK–Japan BIT (1997) (n 20) art 9, para 3.

[22] HK–Finland BIT (2009) (n 20) art 8(2); HK–Arab Emirates BIT (2019) (n 20) art 8(4).

[23] HK–Kuwait BIT (2010) (n 20) art 8(2).

[24] HK–Japan BIT (1997) (n 20) art 9(3); HK–Finland BIT (2009) (n 20) art 8 (2); HK–Arab Emirates BIT (2019) (n 20) art 8 (6).

[25] See generally Ana Ubilava and Luke Nottage, 'Novel and Noteworthy Aspects of Australia's Recent Investment Agreements and ISDS Policy: The CPTPP, Hong Kong, Indonesia and Mauritius Transparency Treaties' in Luke Nottage and others (eds) *New Frontiers in Asia-Pacific International Arbitration and Dispute Resolution* (Alphen aan den Rijn, Wolters Kluwer, 2020).

sector can be witnessed if there were more investors, who come from key financial centres like Japan and Hong Kong, becoming parties to many disputes.

Of 18 cases involving a Hong Kong concern and discussed in this chapter, ten were raised by Hong Kong investors against host states. It can be said that Hong Kong investors have a good command of the rules of investment arbitration and have been mastering those rules freely to protect their interest, creating a series of 'firsts', especially in the ISDS regime. These include the first ICSID annulment proceedings, the first ICSID dispute instituted based on foreign investment law, the first ICSID investment treaty dispute and the first time that a previous decision was reversed because the Respondent was found to have deliberately misled the arbitrators. Moreover, Hong Kong investors raised the first investment claim against Australia and Japan, while a Chinese national with Hong Kong residency instituted an investment claim in the first dispute involving China as a home state.[26] Undeniably, investors from Hong Kong have been the most active or 'best' users of investment arbitration in East Asia Pacific and their behaviours have sometimes even spurred serious policy changes in the states involved.

The dedicated sections or provisions for investment disputes in financial services in Hong Kong's recent IIAs will probably increase the number of finance-related disputes. For example, under the Hong Kong–Canada BIT (2016) and the Hong Kong–Australia investment agreement (2020), in financial service disputes, the appointed arbitrators shall employ the financial services law and, in such conflicts, acknowledge the use of prudent financial measures as a defence.[27]

III. THE ROLE OF FINANCIAL INSTITUTIONS IN RECENT INVESTMENT DISPUTES INVOLVING HONG KONG INVESTORS: TRENDS AND IMPLICATIONS FOR INTERNATIONAL INVESTMENT LAW

The reorganisation of financial institutions and the involvement of juristic persons – corporate entities – seem to be common for recent disputes involving a Hong Kong investor. All publicly known disputes involving a Hong Kong investor can be roughly divided into three groups. As the table below shows, before 1987, HK investors were mainly concerned with the tourism sector, as four out of the five disputes during this period were related to tourism.

Between 1987 and 2010, there were no publicly known disputes involving Hong Kong investors. However, in the past decade, four of six disputes instituted by Hong Kong investors have been based on the same transaction involving the same financial institution – Standard Chartered Bank Hong Kong

[26] *Señor Tza Yap Shum v The Republic of Peru*, ICSID Case No ARB/07/6, Award (7 July 2011).
[27] HK–Canada BIT (2016) (n 20) art 22(2); Hong Kong–Chile BIT (2016) (n 20) art 22.

Table 12.1 Publicly Known Investment Arbitration Cases Involving Hong Kong Investors

	Case	*Institution*	*Year*	*Investment*	*Economic sector(s)*
1	*Hyatt International Corporation & Anor v Iran & Ors*	Iran–US Claims	1979	Management of hotels	Hospitality
2	*Amco Asia Corporation and others v Indonesia*	ICSID	1981	Hotel and office complex investment	Tourism-Hotels and Hospitality
3	*Southern Pacific Properties (Middle East) Limited v Egypt*	ICC	1982	Development of tourist and resort facilities	Tourism
4	*Southern Pacific Properties (Middle East) Limited v Egypt*	ICSID	1984	Development of tourist and resort facilities	Tourism
5	*Asian Agricultural Products Ltd v Sri Lanka*	ICSID	1987	Equity capital in shrimp culture farm	Agriculture
6	*Standard Chartered Bank (Hong Kong) Limited v The United Republic of Tanzania*	ICSID	2014	Loan agreement	Finance and insurance; Electric Power & Other Energy
7	*Philip Morris v Australia*	PCA	2012	Shareholding in Australian subsidiaries engaged in the manufacturing, import, market and distribution of tobacco products	Manufacturing

(continued)

Table 12.1 *(Continued)*

	Case	*Institution*	*Year*	*Investment*	*Economic sector(s)*
8	*Standard Chartered Bank (Hong Kong) Limited v United Republic of Tanzania*	ICSID	2016	Loan agreement	Finance and insurance; Electric Power & Other Energy
9	*Alois Schönberger v Republic of Tajikistan*	ICSID	2019	Cotton purchase agreements signed by the claimant's company incorporated in Hong Kong,	Manufacturing
10	*Shift Energy v Japan*	PCA	2020	Japan's renewable energy subsidy regime	Energy

Source: Compiled by the author using various public sources (UNCTAD, PITAD.org and Investor-State Law Guide in June 2023).

(SCB Hong Kong). It would be worth asking why finance investment disputes have been concentrated in some countries and not others, especially in the past decade.

The trend in Hong Kong disputes since 2010 reflects both the dynamic role played by international investment law in financial services, as well as significant events peculiar to Hong Kong. On the one hand, existing research confirms that the relationship between finance and international investment law has changed radically since the 1990s. Before 2008, the emphasis of most Hong Kong-related cases was on contractual claims or emergency legislation. In sharp contrast, from 2008 onwards, disputes concerning state supervisory and insolvency measures have sprung up; these may be suitable for regulation under the legal structure of international investment law.

IV. EXPLORING THE COMPLEXITIES OF FINANCIAL INVESTMENT DISPUTES IN INTERNATIONAL INVESTMENT LAW: A CASE STUDY OF HONG KONG

International investment law is a constantly evolving field that has significant implications for the global financial sector. In recent years, Hong Kong has emerged as a key player in this area, with a growing number of disputes involving financial institutions and host states. This has raised important questions about the complexities of financial investment disputes and the role of investment treaties in regulating them.

This section aims to present an objective and neutral analysis of the case of Hong Kong, focusing on the common issues that arise in investment treaty claims related to financial investments. The primary objectives are to provide a detailed examination of the jurisprudence of investment treaty claims by Hong Kong subsidiaries, explore the challenges posed by indirect control in financial investments and investment arbitration and discuss the complexities surrounding investment treaties and financial instruments within the global financial sector. The analysis commences by scrutinising the investment structures and shareholding arrangements of Hong Kong subsidiaries, which can be intricate and present unique obstacles in investment arbitration. Subsequently, the focus shifts to the issue of indirect control, a significant concern in financial investments which has implications for the interpretation of investment treaties. Lastly, the section discusses financial instruments and investment treaties, considering recent developments and the challenges they pose for both investors and host states. Through a comprehensive exploration of these complexities, drawing on the case study of Hong Kong, this section aims to shed light on the pressing issues surrounding financial investment disputes in international investment law.

A. Examining the Jurisprudence of Investment Treaty Claims by Hong Kong Subsidiaries: Shareholding and Investment Structures

In the web of global finance, the role of subsidiaries in investment treaty claims, particularly within the context of Hong Kong's dynamic economic landscape, presents a compelling study in international investment law. At the beginning of 2024, the vibrant financial sector of Hong Kong is comprised of a diverse array of institutions: 163 licensed banks, 17 restricted-licence banks, and 13 deposit-taking companies; this is in addition to 42 local representative offices of foreign banking organisations.[28] These entities, hailing from 34 different economies and including 78 of the world's foremost 100 banks, collectively manage an extensive network of about 1,245 local branches – a statistic that notably excludes their principal Hong Kong-based offices.

In the domain of foreign investment, characterised by complex subsidiary structures, investment arbitration panels have increasingly acknowledged the multifaceted nature of these relationships. Notably, in scenarios where a local subsidiary holds a substantial share of its foreign parent company's equity, these tribunals have granted such entities the right to lodge claims as though they were

[28] WTO, 'Hong Kong, The Facts: Financial Services' (*WTO*). Available at: www.gov.hk/en/about/abouthk/factsheets/docs/financial_services.pdf, accessed 10 October 2023.

international investors in their own right. This evolution in legal thought not only reflects the layered realities of foreign investments but also marks a significant shift in the understanding and recognition of subsidiary entities within the ambit of international investment law.

Throughout the past three decades, international tribunals handling disputes involving Hong Kong-based entities have generally mirrored contemporary commercial practices in their rulings. However, recent jurisprudence indicates a discernible, more cautious trajectory, likely in reaction to the increasing scrutiny and criticism levelled at the framework of international investment law. This shift points to a burgeoning cognisance among legal adjudicators of the complexities and potential areas of contention within this legal field, hinting at a more nuanced and possibly more circumspect application of legal principles in the face of evolving challenges in international investment disputes.

A notable example of this evolving approach can be observed in the 1985 interlocutory award of *Hyatt International Corporation v Iran*. In this case, the Iran–US Claims Tribunal determined that Hyatt International Corporation, through its wholly owned subsidiary Hyatt International Corporation (Delaware), held beneficial ownership of the entire capital stock of Hyatt of Hong Kong Limited (a Hong Kong corporation). This Hong Kong entity, in turn, possessed 100% beneficial ownership of the capital stock of both Hyatt Hotel Management Limited and Hyatt Technical Services Company Limited, both Hong Kong corporations.

Consequently, the tribunal acknowledged Hyatt International Corporation's entitlement to bring forth claims on behalf of the Hong Kong corporations based on the Claims Settlement Declaration between Iran and the US. This decision demonstrates the tribunal's willingness to recognise complex ownership structures and adapt its approach in light of emerging concerns surrounding the international investment law landscape.[29]

In a more recent case, *Phillip Morris v Australia*, the claimant was a subsidiary of the Swiss American multinational Phillip Morris International, which commenced operations in Australia in 1954 and was incorporated in Hong Kong in 1994. The claimant, Philip Morris Asia Limited, contended that it had controlled and directed the strategic, budgetary and investment decisions of all its Australian subsidiaries since 2001. However, in its 2015 ruling, the tribunal determined that it lacked jurisdiction to adjudicate the claim, as Philip Morris Asia Limited was deemed to be a non-Hong Kong corporation. More specifically, the tribunal concluded that Philip Morris Asia Limited restructured its corporate entities in 2011 by relocating its Australian operations to Hong Kong. This move was primarily motivated by the intention to leverage the status of a Hong Kong corporation to gain access to investment claims to challenge

[29] *Hyatt International Corporation v Iran*, IUSCT Case No 134, Interlocutory Award (17 September 1985), para 64.

Australia's plain packaging measures, thereby benefiting solely from the ISDS provisions.[30]

In *Standard Chartered v Tanzania*, the claimant Standard Chartered Bank (SCB) Limited argued that it made investments in Tanzania via a loan obtained by its subsidiary, SCB Hong Kong. SCB claimed its ownership to SCB Hong Kong by a minority shareholding of 38.8 per cent and an indirect shareholding of 61.2 per cent. As of May 2010, 38.8 per cent of SCB Hong Kong's shares were directly owned by SCB and the remaining shares of SCB Hong Kong (61.2%) were held by a Hong Kong company SC Sherwood (SC), which was a wholly owned and share-controlled company of SCB. The tribunal declined jurisdiction (*Standard Chartered v Tanzania, 2012*, paras 200-201), concluding that the UK–Tanzania BIT wording demonstrated that only investments made in an active way, rather than via simple passive ownership, are protected by the treaty.[31]

It may be possible to identify the difference between recent investment treaty arbitration cases such as *SCB v Tanzania* and *Phillip Morris* and prior claims made by Hong Kong subsidiaries. *AAPL v Sri Lanka* is the first Hong Kong investment treaty claim but represents a different outcome. In this case, the claimant was a Hong Kong firm and a subsidiary of Serendib, where Serendib has a minority ownership interest of 37 per cent. Probably due to the lack of case law on shareholding and investment in investment treaty claims, the tribunal, in its decision on jurisdiction, did not take into account the size of the shareholding in great depth, in contrast to the approach taken in *SCB v Tanzania* and *Phillip Morris*. Therefore, the existing conflicting jurisprudence on the rights of shareholders has prompted project financiers to carefully structure their investments and manipulate investment treaty protections.

B. Exploring the Challenges of Indirect Control in Financial Investments and Investment Arbitration: Insights from Hong Kong

Indirect control is a challenging issue, whether in disputes involving financial institutions or in investment arbitration and thus, inevitably, the inherent complexity of indirect control is more evident in financial investments.

In practice, it is common to encounter indirect control problems in conflicts involving investors from Hong Kong. In *Amco Asia v Indonesia*, the respondent raised a jurisdiction challenge, stating that Amco Asia was run by Mr Tan, a Dutch national living in Hong Kong; thus, the true controller of PT Amco was not of American nationality. The respondent further claimed that it was unaware of the nationality of the remote controllers of the local company to

[30] *Philip Morris Asia Limited v The Commonwealth of Australia*, PCA Case No 2012-12, Award on Jurisdiction and Admissibility (17 December 2015) para 584.

[31] *Standard Chartered Bank (Hong Kong) Limited v Tanzania Electric Supply Company Limited*, ICSID Case No ARB/10/20, Award (12 Sept 2016) para 225.

be established when it approved the investment and agreed to the arbitration in its decision on jurisdiction. The tribunal emphasised that there were sufficient legal and factual arguments to reject the Respondent's claim and noted that if fraud or misrepresentation had been proved, this would have been a different problem.[32]

Moreover, a recent case shows that the lenders can still enjoy the treaty protection in the same way as equity suppliers, even though there was not a direct legal connection between the lenders and the host states. On the other hand, as host states' respond to some extent, some recent IIAs are attempting to prevent 'shell' corporations from abusing treaty protections by stipulating that only investors conducting substantial commercial activity in the territory of the contracting party can be protected by the treaty.

C. Navigating the Grey Area: Understanding Investment Treaties and Financial Instruments in the Global Financial Sector

International financial instruments, which can take the form of promissory notes, government-guaranteed loans, subordinated debentures, hedging arrangements and sovereign bonds, are often involved in foreign investments. Although investment arbitration tribunals have acknowledged financial instruments as covered investments, the specific financial instruments that constitute an investment under investment treaties remain ambiguous. This uncertainty is due to inconsistent investment jurisprudence and evolving investment treaty drafting practices.

Recent arbitral decisions suggest that bonds and other overseas-issued financial instruments may be considered investments. In *Portigon v Spain* (August 2020), the tribunal ruled that project financing in the form of long-term loans and swaps made by financial institutions could be protected under investment treaties. However, this decision contrasts with a series of disputes between SCB and Tanzania, which display internal inconsistencies. For instance, in *SCB v Tanzania* (2016), the tribunal found that extending a loan did not constitute an investment under the investment treaty.[33] Conversely, in *SCB v Tanzania* (2016), the tribunal determined that SCB Hong Kong had made an investment by purchasing outstanding debt and assigning the rights under the relevant agreements.[34] In a third arbitration between SCB Hong Kong and Tanzania, the

[32] *Amco Asia Corporation v Republic of Indonesia*, ICSID Case No ARB/81/1, Decision on Jurisdiction (25 September 1983) para 14.

[33] *Standard Chartered Bank (Hong Kong) Limited v Tanzania Electric Supply Company Limited*, ICSID Case No ARB/10/20, Award (12 Sept 2016) para 272.

[34] *Standard Chartered Bank (Hong Kong) Limited v The United Republic of Tanzania*, ICSID Case No ARB/10/12, Decision on Jurisdiction and Liability (12 Feb 2014); *Standard Chartered Bank (Hong Kong) Limited v Tanzania Electric Supply Company Limited*, ICSID Case No ARB/10/20, Award (12 Sept 2016).

tribunal supported the argument that SCB Hong Kong had invested in Tanzania (*SCB v Tanzania* (2019)).[35]

Recent developments in international investment law reveal a nuanced approach towards the inclusion of financial instruments under the protection of investment treaties and dispute resolution mechanisms. Notably, the Hong Kong–Canada BIT (2016) and the 2019 Hong Kong-Australia Investment Agreement acknowledge bonds, debentures, and other debt instruments as legitimate investments of an enterprise, yet they introduce specific limitations. In a more pronounced departure, the Hong Kong–Chile BIT (2016) adopts a restrictive stance, essentially excluding financial services from its ambit, save for certain instances pertaining to investment disputes in financial services.

While the Hong Kong context provides an insightful case study for understanding investment disputes in the financial sector, the analysis of ten such disputes fails to capture the entire spectrum of emerging challenges within the financial services sector. Prior empirical studies have identified state actions in their capacity as financial regulators and supervisors as pivotal in precipitating two primary categories of disputes in this sector. These disputes predominantly arise from the issuance of regulatory decrees introducing new compliance obligations, supervisory decisions that impose fines or penalties, adjudications concerning the issuance of new banking or trading licences, measures undertaken by Central Banks in their role as lenders of last resort, and decisions pertaining to the resolution and insolvency of financial institutions.

In these disputes, emerging economies and developing countries predominantly serve as Respondents. The state's forced acquisition of a Hong Kong investor's interests in loan and security agreements is not directly connected to any of the lawsuits involving that investor. Moreover, none of the cases examined involves the revocation of banking licences or the implementation of prudential or other regulatory actions in response to financial crises. These situations give rise to conflicts between countries and financial institutions. As Hong Kong strives to strengthen its status as a global financial centre, these disputes involving non-Hong Kong investors will set precedents for future conflicts.

This chapter has used Hong Kong as a case study to carefully examine the challenges faced by financial institutions when raising investment arbitration claims against host states. Notably, the key issues addressed in this chapter are not limited to the financial sector, prompting questions about the need for a new standard to regulate banks and financial instruments in IIAs.

[35] *Standard Chartered Bank (Hong Kong) Limited v Tanzania Electric Supply Company Limited*, ICSID Case No ARB/10/20, Award (12 Sept 2016) paras 245–46.

13

Global Tax Tussles: Hong Kong's Strategy for Resolving International Tax Disagreements

INTERNATIONAL TAX DISPUTE resolution refers to the process of resolving disputes that arise between jurisdictions regarding the application of tax laws and regulations. These disputes can arise from a variety of issues, such as double taxation, transfer pricing and the interpretation of tax treaties.[1] The legal and systemic importance of international tax dispute resolution is rooted in the fact that tax laws and regulations are often complex and vary significantly between countries and territories. This can lead to confusion and disputes between foreign companies and countries, as well as a lack of consistency in the application of tax laws. International tax dispute resolution is designed to ensure that these disputes are resolved in a fair and efficient manner and that the rights of all parties involved are protected.

Transitioning into the mechanisms at play, one of the primary tools for international tax dispute resolution is the deployment of tax treaties. These treaties, which are bilateral agreements between countries, set forth the guidelines for taxing income and capital across borders. Importantly, these agreements typically encompass specific provisions dedicated to dispute resolution, including mutual agreement procedures (MAPs) and arbitration. These mechanisms provide a structured framework for addressing and resolving the complex tax disputes that arise between jurisdictions, reflecting the interplay of domestic fiscal policies and international rules.

Hong Kong's tax dispute mechanisms become relevant in the context of the tense trade war between the USA and China. The US–China Double Taxation Agreement stipulates the use of a mutual agreement procedure (MAP) to resolve tax disputes.[2] However, the tense relations between the USA and China may impede cooperation and effective communication between the parties, making

[1] Transfer pricing refers to the prices at which related companies in different countries conduct transactions with each other. International tax laws often require that these transactions be conducted at arm's-length prices, which is the price that would be charged between independent parties. When countries disagree on the arm's-length price, a dispute may arise.

[2] Agreement Between the Government of the People's Republic of China and the Government of the United States of America for the Avoidance of Double Taxation and the Prevention of Fiscal Evasion with Respect to Taxes on Income (China–US) (30 April 1984), art 24.

the MAP process less efficient. The non-inclusion of a mandatory arbitration clause in the Double Taxation Agreements (DTAs)[3] may prevent an early resolution of the dispute. To avoid a similar situation, the mandatory arbitration clause should be adopted in Hong Kong's DTAs. This will ensure not just the protection of taxpayers and the attraction of foreign investment but also make dispute resolution of tax matters more efficient. All of this will, in turn, facilitate the sustainable development of Hong Kong's economy.

Therefore, considering the increasing complexities of the international taxation landscape, particularly with the emergence of the digital economy, the resolution of tax disputes between nations is becoming increasingly important. Rapid globalisation coupled with technological advancements has significantly lowered barriers to entry for businesses operating on a global scale. This evolution has, in turn, necessitated the development of fresh tax laws and regulations. One such initiative is the Base Erosion and Profit Shifting (BEPS) project, designed to tackle the taxation challenges introduced by the digital economy. Consequently, international tax dispute resolution is now a vital component of international economic dispute resolution, serving to ensure that tax disagreements are settled in a fair and efficient manner, safeguarding the rights of all involved parties. By employing tax treaties, MAPs and arbitration, international tax dispute resolution furnishes a formal, binding mechanism for countries to navigate disputes, acting as a buffer to prevent such disagreements from escalating into more significant conflicts.

The chapter begins by discussing the declining importance of MAPs in Hong Kong, highlighting the advantages, challenges and global implications for tax dispute resolution in multinational contexts. It analyses Hong Kong's MAP process and the role of binding arbitration in DTAs with diverse partner countries, exploring the effectiveness of these mechanisms in resolving tax disputes. The chapter then shifts focus to the use of mandatory arbitration in tax disputes, emphasising the potential for enhancing efficiency, neutrality and fairness in resolving double taxation conflicts. It presents a case for adopting this approach as an alternative to the traditional MAP process. Finally, the chapter examines the interplay of MAP, arbitration and mediation in the context of Hong Kong's tax dispute resolution landscape. It provides a comprehensive overview of how these mechanisms interact within the framework of the territory's DTAs and assesses their potential in ensuring an efficient and equitable resolution of tax disagreements.

I. THE DECLINING IMPORTANCE OF MUTUAL AGREEMENT PROCEDURES IN HONG KONG

The procedure for settling tax disputes between nations that are covered by a Double Taxation Agreement (DTA) that is utilised the most often is called the

[3] ibid.

MAP. This process is intended to offer a method for the settlement of disputes that may emerge during the implementation of the DTA. When unilateral action fails, the competent authority may contact the competent authority in the jurisdiction of the contracting party to resolve the tax dispute.[4] This method is MAP. The competent authority 'endeavours' to resolve the dispute.[5] These disagreements may include disagreements over the interpretation or application of the DTA or the domestic laws of the countries concerned. If a taxpayer believes that they have been subjected to double taxation as a result of an issue that is covered by the DTA, they are able to request that their tax authorities enter into negotiations with the tax authorities of the other jurisdiction in an effort to resolve the issue under the terms of a MAP.

A. The Mutual Agreement Procedure: Advantages, Challenges and Global Implications for Tax Dispute Resolution in Multinational Contexts

The procedure for filing a request for relief under the MAP often starts with the taxpayer submitting their request to their domestic tax authority. The request, together with any paperwork that may be relevant, will subsequently be sent from the domestic tax authorities to the tax authorities of the other nation. The request will then be examined by the tax authorities of the other nation, who may ask the taxpayer or the tax authorities of the taxpayer's home jurisdiction for more information. Once the relevant tax authorities have collected all the relevant material, they will begin discussions in an effort to settle the disagreement. This procedure is normally completed within two years, but it might take longer if the disagreement is very complicated.

The MAP is a common practice all over the globe in the context of the settlement of tax disputes because it offers a number of advantages for taxpayers and tax authorities alike. Taxpayers can settle disputes with the tax authorities of other nations by using the MAP system, which was created through tax treaties. It is viewed as a desirable alternative to litigation and is used to settle tax disputes that occur across international borders. When the tax authorities of several countries assert competing claims to tax the same income, a situation known as double taxation may arise.

One of the primary reasons MAP is such a common practice around the globe is because it can assist in preventing double taxation in such situations. This may be especially troublesome for taxpayers who operate their businesses in numerous countries since it can lead to confusion and make it more difficult for them to plan and budget for their tax obligations. As it removes the need for several processes and strives to settle disputes as promptly and effectively as possible, the MAP method is also typically regarded as cost-effective.

[4] The HKSAR double tax agreements share this clause in the respective section, art 24(2).
[5] ibid.

This may assist in reducing the impact that disputes have on taxpayers and their companies. In addition, the MAP can potentially promote greater certainty and predictability for taxpayers who do business in several countries. This is crucial for multinational businesses and investors. Lastly, the MAP may assist in ensuring uniformity in the execution of tax treaties and preventing outcomes that are arbitrary or unfair, both of which contribute to preserving positive relations between nations.[6]

B. An Analysis of Hong Kong's MAP Process and the Role of Binding Arbitration in DTAs with Diverse Partner Countries

The MAP Peer Review Report of Hong Kong and the MAP inventory show a smaller number of new cases.[7] The opening inventory on 1 January 2016 showed only six cases, with only one related to attribution/allocation.[8] During 2016 to 2018, only 13 attribution/allocation and four 'other' cases were submitted; only four attribution/allocation cases and three 'other' cases were resolved, leaving 10 attribution/allocation cases and six 'other cases' unresolved.[9] In respect of closed cases commencing after 1 January 2016, two transfer pricing cases have been resolved by unilateral relief grant, while the remaining case was denied by the MAP process.[10] There was only one other case, which was resolved by unilateral relief grant.

MAP is the first resort for dispute resolution for tax disputes and only when this is unsuccessful should the dispute be submitted to binding arbitration as per Article 25 of the OECD Model Convention.[11] While some Hong Kong DTAs, such as the Hong Kong–Pakistan DTA and the Hong Kong–Canada DTA, include mandatory binding arbitration clauses, others do not.[12] Moreover, the

[6] While the MAP process can help resolve disputes and avoid double taxation, it is not always successful. According to the OECD, the percentage of cases resolved through the MAP process has remained relatively stable over the last few years, with about 60 per cent of cases being resolved each year.

[7] OECD, *Making Dispute Resolution More Effective – MAP Peer Review Report, Hong Kong, China (Stage 1): Inclusive Framework on BEPS: Action 14, OECD/G20 Base Erosion and Profit Shifting Project* (Paris, OECD Publishing, 2019) 9.

[8] ibid 10.

[9] ibid.

[10] OECD, 'MAP Statistics 2018 Hong Kong, China' (OECD, 2018). Available at: www.oecd.org/tax/dispute/2018-map-statistics-hong-kong.pdf, accessed 11 October 2023.

[11] OECD, 'Model Tax Convention on Income and on Capital – Condensed Version 2017' (18 December 2017) art 25 (Model Tax Convention on Income and on Capital – Condensed Version 2017).

[12] Only Inland Revenue (Double Taxation Relief and Prevention of Fiscal Evasion with respect to Taxes on Income) (HK–Italian Republic) (29 November 2013) art 24(5) (HK–Italy double tax agreement (2013)); Inland Revenue (Double Taxation Relief and Prevention of Fiscal Evasion with respect to Taxes on Income) (HK–Jersey) (28 June 2013) art 23(5) (HK–Jersey double tax agreement (2013)); Inland Revenue (Double Taxation Relief and Prevention of Fiscal Evasion with respect to Taxes on Income and Capital) (HK–Principality of Liechtenstein) (7 July 2011) art 24(5) (HK–Liechtenstein

difference in the status of countries has yet to be accounted for. For instance, while Canada is a developed nation and Pakistan is a developing nation, the same dispute resolution provision for both countries has been adopted in the DTAs.[13]

While MAP is the dominant dispute resolution procedure for tax disputes, mandatory binding arbitration has several merits, such as convenient initiation and less bias in awards.[14] Moreover, it can attract foreign investors to Hong Kong with the promise of more rights for investor protection. While only foreign investors can initiate arbitration if MAP fails,[15] only the competent authorities initiate the MAP process under the OECD Model Convention.[16] Further, additional barriers may be imposed on accessing MAP,[17] such as a bar when the dispute has already been submitted to a domestic judicial process.[18] The requirement for both taxpayers to provide information to both competent authorities to initiate MAP[19] may lead to extended timelines, as taxpayers are often required to resubmit information when competent authorities find the information to be incomplete. By contrast, oral statements made by the taxpayers are sufficient in mandatory binding arbitration.[20] Further, the award can be vetoed by the taxpayer whose interests it does not protect.[21] The Model Convention states that: '[u]nless a person directly affected by the case does not accept the mutual

double tax agreement (2011)); Inland Revenue (Double Taxation Relief and Prevention of Fiscal Evasion with respect to Taxes on Income) (HK–Canada) (29 October 2013) art 23(6); Inland Revenue (Double Taxation Relief and Prevention of Fiscal Evasion with respect to Taxes on Income) (UK–Kingdom of the Netherlands) 18 November 2010) art 24(5) (HK–Netherlands double tax agreement (2010)); Inland Revenue (Double Taxation Relief and Prevention of Fiscal Evasion with respect to Taxes on Income) (HK–Guernsey) 29 November 2013) art 23(5) (HK–Guernsey double tax agreement (2013)); Inland Revenue (Double Taxation Relief with respect to Taxes on Income) (HK–Switzerland) (13 July 2012) art 24(5) (HK–Switzerland double tax agreement (2012)); Inland Revenue (Double Taxation Relief and Prevention of Fiscal Evasion with respect to Taxes on Income) (HK–Japan) (12 November 2015) art 24(5) (HK–Japan double tax agreement (2015)); and Inland Revenue (Double Taxation Relief and Prevention of Fiscal Evasion with respect to Taxes on Income) (HK–Islamic Republic of Pakistan) (24 November 2017) art 25(5) (HK–Pakistan double tax agreement (2017)) include mandatory binding arbitration. State sovereignty is the main reason why some countries tend not to include mandatory arbitration in their double tax treaties. See Xueliang Ji, 'The Changing Paradigm of International Tax Dispute Settlement: What Are the Promises and Challenges of Mandatory Arbitration for China?' (2020) 21 *Oregon Review of International Law* 117, 135.

[13] HK–Pakistan double tax agreement (2017) art 25(5); HK–Canada Double Tax agreement (2013), art 23(6).

[14] See generally Michael Lang and Jeffrey Owens (eds), *International Arbitration in Tax Matters* (Amsterdam, IBFD, 2015).

[15] Model Tax Convention on Income and on Capital – Condensed Version 2017 (n 11) 453.

[16] ibid 429.

[17] Julien Chaisse, 'Making Tax Dispute Resolution Mechanisms More Effective –The Base Erosion and Profit Shifting Project and Beyond' (2017) 10(1) *Contemporary Asia Arbitration* J 1, 6.

[18] Model Tax Convention on Income and on Capital – Condensed Version 2017 (n 11) 45.

[19] OECD, 'Commentary on Article 25: Concerning the Mutual Agreement Procedure' (2017) para 75.

[20] UN Department of Economics & Social Affairs, 'Model Double Taxation Convention Between Developed and Developing Countries' (2011) 433 (Model Double Taxation Convention Between Developed and Developing Countries (2011)).

[21] ibid.

agreement that implements the arbitration decision, that decision shall be binding on both Contracting States and shall be implemented notwithstanding any time limits in the domestic laws of these States'.[22]

II. MANDATORY ARBITRATION IN TAX DISPUTES: ENHANCING EFFICIENCY, NEUTRALITY AND FAIRNESS IN RESOLVING DOUBLE TAXATION CONFLICTS

Tax disputes arising from DTAs often present challenges for both taxpayers and competent authorities. In situations where disagreements persist despite efforts to resolve them through the MAP, mandatory arbitration has emerged as an alternative method for dispute resolution. This section explores the role of mandatory arbitration in tax disputes, emphasising its potential to enhance efficiency, neutrality and fairness in resolving conflicts arising from DTAs.

Arbitration serves as an additional avenue for resolving disputes that arise from Double Taxation Agreements (DTAs). In situations where the competent authorities are unable to reach a resolution through the Mutual Agreement Procedure (MAP) within the designated timeframe of two to three years, either party can request arbitration if both parties and the competent authorities provide written agreement. The decision made by the arbitral tribunal will be binding on both parties involved. Arbitration is an alternative method of conflict resolution that allows disputing parties to settle their differences with the assistance of a neutral third party. When tax disputes cannot be resolved through the MAP process, they often proceed to the arbitration phase of the dispute resolution process. The UNCITRAL Arbitration Rules are typically followed to ensure the proper conduct of the arbitration procedure. The first step in the arbitration process usually involves selecting a single arbitrator or a panel of arbitrators. Subsequently, the arbitrator or panel will consider the arguments and evidence presented by the parties before rendering a final and binding decision.

Mandatory arbitration can also be used to offset MAP's defects.[23] In the MAP process, the competent authorities 'endeavour' to resolve the dispute, but there is no guarantee of a definitive resolution[24] and no accountability if the process fails. The minimum requirement of the BEPS Action 14 mandates treaty obligations to be implemented in good faith; however, competent authorities are often seen taking aggressive or unreasonable stands.[25] Even when a resolution

[22] OECD, 'Model Tax Convention on Income and on Capital – Condensed Version' (2008) 38.

[23] See generally Jasmin Kollmann and Laura Turcan, 'Overview of the Existing Mechanisms to Resolve Disputes and Their Challenges' in Michael Lang and Jeffrey Owens (eds), *International Arbitration in Tax Matters* (Amsterdam, IBFD, 2015) 15.

[24] Model Tax Convention on Income and on Capital – Condensed Version 2017 (n 11) 429.

[25] OECD, 'Making Dispute Mechanisms More Effective – Action 14: 2015 Final Report' (5 October 2015) 9.

is reached under MAP, there are no provisions, such as follow-up measures or punitive actions, to guarantee implementation.

The benefits of mandatory arbitration could be a compelling factor for the competent authorities to make the MAP process more efficient. The MAP process may, however, be time consuming.[26] Under the OECD Model Convention, the time for the MAP procedure should not exceed two years and under the UN Model Convention, the time should not exceed three years.[27] It should be noted that arbitration cannot be initiated until the MAP process ends. Further, the MAP process is initiated not for a single case but for a group of cases to be resolved simultaneously, which may lead to the profits of one taxpayer being sacrificed to protect the interests of the state.

Additionally, competent authorities may give different interpretations of the same clause.[28] Mandatory arbitration, which can protect the interests of all stakeholders, can serve as the answer to all these dilemmas. It can provide a stable investing environment. It is a more neutral process than MAP, as competent authorities may ignore the interests of taxpayers to further the interests of the contracting states. Mandatory arbitration is also a more independent process and the OECD Model Sample even mandates this.

Moreover, such a clause may also help to ensure the efficacy of the MAP process. For instance, the MAP process fails to be completed within two years[29] as this time can be suspended in the circumstances such as aggrieved taxpayers requesting such suspension, competent authorities awaiting an award from a court or administrative organisation, or the time period being deemed too short by the competent authorities. The taxpayers are simply informed of the suspension in most cases; they do not have any say. However, the MAP process may be concluded on time with the pressure of ceding to a regular authority in mandatory binding arbitration.

Moreover, arbitration in tax disputes is preferable for controversial or sensitive issues.[30] Taxpayers can make greater profits even after the award is passed. If the award does not satisfy them, they can veto it.[31] This veto need not be done explicitly;[32] if the taxpayer does not withdraw their case from local consideration

[26] Luciana Nobrega and Silva Loureiro, 'Mutual Agreement Procedure: Preventing the Compulsory Jurisdiction of the International Court of Justice?' (2009) 37 *Intertax* 529, 539.

[27] OECD, 'Model Tax Convention on Income and on Capital 2014 – Full Version' (30 October 2015), art 25(b) (Model Tax Convention on Income and on Capital 2014 – Full Version); Model Double Taxation Convention Between Developed and Developing Countries (2011), art 25(b).

[28] See OECD, 'Commentaries on the Articles of the Model Tax Convention' (2010). Available at: www.oecd.org/berlin/publikationen/43324465.pdf, 369.

[29] See Model Tax Convention on Income and on Capital – Condensed Version 2017 (n 11) 456–57.

[30] See generally Brian J Arnold, 'The Scope of Arbitration Under Tax Treaties' in Michael Lang and Jeffrey Owens (eds), *International Arbitration in Tax Matters* (Amsterdam, IBFD, 2015) 111, 114.

[31] See Model Tax Convention on Income and on Capital 2014 – Full Version (n 27) art 25, M-60-61.

[32] See Model Tax Convention on Income and on Capital – Condensed Version 2017 (n 11) 459.

this would be interpreted as a refusal of the award. If the taxpayers accept the award, it will become binding on the competent authorities and a mutual agreement to implement the award will have to be reached.

There is no time limit for implementation. If the dispute is already resolved through litigation in a domestic or international court, arbitration cannot be initiated under section 25(5) of the OECD Model Convention.[33] If an award is made in a lower court, the taxpayers can still adopt mandatory arbitration. Thus, by adopting arbitration, taxpayers can avoid the time and expense required by litigation. Further, an arbitral tribunal may be more efficient in terms of qualified staff and resources than a domestic court.

In conclusion, mandatory arbitration offers a valuable alternative to the MAP process for resolving tax disputes arising from double taxation agreements. By providing a neutral, independent and efficient mechanism for dispute resolution, arbitration addresses many of the shortcomings inherent in the MAP process. Furthermore, arbitration allows for the protection of taxpayer interests and facilitates the resolution of controversial or sensitive issues in a more streamlined manner. Ultimately, the adoption of mandatory arbitration in tax disputes can lead to a more stable and predictable investment environment, benefiting both taxpayers and competent authorities.

III. NAVIGATING TAX DISPUTE RESOLUTION IN HONG KONG: EXAMINING THE INTERPLAY OF MAP, ARBITRATION AND MEDIATION IN DOUBLE TAX AGREEMENTS

As a major financial and economic hub, Hong Kong plays a significant role in the global economy. Its 'one country, two systems' status allows it to enjoy a certain degree of international legal sovereignty. Within this context, the territory faces various tax dispute resolution challenges arising from its extensive network of DTAs. This section examines the interplay of MAP, arbitration and mediation in resolving tax disputes under Hong Kong's DTAs, highlighting the importance of these mechanisms in maintaining its status as a leading international financial centre.

The settlement of disagreements between parties may alternatively be achieved via the use of mediation, which is a way of conflict resolution that is both less formal and less confrontational. For instance, Article 24 of Hong Kong DTA provides for unilateral action and states: '[w]here a person considers that the actions of one or both of the Contracting Parties result or will result for him in taxation not in accordance with the provisions of this Agreement, he may, irrespective of the remedies provided by the domestic laws of those Parties,

[33] See OECD, 'Model Tax Convention on Income and on Capital 2010 – Full Version' (6 August 2012), art 25(5).

present his case to the competent authority of the Contracting Party of which he is a resident.'[34]

In most cases, the first step in the mediation process is the selection of a mediator, who plays the role of an impartial third party to assist in facilitating the settlement of the conflict. The mediator guides the parties through a process that identifies the issues at stake in the conflict and brainstorms potential resolutions. The action will begin 'from the first notification of the action resulting in taxation not in accordance with the provisions of this Agreement' and the limitation period differs across different DTAs.[35] The process is entirely voluntary, and the parties are empowered to arrive at a solution that is acceptable to both. This solution is then memorialised in the form of a mediation agreement.

In sum, the MAP, arbitration and mediation are the three primary processes used to settle disputes about tax issues that arise from DTA. When it comes to settling tax disputes between nations that are covered by a DTA, MAP is the approach that is employed most often. Its purpose is to offer a way to resolve disputes that may emerge while applying the DTA and its design reflects this purpose. When the parties to a DTA are unable to settle a problem via the MAP procedure, they may instead choose to resolve it through arbitration, which is one of the methods that can be utilised to resolve disputes under DTAs. The settlement of disagreements between parties may often be achieved via the use of mediation, a less formal and less confrontational conflict resolution approach.

Although Hong Kong is a small territory in China, its 'one country, two systems' status gives it some international legal sovereignty. Hong Kong's status as a financial and economic hub has been strengthened due to this shared international legal sovereignty. At the same time, Hong Kong's sovereignty remains relatively untapped, as it has failed to actively use its IDS powers and rights. In the current context, US actions like the withdrawal of Hong Kong's special treatment may result in a breach of WTO rules and instability in Hong Kong's economy. This could trigger an economic decline and result in a rise in ISDS claims against Hong Kong. Ultimately, to protect its legitimate interests, Hong Kong may be compelled to utilise its IDS rights, including dispute resolution processes in DTAs.

In conclusion, Hong Kong's position as a small territory with international legal sovereignty within China's 'one country, two systems' framework presents both opportunities and challenges in tax dispute resolution. By understanding and effectively utilising the available dispute resolution mechanisms, such as MAP, arbitration and mediation, Hong Kong can not only protect its legitimate interests but also ensure the stability of its economy and maintain its status

[34] The HKSAR double tax agreements share this clause in the respective section, art 24(1).

[35] HK–Italy double tax agreement (2013), art 24(1) stipulates two years; the remaining tax agreements require three years.

as a global financial hub. As the international landscape continues to evolve, Hong Kong must remain proactive in engaging with IDS powers and rights, adapting its strategies to address potential threats and capitalise on opportunities that arise in the realm of tax dispute resolution under its DTAs.

PART IV CONCLUSION

The main findings of Part IV shed light on the mechanisms and processes employed by Hong Kong to effectively manage and resolve economic disputes in its international relations, thereby contributing to its economic resilience and adaptability. Hong Kong's success in this area can be attributed to several key factors:

- Hong Kong's expertise extends to resolving complex international tax disputes. Through mechanisms like MAP in taxation, Hong Kong has demonstrated its capacity to effectively address cross-border tax issues, a critical aspect in today's globalised economy.
- Hong Kong's involvement in WTO dispute resolution, albeit limited in number, is marked by a focus on cases that have broader implications for international trade norms and practices. This targeted approach demonstrates understanding of the intricacies of WTO law and its impact on global trade dynamics. By engaging in pivotal cases, Hong Kong contributes to the development of precedent-setting decisions, thereby influencing the interpretation and application of WTO agreements in future disputes. Moreover, Hong Kong's involvement in the WTO system exemplifies its commitment to multilateralism and a rules-based international order. This stance not only reinforces the legitimacy and authority of the WTO system but also promotes a stable and predictable global trading environment. Hong Kong's engagement in the realm of ISDS under IIAs also presents a scenario of limited but impactful involvement. The restrained use of ISDS by Hong Kong investors against foreign states, and conversely, the limited instances where Hong Kong investors rely on IIAs in disputes with host states, reveal a unique status for Hong Kong as an international economic actor. Firstly, the cautious approach of Hong Kong investors in invoking ISDS mechanisms under IIAs is reflective of broader strategic considerations. This restraint stems from a preference for diplomatic and business-oriented solutions to investment disputes, aligning with Hong Kong's reputation as a global financial center that values stability and long-term relationships. Simultaneously, foreign investors' reluctance to initiate lawsuits against Hong Kong can largely be attributed to the territory's investor-friendly environment. Known for its robust legal framework and strong adherence to the rule of law, Hong Kong provides a highly conducive and stable milieu for foreign investments.

Its legal system reduces the potential for disputes that might typically necessitate arbitration. Furthermore, Hong Kong's economic policies, notably welcoming to foreign investment, feature minimal restrictions and an open market economy. This framework, coupled with a reliable and predictable regulatory regime, fosters a climate of trust and confidence among foreign investors. Consequently, the need for resorting to legal action against the Hong Kong government is substantially lessened, as the territory's commitment to maintaining a supportive business environment pre-empts many of the issues that might otherwise lead to investor-state disputes.

- More generally, Hong Kong has established a comprehensive legal framework and has a strong tradition of upholding the rule of law. This solid foundation provides a conducive environment for the resolution of economic conflicts involving the territory and its international partners. The adherence to legal principles and the fair administration of justice bolster Hong Kong's credibility in dispute settlement.

However, it is important to acknowledge that there are criticisms and challenges that warrant attention in Hong Kong's dispute settlement mechanisms:

One significant issue is the ongoing crisis in WTO, particularly the suspension of the WTO Appellate Body. This development has profound implications for the global trade dispute resolution system, in which Hong Kong actively participates. The suspension has raised concerns about the effectiveness and future of dispute resolution at the WTO, potentially undermining the predictability and stability of the international trade law system. Hong Kong, like other small jurisdictions, faces the challenge of navigating this uncertain landscape where definitive settlement of trade disputes may be hindered, affecting the efficacy of its engagement in this forum.

Additionally, there is growing criticism towards ISDS mechanisms, a key component of IIAs where Hong Kong has shown a measured involvement. Critics argue that ISDS processes often lack transparency, are overly costly, and can lead to inconsistent or biased rulings. There is also concern about the potential for ISDS to undermine national sovereignty, particularly in areas of public policy and regulation. In response to these challenges, the UNCITRAL Working Group III is actively engaged in reform efforts. These reforms aim to address the systemic issues within the ISDS framework, seeking to enhance transparency, accountability, and consistency in rulings. As a participant in the global economic system, Hong Kong will need to navigate these potential reforms and adapt its approach to dispute resolution accordingly.

Recent socio-political developments and tensions have raised concerns about Hong Kong's autonomy and their potential implications for dispute settlement processes. These factors may affect the perceived impartiality and independence of Hong Kong's dispute resolution mechanisms, which could impact the confidence of international investors and trading partners.

Hong Kong's success in managing economic disputes is rooted in its strategic alignment of unilateral foundations, bilateral treaties, multilateral engagement and effective dispute resolution mechanisms. This rather cautious, but cohesive and comprehensive approach enables the territory to navigate the complexities of the global economic landscape and maintain its status as a leading financial centre. However, addressing criticisms and challenges will be crucial to ensuring inclusivity, upholding public trust and sustaining Hong Kong's reputation as a reliable hub for international business.

14

Conclusion

THIS BOOK PROVIDES a detailed analysis of Hong Kong's participation in International Economic Law (IEL), adopting a constructivist perspective. It explores the interplay between Hong Kong's political and legal specifics and its strategies within IEL, particularly focusing on the intersection of multilateralism, bilateralism and unilateralism. The methodology integrates theoretical insights with empirical research to shed light on the various facets of Hong Kong's engagement in the global economic arena. This exploration reveals how the distinctive historical, political and legal background of Hong Kong significantly shapes its role in IEL. Through this constructivist lens, the book presents Hong Kong' economic policies as more than just reflexive responses to global economic forces; they are actively crafted, influenced by a wide range of ideational, political and social factors. In the broader context of IEL, Hong Kong's approach illustrates the evolving nature of international economic relations, where small but strategically positioned regions can wield significant influence. Hong Kong challenges the traditional narratives of economic power, showing that influence in IEL is not solely determined by size or military might but also by strategic economic positioning, legal and policy innovation and adaptability to global changes. This is particularly relevant in a world where economic centres are increasingly interconnected and where regional players can have global impacts.

The main thesis, intricately woven through the constructivist lens, illustrates how Hong Kong's economic policies, deeply embedded in its historical and institutional milieu, are not merely reactions to global economic forces but are actively shaped by a myriad of ideational and social factors.'. Part I of the book explored the territory's unilateral economic policies, including its domestic trade, foreign investment and tax regimes. The free port status of Hong Kong, a policy wherein no tariffs are imposed on imported goods, along with minimal trade barriers, positions the region as a pivotal logistics and trans-shipment hub while fostering an environment conducive to free trade. This free port policy is relatively rare globally and enhances Hong Kong's appeal as a global trading centre. Simultaneously, Hong Kong's open investment climate is marked by the absence of restrictions on inward or outward investment, a lack of nationality restrictions on corporate ownership and an unfettered flow of capital, making it a haven for foreign investors. Moreover, the tax system in Hong Kong, characterised by its low tax rates, absence of VAT/GST, capital gains and inheritance tax, coupled with its simplicity and predictability, makes it particularly attractive for businesses and individuals alike. The territorial basis of taxation, whereby only income derived in Hong Kong is taxed, further cements its status as a favourable environment for international businesses. These policies underscore Hong Kong's unique position as a nexus between the East and West, shaped by the region's historical context, geographical positioning and its status as a Special Administrative Region of China. This unique amalgamation of Eastern and Western business practices and legal systems facilitates Hong Kong's role as a gateway for foreign businesses entering mainland China and Asian markets and for Chinese businesses reaching out to the world. This nexus, fostered by continuous social interactions among policymakers, businesses and civil society, exemplifies the constructivist assertion of norm creation and diffusion within IEL. However, these policies also propel Hong Kong to become one of the world's most significant financial centres and trading economies, attracting multinational corporations, banking institutions and investors while integrating deeply into the global economy. This integration serves as a strategic gateway for China's economic engagement with the world. Concurrently, they create competitive pressures on local businesses and the labour market, necessitating continuous innovation and adaptation. The open economy of Hong Kong, heavily reliant on international trade and investment, renders it particularly susceptible to global economic fluctuations and geopolitical tensions, balancing the benefits of an open, liberal economic system with the challenges of maintaining competitiveness and stability in a rapidly changing world.

In Part II, the focus shifted to the bilateral aspects of Hong Kong's international economic relations, examining its trade agreements, bilateral investment treaties and tax treaties. The constructivist view highlights Hong Kong's role in shaping these norms, reflecting its unique position as a Special Administrative Region of China. The findings underscore the importance of these relationships in shaping Hong Kong's economic policies. Hong Kong's approach to bilateral economic treaties, particularly in trade, foreign investment and tax-related international agreements, distinctively marks its position in the global economy. These bilateral engagements are a crucial part of its strategy, reinforcing Hong Kong's role as a hub for international commerce and finance, blending Eastern and Western economic practices. The region's trade agreements are designed to facilitate trade liberalisation and economic cooperation, significantly reducing tariffs and simplifying customs procedures. Simultaneously, Hong Kong's investment treaties focus on protecting investments and promoting foreign direct investment, featuring key provisions for fair treatment, protection from expropriation and dispute resolution. These treaties not only secure Hong Kong's economic interests but also affirm its status as a vital conduit for international business, especially in bridging mainland China with other global markets. In taxation, Hong Kong has formed several Double Taxation Agreements (DTAs) to prevent double taxation of income and to enhance cross-border trade and investment. These DTAs, which also target tax evasion and promote fiscal transparency, enhance Hong Kong's attractiveness as a hub for international business. The uniqueness of Hong Kong's bilateral economic policies is grounded in its strategic positioning as a global financial centre and a gateway to China. Operating under the 'one country, two systems' principle, Hong Kong leverages its autonomous legal system and economic framework to negotiate agreements that cater to its specific needs. This autonomy allows for a high degree of tailoring in its treaties, setting Hong Kong apart from other regions and countries and reinforcing its pivotal role in the global economic landscape.

Part III discussed Hong Kong's multilateral economic relations, within which Hong Kong showcases a strategy that underscores its unique position in the global economy, particularly in areas of trade, foreign investment and international tax treaties. As a separate customs territory and a member of the World Trade Organisation (WTO), Hong Kong aligns itself with global trade norms while championing free trade and open markets. This involvement ensures that Hong Kong is not only a participant in shaping global trade policies but also benefits from the stability and predictability these international frameworks provide. In the realm of foreign investment, Hong Kong's engagement in multilateral discussions and agreements reflects its dedication to fostering a stable international investment environment. This proactive stance in multilateral investment platforms reinforces Hong Kong's status as a global hub for trade and investment. Hong Kong's participation in international tax cooperation further exemplifies its commitment to global economic integration. By being part of various multilateral agreements focused on tax cooperation and information exchange, Hong Kong adheres to international standards, contributing to efforts against tax evasion and promoting fiscal transparency. The uniqueness of Hong Kong's engagement in these multilateral treaties lies in its ability to leverage its status as a Special Administrative Region of China, which allows it to operate with a degree of autonomy in international affairs. This unique positioning enables Hong Kong to tailor its participation in ways that specifically benefit its economic landscape while aligning with broader global economic objectives. This aligns with the constructivist emphasis on the fluidity of norms and Hong Kong's role in their development and adaptation. The consequences of these policies are multifaceted. On one hand, they position Hong Kong as a key player in the international economic arena, enhancing its global connectivity and influence. On the other hand, this active participation in multilateral frameworks requires Hong Kong to often adapt to the evolving international economic landscape, balancing its own interests with global economic trends and obligations.

Finally, Part IV analysed Hong Kong's involvement in international economic dispute resolution mechanisms, including the WTO Dispute Settlement Mechanism, investor-state dispute settlement and international tax disputes. While these mechanisms are integral to the global economic governance framework, Hong Kong's direct involvement, particularly in the WTO DSB and ISDS, has been relatively limited, raising questions about the effectiveness and reach of these systems in the region's specific context. In the realm of the WTO DSB, despite Hong Kong's status as a separate customs territory and active WTO member, its participation in dispute settlements has been notably infrequent. This limited involvement could be attributed to a variety of factors, including Hong Kong's trade strategies, its economic relationships and possibly its reliance on diplomatic channels over formal dispute resolution processes. This raises questions about the extent to which Hong Kong leverages this mechanism to defend and advance its trade interests on the global stage. Similarly, the use of ISDS by Hong Kong-based investors appears to be relatively modest. This could be reflective of several underlying dynamics, such as the nature of Hong Kong's outbound investments, investor confidence in the legal systems of host countries, or a preference for alternative dispute resolution methods. The limited reliance on ISDS suggests a potential underutilisation of this mechanism by Hong Kong investors, possibly indicating a need for greater awareness or accessibility. The MAP framework, often incorporated in Hong Kong's network of Double Taxation Agreements, stands as a more frequently utilised tool for resolving tax-related disputes. This suggests a more active role in addressing cross-border tax issues, likely due to the direct and often significant impact of such disputes on businesses and government revenues. The critical analysis of Hong Kong's engagement with these international dispute resolution mechanisms reveals a mixed picture. While these frameworks are essential components of the global economic system, their actual impact and utilisation in the Hong Kong context appear to be limited in certain areas. This scenario underscores the need for a deeper understanding of Hong Kong's strategies and preferences in international economic dispute resolution and perhaps a re-evaluation of how these mechanisms can be made more relevant and effective for Hong Kong's unique economic landscape.

Reflecting critically on Hong Kong's engagement in International Economic Law (IEL), the analysis presented in this book brings forth substantive lessons and expert insights, crucial for understanding and enhancing Hong Kong's role in this domain. One significant lesson is the strategic importance of Hong Kong's unique legal and economic position under the 'one country, two systems' framework. This distinct status presents both opportunities and challenges in IEL. On the one hand, it allows Hong Kong to act autonomously in international economic affairs but, on the other hand, it requires careful navigation to align with broader economic policies of mainland China while maintaining its own economic identity. This delicate balancing act is crucial for Hong Kong's continued effectiveness and credibility in international economic negotiations and dispute resolutions. Another critical insight pertains to Hong Kong's engagement with international dispute resolution mechanisms. The limited utilisation of platforms like the WTO DSB and ISDS by Hong Kong suggests a potential re-evaluation of these mechanisms. There's a need for Hong Kong to develop more proactive strategies to leverage these international legal instruments effectively. This includes building stronger legal expertise in international economic law and enhancing its diplomatic engagement in these forums to better protect its economic interests. Moreover, the findings emphasise the importance of adaptability in Hong Kong's economic policy formulation, particularly in response to the rapidly changing landscape of global trade and investment. This adaptability is not just about reactive changes but also about anticipating future trends and challenges in IEL. Hong Kong's ability to foresee and adapt to shifts such as digital trade, sustainable development and evolving norms of international taxation will be pivotal in maintaining its status as a global economic hub. Lastly, the book's analysis underscores the significance of Hong Kong's proactive participation in both bilateral and multilateral economic treaties. It highlights the need not only for Hong Kong to engage in these treaties but also to continuously assess their impact and effectiveness. This involves a constant review and update of its treaty commitments to ensure they align with its evolving economic interests and the changing dynamics of international economic relations.

However, the book also presents an optimistic perspective on Hong Kong's future role in the international economic arena. It highlights that, despite the challenges, Hong Kong's economic importance and influence on global trade, investment and tax policies are poised for significant growth in the coming years. The territory's continually enhancing expertise in negotiating trade, investment and tax treaties, bolstered by its unique legal system, highly skilled professionals and commitment to the rule of law, has proven instrumental in securing favourable agreements.

The book's insights into the adaptability of Hong Kong's economic policies in response to global shifts and the balancing act between autonomy and integration, further embody the constructivist idea of the continuous construction and reconstruction of norms and policies. The Asia-Pacific region has experienced significant economic growth driven by technological advances, increased consumer spending and the emergence of new markets. Hong Kong, as a gateway to this thriving economic landscape (through, for instance, the RCEP) is well positioned to capitalise on these opportunities and bolster its own economic growth. The Greater Bay Area, with its substantial population and GDP, offers a vast market for Hong Kong's businesses. By leveraging its strategic position, Hong Kong can facilitate trade, investment and innovation between the Greater Bay Area and the rest of the world, further solidifying its role as a key player in global trade, investment and tax policy. The ongoing tensions between the United States and China have also, paradoxically, contributed to Hong Kong's increasing economic influence. As countries seek alternatives in trade and investment due to the geopolitical climate, Hong Kong's legal framework, financial sector and adherence to international standards makes it an attractive destination for business. Its reputation for openness, transparency and expertise in global finance maintains Hong Kong as a favourable choice for diversifying operations and navigating the complexities of the current geopolitical landscape.

In its essence, this book transcends a mere descriptive account of Hong Kong's role in IEL, venturing into the deeper realms of how ideational forces and normative frameworks converge to sculpt the contours of international economic governance. Through the prism of constructivism, the analysis has unravelled the ways in which Hong Kong's economic policies and actions, far from being static or predetermined, emerge as dynamic constructs. These policies are continually reshaped by multiple influences – economic integration, historical legacies, economic pacts and the interplay of local and global ideas. This perspective brings to the fore the fluidity and malleability of Hong Kong's economic stance, challenging conventional views of legal and economic determinism. The constructivist lens reveals how Hong Kong's unique international trajectory, coupled with its distinct political and legal status, spawns a unique set of norms and practices within IEL. These norms and practices are not static; they are subject to continuous reinterpretation and re-negotiation within the broader context of shifting global power dynamics, emerging technological paradigms and evolving international trade, tax and investment norms.

The insights gleaned from this analysis bear significant implications for understanding Hong Kong's future trajectory in the global economic landscape. They highlight the criticality of ongoing, nuanced engagement with the evolving nature of international economic law and policy. This is particularly pertinent in an era marked by rapid changes in global trade structures, the ascendancy of digital economies and increasing geopolitical complexities. In this light, Hong Kong's journey within IEL serves as a microcosm of the broader challenges and opportunities faced by dynamic economies navigating the intricate web of twenty-first-century international economic governance.

Bibliography

BOOKS

Bello W, *Deglobalization: Ideas for a New World Economy* (London, Zed Books, 2002).

Chiu T, *The Port of Hong Kong: A Survey of its Development* (Hong Kong, Hong Kong University Press, 1973).

Dolzer R and Stevens M, *Bilateral Investment Treaties* (Leiden, Martinus Nijhoff Publishers, 1995).

Donald D, Wang J and Vanderwolk J, *A Financial Centre for Two Empires: Hong Kong's Corporate, Securities and Tax Laws in its Transition from Britain to China* (Cambridge, Cambridge University Press, 2014).

Dugan CF and others, *Investor State Arbitration* (New York, Oxford University Press, 2008).

Eckart C, *Promises of States under International Law* (Oxford, Hart Publishing, 2012).

Gantz DA, *Liberalizing International Trade after Doha: Multilateral, Plurilateral, Regional and Unilateral Initiatives* (New York, Cambridge University Press, 2013).

Ghai Y, *Hong Kong's New Constitutional Order: The Resumption of Chinese Sovereignty and the Basic Law* (Hong Kong, Hong Kong University Press, 1997).

Ghai Y, *Hong Kong's New Constitutional Order: The Resumption of Chinese Sovereignty and the Basic Law* (2nd edn, Hong Kong, Hong Kong University Press, 1999).

Gibson E, *A Regulatory Design for Financial Stability in Hong Kong* (Cambridge, Cambridge University Press, 2022).

Gittings D, *Introduction to the Hong Kong Basic Law* (2nd edn, Hong Kong, Hong Kong University Press, 2013).

Gwartney J and others, Economic Freedom of the World: 2021 Annual Report (Fraser Institute, 2021).

Jones K, *Reconstructing the World Trade Organisation for the 21st Century: An Institutional Approach* (New York, Oxford University Press, 2014).

Kostakopoulou D, *Institutional Constructivism in Social Sciences and Law: Frames of Mind, Patterns of Change* (Cambridge, Cambridge University Press, 2018).

Lang M and Owens J (eds), *International Arbitration in Tax Matters* (Amsterdam, IBFD, 2015).

Lee CW, *Hong Kong: Global China's Restive Frontier* (Cambridge, Cambridge University Press, 2022).

Li PK, *Hong Kong from Britain to China: Political Cleavages, Electoral Dynamics and Institutional Changes* (Abingdon, Routledge, 2001).

Lo SHC, Cheng KK and Chui WH, *The Hong Kong Legal System* (2nd edn, Cambridge, Cambridge University Press, 2019).

Lowenfeld AF, *International Economic Law* (Oxford, Oxford University Press, 2008).

MacPherson A and Laird G, *Hong Kong Taxation Law and Practice* (Hong Kong, The Chinese University of Hong Kong Press, 2010).

McCourt DM, '*The New Constructivism in International Relations Theory*' (Bristol, Bristol University Press, 2022).

McLachlan C and others, *International Investment Arbitration: Substantive Principles* (Oxford, Oxford University Press, 2007).

Mills L, *Protecting Free Trade: The Hong Kong Paradox 1947–1997* (Hong Kong, Hong Kong University Press, 2012).

Mushkat R, *One Country, Two International Legal Personalities: The Case of Hong Kong* (Hong Kong, Hong Kong University Press, 1997).

OECD, *Making Dispute Resolution More Effective – MAP Peer Review Report, Hong Kong, China (Stage 1): Inclusive Framework on BEPS: Action 14, OECD/G20 Base Erosion and Profit Shifting Project* (Paris, OECD Publishing, 2019).

OECD, *OECD Business and Finance Outlook 2018* (Paris, OECD Publishing, 2018).

PECC Secretariat, *State of the Region Report, 2014–2015* (Pacific Economic Cooperation Council 2014).

Perl SK, *The Protection of National Security in International Economic Law – US Policy on Steel and Aluminium in the Light of WTO Law* (Beiträge zum Transnationalen Wirtschaftsrecht, 2022).

Schreuer CH and others, *The ICSID Convention: A Commentary* (1st edn, Cambridge, Cambridge University Press, 2001).

Schreuer CH and others, *The ICSID Convention: A Commentary* (2nd edn, Cambridge, Cambridge University Press, 2009).

Sung YW, *The China-Hong Kong Connection: The Key to China's Open Door Policy* (Cambridge, Cambridge University Press, 2011).

Van den Berg A, *The New York Convention of 1958: Towards a Uniform Judicial Interpretation* (Boston, Kluwer Law and Taxation, 1981).

Wang S, *Introduction to the Basic Law of the Hong Kong Special Administration Region* (Central Party School of the CPC Press, 1997).

Wendt A, *Social Theory of International Politics* (Cambridge, Cambridge University Press, 1999).

World Bank Group, *The World Bank Group A to Z* (World Bank Publications, 2014).

CONTRIBUTIONS TO EDITED BOOKS

Arnold B, 'The Scope of Arbitration Under Tax Treaties' in Lang M and Owens J (eds), *International Arbitration in Tax Matters* (Amsterdam, IBFD, 2015).

Arts B, 'Non-state Actors in Global Environmental Governance: New Arrangements Beyond the State' in Koenig-Archibugi M and Zürn M (eds), *New Modes of Governance in the Global System* (London, Palgrave Macmillan, 2005).

Baldwin R and Carpenter T, 'Regionalism: Moving from Fragmentation towards Coherence' in Cottier T and Delimatsis P (eds), *The Prospects of International Trade Regulation: From Fragmentation to Coherence* (Cambridge, Cambridge University Press, 2011).

Bièvre DD and Hanegraaff M, 'Non-state Actors in Multilateral Trade Governance' in Reinalda B (ed), *Ashgate Research Companion to Non-state Actors* (London, Routledge, 2011).

Bowring P, 'Hong Kong as an International Commercial Center' in Cohen W and Zhao L (eds), *Hong Kong under Chinese Rule: The Economic and Political Implications of Reversion* (Cambridge, Cambridge University Press, 1997).

Burgstaller M, 'Sovereign Wealth Funds and International Investment Law' in Brown C and Miles K (eds), *Evolution in Investment Treaty Law and Arbitration* (Cambridge, Cambridge University Press, 2011).

Claussen K, 'Sovereignty's Accommodations: Quasi-States as International Lawmakers' in Scott KN and others (eds), *Changing Actors in International Law* (Leiden, Brill Nijhoff, 2020).

Crawford J and Baetens F, 'The Influence of International Trade Law on International Law' in Bethlehem D, McRae D, Neufeld R and Damme IV (eds), *The Oxford Handbook of International Trade Law* (2nd edn, New York, Oxford University Press 2022).

Cullen R and Wong A, 'Globalization and the Hong Kong Revenue Regime', in Cockfield AJ (ed), *Globalization and Its Tax Discontents: Tax Policy and International Investments* (Toronto, University of Toronto Press, 2010).

Di-Benedetto S, 'The National Security Clauses in International Economic Agreements: A Loophole for States to Escape Their Obligations?' in Mauro MR and Pernazza F (ed), *State and Enterprise: Legal Issues in the Global Market* (Cham, Springer International Publishing, 2023).

Dimitropoulos G, 'National Security: The Role of Investment Screening Mechanisms' in Chaisse J, Choukroune L and Jusoh S (eds), *Handbook of International Investment Law and Policy* (Singapore, Springer 2019).

Hillion C and Wessel RA, 'The European Union and International Dispute Settlement: Mapping Principles and Conditions' in Cremona M, Thies A, Wessel RA (eds), *The European Union and International Dispute Settlement* (1st edn, Portland, Hart Publishing 2017).

Hirsch M, 'Linkages Between International Economic Law and Foreign Policy' in Broude T and others (eds), *The Politics of International Economic Law* (Cambridge, Cambridge University Press, 2011).

Kao CC, 'The Inclusion of Investment Court System into the EU-China BIT: Innovations, Prospects and Problems' in Chaisse J (ed), *China–European Union Investment Relationships: Towards a New Leadership in Global Investment Governance?* (Cheltenham, Edward Elgar Publishing, 2018).

Kollmann J and Turcan L, 'Overview of the Existing Mechanisms to Resolve Disputes and Their Challenges' in Lang M and Owens J (eds), *International Arbitration in Tax Matters* (Amsterdam, IBFD, 2015).

Kriner D, 'Unilateralism Unleashed?: Polarization and the Politics of Executive Action' in Lieberman R, Mettler S and Roberts K (eds), *Democratic Resilience: Can the United States Withstand Rising Polarization?* (Cambridge, Cambridge University Press, 2021).

Lai A, 'State Immunity in the Context of Enforcement of Investment Arbitration Awards' in Chaisse J, Choukroune L and Jusoh S (eds), *Handbook of International Investment Law and Policy* (Singapore, Springer, 2021).

Littlewood M, 'Tax Treaty Disputes in Hong Kong' in Baistrocchi E (ed), *A Global Analysis of Tax Treaty Disputes* (Cambridge, Cambridge University Press, 2007).

Murray MN, 'Would tax evasion and tax avoidance undermine a national retail sales tax?' in Slemrod J (ed), *Tax Policy in Real World* (Cambridge, Cambridge University Press, 2010).

Nie GM and Wang E, 'Hong Kong, The World's Freest Economy and its Liberal Policy' in Nagel S (ed), *Handbook of Global Economic Policy* (New York, Routledge, 2000).

Owen J, 'Economic Interdependence and Regional Peace' in Paul TV (ed), *International Relations Theory and Regional Transformation* (Cambridge, Cambridge University Press, 2012).

Pantaleo L, 'Lights and Shadows of the TTIP Investment Court System' in Pantaleo L and others (eds), *Tiptoeing to TTIP: What Kind of Agreement for What Kind of Partnership?* (CLEER Paper 2016).

Pelc KJ, 'Twenty Years of Third-Party Participation at the WTO: What Have We Learned?' in Elsig M, Hoekman B and Pauwelyn J (eds), *Assessing the World Trade Organization: Fit for Purpose?* (New York, Cambridge University Press, 2017).

Stephanie Switzer, 'The World Trade Organization Dispute Settlement Mechanism' in Sobenes E, Mead S, Samson B (eds), *The Environment Through the Lens of International Courts and Tribunals* (The Hague, TMC Asser Press, 2022).

Tao J and Zhong M, 'The Changing Rules of International Dispute Resolution in China's Belt and Road Initiative' in Zhang W, Alon I, Lattemann C (eds), *China's Belt and Road Initiative – Changing the Rules of Globalization* (London, Palgrave Macmillan, 2018).

Ubilava A and Nottage L, 'Novel and Noteworthy Aspects of Australia's Recent Investment Agreements and ISDS Policy: The CPTPP, Hong Kong, Indonesia and Mauritius Transparency Treaties' in Nottage L and others (eds), *New Frontiers in Asia-Pacific International Arbitration and Dispute Resolution* (Alphen aan den Rijn, Wolters Kluwer, 2020).

Undurraga CP and Chiffelle CR, 'Investment Promotion Agencies: Investment Attraction, Policy Role, and Response to Crises' in Chaisse J, Choukrone L and Josh S (eds), *Handbook of International Investment Law and Policy* (Singapore, Springer, 2021).

Viner J, 'The Economics of Customs Unions' in Oslington P (ed), *The Customs Union Issue* (Oxford, Oxford University Press, 2014).

Wehland H, 'Jurisdiction and Admissibility in Proceedings under the ICSID Convention and ICSID Additional Facility Rules' in Baltag C (ed), *ICSID Convention after 50 Years: Unsettled Issues: Unsettled Issues* (Alphen aan den Rijn, Kluwer Law International, 2017).

Wolfrum R and Stoll PT, 'General Agreement on Tariffs and Trade 1994', in Wolfrum R and Stoll PT (eds) *Max Planck Comment. On World Trade Law, WTO-Institutions and Dispute Settlement* (Leiden, Brill Nijhoff 2006).

Zagel G, 'Achieving sustainable development objectives in international investment law' in Chaisse J, Choukrone L and Josh S (eds), *Handbook of International Investment Law and Policy* (Singapore, Springer, 2021).

ENCYCLOPEDIAS

Thiel M and Maslanik J, 'Transnational Actors' (2017 Print version) (New York, Oxford Research Encyclopaedia of International Studies).

JOURNALS

——, 'Trade Policy Review Body – Hong Kong, China' (1999) 11 *World Trade and Arbitration Materials* 92.

Agosin MR and Machado R, 'Foreign Investment in Developing Countries: Does it Crowd in Domestic Investment? (2005) 33 *Oxford Development Studies* 149.

Alstadsæter A, Barrios S, Nicodeme G, Skonieczna AM, Vezzani A, 'Patent Boxes Design, Patents Location, and Local R&D' (2018) 33 *Economic Policy* 131.

Au-Yeung A, 'Understanding the Hong Kong Tax System' (1982) 8 *International Tax Journal* 337.

Baldwin RE, 'Failure of the WTO Ministerial Conference at Cancun: Reasons and Remedies' (2006) 29 *The World Economy* 677.

Boswell C, 'Migration Control in Europe After 9/11: Explaining the Absence of Securitization' (2007) 45 *Journal of Common Market Studies* 589.

Brauner Y, 'What the BEPS?' (2014) 16 *Florida Tax Review* 55.

Brauner Y, 'Treaties in the Aftermath of BEPS' (2016) 41 *Brooklyn Journal of International Law* 973.

Bronckers M, 'Is Investor-State Dispute Settlements (ISDS) Superior to Litigation Before Domestic Courts? An EU View on Bilateral Trade Agreements' (2015) 18 *Journal of International Economic Law* 655.

Broome SA, 'Conflicting Obligations for Oil Exporting Nations?: Satisfying Membership Requirements of both OPEC and the WTO' (2006) 38 *George Washington International Law Review* 409.

Burnay M and Florian C, 'One Country, Two International Status? The Evolution of Hong Kong's International Positioning from Western Imperialism to Chinese Authoritarianism' (2022) 64 *German Yearbook of International Law* 243.

Cavelti LU, Jaag C and Rohner TF, 'Why Corporate Taxation Should Mean Source Taxation: A Response to the OECD's Actions against Base Erosion and Profit Shifting' (2017) 2017 *World Tax Journal* 352.

Chaisse J, 'Assessing the Exposure of Asian States to Investment Claims' (2013) 6 *Contemporary Asia Arbitration Journal* 187.

Chaisse J, 'The Treaty Shopping Practice. Corporate Structuring and Restructuring to Gain Access to Investment Treaties and Arbitration' (2015) 11 *Hastings Business Law Journal* 225.

Chaisse J, 'Investor State Arbitration in International Tax Dispute Resolution – A Cut above Dedicated Tax Dispute Resolution?' (2016) 41 *Virginia Tax Review* 149.

Chaisse J, 'Making Tax Dispute Resolution Mechanisms More Effective – The Base Erosion and Profit Shifting Project and Beyond' (2017) 10 *Contemporary Asia Arbitration Journal* 1.

Chaisse J and Dimitropoulos G, 'Special Economic Zones in International Economic Law: Towards Unilateral Economic Law' (2021) 24 *Journal of International Economic Law* 229.

Chaisse J and Dimitropoulos G, 'Domestic Investment Laws and International Economic Law in the Liberal International Order' (2023) 22 *World Trade Review* 1.

Chaisse J and Ji X, '"Soft Law" in International Law-Making: How Soft International Taxation Law is Reshaping International Economic Governance' (2018) 13 *Asian Journal of WTO Law and Health Policy* 463.

Chaisse J and Ji X, 'Rethinking Hong Kong's Tax Agreements: Challenges of Transparency, Harmonisation and Global Tax Reform' (2021) 51 *Hong Kong Law Journal* 405.

Chaisse J and Ji X, 'Hong Kong's Participation in International Dispute Settlement: Deviations from Conventional Sovereignty' (2022) 17 *Asian Journal of WTO and International Health Law and Policy* 287.

Chaisse J and Kirkwood J, 'Chinese Puzzle: Anatomy of the (Invisible) Belt and Road Investment Treaty' (2020) 23 *Journal of International Economic Law* 245.

Chaisse J and Matsushita M, 'Maintaining the WTO's Supremacy in the International Trade Order: A Proposal to Refine and Revise the Role of the Trade Policy Review Mechanism' (2013) 16 *Journal of International Economic Law* 9.

Chaisse J and Matsushita M, 'China's "Belt and Road" Initiative – Mapping the World Trade Normative and Strategic Implications' (2018) 52 *Journal of World Trade* 163.

Chan J, 'State Succession to Human Rights Treaties: Hong Kong and the International Covenant on Civil and Political Rights' (1996) 45 *The International and Comparative Law Quarterly* 928.

Chan ZT and Meunier S, 'Behind the Screen: Understanding National Support for a Foreign Investment Screening Mechanism in the European Union' (2021) 17 *The Review of International Organizations* 1.

Chen AHY, 'The Basic Law and The Development of The Political System in Hong Kong' (2007) 15 *Asia Pacific Law Review* 19.

Chen AHY, 'The Executive Authorities and the Legislature in the Political Structure of the Hong Kong SAR' (2014) 6 *Academic Journal of Once Country, Two Systems* 80.

Cheng T, 'From Special Economic Zones to Greater Special Economic Region – Hong Kong Special Administrative Region as a Model for Legal Infrastructure Design' (2019) 26 *Transnational Corporations Journal* 63.

Chin GT, 'Geopolitics and Hong Kong as International Financial Centre: A Dynamic IPE Perspective' (2022) 28 *Asia Pacific Business Review* 660.

Chowdhury A, Liu X, Wang M, and Wong MCS, 'The Role of Multilateralism of the WTO in International Trade Stability' (2021) 20 *World Trade Review* 668.

Clausing KA, 'Trade Creation and Trade Diversion in the Canada – United States Free Trade Agreement' (2001) 34 *The Canadian Journal of Economics* 677.

Dabner J, 'Are Taxation Incentives Designed to Attract Regional Corporate Headquarters Likely to Be Effective' (1996) 2 *International Trade and Business Law Annual* 21.

Davey WJ, 'The WTO and Rules-Based Dispute Settlement: Historical Evolution, Operational Success, and Future Challenges' (2014) 17 *Journal of International Economic Law* 679.

Denza E, and Brooks S, 'Investment Protection Treaties: United Kingdom Experience' (1987) 36 *International & Comparative Law Quarterly* 908.

Dian M, 'The Strategic Value of the Trans-Pacific Partnership and the Consequences of Abandoning it for the US Role in Asia' (2017) 54 *International Politics* 583.

Diego-Fernández M, 'Trade Negotiations Make Strange Bedfellows' (2008) 7 *World Trade Review* 423.

Ellis SL and Shea L, 'Foreign Commercial Dispute Settlement in the People's Republic of China' (1980) 6 *International Trade Law Journal* 155.

Fan K, 'Mediation of Investor-State Disputes: A Treaty Survey' (2020) 2 *Journal of Dispute Resolution* 327.

Feng Y, 'China and the Multilateral Investment Guarantee Agency' (1999) *Policy Research Working Paper 1763* 1.

Finnemore M and Sikkink K, (2001), 'Taking Stock: The Constructivist Research Program in International Relations and Comparative Politics' 4 *Annual Review of Political Science* 391.

Flach L and others, 'The Regional Comprehensive Economic Partnership Agreement and Its Expected Effects on World Trade' (2021) 56 *Inter-economic Review of European Economic Policy* 92.

Fong BCH, 'Practicing Autonomy Within a Communist State: Hong Kong's Autonomy from Handover to Anti-Extradition Bill Movement, 1997–2019' (2020) 53 *Communist and Post Communist Studies* 68.

Gaillard E and Penushliski IM, 'State Compliance with Investment Awards' (2021) 35 *ICSID Review – Foreign Investment Law Journal* 540.

Gottwald E, 'Leveling the Playing Field: Is It Time for a Legal Assistance Centre for Developing Nations in Investment Treaty Arbitration?' (2007) 22 *American University International Law Review* 237.

Greenwood J, 'The Monetary Framework Underlying the Hong Kong Dollar Stabilization Scheme' (2009) 99 *The China Quarterly* 631.

Gu X, Lian Z, Peng L and Zhao Q, 'A Comparative Study of Bank Efficiency in Three Chinese Regions: Mainland China, Hong Kong, and Macao' (2023) 46 *Journal of Financial Research* 547.

Guo Y, 'From Conventions to Protocols: Conceptualizing Changes to the International Dispute Resolution Landscape' (2020) 11 *Journal of International Dispute Settlement* 217.

Ha J, Fan K and Shu C, 'Export Performance in Hong Kong – Offshore Trade and Re-Exports' (2003) *Hong Kong Monetary Authority Quarterly Bulletin* 5.

Hailes O, 'Lithium in International Law: Trade, Investment, and the Pursuit of Supply Chain Justice' (2022) 25 *Journal of International Economic Law* 148.

Halkyard A, 'Treating Taxpayers Right: Taxpayers' Rights with Special Reference to Hong Kong' (2001) 9 *Asia Pacific Law Review* 133.

Hamanaka S, 'TPP versus RCEP: Control of Membership and Agenda Setting' (2014) 18 *Journal of East Asian Economic Integration* 163.

Ho D, 'Boosting Hong Kong's Competitiveness in the BEPS Era' (2017) 43 *International Tax Journal* 17.

Hoekman B and Vines D, 'Multilateral Trade Cooperation: What Next?' (2007) 23 *Oxford Review of Economic Policy* 311.

Howse R and Langille J, 'Continuity and Change in the World Trade Organization: Pluralism Past, Present, and Future' (2023) 117 *American Journal of International Law* 1.

Hu J and Huang J, 'Dispute Resolution Mechanisms and Organizations in the Implementation of "One Belt, One Road" Initiative: Whence and Whither' (2018) 52 *Journal of World Trade* 815.

Hua S and Cai Y, 'On the Role and Limitation of the MIGA in BOT Investment Mode for the Belt and Road Initiative' (2019) 9 *Journal of WTO and China* 88.

Hunter RJ, Jr. Lozada HR and Shannon JH, 'The Debate on Reforms of the WTO Appellate Process: A Proxy for a More Serious Discussion of the Future of the WTO' (2023) 6 *Education Quarterly Reviews* 86.

Jackson NC, 'The Legal Regime of Hong Kong after 1997: An Examination of the Joint Declaration of the United Kingdom and the People's Republic of China' (1987) 5 *International Tax & Business Lawyer* 377.

Jao YC, 'Building Prosperity: A Five-Part Economic Strategy for Hong Kong's Future. By Sri International' (2009) 122 *The China Quarterly* 329.

Ji X, 'The Changing Paradigm of International Tax Dispute Settlement: What Are the Promises and Challenges of Mandatory Arbitration for China?' (2020) 21 *Oregon Review of International Law* 117.

King W, 'The Lease Convention between China and the Foreign Powers' (1916) 1 *Chinese Social and Political Science Review* 24.

Knight J, 'Education Hubs: International, Regional and Local Dimensions of Scale and Scope' (2013) 49 *Comparative Education* 374.

Krasner SD, 'State Power and the Structure of International Trade' (1976) 28 *World Politics* 317.

Krasner SD, 'The Hole in the Whole: Sovereignty, Shared Sovereignty, and International Law' (2004) 25 *Michigan Journal of International Law* 1095.

Krugman P, 'The Move Towards Free Trade Zones' (1991) 76 *Economic Review* 5.

Lai K, 'National Security and FDI Policy Ambiguity: A Commentary' (2021) *Journal of International Business Policy* 496.

Lauterpacht E, 'International Law and Private Foreign Investment' (1997) 4 *Indiana Journal of Global Legal Studies* 259.

Lenz H, 'Aggressive Tax Avoidance by Managers of Multinational Companies as a Violation of Their Moral Duty to Obey the Law: A Kantian Rationale' (2020) 165 *Journal of Business Ethics* 681.

Lewis MK, 'The Prisoners' Dilemma Posed by Free Trade Agreements: Can Open Access Provide an Escape?' (2010) 11 *Chicago Journal of International Law* 631.

Li C and Li D, 'When Regional Comprehensive Economic Partnership Agreement (RCEP) Meets Comprehensive and Progressive Trans-Pacific Partnership Agreement (CPTPP): Considering the "Spaghetti Bowl" Effect' (2022) 58 *Emerging Markets Finance and Trade* 1988.

Lindsay P, 'The Ambiguity of GATT Article XXI: Subtle Success or Rampant Failure' (2002) 52 *Duke Law Journal* 1277.

Liu S, 'Hong Kong: A Survey of Its Political and Economic Development over the Past 150 Years' (1997) 151 *The China Quarterly* 583.

Lo M and Wu C, 'From USHKPA to HKHRDA and HKAA: The Turnings of U.S.–China Policy and the End of Hong Kong's Full Autonomy' (2021) 25 *UCLA Journal of International Law and Foreign Affairs* 93.

Lung WP, 'Application and Conclusion of Treaties in the Hong Kong Special Administrative Region of the People's Republic of China: Sixteen Years of Practice' (2013) 12 *Chinese Journal of International Law* 589.

M'Bow AM, 'The Practice of Consensus in International Organization' (1978) 30 *International Social Science Journal* 893.

Makki SS and Somwaru A, 'Impact on Foreign Direct Investment and Trade on Economic Growth: Evidence from Developing Countries' (2004) 86 *American Journal of Agricultural Economics* 795.

Mansfield ED, Milner HV, and Rosendorff PB, 'Why Democracies Cooperate More: Electoral Control and International Trade Agreements' (2002) 56 *International Organization* 477.

Mau SD, 'Hong Kong's Experience with the New York Convention: An Introduction' (1996) 9 *Global Business & Development Law Journal* 393.

McHugh P, 'The Case for a Global Excess Profits Tax: A Response to Dr. Tarcisio Diniz Magalhaes & Professor Allison Christians' (2022) 29 *Indiana Journal of Global Legal Studies* 231.

Miglani AS, 'A Contemporary Contextualization of Security Under Article XXI of the GATT' (2022) 17 *Global Trade and Customs Journal* 485.

Mignolli A, 'The European Union Faces the Crisis of the WTO Dispute Settlement System: Tensions Between Multilateralism and Unilateralism in International Trade Law' (2020) 3 *International Legal Order and Human Rights* 485.

Miškinis A and Byrka M, 'The Role of Investment Promotion Agencies in Attracting Foreign Direct Investment' (2014) 93 *Ekonomika* 41.

Mitchell AD and Munro J, 'Someone Else's Deal: Interpreting International Investment Agreements in the Light of Third-party Agreements' (2017) 28 *European Journal of International Law* 669.

Mitchell AD and Samlidis T, 'Cloud Services and Government Digital Sovereignty in Australia and Beyond' (2022) 30 *International Journal of Law and Information Technology* 1.

Moreno AB and Brauner Y, 'Taxing the Digital Economy Post-BEPS … Seriously' (2019) 58 *Columbia Journal of Transnational Law* 121.

Morriss AP, 'Forward down the Road to Serfdom: International Tax Law as a Means of Central Planning' (2022) 17 *Journal of Law, Economics & Policy* 454.

Mushkat R, 'Scrapping Hong Kong Legislature: An International Law Perspective' (1997) 27 *Hong Kong Law Journal* 12.

Mushkat R, 'The Future of Hong Kong's International Legal Personality: Does International Law Matter – A Post-Handover Snapshot' (1998) 22 *Southern Illinois University Law Journal* 291.

Mushkat R, 'The Dynamics of International Legal Regime Formation: The Sino-British Joint Declaration on the Question of Hong Kong Revisited' (2011) 22 *European Journal of International Law* 1119.

Mustafa Z, 'The Principle of Self-Determination in International Law' (1971) 5 *International Lawyer* 479.

Nobrega L and Loureiro, S, 'Mutual Agreement Procedure: Preventing the Compulsory Jurisdiction of the International Court of Justice?' (2009) 37 *Intertax* 529.

Odumosu IT, 'The Antinomies of the (Continued) Relevance of ICSID to the Third World' (2007) 8 *San Diego International Law Journal* 345.

Pauwelyn J, 'New Trade Politics for the 21st Century' (2008) 11 *Journal of International Economic Law* 559.

Penn O and others, 'Session 5: Tax Regimes in Other High GDP Countries' (2008) *Tax Magazine* 8.

Petkova K, Stasio A and Zagler M, 'On the Relevance of Double Tax Treaties' (2020) 27 *International Tax and Public Finance* 590.

Piantavigna P, 'Tax Abuse and Aggressive Tax Planning in the BEPS Era: How EU Law and the OECD Are Establishing a Unifying Conceptual Framework in International Tax Law, despite Linguistic Discrepancies' (2017) 2017 *World Tax Journal* 47.

Pinchis-Paulsen M, 'Let's Agree to Disagree: A Strategy for Trade-Security' (2022) 25 *Journal of International Economic Law* 527.

Previtera P, Boyle B and Kent M, 'Optimizing Asian Operations through Hong Kong's Double Tax Agreement Network' (2011) 61 *Tax Notes International* 859.

Rand W and others, 'ICSID's Emerging Jurisprudence: The Scope of ICSID's Jurisdiction' (1986–1987) 19 *NYU Journal of International Law and Politics* 33.

Reinisch A, 'European Court Practice Concerning State Immunity from Enforcement Measures' (2006) 17 *European Journal of International Law* 803.

Repousis OG, 'On Territoriality and International Investment Law: Applying China's Investment Treaties to Hong Kong and Macao' (2015) 37 *Michigan Journal of International Law* 113.

Rüstəmov X and Rustamov K, 'Contemporary Trends in China's Foreign Trade' (2022) 135 *Scientific Collection "InterConf"* 37.

Sacerdoti G and Borlini L, 'Systemic Changes in the Politicization of the International Trade Relations and the Decline of the Multilateral Trading System' (2023) 24 *German Law Journal* 17.

Sawyer A, 'Hong Kong Special Administrative Region's Developing Double Tax Agreement Regime: A Case Study of The Hong Kong Special Administrative Region–New Zealand Double Tax Agreement' (2011) *Asian Institute of International Financial Law Working Paper No 7*, 14.

Scanlon B, 'The Geopolitics of Infrastructure and the Unmaking of an Island: The Hong Kong-Zhuhai-Macau Bridge' (2023) *Geopolitics* 1.

Sedlak DR, 'ICSID's Resurgence in International Investment Arbitration: Can the Momentum Hold' (2004) 23 *Penn State International Law Review* 147.

Sekine T, 'Enhanced Third Party Rights Under the WTO Dispute Settlement System' (2018) 15 *Manchester Journal of International Economic Law* 354.

Shan W, 'EU Enlargement and the Legal Framework of EU-China Investment Relations' (2005) 6 *Journal World Investment and Trade* 237.

Sharkey N and Bain K, 'An Australia-Hong Kong Double Tax Agreement: Assessing the Costs and Benefits' (2011) 9 *eJournal of Tax Research* 269.

Shell GR, 'Trade Legalism and International Relations Theory: An Analysis of the World Trade Organization' (1995) 44 *Duke Law Journal* 829.

Shen J, 'Cross-Strait Trade and Investment and the Role of Hong Kong' (1997) 16 *Wisconsin International Law Journal* 66.1

Shi J, 'Autonomy of the Hong Kong Special Administrative Region' (2004) 10 *Leiden Journal of International Law* 491.

Slawotsky J, 'The Weaponization of Human Rights in US–China Trade Policy: Impacts and Risks' (2022) 56 *Journal of World Trade* 547.

Supnik KM, 'Making Amends: Amending the ICSID Convention to Reconcile Competing Interests in International Investment Law' (2009) 59 *Duke Law Journal* 343.

Sykes AO, 'The Law, Economics and Politics of Preferential Trading Arrangements: An Introduction' (2010) 46 *Stanford Journal of International Law* 171.

Timini J, 'Revisiting the 'Cobden-Chevalier Network' Trade and Welfare Effects' (2022) *Explorations in Economic History* 1.

Ting AKF and Ho DHK, 'Tax Consolidation: Does It Have to Be Complex for Hong Kong' (2012) 42 *Hong Kong Law Journal* 158.

Wan TW and others (eds), 'An Interview with Mr. Stuart Harbinson – Trump, Covid-10 and "Free-Riding": Where Is the World Trade Organisation Headed' (2020) *Public Jurist* 14.

Wang C, 'Invocation of National Security Exceptions Under GATT Article XXI: Jurisdiction to Review and Standard of Review' (2019) 18 *Chinese Journal of International Law* 695.

Wang G, 'The Belt and Road Initiative in Quest for a Dispute Resolution Mechanism' (2017) 25 *Asia Pacific Law Review* 1.

Wang Q, 'The Perfection of Subrogation System in Overseas Investment Insurance System' (2022) 6 *Journal of Humanities, Arts and Social Science* 479.

Weinhardt C and Schöfer, T, 'Differential Treatment for Developing Countries in the WTO: The Unmaking of the North–South Distinction in a Multipolar World' (2022) 43 *Third World Quarterly* 74.

Williams M, 'Foreign Investment in China: Will the Anti-monopoly Law Be a Barrier or a Facilitator?' (2009) 45 *Texas International Law Journal* 127.

Wilson JD, 'Mega-Regional Trade Deals in the Asia-Pacific: Choosing Between the TPP and RCEP?' (2015) 45 *Journal of Contemporary Asia* 345.

Witherell WH, 'The OECD Multilateral Agreement on Investment' (1995) 4 *Transnational Corporations* 1.

Xiao Y, 'Competitive Mega-regional Trade Agreements: Regional Comprehensive Economic Partnership (RCEP) vs. Trans-Pacific Partnership (TPP)' (2015) *College Undergraduate Research Electronic Journal* 5.

Xu X and Wilson GD, 'The Hong Kong Special Administrative Region as a Model of Regional External Autonomy' (2000) 32 *Case Western Reserve Journal of International Law* 1.

Yang S, 'Investment Dispute Settlement Mechanism in the Context of the Belt and Road Initiative' (2022) 126 *Journal of Law, Policy and Globalization* 29.

Yeo S and Seitz S, 'Common Reporting Standards' (2016) 9 *International In-House Counsel Journal* 1.

Yu J, 'The United States' Ineffective Response Towards Hong Kong's National Security Law' (2022) 73 *Hastings Law Journal* 161.

Yu JTC, 'The Struggle with Foreign Powers, 1840–1914' (1927) 26 *Current History* 383.

Zawahri NA and Mitchell SM, 'Fragmented Governance of International Rivers: Negotiating Bilateral versus Multilateral Treaties' (2011) 55 *International Studies Quarterly* 835.

Zeller B and Lightfoot R, 'Good Faith: An ICSID Convention Requirement' (2018) 8 *Victoria University Law & Justice Journal* 19.

Zeng H, 'Initiative and Implications of Hong Kong's Bilateral Investment Treaties' (2010) 11 *The Journal of World Investment & Trade* 669.

Zhang Y, 'The Reasons for and Basic Principles in Formulating the Hong Kong Special Administrative Region Basic Law and its Essential Contents and Mode of Expression' (1988) 2 *Journal of Chinese Law* 5.

Zhang Y, 'The Revival of Spectre: Voluntary Import Expansions and the WTO Compatibility' (2023) 18 *Asian Journal of WTO and International Health Law and Policy* 231.

Zhou W, Jiang H and Chen Z, 'Trade vs. Security: Recent Developments of Global Trade Rules and China's Policy and Regulatory Responses from Defensive to Proactive' (2022) 22 *World Trade Review* 193.

ONLINE JOURNALS

——, 'Report Published on Efficacy of EU's Framework for Foreign Direct Investment Screening' (HKTDC Research, 14 September 2022). Available at: research.hktdc.com/en/article/MTE2OD-I1NTA5MQ, accessed 25 May 2024.

CGCC, 'Wing Chu: RCEP Likely to Help Hong Kong Establish Status as Hub for Re-exports' (2022) CGCC Vision 1. Available at: www.cgcc.org.hk/files/file/1666080744_f2.pdf, accessed 25 May 2024.

Cheng T, 'National Security Law – A New Horizon for the Successful Implementation of "One Country, Two Systems"' (2020) 4 *China Law Magazine* Available at: www.doj.gov.hk/en/community_engagement/speeches/20200824_sj1.html, accessed 25 May 2024.

Danzman SB and Meunier S, 'The Big Screen: Mapping the Diffusion of Foreign Investment Screening Mechanisms' (28 August 2021) Princeton School of Public and International Affairs. Available at: www.internationalpoliticaleconomysociety.org/sites/default/files/paper-uploads/2021-10-20-00_43_32-sbauerle@indiana.edu.pdf, accessed 25 May 2024.

Grossman GM, 'The Purpose of Trade Agreements' (2016) NBER Working Paper No 22070. Available at: www.nber.org/system/files/working_papers/w22070/w22070.pdf, accessed 25 May 2024.

Hsieh PL, 'The RCEP, New Asian Regionalism and the Global South' (2017) IILJ Working Paper 2017/4, Available at: www.iilj.org/wp-content/uploads/2017/12/Hsieh-IILJ_2017_4_MegaReg.pdf, accessed 25 May 2024.

IRC Trade Task Force, 'Understanding the Weakness in Global Trade: What is the New Normal?' (Occasional Paper Series No 178, September 2016). Available at: www.ecb.europa.eu/pub/pdf/scpops/ecbop178.en.pdf, accessed 25 May 2024.

Kawai M and Wignaraja G, 'Asian FTAS: Trends and Challenges' (2009) ADBI Working Paper Series No 144, Available at: www.adb.org/sites/default/files/publication/155999/adbi-wp144.pdf, accessed 25 May 2024.

Murrill BJ, 'The "National Security Exception" and the World Trade Organization' (*Congressional Research Service*, 28 November 2018). Available at: www.fas.org/sgp/crs/row/LSB10223.pdf, accessed 25 May 2024.

Overholt WH, 'A Decade Later: Hong Kong's Economy Since 1997' (2007) Hong Kong Journal. Available at: https://carnegieendowment.org/hkjournal/PDF/2007_fall/4.pdf.

Park I, 'Comparison of the Regional Comprehensive Economic Partnership (RCEP) and Other Free Trade Agreements (FTAs)' (August 2022) ERIA Discussion Paper Series No 439, Available at: www.eria.org/uploads/media/discussion-papers/FY22/Comparison-of-the-Regional-Comprehensive-Economic-Partnership-(RCEP)-and-Other-Free-Trade-Agreements-(FTAs).pdf, accessed 25 May 2024.

Petersmann EU, 'Neo-liberal, State-Capitalist and Ordo-Liberal Conceptions of World Trade: The Rise and Fall of the WTO Dispute Settlement System' (2020) EUI Department of Law Research Paper No 2020/16, Available at: www.ssrn.com/abstract=3727995, accessed 25 May 2024.

Sacerdoti G, 'The WTO and its Dispute Settlement System in 2022: From the First Appellate Arbitrations to the Unsuccessful Invocation of the Security Exception' (2023) Bocconi Legal Studies Research Paper No 4369702. Available at: www.papers.ssrn.com/sol3/papers.cfm?abstract_id=4369702, accessed 25 May 2024.

Sejko D, 'UNCITRAL Working Group III on ISDS Reform Virtual Pre-Intersessional Meeting on the Use of Mediation in ISDS Background Paper for Session 3 – Hybrid Models of Arbitration and Mediation' (2020) 7 Available at: www.aail.org/wp-content/uploads/2020/11/2020_UNCITRAL_WGIII_Background_Paper_Session_3.pdf, accessed 25 May 2024.

Wells LT and Jr. Wint AG, 'Marketing a Country: Promotion as a Tool for Attracting Foreign Investment' (2000) Foreign Investment Advisory Service Occasional Paper No 13, World Bank Group Available at: www.documents.worldbank.org/en/publication/documents-reports/documentdetail/884891468763824660/marketing-a-country-promotion-as-a-tool-for-attracting-foreign-investment-revised-edition, accessed 25 May 2024.

COMMAND PAPERS AND LAW COMMISSION REPORTS

APEC Policy Support Unit, 'Trends and Developments in Provisions and Outcomes of RTA/FTAs Implemented in 2018 by APEC Economies' (*APEC*, March 2020). Available at: www.apec.org/docs/default-source/publications/2020/3/trends-and-developments-in-provisions-and-outcomes-of-rta-ftas-implemented-in-2018-by-apec-economies/220psutrends-and-developments-in-provisions-and-outcomes-of-rtaftas-implemented-in-2018-by-apec-econ.pdf?sfvrsn=19cd760d_1, accessed 25 May 2024.

Congressional Research Service, 'Free Trade Agreements and the WTO Exceptions' (Congressional Research Service, 2 July 2008). Available at: www.everycrsreport.com/files/20080702_RS21554_79458f5c4fb11a879a916b4b60cd2ba87b525df9.pdf, accessed 25 May 2024.

Congressional Research Service, 'Regional Comprehensive Economic Partnership (RCEP)' (Congressional Research Service, 17 October 2022). Available at: crsreports.congress.gov/product/pdf/IF/IF11891, accessed 25 May 2024.

Directorate-General for External Policies, Policy Department, 'Short Overview of the Regional Comprehensive Economic Partnership' (*European Parliament*, February 2021). Available at: www.europarl.europa.eu/RegData/etudes/BRIE/2021/653625/EXPO_BRI(2021)653625_EN.pdf, accessed 25 May 2024.

Directorate-General for External Policies, Policy Department, 'Workshop: Trade and Economic Relations with Asia' (*European Parliament*, 7 March 2016). Available at: www.europarl.europa.eu/RegData/etudes/STUD/2016/535024/EXPO_STU(2016)535024_EN.pdf, accessed 25 May 2024.

ESCAP, 'Preferential Trade Agreements in Asia and the Pacific 2022/2023: Trends and Developments' (*ESCAP*, 18 June 2023). Available at: www.repository.unescap.org/rest/bitstreams/756c42fd-3d72-4aa5-b9bc-229f806239c9/retrieve, accessed 25 June 2024.

European Commission, 'Joint Report to the European Parliament and the Council – Hong Kong Special Administrative Region: Annual Report 2017' JOIN(2018) 7 final 1.

International Law Commission Report on the Work of its Forty-Third Session (UN Doc A/46/10, 1991).

Miller T, Kim AB and Roberts JM, '2018 Report of Index of Economic Freedom' (The Heritage Foundation).

Ministry of Foreign Affairs of Japan, 'Global Trend Towards Regional Trade Agreements (RTA)' (Ministry of Foreign Affairs of Japan) 8. Available at: www.mofa.go.jp/region/asia-paci/korea/fta/report0310-3.pdf, accessed 25 May 2024.

OECD, 'Countering Harmful Tax Practises More Effectively, Taking into Account Transparency and Substance – Action 5: 2015 Final Report' (OECD, 2015). Available at: www.oecd-ilibrary.org/docserver/9789264241190-en.pdf?expires=1654515968&id=id&accname=guest&checksum=4A9F63CCAF309028752DC034C5253C29, accessed 25 May 2024.

OECD, 'Harmful Tax Practises– Peer Review Results' (*OECD*, January 2022). Available at: www.oecd.org/tax/beps/harmful-tax-practices-consolidated-peer-review-results-on-preferential-regimes.pdf, accessed 25 May 2024.

OECD, 'Making Dispute Mechanisms More Effective – Action 14: 2015 Final Report' (5 October 2015).

OECD, 'Two-Pillar Solution to Address the Tax Challenges Arising from the Digitalisation of the Economy' (OECD, October 2021). Available at: www.oecd.org/tax/beps/brochure-two-pillar-solution-to-address-the-tax-challenges-arising-from-the-digitalisation-of-the-economy-october-2021.pdf, accessed 25 May 2024.

OECD, Making Dispute Resolution More Effective – MAP Peer Review Report, Hong Kong, China (Stage 1): Inclusive Framework on BEPS: Action 14 (2019).

UK Parliament, Hong Kong: Recent Developments and the UK Response, (*CBP-8616*, 2021).

UNCITRAL Working Group III, 'Possible Reform of Investor-State Dispute Settlement (ISDS) – Submission from the Government of China – Note by the Secretariat' (19 July 2019) UN Doc A/CN.9/WG.III/WP.177.

UNCITRAL Working Group III, 'Possible Reform of Investor-State Dispute Settlement (ISDS) – Note by the Secretariat' (18 September 2017) UN Doc A/CN.9/WG.III/WP.142.

UNCITRAL Working Group III, 'Possible Reform of Investor-State Dispute Settlement (ISDS) – Draft Codes of Conduct and Commentary – Note by the Secretariat' (23 November 2022) UN Doc A/CN.9/WG.III/WP.223.

UNCITRAL Working Group III, 'Possible Reform of Investor-State Dispute Settlement (ISDS) – Note by the Secretariat – Addendum' (30 July 2019) UN Doc A/CN.9/WG.III/WP.166/Add.1.

UNCITRAL Working Group III, 'Report of Working Group III (Investor-State Dispute Settlement Reform) on the work of its forty-fourth session (*Vienna*, 23–27 January 2023)' (7 February 2023) UN Doc A/CN.9/1130.

UNCTAD, 'A New Centre of Gravity: The Regional Comprehensive Economic Partnership and its Trade Effects' (*UNCTAD*, 2021) 1, 12 Available at: www.unctad.org/system/files/official-document/ditcinf2021d5_en_0.pdf, accessed 9 January 2024.

UNCTAD, 'World Investment Report 2022: International Tax Reforms and Sustainable Investment' (2022).

UNCTAD, 'Dispute Settlement: World Trade Organization' (2003), UN Doc UNCTAD/EDM/Misc.232/Add.11.

UNGA, 'Report of the United Nations Commission on International Trade Law' UNCITRAL 50th Session Supp No 17 UN Doc A/72/17.

REPORTS FROM DEPARTMENTS OF THE HONG KONG GOVERNMENT

Bureau of East Asian and Pacific Affairs, '2020 Hong Kong Policy Act Report' (US Department of State, 28 May 2020). Available at: www.state.gov/2020-hong-kong-policy-act-report/, accessed 25 May 2024.

Bureau of East Asian and Pacific Affairs, '2021 Hong Kong Policy Act Report' (US Department of State, 31 March 2021). Available at: www.state.gov/2021-hong-kong-policy-act-report/, accessed 25 May 2024.

Bureau of Economic and Business Affairs, '2021 Investment Climate Statements: Hong Kong' (US Department of State, 22 July 2021). Available at: www.state.gov/reports/2021-investment-climate-statements/Hong-Kong/, accessed 25 May 2024.

Bureau of Economic and Business Affairs, '2022 Investment Climate Statements: Hong Kong' (US Department of State, 29 July 2022). Available at: www.state.gov/reports/2022-investment-climate-statements/Hong-Kong/, accessed 25 May 2024.

Commerce and Economic Development Bureau, 'Legislative Council Panel on Commerce, Industry, Innovation and Technology, 2022 Policy Address – Policy Initiatives of Commerce and Economic Development Bureau' (Legislative Council of the Hong Kong Special Administrative Region of the People's Republic of China, October 2022) LC Paper No CB(1)718/2022(03) 1, 7 Available at: www.legco.gov.hk/yr2022/english/panels/ci/papers/ci20221107cb1-718-3-e.pdf, accessed 25 May 2024.

Commerce and Economic Development Bureau, 'Legislative Council Panel on Commerce, Industry, Innovation and Technology, 2021 Policy Address – Policy Initiatives of Commerce, Industry and Tourism Branch, Commerce and Economic Development Bureau' (Legislative Council of the Hong Kong Special Administrative Region of the People's Republic of China, February 2022) LC Paper No CB(1)50/2022(01) 1, 6. Available at: www.legco.gov.hk/yr2022/english/panels/ci/papers/ci20220211cb1-50-1-e.pdf, accessed 25 May 2024.

Commonwealth Secretariat and Patchett, KW, 'The New York Convention on the Recognition and Enforcement of Foreign Arbitral Awards: Explanatory Documentation Prepared for Commonwealth Jurisdictions' (Commonwealth Secretariat 1981). Available at: www.uncitral.un.org/sites/uncitral.un.org/files/media-documents/uncitral/en/new-york-convention-commonwealth.pdf, accessed 25 May 2024.

Department of Justice, 'Legislative Council Panel on Administration of Justice and Legal Services – Professional Development for Legal Profession – International Organisation Secondment Programmes' (Legislative Council of the Hong Kong Special Administrative Region of the People's Republic of China, September 2021) LC Paper No CB(4)1549/20-21(03) 1, 5. Available at: www.doj.gov.hk/en/legco/pdf/ajls20210927e1.pdf, accessed 25 February 2024.

Economic Analysis Division, Economic Analysis and Business Facilitation Unit, Financial Secretary's Office, 'Third Quarter Economic Report 2016' (Government of the Hong Kong Special Administrative Region, November 2016) 1, 38. Available at: www.hkeconomy.gov.hk/en/pdf/er_16q3.pdf, accessed 8 January 2024.

GovHK, 'Consultation Paper on Measures to Counter Base Erosion & Profit Shifting' (GovHK). Available at: www.gov.hk/en/residents/government/publication/consultation/docs/2016/BEPS.pdf, accessed 25 May 2024.

HKSAR Government, 'Hong Kong's Response to Written Questions from the United States on Hong Kong's Implementation of the World Trade Organization Agreement on Subsidies and Countervailing Measures' (February 2022).

Legislative Council, 'Official Report of Proceedings' (Hong Kong Legislative Council, 16 June 1982). Available at: www.legco.gov.hk/yr81-82/english/lc_sitg/hansard/h820616.pdf, accessed 25 May 2024.

Legislative Council Panel on Constitutional Affairs, 'Constitutional Affairs (Papers) 16 Dec 96' (Legislative Council of the Hong Kong Special Administrative Region of the People#x2019;s Republic of China). Available at: www.legco.gov.hk/yr96-97/english/panels/ca/papers/xx1612x3.htm#E16E2, accessed 25 May 2024.

Legislative Council Secretariat Research and Library Services Division, 'Information Note – Government Procurement Agreement of the World Trade Organization' (30 April 2003) IN23/02-03 1.

Ministry of Economy, Trade and Industry, 2008 Report on Compliance by Major Trading Partners with Trade Agreements – WTO, FTA/EPA, BIT.

Trade and Industry Department Multilateral Division, 'Hong Kong, China's Services Commitments under the World Trade Organisation (WTO) General Agreement on Trade in Services (GATS)' (Trade and Industry Department, The Government of the Hong Kong Special Administrative Region, January 2015). Available at: www.tid.gov.hk/english/trade_relations/tradefora/files/hkc_services_commitment.pdf, accessed 16 November 2022.

FROM THE US

Commerce between United States and Hong Kong, 22 USC §5713.

Continued application of United States law, 22 USC §5721(a).

Country of Origin Marking of Products of Hong Kong, 62 Fed Reg 30927 (5 June 1997).

Country of Origin Marking of Products of Hong Kong, 85 Fed Reg 48551 (11 August 2020).

Exec Order No 13936, 85 Fed Reg 43413 (17 July 2020). Available at: www.federalregister.gov/documents/2020/07/17/2020-15646/the-presidents-executive-order-on-hong-kong-normalization.

Federal Law No 57 of 2008, 'Procedures for Foreign Investments in the Business Entities of Strategic Importance for Russian National Defence and State Security'.

Marking of imported articles and containers, 19 USC § 1304(a).

Participation in multilateral organizations, rights under international agreements, and trade status, 22 USC §5712(3).

Presidential Order, 22 US Code § 5722.

Secretary of State report regarding the autonomy of Hong Kong, 22 USC §§5725; Reporting requirement, §§5731.

US Congress, 'S.1731 – United States-Hong Kong Policy Act of 1992' (Congress.gov). Available at: www.congress.gov/bill/102nd-congress/senate-bill/1731/actions/, accessed 25 May 2024.

United States–Hong Kong Policy Act of 1992, 22 USC §5701. US Department of State, '2022 Hong Kong Policy Act Report' (*US Department of State*, 31 March 2022). Available at: www.state.gov/2022-hong-kong-policy-act-report/, accessed 25 May 2024.

WEBSITES AND BLOGS

UNCITRAL, 1958 New York Convention Guide, 'Introduction' (1958 New York Convention Guide). Available at: newyorkconvention1958.org/index.php?lvl=cmspage&pageid=10&menu=674&opac_view=-1, accessed 25 May 2024.

ADB, 'RCEP Agreement to Enter into Force on 1 January 2022' (*ADB SEADS*, 11 November 2021). Available at: www.seads.adb.org/news/rcep-agreement-enter-force-1-january-2022/, accessed 25 May 2024.

ADB, 'Table 3 FTAs by Scope (cumulative)' (ADB, 26 August 2022). Available at: aric.adb.org/fta-trends-by-scope, accessed 25 May 2024.

ADB, 'Table 7 FTAs in effect with investment chapter or clause (2008–2015)' (*ADB*, December 2016). Available at: www.aric.adb.org/fta-trends-with-investment, accessed 25 May 2024.

AHK Hong Kong, 'Back to the Future: Re-industrialisation in Hong Kong, (*German Industry and Commerce*, 29 May 2019). Available at: hongkong.ahk.de/news/news-details/back-to-the-future-re-industrialisation-in-hong-kong, accessed 25 May 2024.

Arcibal C, 'Once a shining light, foreign investors abandon Hong Kong office space as slowing economy weighs on sentiment' (South China Morning Post, 13 May 2022). Available at: www.scmp.com/business/article/3177531/once-shining-light-foreign-investors-abandon-hong-kong-office-space, accessed 25 May 2024.

Arentsen N and Weber MS, 'UNCITRAL Model Law: Still a Model or Second Best?' (Kluwer Arbitration Blog, 1 July 2014). Available at: http://arbitrationblog.kluwerarbitration.com/2014/07/01/uncitral-model-law-still-a-model-or-second-best/, accessed 25 May 2024.

ASEAN, 'ASEAN Hits Historic Milestone with Signing of RCEP' (*ASEAN*, 15 November 2020). Available at: www.asean.org/asean-hits-historic-milestone-with-signing-of-rcep/, accessed 9 January 2024.

Ashurst, 'Australia-Hong Kong Free Trade Agreement & Investment Agreement (2019)' (Ashurst, 4 July 2019). Available at: www.ashurst.com/en/news-and-insights/legal updates/australia-hong-kong-free-trade agreement and-investment-agreement-(2019)/, accessed 25 May 2024.

Asia Times, '*Asia Pacific Tax* Hub an open and inclusive forum' (*Asia Times*, 13 April 2022). Available at: asiatimes.com/2022/04/asia-pacific-tax-hub-an-open-and-inclusive-forum/, accessed 25 May 2024.

Australian Border Force, 'Regional Comprehensive Economic Partnership Agreement' (Australian Border Force, 15 December 2022). Available at: www.abf.gov.au/free-trade-agreements/Pages/regional-comprehensive-economic-partnership-agreement.aspx, accessed 25 May 2024.

Baliño S and Bernasconi-Osterwalder N, 'Investment Facilitation at the WTO: An Attempt to Bring a Controversial Issue into an Organisation in Crisis' (*Investment Treaty News*, 27 June 2019). Availableat: www.iisd.org/itn/en/2019/06/27/investment-facilitation-at-the-wto-an-attempt-to-bring-a-controversial-issue-into-an-organization-in-crisis-sofia-balino-nathalie-osterwalder/, accessed 25 May 2024.

Baliño S and others, 'Investment Facilitation: History and the Latest Developments in the Structured Discussions' (*IISD*, 31 January 2020) 1, 7. Available at: www.iisd.org/publications/report/investment-facilitation-history-and-latest-developments-structured-discussions, accessed 19 February 2024.

BBC, 'Hong Kong's Tough Covid Laws Threatened by Virus Surge' (*BBC*, 10 February 2022). Available at: www.bbc.com/news/world-asia-china-60329578, accessed 25 May 2024.

BBC, 'Hong Kong-China Extradition Plans Explained' (*BBC*, 13 December 2019). Available at: www.bbc.com/news/world-asia-china-47810723, accessed 25 May 2024.

BBC, 'Trump Targets China over Hong Kong Security Law' (*BBC News*, 30 May 2020). Available at: www.bbc.co.uk/news/world-us-canada-52856876, accessed 14 May 2024.

Belt and Road Initiative, 'Trade' (*Belt and Road Initiative*). Available at: http://onebeltoneroad.com/en/intro/trade, accessed 25 May 2024.

Bermingham F, 'Hong Kong's Status as Trade Hub Based on Political Stability, EU Figures in Protest-Racked Territory Warn' (*South China Morning Post*, 27 November 2019). Available at: www.scmp.com/economy/china-economy/article/3039610/hong-kongs-status-trade-hub-based-political-stability-eu, accessed 25 May 2024.

Bermingham F, 'Hong Kong warned WTO challenge to potential US trade sanctions could be "counterproductive"' (*South China Morning Post*, 29 May 2020). Available at: www.scmp.com/economy/china-economy/article/3086713/hong-kong-warned-wto-challenge-potential-us-trade-sanctions, accessed 25 May 2024.

Boeglin N, 'ICSID and Latin America: Criticisms, Withdrawals and Regional Alternatives' (bilaterals.org, June 2013). Available at: www.bilaterals.org/?icsid-and-latin-america-criticisms&lang=fr, accessed 25 May 2024.

BrandHK, 'Trade Agreements' (BrandHK, 31 August 2021). Available at: www.brandhk.gov.hk/en/doing-business/trade-agreements, accessed 25 May 2024.

Buckley C and others, 'New Security Law Gives China Sweeping Powers Over Hong Kong', (*New York Times*, 29 June 2020). Available at: www.nytimes.com/2020/06/29/world/asia/china-hong-kong-security-law-rules.html, accessed 25 May 2024.

Bureau of East Asian and Pacific Affairs, '2020 Hong Kong Policy Act Report' (US Department of State, 28 May 2020). Available at: www.state.gov/2020-hong-kong-policy-act-report/, accessed 25 May 2024.

Bureau of East Asian and Pacific Affairs, '2020 Hong Kong Policy Act Report' (US Department of State, 28 May 2020). Available at: www.state.gov/2020-hong-kong-policy-act-report/, accessed 25 May 2024.

Centre for Food Safety, 'Import Control – Imported Food Control' (Centre for Food Safety, The Government of the Hong Kong Special Administrative Region, 26 October 2022). Available at: www.cfs.gov.hk/english/import/import_ifc.html, accessed 25 May 2024.

Centre for Food Safety, 'Nutrition Labelling – FAQ for General Public' (Centre for Food Safety, The Government of the Hong Kong Special Administrative Region, 1 February 2021). Available at: www.cfs.gov.hk/english/faq/faq_14.html, accessed 25 May 2024.

Chaisse J, 'The Case for Hong Kong Joining RCEP' (East Asia Forum, 2 September 2021). Available at: www.eastasiaforum.org/2021/09/02/the-case-for-hong-kong-joining-rcep/, accessed 25 May 2024.

Chaisse J, 'Hong Kong's Case for RCEP membership' (East Asia Forum, 7 May 2022). Available at: www.eastasiaforum.org/2022/05/07/hong-kongs-case-for-rcep-membership/, accessed 25 May 2024.

Chaisse J and Olaoye K, 'Hong Kong, SAR China's New Approach to Investment Treaty Arbitration' (Kluwer Arbitration Blog, 10 July 2021). Available at: arbitrationblog.kluwerarbitration.com/2021/07/10/Hong-Kong-sar-chinas-new-approach-to-investment-treaty-arbitration/, accessed 25 May 2024.

Chan L, 'Georgia: A Free Trade Partner' (HKTDC Research, 19 July 2018). Available at: www.research.hktdc.com/en/article/NDMxNDMyNDMw#:~:text=Under%20the%20Sino%2DGeorgia%20FTA,total%20imports%20from%20Mainland%20China, accessed 25 May 2024.

Cheung E, 'Hong Kong Extradition: How Radical Youth Forced the Government's Hand' (BBC, 17 June 2019). Available at: www.bbc.com/news/world-asia-china-48655474, accessed 25 May 2024.

Choong J and Liu X, 'Enforcing Arbitration Awards in China' (*Thomson Reuters Practical Law*, February 2023). Available at: www.ca.practicallaw.thomsonreuters.com/6-381-9839?transitionType=Default&contextData=(sc.Default)&firstPage=true, accessed 25 May 2024.

Choong W, 'Singapore and the United States: Speaking Hard Truths as a Zhengyou' (Fulcrum, 7 April 2022). Available at: fulcrum.sg/singapore-and-the-united-states-speaking-hard-truths-as-a-zhengyou/, accessed 25 May 2024.

Clynch H, 'Saudi Arabia's Aramco IPO: The Mega-Deal Hong Kong Needs?' (Disruption Banking, 2 March 2023). Available at: www.disruptionbanking.com/2023/03/02/saudi-arabias-aramco-ipo-the-mega-deal-hong-kong-needs/, accessed 25 May 2024.

Commerce and Economic Development Bureau 'Participation in International Organisations'. Available at: www.cedb.gov.hk/en/trade-and-investment/participation-in-international-organisations.html, accessed 25 May 2024.

Commerce and Economic Development Bureau, 'Economic and Trade Offices' (Commerce and Economic Development Bureau, The Government of the Hong Kong Special Administrative Region, 1 July 2022). Available at: www.cedb.gov.hk/en/trade-and-investment/economic-and-trade-offices.html, accessed 25 May 2024.

Commerce and Economic Development Bureau, 'Our Portfolio' (Commerce and Economic Development Bureau, The Government of the Hong Kong Special Administrative Region, 1 July 2022). Available at: www.cedb.gov.hk/en/about-us/our-portfolio.html, accessed 25 May 2024.

Commerce and Economic Development Bureau, 'Permanent Secretary for Commerce and Economic Development' (Commerce and Economic Development Bureau, The Government of the Hong Kong Special Administrative Region, 1 July 2022). Available at: www.cedb.gov.hk/en/about-us/permanent-secretary-for-commerce-and-economic-development.html, accessed 25 May 2024.

Congressional Research Service, 'Revoking Hong Kong's Preferential Trade Status: Legal Framework and Implications' (Updated 2 April 2021). Available at: crsreports.congress.gov/product/pdf/lsb/lsb10488, accessed 25 May 2024.

Customs and Excise Department, 'Types and Duty Rates' (Customs and Excise Department, The Government of the Hong Kong Special Administrative Region, 24 February 2016). Available at: www.tid.gov.hk/english/ito/wto/wto_overview.html, accessed 25 May 2024.

Department of Foreign Affairs and Trade, 'About FTAs' (*Australian Government, Department of Foreign Affairs and Trade*). Available at: www.dfat.gov.au/trade/about-ftas/about-free-trade-agreements, accessed 25 May 2024.

Department of Justice, 'International Law Division' (*Department of Justice, The Government of Hong Kong Special Administrative Region*, 14 November 2022). Available at: www.doj.gov.hk/en/about/orgchart_ild.html, accessed 25 May 2024.

Department of Justice, 'Multilateral Agreements' (*Department of Justice, The Government of the Hong Kong Special Administrative Region*, 1 December 2022). Available at: www.doj.gov.hk/en/external/treaties.html, accessed 25 May 2024.

Department of Justice, 'Multilateral Agreements' (*Department of Justice, The Government of the Hong Kong Special Administrative Region*, 9 January 2024). Available at: www.doj.gov.hk/en/external/treaties.html, accessed 21 January 2024.

DG Trade, 'What does "Mode of Supply" for Services Mean?' (*European Commission | DG Trade*). Available at: trade.ec.europa.eu/access-to-markets/en/faqs/what-does-mode-supply-services-mean, accessed 25 May 2024.

Dubai Chamber, 'Dubai Chambers Inaugurates New Office in Hong Kong to Drive Mutual Economic and Business Growth' (*Dubai Chamber*, 9 February 2023). Available at: www.dubaichamber.com/en/media-center/news/dubai-chambers-inaugurates-new-office-in-hong-kong-to-drive-mutual-economic-and-business-growth/, accessed 25 May 2024.

EFTA, 'EFTA States and Hong Kong, China sign Free Trade Agreement' (*EFTA*, 21 June 2011). Available at: www.efta.int/Free-Trade/news/EFTA-States-and-Hong-Kong-China-sign-Free-Trade-Agreement-808, accessed 25 May 2024.

English.www.gov.cn, 'RCEP to Benefit China and the World' (*The State Council, The People's Republic of China*, 21 March 2022). Available at: www.english.www.gov.cn/news/videos/202201/01/content_WS61cfc871c6d09c94e48a304d.html, accessed 25 May 2023.

Enterprise Singapore, 'United States (USSFTA) Legal Text' (Enterprise Singapore, September 2022). Available at: www.enterprisesg.gov.sg/-/media/esg/files/non-financial-assistance/for-companies/free-trade-agreements/ussfta/legal-text/ussfta_legal_text.pdf, accessed 25 May 2024.

European Commission, 'EU – Hong Kong Customs Cooperation' (*European Commission*). Available at: ec.europa.eu/taxation_customs/customs-4/international-affairs/third-countries/hong-kong_en, accessed 25 May 2024.

European Parliament, 'The EU's Role in International Economic Fora' (*European Parliament*, 2015). Available at: www.europarl.europa.eu/RegData/etudes/BRIE/2015/563475/IPOL_BRI(2015)563475_EN.pdf, accessed 25 May 2024.

Executive Council, 'Executive Council' (*Executive Council, The Government of the Hong Kong Special Administrative Region*, 8 April 2022). Available at: www.ceo.gov.hk/exco/eng/index.html, accessed 25 May 2024.

FATF, 'Hong Kong, China's measures to combat money laundering and terrorist financing' (2019). Available at: www.fatf-gafi.org/en/publications/Mutualevaluations/Mer-hong-kong-china-2019.html, accessed 25 May 2024.

Feng Z, 'Trump Targets China over Hong Kong Security Law' (*BBC News*, 30 May 2020). Available at: www.bbc.com/news/world-us-canada-52856876, accessed 25 May 2024.

Financial Secretary, 'Duty Visit to Saudi Arabia and Bahrain' (*Financial Secretary, Deputy Financial Secretary, The Government of the Hong Kong Special Administrative Region*, 30 October 2022). Available at: www.fso.gov.hk/eng/blog/blog20221030.htm, accessed 25 May 2024.

Financial Services and the Treasury Bureau, 'Five Major Revenue Sources of the Government' (*Financial Services and the Treasury Bureau*). Available at: www.fstb.gov.hk/en/treasury/general/five-major-revenue-sources-of-the-government.htm, accessed 25 May 2024.

Financial Services and the Treasury Bureau, 'Guide to Procurement' (*Financial Services and the Treasury Bureau, The Government of the Hong Kong Special Administrative Region*). Available at: www.fstb.gov.hk/en/treasury/gov_procurement/guide-to-procurement.htm#topic-2, accessed 14 November 2022

Financial times, 'The Doha Round Finally Dies a Merciful Death' (*Financial Times*, 21 December 2015). Available at: www.ft.com/content/9cb1ab9e-a7e2-11e5-955c-1e1d6de94879, accessed 25 May 2024.

Foreign Investment Watch, 'Multi-jurisdiction guide for screening of foreign investments' (August 2019). Available at: foreigninvestmentwatch.com/guidance/, accessed 25 May 2024.

Gan N, 'China Approves Controversial National Security Law for Hong Kong' (CNN, 28 May 2020). Available at: edition.cnn.com/2020/05/28/asia/china-npc-hk-security-law-intl-hnk/index.html, accessed 25 May 2024.

Global Affairs Canada, 'World Trade Organisation Joint Statement Initiative on Investment Facilitation for Development' (*Government of Canada | Gouvernement du Canada*, 3 June 2021). Available at: www.international.gc.ca/world-monde/international_relations-relations_internationales/wto-omc/investment-facilitation-investissements.aspx?lang=eng, accessed 25 May 2024.

Government of Dubai Media Office, 'Dubai Chamber Launches Online Tool to Identify Export Gaps in Promising Markets' (*Government of Dubai*, 9 August 2021). Available at: www.mediaoffice.ae/en/news/2021/August/09-08/Dubai-Chamber, accessed 25 May 2024.

GovHK, 'Government Structure' (*GovHK, The Government of the Hong Kong Special Administrative Region*, September 2022). Available at: www.gov.hk/en/about/govdirectory/govstructure.htm, accessed 25 May 2024.

GovHK, 'Objections and Appeals' (*GovHK*). Available at: www.gov.hk/en/residents/taxes/taxfiling/object/objections.htm, accessed 25 May 2024.

GovHK, 'Organisation Chart of the Government of the Hong Kong Special Administrative Region' (*GovHK, The Government of the Hong Kong Special Administrative Region*, 1 July 2022). Available at: www.gov.hk/en/about/govdirectory/govchart/index.htm, accessed 25 May 2024.

GovHK, 'Hong Kong, The Facts: Financial Services' (*GovHK*). Available at: www.gov.hk/en/about/abouthk/factsheets/docs/financial_services.pdf, accessed 27 June 2022.

HKSAR Government, 'CE Begins Visit Programme in Saudi Arabia (with Photos/ Video)' *The Government of the Hong Kong Special Administrative Region Press Releases*, 6 February 2024). Available at: www.info.gov.hk/gia/general/202302/06/P2023020600104.htm, accessed 25 May 2024.

HKSAR Government, 'CE Continues Visit in Abu Dhabi and Starts Dubai Visit (with Photos/ Video)' *The Government of the Hong Kong Special Administrative Region Press Releases*, 9 February

2023). Available at: www.info.gov.hk/gia/general/202302/09/P2023020800799.htm, accessed 25 May 2024.

HKSAR Government, 'CE to Visit Saudi Arabia and UAE' (*The Government of the Hong Kong Special Administrative Region Press Releases*, 2 February 2023). Available at: www.info.gov.hk/gia/general/202302/02/P2023020200473.htm, accessed 25 May 2024.

HKSAR Government, 'HKSAR Government Officially Launches Dispute Settlement Procedures in accordance with WTO Mechanism on US' New Requirement on Origin Marking' (*The Government of the Hong Kong Special Administrative Region Press Releases*, 30 October 2020). Available at: www.info.gov.hk/gia/general/202010/30/P2020103000455.htm?fontSize=1, accessed 25 May 2024.

HKSAR Government, 'HKSARG strongly Objects to US' New Rule on Origin Marking of Hong Kong Products' (*The Government of the Hong Kong Special Administrative Region Press Releases*, 11 August 2020). Available at: www.info.gov.hk/gia/general/202008/11/P2020081100732.htm, accessed 25 May 2024.

HKSAR Government, 'Hong Kong to Commence Free Trade Agreement Negotiation with Peru (with photos)' (*The Government of the Hong Kong Special Administrative Region Press Releases*, 16 November 2022). Available at: www.info.gov.hk/gia/general/202211/16/P2022111600587.htm, accessed 25 May 2024.

HKSAR Government, 'LCQ 17: Impacts of the Revocation of Hong Kong's Special Trade Status' (*The Government of the Hong Kong Special Administrative Region Press Releases*, 17 June 2020). Available at: www.info.gov.hk/gia/general/202006/17/P2020061700355.htm/, accessed 25 May 2024.

HKSAR Government, 'LCQ14: Hong Kong as an International Arbitration Hub' (*The Government of Hong Kong Special Administrative Region*, 18 December 2019). Available at: www.info.gov.hk/gia/general/201912/18/P2019121800402.htm, accessed 25 May 2024.

HKSAR Government, 'LCQ2: The Relationship among the Executive Authorities, the Legislature and the Judiciary' (*The Government of the Hong Kong Special Administrative Region Press Releases*, 27 January 2010). Available at: www.info.gov.hk/gia/general/201001/27/P201001270155.htm, accessed 25 May 2024.

HKSAR Government, 'LCQ4: Regional Comprehensive Economic Partnership' (*The Government of the Hong Kong Special Administrative Region Press Releases*, 1 June 2022). Available at: www.info.gov.hk/gia/general/202206/01/P2022060100534.htm, accessed 14 November 2022.

HKSAR Government, 'One Country, Two Systems' (*The Government of the Hong Kong Special Administrative Region Press Releases*, July 2002). Available at: www.info.gov.hk/info/sar5/e12.htm, accessed 25 May 2024.

HKSAR Government, 'Prevailing Tax Policy' (*Financial Services and the Treasury Bureau*). Available at: www.fstb.gov.hk/en/treasury/general/prevailing-tax-policy.htm, accessed 25 May 2024.

HKSAR Government, 'Public Consultation on Free Trade Agreement with Peru Starts' (*The Government of the Hong Kong Special Administrative Region Press Releases*, 24 November 2022). Available at: www.info.gov.hk/gia/general/202211/24/P2022112200515.htm, accessed 25 May 2024.

HKSAR Government, 'Speech by CE at Kingdom of Saudi Arabia-Hong Kong Investment Forum and Chinese New Year Gala Dinner (English only) (With Photo/Video)' (*The Government of the Hong Kong Special Administrative Region Press Releases*, 6 February 2023). Available at: www.info.gov.hk/gia/general/202302/06/P2023020600055.htm, accessed 25 May 2024.

HKSAR Government, 'Speech by CE at United Arab Emirates-Hong Kong Business Forum and Chinese New Year Gala Dinner (English Only) (With Photos/Videos)' (*The Government of the Hong Kong Special Administrative Region Press Releases*, 9 February 2023). Available at: www.info.gov.hk/gia/general/202302/09/P2023020900034.htm, accessed 10 March 2024.

HKSAR Government, 'Speech by CE-elect at Bauhinia Culture International Forum (English only) (with photos/video)' (*The Government of the Hong Kong Special Administrative Region Press Releases*, 16 June 2022). Available at: www.info.gov.hk/gia/general/202206/16/P2022061600310.htm, accessed 25 May 2024.

HKSAR Government, 'Speech by SJ at Webinar "Why Hong Kong is Irreplaceable" (English only) (with photos)' (*The Government of the Hong Kong Special Administrative Region Press Releases*, 26 February 2021). Available at: www.info.gov.hk/gia/general/202102/26/P2021022600789.htm, accessed 25 February 2024.

GovHK, 'Tax Return Filing, Enquiry & Payment' (*GovHK*). Available at: www.gov.hk/en/residents/taxes/taxfiling/?subcat=taxrates, accessed 25 May 2024.

HKSAR Government, 'Transcript of Remarks by CE at Media Sessions in Dubai (with Photos/Video)' *The Government of the Hong Kong Special Administrative Region Press Releases*, 10 February 2023). Available at: www.info.gov.hk/gia/general/202302/10/P2023021000502.htm, accessed 7 March 2024.

HKSAR Government, 'WTO Members Commend Hong Kong, China for its Free Trade Regime (With Photos)' (*The Government of the Hong Kong Special Administrative Region Press Releases*, 29 November 2018). Available at: www.info.gov.hk/gia/general/201811/29/P2018112900153.htm, accessed 13 November 2022.

HKTDC Media Room, 'Hong Kong's Middle East Mission Lays Groundwork for New Business Opportunities' (*HKTDC*, 10 February 2023). Available at: www.mediaroom.hktdc.com/en/pressrelease/detail/20485/Hong%20Kong%E2%80%99s%20Middle%20East%20mission%20lays%20groundwork%20for%20new%20business%20opportunities, accessed 25 May 2024.

HKTDC Research, 'ASIA: Hong Kong Makes Official Application to Join the RCEP' (*HKTDC Research*, 8 March 2022). Available at: research.hktdc.com/en/article/MTAwNDI3NzY4OA, accessed 25 May 2024.

HKTDC Research, 'Hong Kong Files WTO Case Against U.S. "Made in China" Marking Requirement' (*HKTDC Research*, 3 November 2020). Available at: research.hktdc.com/en/article/NTgwODY0OTUz, accessed 25 May 2024.

HKTDC Research, 'Hong Kong's Trade Policy' (*HKTDC Research*). Available at: research.hktdc.com/en/Article/MzM0NDk2NTI4, accessed 25 May 2024.

Ho, G, 'A Trade Pact Nearly 10 Years in the Making: 5 Things to Know about RCEP' (*The Straits Times*, 15 November 2020). Available at: www.straitstimes.com/asia/a-trade-pact-nearly-10-years-in-the-making-5-things-to-know-about-rcep, accessed 25 May 2023.

Hong Kong Economic and Trade Office (London), 'London ETO Events' (*Hong Kong Economic and Trade Office (London)*, 14 December 2022). Available at: www.hketolondon.gov.hk/london-event.php, accessed 25 May 2024.

Hong Kong Economic and Trade Office (London), 'Our Responsibilities' (*Hong Kong Economic and Trade Office (London), The Government of the Hong Kong Special Administrative Region*, 14 December 2022). Available at: www.hketolondon.gov.hk/responsibilities.php, accessed 25 May 2024.

Hong Kong Economic and Trade Office in Geneva, 'About Us' (*Hong Kong Economic and Trade Office in Geneva*). Available at: www.hketogeneva.gov.hk/en/about/index.html, accessed 24 June 2022.

Hong Kong Government, 'The Port' (2022) Hong Kong: The Facts. Available at: www.gov.hk/en/about/abouthk/factsheets/docs/The-Port.pdf, accessed 25 May 2024.

Hong Kong Monetary Authority, 'Guide to Hong Kong Monetary, Banking and Financial Terms' (*Hong Kong Monetary Authority*, 23 July 2021). Available at: www.hkma.gov.hk/eng/data-publications-and-research/guide-to-monetary-banking-and-financial-terms/world_bank_group/, accessed 25 May 2024.

Hong Kong Monetary Authority, 'Hong Kong as an international finance centre'. Available at: www.hkma.gov.hk/eng/key-functions/international-financial-centre/hong-kong-as-an-international-financial-centre/, accessed 25 May 2024.

Horrigan B and others, 'Australia and Hong Kong Sign New Trade Agreement Containing Investor-State Dispute Resolution Provisions' (Herbert Smith Freehills, 28 March 2019). Available at: hsfnotes.com/arbitration/2019/03/28/australia-and-hong-kong-sign-new-trade-agreement-containing-investor-state-dispute-resolution-provisions/, accessed 25 May 2024.

Horsley J.P., 'Chinese Law Requires Public Consultation in Lawmaking: What Does it Mean for the Hong Kong National Security Legislation?' (*Brookings*, 8 June 2020). Available at: www.brookings.edu/blog/order-from-chaos/2020/06/08/chinese-law-requires-public-consultation-in-lawmaking-what-does-it-mean-for-the-hong-kong-national-security-legislation/, accessed 25 May 2024.

HSBC Expat 'Tax in Hong Kong'. Available at: www.expat.hsbc.com/expat-explorer/expat-guides/hong-kong/tax-in-hong-kong/, accessed 25 May 2024.

ICSID, 'Dr. Anthony Neoh' (*ICSID*). Available at: icsid.worldbank.org/resources/databases/arbitrators-conciliators-ad-hoc-committee-members/profile?cvid=55, accessed 25 May 2024.

ICSID, 'Joining ICSID' (*ICSID*). Available at: www.icsid.worldbank.org/about/member-states/joining-icsid, accessed 25 May 2024.

ICSID, 'Ms. Teresa Cheng' (*ICSID*). Available at: icsid.worldbank.org/resources/databases/arbitrators-conciliators-ad-hoc-committee-members/profile?cvid=602, accessed 25 May 2024.

IFC, 'Hong Kong Ranked as the Third Most Business-Friendly Economy in the World' (*IFC*, 29 October 2014). Available at: pressroom.ifc.org/all/pages/PressDetail.aspx?ID=24957, accessed 25 May 2024.

IMF, 'Why Complementarity Matters for Stability – Hong Kong SAR and Singapore as Asian Financial Centers' (*IMF*, 2014). Available at: www.imf.org/external/pubs/ft/wp/2014/wp14119.pdf, accessed 25 May 2024.

Inland Revenue Department (Hong Kong SAR) 'Comprehensive Double Taxation Agreements Concluded'. Available at: www.ird.gov.hk/eng/tax/dta_inc.htm, accessed 25 May 2024.

Inland Revenue Department, 'Commissioner's Overview' (*Inland Revenue Department*). Available at: www.ird.gov.hk/dar/2007-08/table/eng/ch1.pdf, accessed 25 May 2024.

Inland Revenue Department, 'Comprehensive Double Taxation Agreements concluded' (*Inland Revenue Department*). Available at: www.ird.gov.hk/eng/tax/dta_inc.htm, accessed 25 May 2024.

Inland Revenue Department, 'Departmental Interpretation and Practice Notes' (*Inland Revenue Department*). Available at: www.ird.gov.hk/eng/ppr/dip.htm, accessed 25 May 2024.

Inland Revenue Department, 'Ordinances Administered' (*Inland Revenue Department*). Available at: www.ird.gov.hk/eng/abo/ord.htm, accessed 25 May 2024.

Inland Revenue Department, 'Organization Chart' (*Inland Revenue Department*). Available at: www.ird.gov.hk/eng/abo/org.htm, accessed 25 May 2024.

Inland Revenue Department, 'Penalty Policy' (*Inland Revenue Department*). Available at: www.ird.gov.hk/eng/pol/ppo.htm, accessed 25 May 2024.

International Finance Business Desk, 'RCEP and its Impact on Global Trade' (*International Finance*, 21 March 2022). Available at: internationalfinance.com/rcep-impact-global-trade/, accessed 9 January 2024.

International Trade Administration, 'China – Trade Agreements' (*International Trade Administration*, 4 January 2022). Available at: www.trade.gov/country-commercial-guides/china-trade-agreements, accessed 25 May 2024.

International Trade Administration, 'Free Trade Agreement Overview' (*International Trade Administration*). Available at: www.trade.gov/free-trade-agreement-overview, accessed 25 May 2024.

International Trade Administration, 'Standards for Trade-Hong Kong & Macau' (*International Trade Administration*, 12 March 2021). Available at: www.trade.gov/country-commercial-guides/standards-trade-Hong-Kong-macau, accessed 25 May 2024.

International Trade and Investment Center, 'Reach' (*International Trade and Investment Center*). Available at: www.iticnet.org/reach, accessed 25 May 2024.

InvestHK, 'About InvestHK' (*InvestHK, The Government of the Hong Kong Special Administrative Region*, 6 October 2022). Available at: www.investhk.gov.hk/en/about-investhk.html, accessed 25 May 2024.

InvestHK, 'Hong Kong: Where Work Opportunities Connect'. Available at: www.investhk.gov.hk/sites/default/files/2022.11-corporate-brochure-en.pdf, accessed 25 May 2024.

InvestHK, 'InvestHK Hosts Seminar to Update Foreign Companies about Foreign Investment Policy and Business Environment in Mainland' (*InvestHK, The Government of the Hong Kong Special

Administrative Region, 14 October 2022). Available at: www.investhk.gov.hk/en/news/investhk-hosts-seminar-update-foreign-companies-about-foreign-investment-policy-and-business.html, accessed 25 May 2024.

IRET, 'The Tax System of Hong Kong' (*IRET Policy Bulletin*, 28 December 2010). Available at: http://iret.org/pub/BLTN-95.PDF, accessed 25 May 2024.

Irwin D, 'The Pandemic adds Momentum to the Deglobalisation Trend' (*Voxeu*, 5 May 2020). Available at: voxeu.org/article/pandemic-adds-momentum-deglobalisation-trend, accessed 25 May 2024.

Isayev UT, 'Session VII: Foreign Investment during the Transition: How to Attract It, and How to Make the Best Use of It' (27–28 May 1998). Presentation to the International Monetary Fund-Kyrgyz Republic Conference on Challenges to Economies in Transition: Stabilization, Growth, and Governance (Bishkek) 3–4. Available at: www.imf.org/external/np/eu2/kyrgyz/pdf/isayev.pdf, accessed 25 May 2024.

Kawase K and Coleman Z, 'Hong Kong's Special Trade Status with the US: Five Things to Know' (*Nikkei Asia*, 29 May 2020). Available at: www.asia.nikkei.com/Spotlight/Hong-Kong-protests/Hong-Kong-s-special-trade-status-with-the-US-Five-things-to-know, accessed 25 May 2024.

Kleefeld E, 'Hundreds of Thousands Attend Protest in Hong Kong over Extradition Bill' (*Vox*, 9 June 2019). Available at: www.vox.com/world/2019/6/9/18658650/hong-kong-protest-march-china-extradition-bill-2019, accessed 25 May 2024.

Kryvoi Y, '44th session of the UNCITRAL Working Group III: Code of Conduct for Arbitrators, its Enforcement, Corruption Allegations in ISDS' (*British Institute of International and Comparative Law*, 3 February 2023). Available at: www.biicl.org/blog/53/44th-session-of-the-uncitral-working-group-iii-code-of-conduct-for-arbitrators-its-enforcement-corruption-allegations-in-isds?cookiesset=1&ts=1676204401, accessed 25 May 2024.

Kuo L, 'Chinese Parliament Approves Controversial Hong Kong Security Law' (*The Guardian*, 28 May 2020). Available at: www.theguardian.com/world/2020/may/28/china-vote-npc-national-security-laws-hong-kong-us-protest, accessed 25 May 2024.

Lam E, 'U.S. to Label Hong Kong's Goods as "Made in China" in Blow to Territory' (Bloomberg, 11 August 2020). Available at: www.bloomberg.com/news/articles/2020-08-11/u-s-to-label-hong-kong-s-goods-as-made-in-china-in-blow-to-territory, accessed 25 May 2024.

Lampe M, 'Explaining Nineteenth-Century Bilateralism: Economic and Political Determinants of the Cobden-Chevalier Network' (*World Trade Organization*, 11 January 2011). Available at: www.wto.org/english/res_e/publications_e/wtr11_forum_e/wtr11_11jan11_e.htm, accessed 25 May 2024.

Lee KJ, 'Middle East Visit Heralds Better Times for Hong Kong's Economy and People' (*South China Morning Post*, 13 February 2023). Available at: www.scmp.com/comment/opinion/article/3209941/middle-east-visit-heralds-better-times-hong-kongs-economy-and-people, accessed 25 May 2024.

Lee YN, 'Hong Kong is a "Pawn" in US–China Rivalry, Says Former Diplomat' (CNBC, 28 May 2020). Available at: www.cnbc.com/2020/05/28/hong-kong-is-a-pawn-in-us-china-rivalry-ex-singapore-diplomat-says.html, accessed 25 May 2024.

Legislative Council, 'Legislative Process' in Legislative Council (ed), *A Companion to the History, Rules and Practices of the Legislative Council of the Hong Kong Special Administrative Region* (The Legislative Council Commission 2016). Available at: www.legco.gov.hk/general/english/procedur/companion/chapter_11/chapter_11.html, accessed 25 May 2024.

Legislative Council, Public Engagement in Legislative Council (ed), *A Companion to the History, Rules and Practices of the Legislative Council of the Hong Kong Special Administrative Region* (The Legislative Council Commission 2016) para 16.8. Available at: www.legco.gov.hk/general/english/procedur/companion/chapter_16/chapter_16.html, accessed 25 May 2024.

Leng S and Zheng W, 'China unveils plan to make Hainan a free trade hub like Hong Kong, Singapore as risks of US decoupling loom' (*South China Morning Post*, 2 June 2020). Available at: www.scmp.com/economy/china-economy/article/3087206/china-unveils-plan-make-hainan-free-trade-hub-hong-kong, accessed 25 May 2024.

Lester S, 'Professor Julien Chaisse Discusses Hong Kong's Application to Join RCEP' (*China Trade Monitor*, 8 March 2022). Available at: www.chinatrademonitor.com/professor-julien-chaisse-discusses-hong-kongs-application-to-join-rcep/, accessed 25 May 2024.

Local, 'Aramco Team Series to be Held at Fanling Golf Course in October' (*The Standard*, 7 February 2023). Available at: www.thestandard.com.hk/breaking-news/section/4/200045/Aramco-Team-Series-to-be-held-at-Fanling-golf-course-in-October, accessed 25 May 2024.

MIGA, 'Dispute Resolution' (*MIGA*). Available at: www.miga.org/dispute-resolution, accessed 25 May 2024.

MIGA, 'Projects' (*MIGA*). Available at: www.miga.org/projects?project_status=All&env_category=All&project_type=All&covid_19=All&board_date%5Bmin%5D=&board_date%5Bmax%5D=&title=&guarantee_holder%5B2816%5D=2816&guarantee_holder%5B2821%5D=2821&guarantee_holder%5B2826%5D=2826&guarantee_holder%5B781%5D=781&guarantee_holder%5B782%5D=782&guarantee_holder%5B783%5D=783&guarantee_holder%5B616%5D=616&guarantee_holder%5B950%5D=950&guarantee_holder%5B951%5D=951&guarantee_holder%5B959%5D=959&guarantee_holder%5B2406%5D=2406&project_id=&sip_type=All&page=0, accessed 25 May 2024.

MIGA, 'What We Do' (*MIGA*). Available at: www.miga.org/what-we-do, accessed 25 May 2024.

Millennium Cities Initiative, 'Tools, Techniques and Resources for Investment Promotion'. Available at: http://mci.ei.columbia.edu/initiatives/private-sector-development/overview-of-investment-promotion/#:~:text=Investment%20promotion%20actively%20seeks%20to,as%20well%20as%20foreign%20companies, accessed 25 May 2024.

Ministry of Commerce, People's Republic of China, 'China-Norway FTA' (*China FTA Network*). Available at: http://fta.mofcom.gov.cn/topic/ennorway.shtml, accessed 25 May 2024.

Ministry of Commerce, People's Republic of China, 'Mainland and Hong Kong Closer Economic and Partnership Arrangement' (*China FTA Network*). Available at: http://fta.mofcom.gov.cn/topic/enhongkong.shtml, accessed 25 May 2024.

Ministry of Finance, Support Hainan to Comprehensively Deepen the Reform and Opening up of the Implementation Plan for Fiscal and Taxation Policies. Available at: www.hnftp.gov.cn/zcfg/zcwj/ss/202002/t20200226_3261459.html, accessed 27 August 2020

Ministry of Foreign Affairs of Japan, 'Summary of the Regional Comprehensive Economic Partnership Agreement' (*Ministry of Foreign Affairs of Japan*) 1. Available at: www.mofa.go.jp/mofaj/files/100114908.pdf, accessed 25 May 2024.

Mishra S, 'Hong Kong Ranked the World's Freest Economy by Canadian Think Tank for the 26th Time in a Row' (*Independent*, 9 September 2022). Available at: www.independent.co.uk/asia/east-asia/Hong-Kong-free-economy-fraser-institute-b2163710.html, accessed 13 November 2022

Mullen A, 'Explainer | What is RCEP, the World's Largest Free Trade Deal that is Under Way?' (*South China Morning Post*, 1 January 2022). Available at: www.scmp.com/economy/global-economy/article/3161707/what-rcep-worlds-largest-free-trade-deal-under-way, accessed 25 May 2024.

News.gov.hk, 'CE Begins Abu Dhabi Visit' (news.gov.hk, 8 February 2023). Available at: www.news.gov.hk/eng/2023/02/20230208/20230208_094211_229.html, accessed 25 May 2024.

News.gov.hk, 'CE Begins Visit in Saudi Arabia' (news.gov.hk, 6 February 2023). Available at: www.news.gov.hk/eng/2023/02/20230206/20230206_102337_811.html, accessed 25 May 2024.

News.gov.hk, 'CE Boosts Ties in Saudi Arabia' (news.gov.hk, 7 February 2023). Available at: www.news.gov.hk/eng/2023/02/20230207/20230207_100533_806.html?type=category&name=finance&tl=t, accessed 25 May 2024.

News.gov.hk, 'CE Continues UAE Visit' (news.gov.hk, 9 February 2023). Available at: www.news.gov.hk/eng/2023/02/20230209/20230209_084056_941.html, accessed 25 May 2024.

News.gov.hk, 'CE Meets UAE Officials' (news.gov.hk, 10 February 2023). Available at: www.news.gov.hk/eng/2023/02/20230210/20230210_095500_526.html, accessed 25 May 2024.

News.gov.hk, 'CE to Deliver Policy Address' (News.gov.hk, 17 October 2022). Available at: www.news.gov.hk/eng/2022/10/20221017/20221017_190644_997.html, accessed 25 May 2024.

News.gov.hk, 'Middle East Visit Fruitful: CE' (news.gov.hk, 10 February 2023). Available at: www.news.gov.hk/eng/2023/02/20230210/20230210_135407_131.html, accessed 25 May 2024.

OECD, 'Convention on Mutual Administrative Assistance in Tax Matters' (OECD). Available at: www.oecd.org/tax/exchange-of-tax-information/convention-on-mutual-administrative-assistance-in-tax-matters.htm, accessed 25 May 2024.

OECD, 'International Collaboration to End Tax Avoidance' (*OECD*). Available at: www.oecd.org/tax/beps/, accessed 25 May 2024.

OECD, 'Investment Screening in Times of COVID-19 and Beyond' (7 July 2020). Available at: www.oecd.org/coronavirus/policy-responses/investment-screening-in-times-of-covid-19-and-beyond-aa60af47/, accessed 25 May 2024.

OECD, 'Multilateral Agreement on Investment' (*OECD*). Available at: www.oecd.org/investment/internationalinvestmentagreements/multilateralagreementoninvestment.htm, accessed 16 February 2024.

OECD, 'Multilateral Convention to Implement Tax Treaty Related Measures to Prevent BEPS' (*OECD*). Available at: www.oecd.org/tax/treaties/multilateral-convention-to-implement-tax-treaty-related-measures-to-prevent-beps.htm, accessed 25 May 2024.

OECD, 'OECD Releases Pillar Two Model Rules for Domestic Implementation of 15% Global Minimum Tax' (*OECD*, December 2021). Available at: www.oecd.org/tax/beps/oecd-releases-pillar-two-model-rules-for-domestic-implementation-of-15-percent-global-minimum-tax.htm, accessed 25 May 2024.

OECD, 'Addressing the Tax Challenges of the Digital Economy' (OECD 2014) 32. Available at: www.oecd-ilibrary.org/fundamental-principles-of-taxation_5jxv8zhcggxv.pdf, accessed 25 May 2024.

Office of the Historian, 'Bretton Woods-GATT, 1941–1947' (*Office of the Historian, Foreign Service Institute, United States Department of State*). Available at: www.history.state.gov/milestones/1937-1945/bretton-woods, accessed 25 May 2024.

Ouyang I, 'Chief Executive John Lee's Middle East Delegation Comprises 30 Heavyweights from Finance, Tech and Logistics Sectors' (*South China Morning Post*, 6 February 2023). Available at: www.scmp.com/business/banking-finance/article/3209281/chief-executive-john-lees-middle-east-delegation-comprises-30-heavyweights-finance-tech-and, accessed 25 May 2024.

Pedrosa E, 'Free Trade Agreements in East Asia: A Way toward Trade Liberalization' (*PECC Forum*, 21 January 2011). Available at: www.pecc.org/blog/entry/free-trade-agreements-in-east-asia-a-way-toward-trade-liberalization, accessed 25 May 2024.

Rapoza K, 'Imaging Hong Kong without Its U.S. Special Status Deal' (*Forbes*, 29 May 2020). Available at: www.forbes.com/sites/kenrapoza/2020/05/29/imaging-hong-kong-without-its-us-special-status-deal/?sh=4560f1851c9d, accessed 25 May 2024.

Rivera JCB and Azuga MV, 'Life after ICSID: 10th Anniversary of Bolivia's Withdrawal from ICSID' (*Kluwer Arbitration Blog*, 12 August 2017). Available at: www.arbitrationblog.kluwerarbitration.com/2017/08/12/life-icsid-10th-anniversary-bolivias-withdrawal-icsid/, accessed 25 May 2024.

RTHK, 'NSL not a top concern for investors: InvestHK chief' (*RTHK*, 25 March 2022). Available at: www.news.rthk.hk/rthk/en/component/k2/1640706-20220325.htm, accessed 25 May 2024.

Sacks D, 'Countries in China's Belt and Road Initiative: Who's In and Who's Out' (*Council on Foreign Relations*, 24 March 2021). Available at: www.cfr.org/blog/countries-chinas-belt-and-road-initiative-whos-and-whos-out, accessed 25 May 2024.

The American Chamber of Commerce in Hong Kong, 'Response of Amcham HK to President Trump's Revocation of Hong Kong's Special Trading Status' (*AmCham*, 17 July 2020). Available at: www.amcham.org.hk/news/response-amcham-hk-president-trumps-revocation-hong-kongs-special-trading-status/, accessed 25 May 2024.

The ASEAN Secretariat, 'Regional Comprehensive Economic Partnership' (*RCEP*, 2019). Available at: www.rcepsec.org/legal-text/, accessed 25 May 2024.

The ASEAN Secretariat, 'Summary of the Regional Comprehensive Economic Partnership Agreement' (*RCEP*) 1. Available at: www.rcepsec.org/wp-content/uploads/2020/11/Summary-of-the-RCEP-Agreement.pdf, accessed 9 January 2024.

The Heritage Foundation, '2011 Index of Economic Freedom – Hong Kong'. Available at: www.heritage.org/index/Country/HongKong, accessed 25 May 2024.

The Legal 500, 'Investment Funds' (*The Legal 500*). Available at: www.legal500.com/c/Hong-Kong/investment-funds/, accessed 25 May 2024.

The World Bank, 'Least Developed Countries: UN Classification' (*The World Bank | Data*). Available at: data.worldbank.org/country/XL, accessed 9 January 2024.

Tian S, Lee T and others, 'Hong Kong and Singapore Spar for Green Finance Supremacy in Asia' (*Bloomberg*, 8 December 2022). Available at: www.bloomberg.com/news/articles/2022-12-08/hong-kong-singapore-spar-for-the-green-finance-crown-in-asia?leadSource=uverify%20wall, accessed 25 May 2024.

Timpany J and Lu L, 'Hong Kong SAR: The impact of the OECD's BEPS 2.0 proposals' (*International Tax Review*, 24 August 2021). Available at: www.internationaltaxreview.com/Article/b1t8h4gpjyynn4/Hong-Kong-sar-the-impact-of-the-oecds-beps-20-proposals, accessed 25 May 2024.

Trade and Industry Department, 'Consultation Papers' (*Trade and Industry Department, The Government of the Hong Kong Special Administrative Region*, 24 November 2022). Available at: www.tid.gov.hk/english/aboutus/noticeboard/consultpaper.html, accessed 25 May 2024.

Trade and Industry Department, 'Consultation Papers' (*Trade and Industry Department, The Government of the Hong Kong Special Administrative Region*, 20 July 2022). Available at: www.tid.gov.hk/english/aboutus/noticeboard/consultpaper.html, accessed 25 May 2024.

Trade and Industry Department, 'Environmental Goods Agreement (under negotiation)' (*Trade and Industry Department, The Government of the Hong Kong Special Administrative Region*, 20 July 2022). Available at: www.tid.gov.hk/english/trade_relations/ega/index.html, accessed 25 May 2024.

Trade and Industry Department, 'Free Trade Agreement between Hong Kong, China and Chile' (*Trade and Industry Department, The Government of the Hong Kong Special Administrative Region*, 11 November 2022). Available at: www.tid.gov.hk/english/ita/fta/hkclfta/index.html, accessed 25 May 2024.

Trade and Industry Department, 'Free Trade Agreement between Hong Kong, China and the Member States of the European Free Trade Association' (*Trade and Industry Department, The Government of the Hong Kong Special Administrative Region*, 11 November 2022). Available at: www.tid.gov.hk/english/ita/fta/hkefta/index.html, accessed 25 May 2024.

Trade and Industry Department, 'Free Trade Agreement between Hong Kong, China and the Association of Southeast Asian Nations' (*Trade and Industry Department, The Government of the Hong Kong Special Administrative Region*, 4 January 2023). Available at: www.tid.gov.hk/english/ita/fta/hkasean/index.html, accessed 25 May 2024.

Trade and Industry Department, 'Free Trade Agreement between Hong Kong, China and Georgia' (*Trade and Industry Department, The Government of the Hong Kong Special Administrative Region*, 11 November 2022). Available at: www.tid.gov.hk/english/ita/fta/hkgefta/index.html, accessed 25 May 2024.

Trade and Industry Department, 'Free Trade Agreement between Hong Kong, China and Australia' (*Trade and Industry Department, The Government of the Hong Kong Special Administrative Region*, 11 November 2022). Available at: www.tid.gov.hk/english/ita/fta/hkaufta/index.html#:~:text=Hong%20Kong%20and%20Australia%20commenced,signed%20on%2026%20March%202019, accessed 25 May 2024.

Trade and Industry Department, 'Hong Kong and Chile Sign Investment Agreement' (*Trade and Industry Department, The Government of the Hong Kong Special Administrative Region*, 16 November 2016). Available at: www.tid.gov.hk/english/aboutus/presspeech/press/2016/20161119.html, accessed 25 May 2024.

Trade and Industry Department, 'Hong Kong Special Administrative Region and Macao Special Administrative Region Closer Economic Partnership Arrangement (HK-Macao CEPA)' (*Trade and Industry Department, The Government of the Hong Kong Special Administrative Region,*

11 November 2022). Available at: www.tid.gov.hk/english/ita/fta/hkmacao/index.html, accessed 25 May 2024.

Trade and Industry Department, 'Hong Kong to Negotiate Free Trade Agreements with Georgia and Maldives' (*Trade and Industry Department, The Government of the Hong Kong Special Administrative Region*, 11 November 2022). Available at: www.tid.gov.hk/english/aboutus/noticeboard/maldivesgeorgiafta.html, accessed 25 May 2024.

Trade and Industry Department, 'Hong Kong, China – New Zealand Closer Economic Partnership Agreement' (*Trade and Industry Department, The Government of the Hong Kong Special Administrative Region*, 14 November 2022). Available at: www.tid.gov.hk/english/ita/fta/hknzcep/index.html, accessed 25 May 2024.

Trade and Industry Department, 'Hong Kong's Free Trade Agreements (FTAs)' (*Trade and Industry Department, The Government of the Hong Kong Special Administrative Region*, 24 February 2023). Available at: www.tid.gov.hk/english/ita/fta/index.html, accessed 5 March 2024.

Trade and Industry Department, 'Hong Kong's Investment Promotion and Protection Agreements' (*Trade and Industry Department, The Government of the Hong Kong Special Administrative Region*, 8 November 2022). Available at: www.tid.gov.hk/english/ita/ippa/index.html, accessed 25 May 2024.

Trade and Industry Department, 'Hong Kong's Principal Trading Partners in 2021' (*Trade and Industry Department, The Government of the Hong Kong Special Administrative Region*, 11 November 2022). Available at: www.tid.gov.hk/english/trade_relations/mainland/trade.html, accessed 25 May 2024.

Trade and Industry Department, 'Hong Kong's Trade Policy' (*Trade and Industry Department, The Government of the Hong Kong Special Administrative Region*, 11 November 2022). Available at: www.tid.gov.hk/english/trade_relations/trade_policy/trpolicy.html, accessed 25 May 2024.

Trade and Industry Department, 'Hong Kong's Trade Policy' (*Trade and Industry Department, The Government of the Hong Kong Special Administrative Region*, 20 July 2022). Available at: www.tid.gov.hk/english/trade_relations/trade_policy/trpolicy.html, accessed 13 November 2022.

Trade and Industry Department, 'Hong Kong's Free Trade Agreements (FTAs)' (*Trade and Industry Department, The Government of the Hong Kong Special Administrative Region*, 10 November 2022). Available at: www.tid.gov.hk/english/ita/fta/index.html, accessed 14 November 2022.

Trade and Industry Department, 'Hong Kong's Participation in Plurilateral Trade Agreements' (*Trade and Industry Department, The Government of the Hong Kong Special Administrative Region*, 20 July 2022). Available at: www.tid.gov.hk/english/trade_relations/tradefora/plurilateral_trade_agreements.html, accessed 25 May 2024.

Trade and Industry Department, 'Hong Kong's Participation in Plurilateral Trade Agreements' (*Trade and Industry Department, The Government of the Hong Kong Special Administrative Region*, 20 July 2022). Available at: www.tid.gov.hk/english/trade_relations/tradefora/plurilateral_trade_agreements.html, accessed 25 May 2024.

Trade and Industry Department, 'International Trade Organisations' (*Trade and Industry Department, The Government of the Hong Kong Special Administrative Region*, 11 November 2022). Available at: www.tid.gov.hk/english/ito/index.html, accessed 25 May 2024.

Trade and Industry Department, 'Negotiation of a Free Trade Agreement between Hong Kong and Chile Consultation Document' (*Trade and Industry Department, The Government of the Hong Kong Special Administrative Region*, 11 November 2022). Available at: www.tid.gov.hk/english/aboutus/noticeboard/chile_agreement.html, accessed 25 May 2024.

Trade and Industry Department, 'Our Mission and Values' (*Trade and Industry Department, The Government of the Hong Kong Special Administrative Region*, 11 November 2022). Available at: www.tid.gov.hk/english/aboutus/deptprofile/mission.html, accessed 25 May 2024.

Trade and Industry Department, 'Overview of Mainland and Hong Kong Closer Economic Partnership Arrangement' (*Trade and Industry Department, The Government of the Hong Kong Special Administrative Region*, 11 November 2022). Available at: www.tid.gov.hk/english/cepa/cepa_overview.html, accessed 25 May 2024.

Trade and Industry Department, 'Trade in Services Agreement (under negotiation)' (*Trade and Industry Department, The Government of the Hong Kong Special Administrative Region*, 11 November 2022). Available at: www.tid.gov.hk/english/trade_relations/tradefora/wto_TISA.html, accessed 25 May 2024.

Trade and Industry Department, 'World Trade Organisation (WTO)' (*Trade and Industry Department, The Government of the Hong Kong Special Administrative Region*, 11 November 2022). Available at: www.tid.gov.hk/english/ito/wto/wto_overview.html, accessed 13 November 2022

Trade and Industry Department, 'International Trade Organizations: World Trade Organization' (*Trade and Industry Department, The Government of the HKSAR*). Available at: www.tid.gov.hk/english/ito/wto/wto_overview.html, accessed 25 May 2024.

Tuomi K, 'Review of Investment Incentives Best Practice in Attracting Investment' (*International Growth Centre*, 2012). Available at: www.theigc.org/publication/review-of-investment-incentives-best-practice-in-attracting-investment/, accessed 25 May 2024.

US Congress, 'S.1838 – Hong Kong Human Rights and Democracy Act of 2019' (*Congress.gov*). Available at: www.congress.gov/bill/116th-congress/senate-bill/1838/actions, accessed 25 May 2024.

US Congress, 'S.2710 – A bill to prohibit the commercial export of covered munitions items to the Hong Kong Police Force' (*Congress.gov*). Available at: www.congress.gov/bill/116th-congress/senate-bill/2710, accessed 25 May 2024.

US Department of State, '2022 Investment Climate Statements: Hong Kong' (2022). Available at: www.state.gov/reports/2022-investment-climate-statements/hong-kong/, accessed 25 May 2024.

UNCITRAL, 'Working Group III: Investor-State Dispute Settlement Reform' (*United Nations, United Nations on International Trade Law*). Available at: uncitral.un.org/en/working_groups/3/investor-state, accessed 25 May 2024.

UNCTAD Investment Policy Hub, 'International Investment Agreements Navigator: Hong Kong, China SAR'. Available at: investmentpolicy.unctad.org/international-investment-agreements/countries/93/hong-kong-sar-china, accessed 25 May 2024.

UNCTAD Investment Policy Hub, 'International Investment Agreements Navigator' (*UNCTAD Investment Policy Hub*). Available at: investmentpolicy.unctad.org/international-investment-agreements/by-economy, accessed 25 May 2024.

UNCTAD, 'Evolution of the World's 25 Top Trading Nations' (*UNCTAD*, 6 April 2021). Available at: unctad.org/topic/trade-analysis/chart-10-may-2021, accessed 13 November 2022

UNCTAD, 'Investment Laws Navigator' Available at: investmentpolicy.unctad.org/investment-laws, accessed 25 May 2024.

UNCTAD, 'Investment Policy Hub: Hong Kong, China SAR'. Available at: investmentpolicy.unctad.org/international-investment-agreements/countries/93/hong-kong sar-China, accessed 25 May 2024.

UNCTAD, 'National Security-Related Screening Mechanisms for Foreign Investment' (December 2019) Investment Policy Mentor. Available at: unctad.org/system/files/official-document/diaepcbinf2019d7_en.pdf, accessed 25 May 2024.

UNESCAP, 'Outward Foreign Direct Investment and Home Country Sustainable Development' (20 April 2020) Studies in trade, investment and innovation no 93, 54. Available at: www.unescap.org/publications/studies-trade-investment-and-innovation-no-93-outward-foreign-direct-investment-and, accessed 25 May 2024.

US Department of Commerce, 'Statement from U.S. Secretary of Commerce Wilbur Ross on Revocation of Hong Kong Special Status' (*US Department of Commerce*, 29 June 2020). Available at: www.2017-2021.commerce.gov/news/press-releases/2020/06/statement-us-secretary-commerce-wilbur-ross-revocation-hong-kong.html, accessed 25 May 2024.

US Department of State, '2021 Investment Climate Statements' (2021). Available at: www.state.gov/reports/2021-investment-climate-statements/, accessed 25 May 2024.

US Department of State, '2022 Investment Climate Statements: Hong Kong' (2022). Available at: www.state.gov/reports/2022-investment-climate-statements/hong-kong/, accessed 25 May 2024.

Victor D and Ives M, 'Why Are People Protesting in Hong Kong?' (*The New York Times*, 15 October 2019). Available at: www.nytimes.com/2019/10/15/world/asia/what-are-hong-kong-protests-about.html, accessed 25 May 2024.

Walker A, 'Is Free Trade Good or Bad?' (*BBC*, 18 January 2017). Available at: www.bbc.com/news/business-38209407, accessed 25 May 2024.

Wang X, 'No Second-Rate Trade Deal: What RCEP Means for the Global Economy' (*Asian Global Online*, 30 June 2022). Available at: www.asiaglobalonline.hku.hk/not-second-rate-trade-deal-what-rcep-means-global-economy/, accessed 25 May 2024.

Wilcox D, 'Convergence and Hegemony: The United States and China in the 21st Century' (*Union College*, 2022). Available at: www.digitalworks.union.edu/theses/2654/, accessed 25 May 2024.

Williams M, 'How Much Does Hong Kong's Special Status Matter?' (Capital Economics, 11 November 2019). Available at: www.admin.capitaleconomics.com/publications/china-economics/china-economics-update/how-much-does-hong-kongs-special-status-matter, accessed 25 May 2024.

Wong D and Koty AC, 'The US-China Trade War: A Timeline' (China Briefing, 25 August 2020). Available at: www.chinabriefing.com/news/the-us-china-trade-war-a-timeline/, accessed 25 May 2024.

Wong N, 'Free-Trade Agreement 'Logical Next Step' for Hong Kong and United Arab Emirates, Territory Leader John Lee Says' (*South China Morning Post*, 9 February 2024). Available at: www.scmp.com/news/hong-kong/article/3209568/hong-kong-and-united-arab-emirates-set-commence-talks-bilateral-free-trade-agreement-territory-leader, accessed 25 May 2024.

Wong N, 'Hong Kong must Seize Opportunities with Middle Eastern Investors Eyeing Mainland China Market, Top Banker Says' (*South China Morning Post*, 14 February 2024). Available at: www.scmp.com/news/hong-kong/hong-kong-economy/article/3210089/middle-eastern-investors-keen-put-more-assets-mainland-china-lack-awareness-conduits-hong-kong, accessed 25 May 2024.

World Bank, 'MIGA (Multilateral Investment Guarantee Agency)' (*World Bank*, September 2012). Available at: http://web.worldbank.org/archive/website01363/WEB/0__CO-83.HTM, accessed 25 May 2024.

World Business Outlook, 'Hong Kong and Sharjah Announces a Strategic Investment Alliance' (*World Business Outlook*, 10 February 2024). Available at: www.worldbusinessoutlook.com/hong-kong-and-sharjah-announces-a-strategic-investment-alliance/, accessed 8 March 2024.

World Trade Organization, 'Accession: Explanation, How to Become a Member of the WTO' (*World Trade Organization*). Available at: www.wto.org/english/thewto_e/acc_e/acces_e.htm, accessed 25 May 2023.

World Trade Organization, 'Disputes by Members' (*World Trade Organization*). Available at: www.wto.org/english/tratop_e/dispu_e/dispu_by_country_e.htm, accessed 13 November 2022.

World Trade Organization, 'Groups in the Negotiations by WTO Member' (*World Trade Organization*, 12 April 2021). Available at: www.wto.org/english/tratop_e/dda_e/groups_by_country_e.htm, accessed 13 November 2022.

World Trade Organization, 'Guide to Reading the GATS Schedules of Specific Commitments and the List of Article II (MFN) Exemptions' (World Trade Organization). Available at: www.wto.org/english/tratop_e/serv_e/guide1_e.htm, accessed 25 May 2024.

World Trade Organization, 'Hong Kong, China and the WTO' (*World Trade Organization*). Available at: www.wto.org/english/thewto_e/countries_e/hong_kong_china_e.htm, accessed 29 June 2024

World Trade Organization, 'Hong Kong, China: December 1998' (*World Trade Organization*). Available at: www.wto.org/english/tratop_e/tpr_e/tp095_e.htm, accessed 17 November 2022

World Trade Organization, 'Investment Facilitation for Development' (*World Trade Organization*). Available at: www.wto.org/english/tratop_e/invfac_public_e/invfac_e.htm, accessed 14 November 2022

World Trade Organization, 'Principles of the Trading System' (*World Trade Organization*). Available at: www.wto.org/english/thewto_e/whatis_e/tif_e/fact2_e.htm, accessed 25 May 2024.

World Trade Organization, 'Schedules of Specific Commitments and Lists of Article II Exemptions' (*World Trade Organization*). Available at: www.wto.org/english/tratop_e/serv_e/serv_commitments_e.htm, accessed 25 May 2024.

World Trade Organization, 'Members and Observers' (*World Trade Organization*). Available at: www.wto.org/english/thewto_e/whatis_e/tif_e/org6_e.htm, accessed 25 May 2024.

WorldData.info, 'Indicators of Economy in Hong Kong' (*WorldData.info*). Available at: www.worlddata.info/asia/Hong-Kong/economy.php, accessed 13 November 2022

WorldData.info, 'The 50 Largest Economies in the World' (*WorldData.info*). Available at: www.worlddata.info/largest-economies.php, accessed 14 May 2024

Wright L, 'Fractured Foundations: Assessing Risks to Hong Kong's Business Environment' (*Atlantic Council Geoeconomics Center*, 7 March 2023). Available at: www.atlanticcouncil.org/in-depth-research-reports/report/fractured-foundations-assessing-risks-to-hong-kongs-business-environment/, accessed 25 May 2024.

WTO, 'Circulation of Draft Agreement Marks Major Milestone in Investment Facilitation Talks' (*WTO*, 16 December 2022). Available at: www.wto.org/english/news_e/news22_e/infac_16dec22_e.htm, accessed 25 May 2024.

WTO, 'Dispute Settlement System Training Module: Chapter 1 Introduction to the WTO Dispute Settlement System' (*WTO*). Available at: www.wto.org/english/tratop_e/dispu_e/disp_settlement_cbt_e/c1s4p1_e.htm, accessed 25 May 2024.

WTO, 'Hong Kong, China Initiates Dispute Complaint Against US Origin Marking Requirements' (*WTO*, 3 November 2020). Available at: www.wto.org/english/news_e/news20_e/ds597rfc_03nov20_e.htm, accessed 25 May 2024.

WTO, 'Investment Facilitation Agreement Negotiators Wrap Up Productive Year' (*WTO*, 8 December 2020). Available at: www.wto.org/english/news_e/news20_e/infac_08dec20_e.htm, accessed 25 May 2024.

WTO, 'Investment Facilitation Negotiators Confirm Aim of Finalizing Text-based Talks by End-2022' (*WTO*, 8 July 2022). Available at: www.wto.org/english/news_e/news22_e/infac_08jul22_e.htm, accessed 25 May 2024.

WTO, 'Investment Facilitation Talks Intensify to Conclude Draft Agreement in First Half of 2023' (*WTO*, 1 February 2023). Available at: www.wto.org/english/news_e/news23_e/infac_02feb23_e.htm, accessed 25 May 2024.

WTO, 'Structured Discussions on Investment Facilitation for Development Move into Negotiating Mode' (*WTO*, 25 September 2020). Available at: www.wto.org/english/news_e/news20_e/infac_25sep20_e.htm, accessed 25 May 2024.

WTO, 'Text of the 'July Package' – The General Council's Post-Cancún Decision' (*WTO*, 1 August 2004). Available at: www.wto.org/english/tratop_e/dda_e/draft_text_gc_dg_31july04_e.htm, accessed 25 May 2024.

WTO, 'Workshop on Investment Facilitation for Development' (*WTO*, 10 July 2017). Available at: www.wto.org/english/tratop_e/invest_e/workshopinvestjuly17_e.htm, accessed 25 May 2023

WTO, 'Member Information: Hong Kong, China and the WTO'. Available at: www.wto.org/english/thewto_e/countries_e/hong_kong_china_e.htm, accessed 25 May 2024)

WTO, Regional Trade Agreements Database: Hong Kong, China. Available at: https://rtais.wto.org/UI/PublicSearchByMemberResult.aspx?membercode=344, accessed 25 May 2024.

Xu N, 'Can Hong Kong Leverage Its Special Trade Status against China?' (*The News Lens International Edition*, 19 August 2019). Available at: international.thenewslens.com/feature/hkantielab/123671, accessed 25 May 2024.

Yen Z, 'GFCI 32 Rank' (*Z/Yen*, 22 September 2022). Available at: www.longfinance.net/programmes/financial-centre-futures/global-financial-centres-index/gfci-32-explore-the-data/gfci-32-rank/, accessed 13 November 2022.

Yeung C, 'Economic and Trade Information on Hong Kong' (*HKTDC Research*, 27 October 2022). Available at: research.hktdc.com/en/Article/MzIwNjkzNTY5, accessed 13 November 2022.

Yiu P, 'Global Companies Moving Top Posts out of Hong Kong' (The Nikkei Asia, 17 August 2022). Available at: www.asia.nikkei.com/Spotlight/Coronavirus/Global-companies-moving-top-posts-out-of-Hong-Kong-survey, accessed 25 May 2024.

Zhang M, 'RCEP Developing Toward Asia-Pacific Economic Integration' (*China–US Focus*, 20 November 2019). Available at: www.chinausfocus.com/finance-economy/rcep-developing-toward-asia-pacific-economic-integration, accessed 25 May 2024.

Zhang Y, '*HK – Corporate Taxation*' s. 1.4.4. Available at: www.research.ibfd.org/#/doc?url=/link-resolver/static/cta_hk_auth&refresh=1590284728927#cta_hk_auth, accessed 25 May 2024.

Zheng S, 'Hong Kong's Economy Records Worst Contraction Since 2020' (*Bloomberg*, 31 October 2022). Available at: www.bloomberg.com/news/articles/2022-10-31/hong-kong-s-economy-records-worst-contraction-since-2020#xj4y7vzkg, accessed 25 May 2024.

Zhou C, Tang F and Wang O, 'China Backs Hong Kong to Join RCEP Trade Deal in Potential Boost to Territory's Flagging Logistics Sector' (*South China Morning Post*, 25 June 2021). Available at: www.scmp.com/economy/china-economy/article/3138789/china-backs-hong-kong-join-rcep-trade-deal-potential-boost, accessed 25 May 2024.

OTHERS

AOTCA, 'AOTCA Hong Kong 2016 – International Tax Conference Program'. Available at: www.nichizeiren.or.jp/eng/pdf/AOTCA2016-InternationalTaxConferenceProgram.pdf, accessed 25 May 2024.

Commerce and Economic Development Bureau, 'Legislative Council Panel on Commerce, Industry, Innovation and Technology, 2022 Policy Address – Policy Initiatives of Commerce and Economic Development Bureau' (*Legislative Council of the Hong Kong Special Administrative Region of the People's Republic of China*, October 2022) LC Paper No CB(1)718/2022(03). Available at: www.legco.gov.hk/yr2022/english/panels/ci/papers/ci20221107cb1-718-3-e.pdf, accessed 25 May 2024.

Committee on Regional Trade Agreements, Factual presentation – Free Trade Agreement between Hong Kong, China and Australia – Goods and services – Report by the Secretariat – Revision (16 December 2020) WT/REG400/1/Rev.1. Available at: http://docsonline.wto.org.

Council Business Division 1, Legislative Council Secretariat, 'Legislative Council Panel on Commerce and Industry – Minutes of Meeting held on Friday, 19 February 2021, at 10:45 am in Conference Room 3 of the Legislative Council Complex' (*Legislative Council of the Hong Kong Special Administrative Region of the People's Republic of China*, 15 April 2021) LC Paper No. CB (1)798/20–21 1, 8. Available at: www.legco.gov.hk/yr20-21/english/panels/ci/minutes/ci20210219.pdf, accessed 25 May 2024.

Dispute Settlement Body – Held in the Centre William Rappard on 25 January 2021 – Minutes of Meeting (12 March 2021) WT/DSB/M/448. Available at: http://docsonline.wto.org.

Dispute Settlement Body – Held in the Centre William Rappard on 22 February 2021 – Minutes of Meeting (24 March 2021) WT/DSB/M/449. Available at: http://docsonline.wto.org.

English translation of President Xi Jinping's report at the 19th National Congress of the Communist Party, *Secure a Decisive Victory in Building a Moderately Prosperous Society in All Respects and Strive for the Great Success of Socialism with Chinese Characteristics for a New Era*. Available at: www.hnftp.gov.cn/xwzx/ywsd/202002/t20200224_3260171.html (visited 16 November 2020).

General Council – Held in the Centre William Rappard and in virtual format on 13 October 2020 – Minutes of the Meeting (25 November 2020) WT/GC/M/187. Available at: http://docsonline.wto.org.

General Council – Held in the Centre William Rappard on 10 and 18 May 2017 – Minutes of Meeting (21 July 2017) WT/GC/M/167. Available at: http://docsonline.wto.org.

General Council – Held in the Centre William Rappard on 18 October 2018 – Minutes of Meeting (20 November 2018) WT/GC/M/174. Available at: http://docsonline.wto.org.

General Council – Held in the Centre William Rappard on 27–28 February 2017 and Reconvened on 7 April 2017 – Minutes of Meeting (3 May 2017) WT/GC/M/166. Available at: http://docsonline.wto.org.

General Council – Held in the Centre William Rappard on 28 February 2019 – Minutes of Meeting (15 April 2019) WT/GC/M/176. Available at: http://docsonline.wto.org.

General Council – Held in the Centre William Rappard on 3 March 2020 – Minutes of Meeting (16 April 2020) WT/GC/M/182. Available at: http://docsonline.wto.org.

General Council – Held in Virtual Format on 1–2 and 4 March 2021 – Minutes of Meeting (23 April 2021) WT/GC/M/190. Available at: http://docsonline.wto.org.

General Council – Held in Virtual Format on 27–28 July 2021 – Minutes of Meeting (4 October 2021) WT/GC/M/192 Available at: http://docsonline.wto.org.

Hong Kong – Schedule of Specific Commitments (15 April 1994) GATS/SC/39.

IBRD, 'Doing Business in 2004: Understanding Regulations' (*IBRD*, September 2003) 1, xiv, 89 Available at: www.archive.doingbusiness.org/content/dam/doingBusiness/media/Annual-Reports/English/DB04-FullReport.pdf, accessed 25 May 2024.

IBRD, 'Doing Business in 2005: Understanding Regulations' (*IBRD*, September 2004) 1, 2. Available at: www.archive.doingbusiness.org/content/dam/doingBusiness/media/Annual-Reports/English/DB05-FullReport.pdf, accessed 25 May 2024.

ICSID, 'Guide to Membership in the ICSID Convention' (*ICSID*, 2020) 1, 5 Available at: icsid.worldbank.org/sites/default/files/Guide_to_Membership_in_the_ICSID_Convention_2020.pdf, accessed 25 May 2024.

ICSID, 'List of Contracting States and Other Signatories of the Convention (as of 25 October 2022)' (*ICSID*, 2022) 1. Available at: www.icsid.worldbank.org/sites/default/files/ICSID%203/ICSID-3--ENG.pdf, accessed 25 May 2024.

ICSID, 'Members of the Panels of Conciliators and of Arbitrators' (*ICSID*). Available at: www.icsid.worldbank.org/sites/default/files/ICSID%2010/ICSID-10.pdf, accessed 25 May 2024.

ICSID, 'Number of Arbitrators and Method of Appointment – ICSID Convention (2006 Rules)' (*ICSID*). Available at: www.icsid.worldbank.org/procedures/arbitration/convention/process/appointment/2006, accessed 25 May 2024.

ICSID, 'Practice Notes for Respondents in ICSID Arbitration' (*ICSID*, 2015) 1, 15 Available at: www.icsid.worldbank.org/sites/default/files/publications/Practice%20Notes%20for%20Respondents%20-%20Final.pdf, accessed 25 May 2024.

Ji P, Explanations on "The Basic Law of the Hong Kong Special Administrative Region of the People's Republic of China (Draft)" and Its Related Documents (Addressing the Third Session of the Seventh National People's Congress on 28 March 1990).

John Tsang, 'Budget Speech by the Financial Secretary' (*The Government of the Hong Kong Special Administrative Region Press Releases*, 25 February 2009). Available at: www.info.gov.hk/gia/general/200902/25/P200902250108.htm, accessed 25 May 2024.

Legislative Council, 'Special FC Meeting on 12 April 2022 – Speaking Notes for Secretary for Commerce and Economic Development' (*Legislative Council of the Hong Kong Special Administrative Region of the People's Republic of China*, 12 April 2022) 1, 6. Available at: www.legco.gov.hk/yr2022/english/fc/fc/sp_note/session11-cedb-cit-e.pdf, accessed 25 May 2024.

MIGA, 'Operational Regulations (As amended by the Board of Directors through August 27, 2022)' (*MIGA*) xiv. Available at: www.docs.pca-cpa.org/2016/02/Operational-Regulations-of-the-Multilateral-Investment-Guarantee-Agency-as-amended-through-Aug.-27-2002.pdf, accessed 25 May 2024.

Ministerial Conference – Eleventh Session – Buenos Aires, 10–13 December 2017 – Joint Ministerial Statement on Investment Facilitation for Development (13 December 2017) WT/MIN(17)/59.

Ministry of Foreign Affairs of the People's Republic of China, 'The Ministry of Foreign Affairs. The Chinese Side Firmly Opposes the US Side's Signing of the "Hong Kong Autonomy Act"' (*Ministry of Foreign Affairs of the People's Republic of China*, 15 July 2020). Available at: www.fmprc.gov.cn/mfa_eng/gjhdq_665435/3376_665447/3432_664920/3435_664926/202007/t20200716_590947.html, accessed 25 May 2024.

OECD, 'Jurisdictions Participating in the Convention on Mutual Administrative Assistance in Tax Matters' (*OECD*, May 2022). Available at: www.oecd.org/ctp/exchange-of-tax-information/Status_of_convention.pdf, accessed 25 May 2024.

OECD, 'MAP Statistics 2018 Hong Kong, China' (*OECD*, 2018). Available at: www.oecd.org/tax/dispute/2018-map-statistics-hong-kong.pdf, accessed 25 May 2023.

OECD, 'Members of the OECD/G20 Inclusive Framework on BEPS joining the October 2021 'Statement on a Two-Pillar Solution to Address the Tax Challenges Arising from the Digitalisation of the Economy' (*OECD*, November 2021). Available at: www.oecd.org/tax/beps/oecd-g20-inclusive-framework-members-joining-statement-on-two-pillar-solution-to-address-tax-challenges-arising-from-digitalisation-october-2021.pdf, accessed 25 May 2024.

OECD, 'Signatories and Parties to the Multilateral Convention to Implement Tax Treaty Related Measures to Prevent Base Erosion and Profit Shifting' (*OECD*). Available at: www.oecd.org/tax/treaties/beps-mli-signatories-and-parties.pdf, accessed 25 May 2024.

Office of the Government Economist, Financial Secretary's Office, Government of the Hong Kong Special Administrative Region, 'Box 3.2 RCEP and its Possible Impacts on Hong Kong' (*Government of the Hong Kong Special Administrative Region*, February 2021). Available at: www.hkeconomy.gov.hk/en/pdf/box-20q4-3-2.pdf, accessed 25 May 2024.

RCEP, 'Guiding Principles and Objectives for Negotiating the Regional Comprehensive Economic Partnership' (*RCEP*) 1. Available at: www.rcepsec.org/wp-content/uploads/2019/10/RCEP-Guiding-Principles-public-copy.pdf, accessed 25 May 2024.

The Hong Kong Special Administrative Region of the People's Republic of China, 'Policy Address – International Trade Centre' (*The Hong Kong Special Administrative Region of the People's Republic of China, The Chief Executive's 2022 Policy Address, October 2022*). Available at: www.policyaddress.gov.hk/2022/en/p44.html, accessed 25 May 2023.

The Hong Kong Special Administrative Region of the People's Republic of China, 'The Chief Executive's 2022 Policy Address' (*Legislative Council of the Hong Kong Special Administrative Region of the People's Republic of China, 19 October 2022*). Available at: www.legco.gov.hk/yr2022/english/panels/20221019-policy-e.pdf, accessed 8 January 2024.

Trade Negotiations Committee – Held in the Centre William Rappard on 28 November 2017 – Minutes of Meeting (8 February 2018) TN/C/M/38.

Trade Policy Review Body – 1 and 3 December 2010 – Trade Policy Review – Hong Kong, China – Minutes of the Meeting (26 January 2011) WT/TPR/M/241. Available at: http://docsonline.wto.org.

Trade Policy Review Body – 11 and 13 July 2018 – Trade Policy Review – China – Minutes of the meeting (21 November 2018) WT/TPR/M/375. Available at: http://docsonline.wto.org.

Trade Policy Review Body – 13 and 15 December 2006 – Trade Policy Review – Hong Kong, China – Minutes of the Meeting – Addendum (16 February 2007) WT/TPR/M/173/Add.1. Available at: http://docsonline.wto.org.

Trade Policy Review Body – 16 and 18 December 2002 – Trade Policy Review – Hong Kong, China – Minutes of the Meeting (17 February 2003) WT/TPR/M/109. Available at: http://docsonline.wto.org.

Trade Policy Review Body – 19 and 21 November 2014 – Trade Policy Review – Hong Kong, China – Minutes of the Meeting (19 January 2015) WT/TPR/M/306. Available at: http://docsonline.wto.org.

Trade Policy Review Body – 26 and 28 November 2018 – Trade Policy Review – Hong Kong, China – Minutes of the Meeting (6 March 2019) WT/TPR/M/380. Available at: http://docsonline.wto.org.

Ukpe, AI, *Differentiated Differentiation: Using Progressive Regulation as a Framework for Special and Differential Treatment in the WTO* (Wageningen University, 2022).

WTO, 'Multi-party Interim Appeal Arbitration Arrangement pursuant to Article 25 of the DSU' (30 April 2020) pmbl, WTO Doc JOB/DSB/1/Add.12. Available at: www.hketogeneva.gov.hk/doc/1A12.pdf, accessed 25 May 2023.

WTO, 'WTO Analytical Index GATT 1994 – General (DS Reports)' (December 2022) 6 (WTO Analytical Index GATT 1994).

Government Information Centre, 'The 2005-06 Policy Address' (*Government Information Centre*, 12 October 2005). Available at: www.policyaddress.gov.hk/05-06/eng/p5.htm, accessed 25 May 2024.

Greater Bay Area, 'Outline Development Plan for the Guangdong-Hong Kong-Macao Greater Bay Area' (*Greater Bay Area*, 18 February 2019). Available at: www.bayarea.gov.hk/filemanager/en/share/pdf/Outline_Development_Plan.pdf, accessed 25 May 2024.

HKSAR Government, 'Is Tax Reform Required in Hong Kong' Available at: www.taxreform.gov.hk/eng/pdf/Chapter_01.pdf, accessed 25 May 2024.

Office of the Chief Executive, 'The Chief Executive's 2017 Policy Address – We Connect for Hope and Happiness' (2017). Available at: www.policyaddress.gov.hk/2017/eng/pdf/PA2017.pdf, accessed 25 May 2024.

Office of the Chief Executive, 'The Chief Executive's 2018 Policy Address – Striving Ahead Rekindling Hope' (2018). Available at: www.policyaddress.gov.hk/2018/eng/pdf/PA2018.pdf, accessed 25 May 2024.

Office of the Chief Executive, 'The Chief Executive's 2019 Policy Address – Treasure Hong Kong: Our Home' (2019). Available at: www.policyaddress.gov.hk/2019/eng/pdf/PA2019.pdf, accessed 25 May 2024.

Office of the Chief Executive, 'The Chief Executive's 2021 Policy Address – Building a Bright Future Together' (2021). Available at: www.policyaddress.gov.hk/2021/eng/pdf/PA2021.pdf, accessed 25 May 2024.

Office of the Chief Executive, 'The Chief Executive's 2022 Policy Address – 2022.10.19' (2022) para 36. Available at: www.policyaddress.gov.hk/2022/public/pdf/policy/policy-full_en.pdf, accessed 25 May 2024.

Trade and Industry Department, 'An Introduction to the Trade and Industry Department' (*Trade and Industry Department, The Government of the Hong Kong Special Administrative Region*, April 2022). Available at: www.tid.gov.hk/english/aboutus/deptprofile/files/intro_TID.pdf, accessed 25 May 2024.

Trade and Industry Department, 'Legislative Council Brief – Free Trade Agreement between Hong Kong and Georgia' (*Trade and Industry Department, The Government of the Hong Kong Special Administrative Region*, 28 June 2018) CR WT 324/27/3 1, 4–6. Available at: www.tid.gov.hk/english/ita/fta/hkgefta/files/GEHKFTA_Legco_Brief.pdf, accessed 25 May 2024.

Trade and Industry Department, 'Legislative Council Brief – Free Trade Agreement between Hong Kong and Australia' (*Trade and Industry Department, The Government of the Hong Kong Special Administrative Region*, 28 June 2018) CR WT 324/9/2/2. Available at: www.tid.gov.hk/english/ita/fta/hkaufta/files/legco20190326_e.pdf, accessed 8 January 2024.

Trade and Industry Department, 'Legislative Council Brief – Hong Kong – New Zealand Closer Economic Partnership Agreement' (*Trade and Industry Department, The Government of the Hong Kong Special Administrative Region*, 29 March 2010) CR WT 324/9/1 1, 6–7. Available at: www.tid.gov.hk/english/ita/fta/hknzcep/files/LegCoBriefs_HKC_NZCE.pdf, accessed 25 May 2024.

Trade and Industry Department, 'World Trade Organization: Key Outcomes of the Twelfth Ministerial Conference' (*Legislative Council of the Hong Kong Special Administrative Region of the People's Republic of China*, October 2022) LC Paper No. CB(1)673/2022(05). Available at: www.legco.gov.hk/yr2022/english/panels/ci/papers/ci20221018cb1-673-5-e.pdf, accessed 25 May 2024.

Index

www.ingramcontent.com/pod-product-compliance
Ingram Content Group UK Ltd.
Pitfield, Milton Keynes, MK11 3LW, UK
UKHW020240290926
15470UKWH00002B/646

9 781509 968169